Dr. J. G. M. Ramsey

Dr. J. G. M. Ramsey

From an oil portrait by Lloyd Branson. Picture furnished through courtesy of Dr. Ramsey's great granddaughter, Ellen Le Noir, Baton Rouge, Louisiana. (Frontispiece.)

Dr. J. G. M. Ramsey

Autobiography and Letters

EDITED

BY

William B. Hesseltine

Published by

TENNESSEE HISTORICAL COMMISSION

Nashville

1954

To
FRANK W. PRESCOTT
Citizen of Tennessee
who also has given his energies
to civic improvement.

Preface

Dr. James Gettys McGready Ramsey, Tennessee historian, left a deep and lasting impression on the life of his native and beloved state. Although later generations remembered him only for his historical writing, his contemporaries knew him as a man of exceptional versatility whose varied activities extended from the practice of medicine to the financing of railroads. He was a canal commissioner and a school commissioner, the president of banks and a farmer, a Presbyterian elder and a poet, a register of deeds, a contributor to magazines, a Confederate treasury agent, a postmaster, an operator of a ferry, a trustee of colleges, and a philosopher who thought deeply upon the problems of the South and the nature of Southern people. He was a fit representative of a Southern tradition, running back through Thomas Jefferson even to William Byrd the first, of cultured gentlemen who read the classics in their own libraries, took an active part in politics, contributed to the intellectual advancement of their communities, and stood in the forefront of movements for civic improvement.

"Patriotism," announced Dr. Ramsey as he was called upon to offer a toast at a banquet celebrating the arrival of the first steamboat in Knoxville: "Patriotism;—Something else than party zeal or a selfish scramble for offices." By that definition, Dr. Ramsey was a patriot. He loved his country of East Tennessee, his native state, and the South of which it was a part. He loved the federal union and mourned when selfish partisans scrambling for office seized its government, perverted its constitution, and sent its armies on a mission of plunder, and violence, and arson. "Have I a country to love?" he asked pitiably after the old order had passed away. As a patriot he had loved his land and given his energies, not to partisan zeal, but to social betterment.

His patriotism began with his family. He was proud of his Scotch-Irish ancestors, Alexanders and Ramseys, who had come as pioneers to western North Carolina and Tennessee. They had integrity, a respect

vii

for learning, a sturdy devotion to liberty. They made the Watauga Association, the state of Franklin, and the state of Tennessee. They stood defiant at Alamance, and they adopted, so Dr. Ramsey firmly believed, the Resolves at Mecklenburg which were the first American Declaration of Independence. Part of Dr. Ramsey's patriotism found outlet in preserving from oblivion the story of the heroic deeds of these backwoods patriots.

He raised his own family in the tradition of his ancestors. He surrounded his eleven children with books and learning. He established a school for their instruction, sent his sons to college, and encouraged their intellectual development. He raised them in the rigid piety of the Presbyterians. He took pride in their youthful prowess and their early success in law, and business, and politics. He established them, as they came of age, as landed gentlemen. He gave them to the army of the South, and although he grieved at their misfortunes and he was heartbroken when his youngest son, Arthur, his "Benjamin," fell in battle, he had no self-reproaches. His patriotism and that of his children was the stern heritage of his pioneer ancestors.

In the same patriotic spirit he served his community. He began by studying medicine in Knoxville, and after attending lectures at the University of Pennsylvania he returned home to practice. He built "Mecklenburg" at the juncture of the French Broad and the Holston, maintained a ferry across the Tennessee River, and farmed the land between the two converging rivers. Across the Tennessee in time there arose Riverside, the home of his daughter Margaret Jane and his son-in-law T. Howard Dickson. At Mecklenburg he maintained a library of four thousand volumes and manuscripts and documents of early Tennessee history. There he entertained Presbyterian divines, statesmen and politicians, historians and literary men. Like his father's house at Swan Pond, he made Mecklenburg into a house of prayer and a seat of culture.

Yet his very residence at the exact spot where the Tennessee River began emphasized to him the unique nature of the Tennessee Valley. Throughout American history, settlement had followed the river valleys, and those who came to each successive valley first to occupy the fertile bottoms and control the strategic crossings possessed the wealth-producing locations and became the local leaders. Frequently they, like Dr. Ramsey, became the local aristocrats, dominating church, local government, and the institutions of culture in the community. But the Tennessee River was not like the other rivers of America which flowed into the sea. For all practical purposes the Tennessee River, which began so promisingly at Dr. Ramsey's doorstep, flowed, as a river, only to Moccasin Bend at the foot of Lookout Mountain. A freak of geology had interfered with geographic logic. Lookout Mountain, thrusting its precipitous cliffs across the river's logical path to the Atlantic or the Gulf of Mexico, dispersed its waters and sent them uselessly westward around Moccasin Bend, over unnavigable Muscle Shoals, the Suck and the Boiling Pot. Only in a far-off corner of Alabama did the waters, gathering themselves together, find a channel *northward* to the Ohio. The Tennessee River was two rivers: one that ran from Knoxville to Chattanooga, the other from Florence to Paducah. For long years men of East Tennessee dreamed dreams of dredging a channel or cutting a canal to join these two widely separated rivers which shared the same water but had nothing else in common.

But not Dr. Ramsey. Though he cooperated with his neighbors in efforts to defy the accidents of nature and bring steamboats to Knoxville, and though he became a canal commissioner in futile efforts to salvage the wasted waters of the Tennessee, he put no faith in the river. He knew that the water from Mecklenburg to Moccasin Bend was, in effect, a land-locked lake with no navigable outlet. He turned his gaze away from the beautiful siren which stretched before his door to lure men on to Muscle Shoals. He looked instead across the mountains and saw a vision of a substitute river that ran on iron and could be made to go where men willed.

He succeeded his father on the board of a Knoxville bank, and he joined his brother, William B. A. Ramsey, in business enterprises. But his business instincts told him that water communication with far-off New Orleans was not the answer to the problem of East Tennessee's isolation. He became the leading spokesman for a railroad which would link Knoxville to Charleston. This was the "Mecklenburg Politics," and to promote his ideas Dr. Ramsey went to Charleston and aroused enthusiasm among South Carolina's business leaders. Back in Knoxville, he sponsored public meetings and railroad conventions. When eventually his efforts bore fruit, he became president of a railroad bank, sold Tennessee bonds on the New York market, and bought the equipment for the East Tennessee and Georgia Railroad.

His railroad interests—the whole logic, in fact, of the Mecklenburg politics—bound Dr. Ramsey to the South and to the domain of King

Cotton. But more than interest bound him to the land of Dixie. His whole emotional nature was enlisted in the Southern cause. He exemplified in Mecklenburg the highest ideal of Southern society: the landed gentleman of public and private virtue, of culture, of civic responsibility which was more than a scramble for offices. He was a patriarch guiding the lives of his slaves, his tenants, and his poorer neighbors and responsible to his Creator for their moral growth. He took pride in his Southern ancestors and in their achievements. He believed his own grandfather and his grandfather's neighbors had gathered at Charlotte to write the Mecklenburg Resolves. He believed his Scotch-Irish forebears had struck the first and most valiant blows against British parliamentary absolutism. He studied their history and he wrote the *Annals of Tennessee* in a patriotic effort to glorify their deeds. In politics he was a Democrat, following the states' rights principles of Thomas Jefferson and John C. Calhoun, voting for Andrew Jackson and James K. Polk. His politics and his social orientation combined with his economic interests to make him a Southerner and to lead him into the Southern Confederacy.

But Dr. Ramsey's attachment to the South was not shared by all his East Tennessee neighbors. The people of the thirty mountain counties of East Tennessee were not agreed that their destiny was wrapped up in the Southern cause. Some of them, like "Parson" William Ganaway Brownlow, fiery editor of the Knoxville *Whig,* foresaw industrial potentialities in the coal and iron of the Tennessee hills and the power to turn the wheels of mills in the streams that poured into the Tennessee River. The hopeful industrialists placed their faith in making the Tennessee navigable through federal aid and in attracting Northern capital to the region. Brownlow proclaimed himself an Alexander Hamilton–Henry Clay–Internal Improvement Whig. Others there were like Andrew Johnson, senator who represented the small farmers and the hill folk, who despised the Southern aristocrats like Dr. Ramsey at the same time that they rejected industrialism. For long years Brownlow and Johnson, fit representatives of their divergent interests, fought in the verbal battles of Tennessee politics. Then, on the issue of secession, they united momentarily against the common enemy of cotton capitalism and Southern aristocracy which Dr. Ramsey represented. Yet as soon as secession was stamped out, the two old antagonists sprang again at each other's throats. But, in the meantime, Dr. Ramsey and the Southern tradition which he typified, had gone down in ruin.

Dr. Ramsey might, conceivably, have lived with Andrew Johnson. The agrarian democrat and the landed aristocrat might differ in point of view but they had a common bond in the soil and in the history of East Tennessee. But between Dr. Ramsey and Parson Brownlow there was a fundamental antagonism. Dr. Ramsey had no use for the Northern capitalist, the industrialist, the "Bogus-Aristocrat" of wealth whom he had seen in the Northern cities. He saw no beauty in smokestacks, in blast furnaces, in the power loom. Moreover, as he saw it, the lust for money had perverted the old Puritan into a crass Yankee, cringing, subservient, and grasping. "We are essentially two people," he repeated—heterogeneous, incompatible. For the Brownlows who would industrialize East Tennessee he had only contempt. For Brownlow himself, Dr. Ramsey had a personal hatred. He counted the vituperative editor his greatest—in fact, his only —personal enemy, and he firmly believed that Brownlow had hired the arsonist who burned Mecklenburg. Whatever the facts may have been, in a symbolic sense Dr. Ramsey was right.

When secession and civil war came, Dr. Ramsey was sixty-four years old. Behind him lay a long record of service to his community and substantial achievements, ranging from a railroad to a volume of history, to attest to his efforts for his region's material and cultural well-being. He looked forward to laying aside his civic duties, his professional and business responsibilities, and spending his last days in quiet and honored retirement. Instead, he became a Confederate treasury agent, collecting and paying out funds for a war-torn government. In addition, he followed the armies as a surgeon, ministering to the wounded on the battlefields. When the enemy descended on Knoxville, he carried the funds of his depository and of his bank to Atlanta, and then, driven out before the advancing foe, he went to Augusta, to Charlotte—and even, in the end, planned to flee across the Mississippi.

Meantime, his sons were in the Confederate army, and one of them lost his life. Two of his daughters died,—one, at least, as a result of devotion to the South. His wife and daughters abandoned Mecklenburg, and an arsonist in the federal army set fire to the mansion at the head of the Tennessee River. His youngest daughter was exiled from Knoxville, and his wife, homeless and bereaved, became a refugee. The world of Dr. Ramsey fell apart, and the smoke from the books, the manuscripts, and the records of Mecklenburg mingled in the darkened sky with the smoke from the burning ruins of the Southern way of life.

Dr. Ramsey was sixty-eight when he gathered the remnants of his family under a rented roof in Charlotte, North Carolina, borrowed a horse and a doctor's saddle-bags, and resumed the practice of medicine. He returned to his historical interests, and set about to tell the story of his services to Tennessee in days of peace and to the Confederacy in the long years of the war. He told, in an Autobiography, the story of his own and his family's services, their misfortunes, and their bereavements. He was a historian with a historian's sense of the importance of the record. Carefully he recorded his wanderings, his emotions, his frantic haste to save the money of the government and the people entrusted to him. He added the circumstantial items, told the lore—and carefully distinguished the personally known fact from the story as told to him by others.

But through his Autobiography there ran a theme. It was not alone a recounting of experiences: The experiences added up to a running exposition of the differences between Southern and Northern character. They were, indeed, two peoples. The ancient virtues of the Scotch-Irish, the Presbyterian, the liberty-loving sons of the old border—honor, probity, integrity, social consciousness, learning—were concentrated in the South while their antitheses were Northern characteristics. Instance after instance gave support to the thesis. The lack of chivalry, the ignorance, and the vice displayed by federal soldiers proved again and again that a union of Southern and Yankee could be maintained only by the bayonet.

In March 1870 Dr. Ramsey brought his Autobiography to a close. But even yet he had a contribution to make to history and to culture. A quarter of a century earlier he had come in contact with historian Lyman C. Draper, eighteen years his junior, who was gathering manuscripts and lore on the lives of the pioneers of the period of the American Revolution. Dr. Ramsey sent Draper information about Daniel Boone, John Sevier, the Shelbys, and the men of Watauga. When he wrote his *Annals of Tennessee* he compared notes with Draper. In 1852, Draper moved to Wisconsin, founded and built the State Historical Society, and continued to collect manuscripts, documents, and oral traditions of the "Old Border." A Democrat with pro-southern sympathies, he had much in common with Dr. Ramsey. When the rising "Black Republicans" defeated him for a second term as state superintendent of public instruction, Dr. Ramsey urged him to move to Tennessee, reform the common school system, and invigorate the historical society.

The Civil War brought a momentary halt to the correspondence between the two historians. Then in 1870, just as Dr. Ramsey was completing his Autobiography, Draper wrote him again. For more than a dozen years Dr. Ramsey wrote to Lyman Draper about early Tennessee and Southern history. His own collections of manuscripts, rare imprints, and recorded lore had been destroyed in the holocaust of Mecklenburg, but much that he had gathered remained in his memory where arsonists inspired by personal enmity or war psychosis could not destroy them. These memories he shared with Draper, telling him "nursery tales" he had heard in his boyhood, discussing critical points of fact on the men of Watauga, the signers of the Mecklenburg Resolves, the battles of the Revolution. In 1872 Dr. Ramsey moved back to Knoxville, practicing medicine until a fall from a horse made him a cripple. But even as a pain-wracked invalid he continued his letters. Sometimes he interviewed old residents of Knoxville, and sent their family traditions to Draper. Draper saved them, using them to write his own book on *King's Mountain and its Heroes*—a volume which Dr. Ramsey inspired and blessed.

Thus it was that even as an octogenarian invalid Dr. Ramsey continued to make, as he had made throughout his life, a vital contribution to the culture of his community and of the South. Much that he had done, through a patriotism which was something else than partisan zeal or a scramble for offices, has turned out differently than he had planned. The railroad which he built still runs, and its huge trestle, crossing where Dr. Ramsey's ferry once ran, blocks the view down the Tennessee from the site of old Mecklenburg. The industry which he deplored has come to the very spot where he worshipped, and the dust of a marble quarry sifts down upon Dr. Ramsey's neglected grave in Lebanon churchyard. The river has become navigable and its floods have been harnessed by the federal government and the men of the Brownlow tradition to turn the wheels of other industry. Mecklenburg has gone with the way of life that it represented. But his *Annals,* his Autobiography, and his letters constitute still a lasting contribution which Dr. Ramsey has made to an understanding of the American heritage.

*   *   *

I first met Dr. Ramsey, through his Autobiography, nearly a quarter of a century ago when, as a citizen of Tennessee, I was investigating the impact of the civil war on East Tennessee. Miss Laura Luttrell, then in charge of the McClung Collection in the Lawson McGhee Library in

Knoxville called to my attention the typed copy which Dr. Philip M.
Hamer had obtained for the library. Miss Luttrell and I talked a little
about editing the Autobiography for publication.

Years later, as a resident of Wisconsin, I became interested in the career
of Lyman Copeland Draper, whose collections of historical material on
the early history of the Trans-Allegheny region are the richest treasure of
the State Historical Society of Wisconsin. In Draper's personal correspondence I found Dr. Ramsey's letters to the Wisconsin historian. My search
for Draper's letters to Dr. Ramsey proved futile, but it led me back to
Dr. Ramsey's Autobiography, and the story of the high-minded gentleman, filled with public and private virtue, which it revealed. I was delighted when Miss Pollyanna Creekmore, Miss Luttrell's successor in the
McClung Collection, suggested again that I prepare the Autobiography
for publication. Miss Mary U. Rothrock of Knoxville interested herself in
the proposal, and presented it to Dr. Robert H. White and the Publications Committee of the Tennessee Historical Commission. To each of
these I am grateful for the opportunity to present Dr. Ramsey's story.

In the process I have tried to use Dr. Ramsey's letters to supplement
and to round out the Autobiography. On matters which Dr. Ramsey discussed, I have used his letters, in whole or in part, as footnotes to supplement the text. Dr. Ramsey made only passing reference in his Autobiography to his *Annals of Tennessee*. I have broken the Autobiography
at an appropriate place to insert a chapter of his letters to Draper which
give an intimate picture of the historian at work. Dr. Ramsey attached to
his Autobiography an appendix containing seven letters on the subject of
slavery and reopening the slave trade. Ignoring his strict injunction not
to publish them, I have inserted these letters as a chapter on "The Industrial Necessities of the South." The letters which he wrote to Lyman
Draper after he finished the Autobiography I have used as the later chapters.

For the most part—and certainly for the most valuable part—these letters have not before been seen. Most of them are in the "Draper Correspondence" in the library of the State Historical Society of Wisconsin.
Some are in the "Draper Manuscripts," wherein Draper put his collections on early American history. The criteria for the division are not always clear to his biographer. Items which might well have appeared in
the "Manuscripts" remained in his private "Correspondence." Since cal-
endars of the "Tennessee Papers" in the Draper Manuscripts have been

published and the entire collection is available in various places on micro-
film, I have omitted a few letters and parts of letters which contained
biographical sketches or extracts from printed sources. None of the letters,
whether from the "Correspondence" or the "Manuscripts" have been
printed before.

For permission to publish them here I am grateful to the State Historical Society of Wisconsin. To Dr. Clifford L. Lord, able director of
the Society and worthy successor of Lyman Draper, I am further obli-
gated for the services of a typist to transcribe the letters. To the Department of History of the University of Wisconsin I owe similar thanks for
a typist who copied the Autobiography. To the typists I owe a singular
debt—not for efficiency, but for confirming my belief in the human interest in Dr. Ramsey. Both typists dallied over their keys while they read
ahead in the old doctor's story.

Dr. Ramsey wrote his Autobiography—four hundred and eighty pages
of it—without a break for chapters and frequently without separating it
into paragraphs. Sometimes, too, a chain of thought led him back to add
more information on matters he had discussed before. Such occasions
were rare, but I have rearranged a few pages to bring matter on the same
subject together. I have indicated these places in the footnotes. For convenience of the reader, too, I have divided the Autobiography into chapters
and supplied chapter titles.

The other changes I have made have been few and simple, and, I trust,
do no violence to scholarly standards or to the proper functions of an
editor. Dr. Ramsey was a literate gentleman who knew well enough how
to punctuate, but in his holograph manuscript and his letters he relied
almost exclusively on the dash. I have translated his dashes into more
conventional punctuation marks. I have tried to bring his old-style capi-
talization into conformity to present-day usage. So, too, I have modernized
his spelling, rendering parlour as parlor and neighbour as neighbor. Dr.
Ramsey used two r's in car, two g's in wagon, and doubled the "l" in
scholar. He used an ampersand for and, abbreviated freely, and used
initials in place of names. To have left these things would have offended
the eye and have given a false impression of the writer.

One of Dr. Ramsey's faults in his *Annals of Tennessee* was his failure
to give full names, and sometimes, when more than one person of the
same surname appeared in his history, the account was confusing. His
Autobiography had the same fault, and sometimes he left blanks for

names he could not remember. Occasionally, he had clearly misunder-
stood a name and spelled it wrong. Whenever possible I have supplied
full and corrected names—without using brackets to indicate my additions. Only in a few cases have I felt it necessary to identify further the
names in the Autobiography or the letters. For aid in supplying such
data, as well as for proofreading and supervising typists, I am especially
indebted to Larry Gara, able and efficient research assistant in history at
the University of Wisconsin.

The original of the Autobiography was in the hands of Dr. J. R. Alexander of Charlotte, North Carolina, when Dr. P. M. Hamer, sometime
professor of history in the University of Tennessee, copied it for the
McClung Collection. I have worked from the carefully prepared and col-
lated typescript which Dr. Hamer made. A small part of the Autobiography was published by Samuel G. Heiskell in his *Andrew Jackson and
Early Tennessee History* in 1920. (Cf. 2:82–122.) The entire story as it
came from Dr. Ramsey's pen, and his letters relating to Tennessee history
deserve a wider audience, and I am happy to have been the agent to prepare them for publication.

WILLIAM B. HESSELTINE

Madison, Wisconsin
January 11, 1953

Contents

CHAPTER I

Heritage and Youth

My paternal grandfather was Reynolds Ramsey. It is believed that his parents were Scotch Irish Presbyterians, and that his father on coming to America settled at New-Castle, Delaware. It is a tradition but fully believed by their son Reynolds that on their passage across the Atlantic the mother fell overboard and was drowned. Her body could be seen floating on the sea some time after the accident, being buoyed above the waves by the stuffed or quilted dresses which ladies wore at that early period in the high latitude from which they came. Their son Reynolds was a good English scholar and had been well raised and piously trained. He was tall and graceful. I can even now recollect his polite bearing when yet an old man and especially to ladies. He never entered a room with his hat on and never retired from it without a graceful bow and a modest and sincere adieu. The date of his birth is not here and now known but it can be found in the old family Bible where I have seen it at Robert Swan's Esquire, near Cleveland, Tennessee. Mrs. Swan was his granddaughter and thus came into possession of the family records.

Reynolds Ramsey married Naomi Alexander, daughter of Francis Alexander, on the _____ day of _____ 17__. (These and other similar blanks can be filled by examining Mrs. Swan's Bible.) Her father was a member of influence and position in _____ Church Pa. or New Jersey and his name appears often in the early ecclesiastical records of the presbytery of _____ to which he belonged. His daughter Naomi was a rigid Calvinist and had been well indoctrinated in the creed of the Presbyterian Church. After her marriage she with her husband removed to and settled upon Marsh Creek then in York County Pa. (now Adams County) six or eight miles westward from the present Gettysburg. Thrift followed the industrious and frugal habits of this young couple. He erected a merchant mill upon Marsh Creek and his neighborhood was soon settled by pious and intelligent immigrants. A small village, Miller's Town, soon sprang up in which soon after was organized a Presbyterian Church. Of

1

this Reverend William Paxton afterwards (1806) was the pastor. The congregation was distinguished rather for its piety and intelligence than for wealth and refinement. Good schools and the living ministry were always well sustained and encouraged. A respect for the laws and order of good society, for parental authority and for filial obedience and a strict regard to the teaching of the Bible and of the protestant religion everywhere prevailed.

In such a community was the rising family of Reynolds and Naomi Ramsey trained. They had three or four sons and one daughter. Of these Francis Alexander Ramsey was probably the eldest and was born May 31, 1764. He was the father of this writer. Early in life he manifested great mental activity and excelled especially in mathematical studies. His chirography was not excellent only, it was elegant. He drew well and was especially skilled in trigonometry and surveying. To these attainments were super-added a gentle and amiable disposition, frank and urbane manners, pure morals and an ambition, well regulated and lofty, to make a mark for himself upon his age and posterity. No theater presented itself for the exhibition of his capacities in the secluded neighborhood where his youth and early manhood had been spent, and he remained, therefore, with his parents only till his nineteenth year.

Of two brothers of his, John and William, nothing further is known, than that they died early, one of them of consumption in Charleston, South Carolina in the house and kind family of Dr. David Ramsay of that city, whose professional aid he had sought under what proved to be an incurable disease.

Another brother, believed to be the youngest son of his parents, Samuel Ramsey received his academic education in his father's neighborhood and finished his collegiate studies at Liberty Hall, afterwards Washington College in Lexington, Virginia under the Presidency of Reverend William Graham. He studied divinity under the same learned divine. After his licensure he missionated in Virginia a short time. Such was his admiration of his great teacher, that he assumed the name of Graham as part of his own and in all after-life was known as S. G. Ramsey. He married the widow of Reverend Carey Allen, Mrs. Elizabeth Christian, daughter of Dr. William Fleming who was surgeon and for a part of the day colonel commandant under General Lewis at the great Indian Battle of the Kanawha, October 1774. He afterwards about 1793 removed to Knox County, now Tennessee, and became the founder and pastor of several churches in the new county and an approved teacher in Ebenezer Academy, which he established on his own farm. He had hemorrhage of the lungs which terminated in dropsy June or July 1817. An extended memoir of his useful life, his ministerial labors and his educational enterprises was published in 1867-8 in the (Richmond) *Christian Observer* written by this writer under the signature of "Mnemonika" to which the reader is respectfully referred.

The remaining member of the children of Reynolds and Naomi Ramsey was their only daughter, Amelia (Naomi). She married James King who died after the birth of Amelia King and James King. During her widowhood she resided with her parents while they remained in Pennsylvania.

My maternal grandfather was John McKnitt Alexander. His father's name I do not know, but I believe it was James. I think he lived in Hopewell Church in either New Jersey, or Pennsylvania and was a man of position and influence, both in church and state. His wife's maiden name was McKnitt. They had a large family of sons and two daughters. Of the former the names were Hezekiah, John McKnitt, _____, _____, _____, and the youngest Ezekiel. The daughters were Jemima who married James Sharpe, who was a major in the Revolutionary war, and Elizabeth, who married _____ Sample. My grandfather, John McKnitt Alexander married Jane Baine in Pennsylvania and he, his brothers and sisters, were among the first emigrants who from 1740 to 1760 crossed the Yadkin in search of a new home in North Carolina. They founded several Presbyterian churches in what afterwards became Mecklenburg County. Of these, John McKnitt and another brother became elders in the present Hopewell. Major Sharpe and Mr. Sample and their wives were members of the same organization. The name Hopewell was given, it is said, to the infant congregation in fond remembrance of the old church from which they emigrated. In like manner, Hezekiah Alexander became the founder and a ruling elder in Sugar Creek Church. The whole tribe of these Alexanders were remarkable for the tenacity with which they adhered to the doctrines and order of presbytery. They always had a learned clergy, were always the patrons of schools and the institutions of learning, always jealous of their rulers, men of intelligence and public spirit and advocates of the rights of self-government, of conscience and of liberty. Not strange was it, therefore, that when taxation without representation was attempted by the British ministry and enacted by the British parliament, when indeed parliamentary supremacy was claimed as a part and the essence of the British government, not strange we repeat, was it that the first of the first voice of resistance to the exercise of these arbitrary and unconstitutional powers and exactions, was found to arise from the free, enlightened and virtuous community then starting into life between the Yadkin and Catawba rivers. It was so. That community acted as one man and resolved to separate themselves from the mother country. They elected deputies and invested them with unlimited powers. These assembled at Charlotte on the nineteenth of May 1775, and on the twentieth united in a unanimous Declaration of Independence. Of this convention of deputies, not less than six were named Alexander. Their secretary was John McKnitt Alexander. The whole tribe were active Whigs in the war of the American Revolution which succeeded. My grandfather was beyond the age for military operations and services, yet he was selected by General Greene as a quasi aide de camp, was often pilot of his army and by his influence and his money contributed much to the success of the American arms in the southern states. His eldest son, William Baine Alexander, then below the military age, saw active service during the occupancy of Charlotte by Lord Cornwallis. His (J. McK. A.) three daughters were Peggy Alexander, who was born on the third of April 1766 and Polly, and Abigail Baine. The former was married on the seventh of April 1789, to Francis Alexander Ramsey, who has already been mentioned. The youngest child of John McKnitt Alexander was Joseph McKnitt, who was educated at Princeton, N. J., studied medicine, and settled near the old family mansion of his father, now known as Alexandriana, at the head of Long Creek, on the south side of the Statesville railroad. He had an extensive practice. He married Dovey Winslow. His brother, William B. Alexander, already mentioned, inherited the old homestead and mansion. He married Miss Violet Davidson, and had sons Joseph, Robert D., James McKnitt, John Ramsey, and George W. and _____, and daughters Jane Baine who married John Sharpe then of Tennessee, Peggy who married David Henderson, Rebecca who married _____ McCoy, and _____ who married Dr. Isaac Wilson. . . .

The third daughter of John McKnitt Alexander, Abigail, married Reverend S. C. Caldwell, once pastor of Hopewell and Sugar Creek. They had one daughter Jane Baine and one son Thomas. Jane became the wife of Reverend Walter Smilie Pharr. They had an only child, the present Reverend S. C. Pharr, D.D. Thomas became a Doctor of Medicine, lived near Charlotte. He married a daughter of Honorable _____ Johnson,[1] formerly a member of Congress from the Mecklenburg District. The other daughter of J. McKnitt Alexander, Polly, married Reverend James Wallis, pastor of Providence congregation. They had seven sons, William B. A. John McKnitt A. Ezekiel A., James, Joseph McKnitt, and _____.

The wife of John McKnitt Alexander died in the spring of 1789 a short time before the marriage of her first daughter, Peggy to Colonel Ramsey. The husband never married again, but continued a widower and resided in the old mansion with his son, W. B. Alexander till 1817. He had been exceedingly fond of books, read early and late with intense avidity, and lost his eyesight, and was blind for several years before his death. He lies interred in Hopewell graveyard, surrounded by the remains of his wife and of a numerous posterity. Many incidents in the life of my maternal grandfather, J. McKnitt Alexander are here omitted, as they may be found elsewhere, viz., in Foote's *Sketches of North Carolina Presbyterianism,* under the head of Hopewell, the Charlotte Convention; H. Jones, *Defense of North Carolina.* Wheeler's *North Carolina,* Ramsey's *Annals of Tennessee,* and several articles in the "Land We Love" contributed by this writer.[2] He was a man of great public spirit and enterprise. Had a vigorous intellect, had most of the attributes of genius, was self-reliant and energetic. Remarkable for probity and for public and private virtue. He was nearly six feet high, very symmetrical in his person, had a fine forehead and the most brilliant black eyes I have ever seen. His manner of speaking was calm and deliberate, but exceedingly earnest and emphatic. With greater culture, his intellect would have equaled that of Calhoun while in the majesty of his virtue and of his unselfish patriotism, he was not a whit behind that most illustrious statesman and esteemed patriot.

This brings to mind what I should have mentioned when speaking of Reynolds Ramsey on a preceding page. During the war of the Revolution he was a soldier and compatriot of Washington. He was at Valley Forge, at Trenton and at Princeton. I have heard him say that it was no exaggeration when the historians of those great events represent that the ice across

---

[1] Charles Johnson of Chowan County, North Carolina, who served in the Seventh Congress from March 4, 1801 until his death July 23, 1802 is the only North Carolina representative of this name. *Biographical Dictionary of the American Congress 1774–1949* (1950), 1374.
[2] Cf. Mnemonika [J. G. M. Ramsey], "Sketch of Mecklenburg County," *Land We Love,* 2:129–145 (December, 1866).

Delaware River and the frozen roads the soldiers traveled were marked
by the blood from their naked feet. He supplied the Republican army
with flour from his mill on Marsh Creek and refused British gold for his
breadstuffs, when offered by those he had reason to believe were in the
interest of the enemies of his country. I have heard him say that he was
as poor in 1781 as at the commencement of the war, and when counting
over and examining his box of Continental money left on his hands worthless as waste paper, I have seen his eyes glisten with patriotic joy at the
recollection of his sacrifices and self-denial which had made him penniless.
That was the price he paid for American liberty and independence.

When his sons had left him and emigrated to the West, my grandfather
sold out his mills on Marsh Creek and removed to Gettysburg, now a
flourishing inland village. It was laid out by Samuel Gettys, Esquire, who
had married his (Ramsey's) sister. He resided in that town several years
but still retained his membership in his old church at Miller's Town. Summer, winter, with his wife and daughter, Mrs. King, and her two children
he drove out there every Sabbath in his plain old-fashioned carriage and
listened to Mr. Paxton, his old minister. He was a devout and attentive
worshiper in the house of God, as well as in his own family. I have often
heard him mention the names of Davies, Blair, Smith, the Tennants and
others of the earlier Presbyterian divines.[3] He was a humble, and very
pious man, a good citizen, a conscientious public officer, fond of good
men and good books. In these he delighted. He reached his three score
and ten with few of the infirmities of age. After that period he found it
necessary and advisable to comply with the earnest and dutiful request of
his two sons in Tennessee to follow them there to spend the evening of
life with or near them. This he carried into effect in 1808. There for the
present I shall leave him. I intend hereafter on another page to resume
his history.

On [an earlier] page of these sheets it has been mentioned that the
eldest son of the family Francis A. Ramsey had found in the seclusion
of his father's neighborhood, no suitable theater for the exercise of his
capacities and his attainments. A brother of his mother, John Alexander,
had already removed to and occupied a pleasant farm situated on Big

---

[3] William Tennant (1673-1745), founder of the "Log College" at Neshaminy, Pennsylvania, his sons Gilbert (1703-1763) and William (1705-1777), his pupil Samuel Blair
(1712-1751), Blair's pupil Samuel Davies (1723-1761) and Blair's son-in-law Robert Smith
were leaders in the evangelical movement in the Presbyterian Church and founders of "New
School" Presbyterianism in 1741. Cf. C. H. Maxson, *The Great Awakening in the Middle
Colonies* (1920).

Limestone Creek in Washington County of North Carolina. Other Pennsylvanians had settled near him and formed the nucleus of a good congregation of Presbyterians and of an enlightened society. The uncle invited his young and aspiring nephew to come to the backwoods as the frontier is always called. His neighbors united in the same invitation. It comported exactly with the disposition and choice of the young man now in his nineteenth year. With tears in his eyes and with a heavy heart he bade adieu to his fond parents and other members of the affectionate family on Marsh Creek. I have often heard my father tell the sorrowful feelings he endured on leaving the home of his youth on a journey of five hundred miles to the unknown wilds of the western wilderness—infested then and for many years afterwards by unfriendly tribes of Indians and by white men also, little in advance of savages, in civilization, and observance of law and order. On an extreme frontier everywhere there are always found a few lawless and desperate men who resort thither to avoid the penalty of crime, and to find an immunity from punishment awarded to the wrongdoer, in older and better regulated communities. Happily for the world however, the destructive principle is counteracted or is weakened by the conservative. Upon Holston and Chucky, as the then new settlements were designated, the large mass of the new settlers were eminently conservative and law-abiding. Perhaps in no other frontier community was there ever exhibited a simplicity as primitive or a patriotism as genuine and efficient as then existed in Washington County of North Carolina. There our young and adventurous immigrant found a home first in the house of his mother's brother. At an early period, after his arrival there, it became known that he understood surveying. His compass and chain he had brought with him. With his horse these constituted his entire fortune. He needed nothing further. These gave him at once employment, competency and position. Either as principal or as deputy, he held at the same time the office of surveyor, sheriff and clerk. He was nineteen years old when he left Pennsylvania but the minor age worked no disqualification for office. Every inhabitant and many non-residents were entering their land warrants on the vacant territory and the compass became an instrumentality in extending the new settlements, not less necessary and effective than the axe and the rifle.

When in 1784 the cession to congress by the legislature of North Carolina of her western counties had produced general excitement and dissatisfaction west of the Alleghenies, Francis A. Ramsey took sides with the

insurgents. He was secretary of one of the conventions whose action withdrew the allegiance of the western people from the mother state and established for them a new commonwealth thereafter known as the State of
Franklin. Under this anomalous government he held offices both civil and
military. He was one of the council of state and was sent by the Franklin
authorities on an embassy to negotiate the terms of separation between the
two now antagonistic and rival governments. During these civil commo-
tions, when Franklin had ceased to be and the western people had returned to their allegiance to North Carolina, passing on official business to
New Bern through Mecklenburg County Colonel Ramsey formed the acquaintance of Miss Peggy, eldest daughter as has been mentioned, of
John McKnitt Alexander. On the seventh of April 1789 she became his
wife. Soon after this date they moved across the mountain and settled on
Little Limestone Creek. The property has since been occupied by Mr.
Broils, I believe, and is not far from the present cross of the E. T. & V. R. R.
They had both previous to their marriage been members of the Presbyte-
rian Church. They were now within the bounds of Salem Congregation of
which Reverend Samuel Doak was the pastor. Here my oldest brother
William Baine Alexander was born on the twenty-sixth of March 1791.
During the next or the succeeding year my parents removed to the Swan
Pond in the present Knox County, Tennessee. The authorities of the
Southwestern Territory had organized a court for the District of Hamilton. Of this court my father was made the clerk. It held its sessions at
Knoxville, a recently established town and now the seat of the territorial
government. My father had made several most eligible locations of land in
this county. On several accounts the Swan Pond was the most desirable
location for a residence. It was the center and nucleus of a Presbyterian
congregation—the uplands were exceedingly fertile, a good proportion of
lowland suitable for meadows, a small clear lake of four or five feet depth
spread its beautiful expanse south of a peninsula sufficiently large for the
yard and grounds around the site of the buildings and also for a large
garden and orchard. On this peninsula he determined to erect a mansion
for a permanent home. Apprehending malaria from the exhalation of such
an extent of water, he cut through the beaver dam, which by obstructing
the branches above it had formed the little lake, and by suitable ditches
succeeded in draining it off so as to bring all the submerged land into
tillage or grass. In place of the beautiful Swan Pond, as known to hunters
and peltrymen for more than a hundred years, it has now the verdure and

beauty of a Pennsylvania meadow, unsurpassed in the luxuriance of its grasses and the depth of its alluvial soil.

At first Colonel Ramsey erected a temporary residence twenty feet by twenty feet a little in the rear and east of the site he had selected for his family mansion. It was of hewn logs, one story high, a stone chimney in one corner, and covered with lap shingles. (In this cabin I was born March 25, 1797.) [4]

My second brother John McKnitt Alexander was born the second of May 1793 and probably at this place. My third brother Samuel Reynolds, was born August 9, 1795, and this writer, James Gettys McGready, was born on the twenty-fifth of March 1797.

In the meantime Colonel Ramsey, in pursuance of his original purpose, had contracted with an architect and carpenter, Thomas Hope, who had learned his trade in London. The first work he did in Tennessee was on my father's house. It was a large stone structure, a deep basement, and an attic besides two tall stories. Its corners, its arches, the top of its chimneys, and one row of building rocks, midway between the ground and the top of the square, were built of pure blue limestone, while the wall through-out, was built of red granite. Its style was Gothic, long narrow windows, cornices richly carved in wood, but painted to resemble stone, massive, elaborately finished and ornamented. It is even yet a tasteful and imposing structure. At the census of 1800 it was the most costly and most admired building in Tennessee. This, his first job in the state, soon brought to Mr. Hope more work than he could execute. Dr. Joseph Churchill Strong, Colonel Charles McClung and Captain John Kain afterwards employed him on their mansions. He was not only an architect, but also a cabinet-maker, and an upholsterer. The tall and elegant secretary and bookcase in which the fancy volumes of Colonel Ramsey's library were placed and a massive bureau were made by Mr. Hope also. In the construction he used as embellishments some American woods he had never seen before (sumac was one of them). As may well be excused in an English mechanic, he put upon his workmanship on the top of Colonel Ramsey's secretary the English lions and the unicorn. Colonel Ramsey refused to receive the work till he had placed the American eagles in suitable propinquity to and above the armorials of British royalty.

This old-time honored family mansion is six miles east of Knoxville

---

[4] In 1927 the Bonny Kate Chapter of the Daughters of the American Revolution erected a marble monument on the site of the cabin to mark Dr. Ramsey's birthplace.

and on the road to Dandridge. For twenty-three years it was occupied by
its first proprietor and was up to the time of his death in November 1820
a center of a generous hospitality, refined and elegant and not less sincere,
unostentatious and cordial. After his decease it became the distributive
share of my father's large real estate to my brother Colonel W. B. A. Ramsey since secretary of state at Nashville. At his removal to the seat of government he sold the property to me. I conveyed it to my son Colonel
Francis A. Ramsey, thus named for his grandfather. He occupied it several
years before the Confederate War. While he was in that service it was sold
and it now belongs to a stranger. *Sic transit gloria mundi*. It was a house
of prayer, and of praise. A home for the minister of religion, the stranger,
the widow, the orphan, the exile and the homeless! That old Mansion!
with its pointed gables, quaint cornices and antique windows! Dear old
home with its gay dreams and sunny hours, and cloudless skies, and visions of bliss and glorious happiness gone! All gone! gone! [5]

[5] Later in his *Autobiography* Dr. Ramsey made further comments about his father's house.
"It was" he said, "almost the oldest North Carolina grant in this section of the country. My
father had entered it in 1786 when he, General White, and Colonel Love were the first to
explore that frontier. . . . The place is a little historical. Beavers had constructed their dam
below the confluence of two small streams. This formed a pond covering perhaps two hundred acres. To this vast quantities of aquatic birds resorted especially in winter, amongst
others the swan in large droves. At a very early day French and Spanish traders ascended the
river to the *Fork* (afterwards Mecklenburg) a mile from it and procured valuable cargoes of
feathers, furs, and peltries generally. Within my own recollection the traders' path could
still be seen. The remains of an old house built by a Mr. Evans, the pioneer hunter and
peltryman, are also within my recollection. It stood on Mrs. Breck's part of the same plantation on an eminence commanding a view of the house and Cumberland mountains on the
north and the Alleghaneys on the south. When I first saw these remains there were bearing
peach trees standing near them. Their fruit was most delicious. It was then called the French
peach, and from it the large silver colored and juicy peach still in the neighborhood is believed to be derived. These vestiges have long since disappeared. They were not far from a
more recent structure occupied by Mr. Jeremiah M. Monday. It can be made the most beautiful place in Knox County.
"Swan Pond is historical furthermore as the oldest, finest, and most costly structure erected
in this part of Tennessee. At the close of the administration of Washington my father began it. The architect was from London, Thomas Hope, a regularly trained worker and
carver in wood. At the census of 1800 it was the best house in the state. Its style is Gothic.
Its corners are all blue limestone while the arches and the [row] of stone above and next
to them are of the same material. For twenty years it was the home of the pioneer, the
stranger, the widow and the orphan. It was also the home of the Christian minister. A
whole Presbytery held its synod in its ancient and venerable hall. For the same length of
time it was the house of prayer. Morning and evening it was vocal with the reading of
God's word, singing his praises, and with the incense of prayer around the family altar
erected for His worship. These memories of the past would be pleasant especially to this
writer but for the reflection that within the last ten years the house has been desecrated often
to the vapid inroads of the rude, the vulgar, and uncultivated,—often to the fun, folly,
frolic and vulgarity of vagrant—and perhaps, too, often to the purposes of licentiousness
and crime. Such is the history though of the world and of man. The ashes of the Father of
the Faithful are surrounded now by pagans and idolaters. Mount Zion is now a Turkish
harem. The primitive churches planted by Christ's apostles no longer exist and have been
supplanted by the temples of the heathen, of Gentile, the infidel, the licentious and the pro-
fane. It is so ordained of Heaven. It is *quoad hoc* all right. I yield to it and submit."

Thou art tumbling to the dust, old pile
Thou art hastening to thy fall;
And round thee in thy loneliness
Clings the ivy to thy wall
The occupants are scattered now
Who knelt before thy shrine,
And silence reigns where anthems rose
In days of Auld Lang Syne.

And sadly sighs the wandering wind
Where oft in years gone by
Prayers rose from many hearts to Him
The Highest of the High.
The tramp of many a busy foot
That sought thy halls is o'er
And many a weary heart around
Is still forever more.

How doth Ambitions, hope take wing!
How droops the spirit now!
We hear the distant city's din,
The dead are mute below.
The Sun which shone upon their paths
Now gilds their lowly graves—
The zephyrs which once fanned their brow
The grass above them waves.

Oh! could we call the many back
Who've gathered here in vain;
Who've careless roved where we do now
Who'll never meet again—
How would our very souls be stirred
To meet the earnest gaze
Of the lovely and the beautiful;
The lights of other days!

This digression from the main object of the writer of these pages, has been suggested by the fond recollections of his early home, and of the dear parents and other near relatives whose remains are mouldering in the cemetery nearest to the Old Stone House. The family genealogy is resumed.

My next brother, William Baine Alexander, was born November 28, 1801. Francis Alexander Ramsey, the last child of my own mother, was born October 18, 1804.

My mother, Peggy Alexander died of consumption July 9, 1805, aged thirty-nine years three months and four days. I was then eight years old, but can distinctly recollect the whole scene and it is still vividly impressed upon my memory. Her life and character as a lady, as a wife, a mother and as a Christian, have been fully portrayed in a funeral sermon by Reverend Robert Henderson, her favorite preacher. That sermon preached from a text of her own selection and another preached at her own request in her sick chamber and entitled "The Christian Hope" were both published by my disconsolate and bereaved father in pamphlet form and were extensively distributed among her relations and religious acquaintants. They were afterwards published in book form in "Sermons by Reverend Robert Henderson, of Murfreesboro, Tennessee, in eleven volumes." The reader is referred to them.

After the death of his wife Colonel Ramsey was inconsolable and bereaved. She had hung around his neck like a jewel. Of their children three sons had preceded her to the grave, viz. William Baine Alexander Ramsey died March 21, 1799 nearly eight years old. His name was given to an infant son not yet named. Samuel Reynolds Ramsey died September 16, 1800 suddenly aged five years and Francis Alexander Ramsey died November 23, 1804 aged five weeks. These heavy bereavements were tolerable compared with that occasioned by the death of the mother of his living and dead children. The pang was for a time too heavy to be borne. His solitude became insufferable. His father-in-law wrote to him to visit Alexandriana with his four now motherless children. He did so and in the fall of 1805 he with them spent a few weeks in Mecklenburg County, North Carolina. Returning to his desolated home at Swan Pond he received a similar request from his aged parents to bring his children to Gettysburg, Pennsylvania to see their grandparents who now lived in that village. In the spring of 1806 that visit was accomplished. He took his children from there on a visit to some friends in Baltimore. Coming back to Gettysburg he renewed his acquaintance with Mrs. Ann Fleming, widowed daughter of Judge Agnew. They were married in the fall and removed soon after to Swan Pond. Soon after this my brother John McKnitt A. Ramsey, at the time a student of Blount College in Knoxville, died in that city. My stepmother on the birth of a son soon after, named her own son for my deceased brother, John McKnitt Alexander.

My grandparents at Gettysburg began to feel the infirmities of age aggravated by the absence of their two sons in Tennessee. The sons invited them to come and spend the evening of their life with them. They came accordingly, but the milder climate of their adopted state rejuvenated them so much that they again took up house on a small farm in the Grassy Valley near Ebenezer Church of which their son, Reverend S. G. Ramsey was pastor. Their widowed daughter, Mrs. King, lived with them and married soon after a Mr. Taylor. My aunt did not survive long after this event, dying of puerperal convulsions. She was buried in Ebenezer Church yard. This heavy bereavement drove the aged couple back to my father's house where in happy tranquillity they passed the remainder of their days. My father's uncle, John Alexander, who had been kind to him when he came a boy and a stranger to the new country on Chucky in 1783, had now become infirm, blind and poor. His past kindnesses to the nephew were now amply repaid. He had him brought from Limestone, settled him on his own farm, and near to the old mansion in a neat frame cottage where he ended his days at an advanced age. He was the grandfather of the late Chancellor Samuel Ramsey Rodgers, of Knoxville. Besides these benefactions my father brought around him other distant relatives, old, destitute and infirm: Hannah Moreton, Mrs. Patton, and Mrs. Hawthorn and others. His religion was a religion of deeds of charity and kindness to all but especially to those of the house-hold of faith.

My grandmother died in my father's house about 1814, my grandfather in March 1817. They were gathered to their fathers at an extreme old age and were interred in the family burying ground at the Fork (Lebanon) Church.

Colonel Ramsey was a steady patron of schools and learning in his neighborhood. Common school teachers on the frontier were not always at hand and were often incompetent. To supply this great deficit he often employed educated young men as clerks in his office (then kept according to law in his house and in the country) and as instructors of his children. The first of these was John Naylor Gamble from Pennsylvania. His penmanship was elegant, and may still be seen in the records of Hamilton District and other courts in Knoxville. The second was William Smith from New England and a third, Mr. Lyle Humphreys from Limestone near Washington College. These were all good tutors, the latter a classical scholar with whom my brother William and myself began our Latin studies. About 1809 we were sent to Ebenezer Academy then revived under the care and instruction of our uncle Reverend S. G. Ramsey. He had quite a large class, the sons of gentlemen and the elite of the country. James Houston, a graduate of Washington College and a great linguist— a student of theology under my uncle and a rigid disciplinarian was employed as assistant teacher in the academy. I have always thought that my knowledge of classical literature might be mainly ascribed to his attainments in Latin and Greek. The health of our principal was precarious and I had often the duty assigned me of hearing the recitations of the more advanced young men. I found this very conducive to my own progress. My brother and myself were throughout the whole of our course of studies then and afterwards, kept in the same class. We remained at Ebenezer till October 1814, having been there five years, when we were sent to Washington College. We took an advanced position even in Dr. Doak's classes. He was a graduate of Nassau Hall in its palmiest days under John Witherspoon D.D. its accomplished president. Being in advance of most of the members of the class we devoted some time to the study of Hebrew and at the commencement, March 1816, we received the degree of Bachelor of Arts—I in my nineteenth and my brother in his seventeenth year. Returning home I availed myself one year of the miscellaneous reading my father's large library afforded. In the early summer of 1817 I entered the office of my never to be forgotten *Medicae Preceptor* Joseph Churchill Strong M. D. the senior physician of Knoxville, Tennessee. In the meantime I had though under age been elected register of Knox County. This afforded an agreeable diversity of employment and some emolument.

During my first year's study under Dr. Strong my step-mother lost her health and in November she died during my absence to Salem, North Carolina whither I had gone for the purpose of bringing home my sister Eliza who had been sent there to school. On our return we found our father the second time a widower.

I continued to reside in the family of Dr. Strong, studying medicine, attending to his drug-store, keeping his books and writing in my office. I was the favorite of the doctor's students and had charge of his keys, his bank deposits and sometimes visited his patients. He was an excellent teacher of medicine—was the senior physician of the country and his practical remarks had always the validity of medical axioms. After more than two years of diligent application to medical studies, in the October of 1819 I went on horse back to Gettysburg where I left my horse and took the stages to Philadelphia. Dr. Strong gave me letters of introduction to the medical faculty of the University of Pennsylvania.[6] In the class of 1819

---

[6] One of the letters, addressed to Dr. N. Chapman, and dated September 21, 1819, read: "I take the liberty to introduce to you Doctor James Ramsey a Student of Medicine. He has resided with me for two years past and now wishes to attend the Lectures at Philadelphia. From the encouragement you gave me when at your house in the fall of 1816 to introduce

and 1820 I never lost a day—not even one lecture. I took notes of all the lectures of all the professors except Dr. Robert Hare on chemistry. I laid in a good medical library in the city. Returning to Knoxville I went to Memphis, then only a hamlet—to Brownsville, and other very infant villages intending to settle somewhere in the Western District.

My father in the meantime had married in April of 1820 his third wife, Mrs. Margaret Humes of Knoxville. A few months afterwards he received the appointment of president of the new state bank then first organized. Preparing to put his bank into operation he remained late and early in the office of (Scotch) James Campbell, the cashier. It stood at the corner of Cumberland and Water street not far from First Creek and Kennedy's mill dam. Here he contracted malarial fever. Unwilling to prescribe where the patient was my father I invited Dr. Strong to take the case. Dr. King was called in consultation. They attended him faithfully but on the fifth of November 1820 he breathed his last. His remains were taken from Knoxville followed by a large concourse of mourning citizens and friends to the family burying ground at Lebanon.[7]

The death of Colonel Ramsey produced a general sorrow in the community of which he had been so long a prominent member. The Presbyterian Church had lost one of its brightest ornaments—his own congregation, Lebanon, had been deprived of one of its founders and its most distinguished, as he was the most zealous and exemplary, of its elders. The poor and the friendless had lost their benefactor and their sympathising friend and counsellor. To the stranger he had always extended a cordial welcome —a warm hand and an open purse. In all the relations of life—a son, a brother, a husband, a father, neighbor, citizen, public officer and patriot he was dutiful, faithful—active, useful, exemplary—public spirited and enterprising—enlightened, a true lover of his country and a good man. He cared not for wealth only as a means of benevolence and beneficence to others. From his first arrival on the frontier in 1783 to the time of his death in 1820—a period of thirty-seven years he was never without office. Offices were showered upon him and he proved himself competent and worthy of them: offices which implied ability, probity, efficiency and zeal in the public service, and high personal character. It is no indelicacy in this writer to refer thus to the character of a deceased father, indeed to have omitted

students to you, I now with pleasure recommend to your friendly attention the young gentleman who is the bearer of this. His correct deportment, industry, integrity and moral conduct cannot fail to give satisfaction to his Preceptors."

[7] Knoxville *Register,* November 7, 1820.

what has here been said of him would have been infidelity to historical truth and in this writer a filial impiety. For a more special account of the deceased the reader is referred to "Ramsey's Annals of Tennessee" passim.[8]

[8] Cf., John T. Fain, *Fain's Critical and Analytical Index and Genealogical Guide to Ramsey's Annals of Tennessee* (1920). For further details about many of the people mentioned in the Autobiography, consult the East Tennessee Historical Society's *The French Broad–Holston Country* (1946).

CHAPTER II

Mecklenburg Politics

I have already mentioned that I intended to seek a theatre of practice in the Western District. I was preparing to execute this intention in the summer of 1820. To this my father interposed the objection that he was getting old and preferred that I should remain near him. To this preference was added that of Dr. Strong with the advice that I should settle in Knoxville. I opened an office, therefore, on Main street between Water and State August 1, 1820.[1] In November my father died. My brother W. B. A. Ramsey and myself had to administer on his estate. On the first of March 1821 I was married to the present Mrs. Ramsey, Peggy Barton Crozier,[2] eldest daughter of Captain John and Hannah Crozier then living at Fruit Hill near Knoxville. After a bridal tour of several weeks we returned and prepared for house-keeping. We lived in Knoxville till January 7, 1823, when we removed to a building I had erected on one of my father's farms around Gilliam's Station immediately in the fork of Holston and French Broad Rivers.

Connecting agricultural with professional pursuits I began to investigate the non-remunerative character of East Tennessee farming. Nearly 3,000 miles of river navigation intervened between our section of the state and the Gulph of Mexico, while in the other direction the Alleghany Range interposed their formidable heights as an insuperable impediment to our commercial intercourse by land with the South Atlantic harbors and through them with the markets of the world. It will scarce be believed at this day of railroads and steamboats that the insulated position of East Tennessee fifty years ago made farming there, even with the greatest industry and the strictest frugality, so unproductive and unremunerating. I

---

[1] His "card" in the Knoxville *Register*, October 10, 1820 stated, however, that "he may be called upon at his shop on Market Street nearly opposite the dwelling house of William Bowen." The following February 13, the *Register* carried a notice that "Dr. Ramsey has received from Philadelphia the recent vaccine matter" with the editor's added admonition that everyone should be vaccinated.

[2] Mrs. Ramsey was born in 1801. She survived her husband five years, dying in Knoxville in 1889.

have known corn to sell at that early period at 6d [or] 8⅓ cents per bushel on the stock and 16⅔ or 20 cents husked. Wheat was often sold for 33⅓ per bushel and for want of purchasers was sometimes thrown out of the stacks as food for the hogs. Meat was correspondingly low: pork $2.50 beef $2.25 or if stall-fed $2.50. At these prices there was no requital for the toil of the husbandman. The capital invested in real estate was wholly unproductive. There was no demand for labor. This produced a constant emigration of the industrious and the enterprising from East Tennessee to sections of the country having greater commercial facilities. The prevalent opinion was that these embarrassments to our agriculture and our commerce could be traced to the obstructions of our navigation and that if the Muscle Shoals were so improved as to admit of the passage of steamboats through them our products would find a market below them. I on the other hand after a patient examination of the whole subject held a very different opinion. I insisted that East Tennessee was essentially an Atlantic country and that the true theory of our trade was to reach the south Atlantic seaports with our products and through them a foreign market. A land communication with Charleston and Augusta I believed would be more promotive of our agricultural interests than a circuitous and long voyage of river navigation, subjecting our cereals to certain deterioration of the raw material, and imposing upon our traders the heavy competition their cargoes would encounter with the products of the whole West and Northwest. I availed myself of every opportunity of impressing these views upon the good judgment of my intelligent countrymen. The arrival of a small steamboat—the *Atlas*—Captain William Conner of Cincinnati, in 1826 at Knoxville was hailed with lively enthusiasm as the dawn of a better day upon the industrial interests of East Tennessee. I, too, admired the enterprise of the fearless navigator. I contributed to the dinner and to the purse too by which he was feted. I invited him to bring his little craft higher up the river to Mecklenburg—the name I had given to my private residence at the confluence of the two principal streams of East Tennessee. On the day appointed the *Atlas* with most of the Knoxville people on board arrived at my landing—an immense concourse of citizens from the surrounding country had come in to witness the triumphs of the genius of Fulton amidst our shoal rivers and our mountain seclusions. From a rostrum erected on the bank of the French Broad I gave Captain Conner and his voyageurs a hearty welcome to my house and its hospitalities, but took the occasion of such an assemblage of my countrymen as were present to expatiate at some length on the theory of our trade as already on a preceding page has been briefly stated.[3] My address was published in the first issue of a Knoxville paper, was extensively read—analysed and calmly examined. The politicians spoke against my theory—journalists wrote against it. From that day onward my theory was designated or condemned as the *Mecklenburg Politics*. I was misrepresented as an opposer of river-improvement when in fact I favored the removal of the obstructions at the Muscle Shoals by federal appropriations, denying, however, in toto that it would essentially contribute to our commercial relief or improve our trading facilities.

With a good deal of tenacity of purpose I continued to advocate my pet theory. Under assumed names I defended it in several newspapers. I had correspondents at home and abroad—in Tennessee, the Carolinas and Georgia. They all responded favorably and promised their aid and cooperation. The opponents of the scheme were active also against *land* communications. A member of Congress—a talented and virtuous public servant—did not hesitate to declare upon the stump that he must be a monomaniac that with so large a stream as the Tennessee running to New Orleans (3,000 miles of difficult and dangerous navigation) would suggest transportation (3 or 400 miles) to the Atlantic as either advisable or practicable. The friends of the new scheme—increasing daily in numbers, intelligence and public spirit—survived this unworthy and weak insinuation. A convention of delegates from the counties in Tennessee most interested in the scheme was called by me (anonymously) to meet at Dandridge. Of this small body General Tiglman A. Howard of Newport acted as chairman and I as secretary. By direction of this convention the secretary was instructed to open a correspondence with other communities and to propose that a similar convention should meet at Asheville and deliberate on the general subject.

Wishing to do everything in favor of my theory I went in November of

---

[3] The date was March 6, 1828. Dr. Ramsey's address began with the unpopular declaration that "I cannot conceal my conviction that an entire water communication through the Tennessee River, to our section of the State is not only impracticable, but would be, if effected, destructive of her best interest—that if it should facilitate our trade to New Orleans, it will be but in a limited extent, and that any advantage that measure might afford, will be far overbalanced by the actual injury it will do to all the interests of East Tennessee." It would, he explained, only bring East Tennessee produce into competition with the agricultural output of the west. "The market for East Tennessee is Charleston or Savannah," he asserted, "and the channel of communication is the Savannah River." Cotton brought higher prices in Charleston than in New Orleans, and the region between Charleston and the mountains was a better market for foodstuffs produced in East Tennessee. Cf. Knoxville *Register*, March 12, 1828.

1828 to Charleston, South Carolina for the purpose of securing the co-operation of the citizens of that city and state.⁴ I called upon Honorable H. L. Pinkney, the editor of the Charleston *Mercury,* and made known to him my mission. He politely offered me the use of its columns. About the last of December 1828 or first January 1829 I began a series of num-bers, signed Clinton, urging the connection between South Carolina and the navigable waters of the West.⁵ I had been politely introduced by Dr. Frederick Rutledge to the privileges of the Charleston Library and was often in it. One day I saw several gentlemen standing around a table ex-amining with great care a large map before them, and mentioning Knox-ville, the French Broad, and other localities designated in my articles as published in the *Mercury.* The librarian, Mr. Logan, was the only one present who knew me and coming to the end of the library where I was he said he wished to introduce me to the cluster of gentlemen across the room. He went with me and made me acquainted with Major Alexander Black, Mitchell King, Kerr Boyce and other friends of internal improve-ment. One of them said they had been informed that they were indebted to my pen for the articles in the *Mercury* signed Clinton and that they had been searching the map to find the places named in my pieces. I had not before that day avowed myself as the writer, but admitted that I was, and felt as a citizen of the West a deep interest in the subject of uniting our two sections of the union by a commercial identity. Looking over the map, I was surprised to find that gentlemen who knew every sea-port and trading centre in Europe had so little knowledge of western topography that I had to show them the sources of the Tennessee River and its in-osculatings with the Savannah and their other rivers. I met them con-

⁴ He carried with him a letter of Dr. Strong, October 24, 1828, which certified that "Doctor J. G. M. Ramsey was formerly a student of Medicine with me, and afterwards at-tended the Medical Lectures at the University of Pennsylvania, Since which he has been engaged in the practice of Medicine in this County, with much success and usefulness.
   "He is distinguished for his correct conduct, and I can with confidence recommend him as a Gentleman of the strictest integrity.
   "Dr. Ramsey's health being somewhat impaired he contemplates spending the winter in Charleston and he, with many of our Citizens feel much interested in promoting the facul-ties of intercourse between Charleston and East-Tennessee and we sincerely wish him success in his enterprise."
   Dr. Strong was then Mayor of Knoxville and this introduction, in Ramsey's opinion, "gave an official authority to my mission to Charleston."
   He carried, too, a letter from Hugh Lawson White to Robert Y. Hayne, saying "I ask leave to introduce to your acquaintance my friend, Doctor Ramsey, a native of this county. You will find him a worthy, intelligent, man." To this, White added a postscript which established Dr. Ramsey's political rectitude: "This is said to be an Adams District—The Ad-ministration candidate cannot in my opinion receive more than one tenth of the votes."
⁵ They were reprinted in the Knoxville *Register,* February 4, 11, 1829.

stantly afterwards. They took me up to the Neck where I saw a model of railroad whose car was put in motion by horse power. I every day received assurances of earnest cooperation in extending their improvements towards Tennessee.[6]

---

[6] January 14, 1829, Dr. Ramsey wrote his brother, W. B. A. Ramsey, a fuller account of his activities in Charleston. The letter illustrates Dr. Ramsey's zeal for his railroad projects and his talents as a promoter. It follows:

Charleston January 14, 1829

Dear Brother

Yours of _____ I handed over to your friend Conner whose minute acquaintance with one subject to which it referred will enable him to answer you more fully and accurately than I could have done. That of December 31, I received last Saturday night—the supplement to it by Mrs. Ramsey enhances its value 100 per cent. I wrote her last week and hope she has received it in due time. As you requested, I have made Mr. William Kennedy a subscriber to the *Southern Review* by paying in advance for the current year $5.00, if he wishes the first volume it can yet be had by signifying a wish to that effect. I will also be able to procure for you Swift on Evidence, with the treatise on promissory notes. The edition however is old (1810). I hope your own review has been received. Your sagacity will soon notice in the last number an article on "Internal Improvement." You will notice in it especially that my scheme of connecting this sea-port with the Tennessee River is ably advocated in the general, but that in detail the router, from mistaken conceptions of the geography and localities of the intervening country, has located the road in a position from which East Tennessee will be able to derive less advantage than from the plan suggested in my steam-boat-address and the various numbers of Clinton, Morgan, etc., in the Knoxville papers a few years back. I say East Tennessee, not because I believe she alone will experience less advantage from the route by Florence to Augusta (for I think the West in general will participate with her in the diminished facilities of that improvement), but because I wish East Tennessee, and especially Knoxville, to act immediately on this subject. The railroad from this place to Augusta will soon be put under contract. The United States engineers are now engaged in making the necessary surveys and examinations for its location. It will be continued further, and probably the present corpse of engineers may be instructed to continue their reconnaisance of the intervening country to the Tennessee. Hence it is important that the claims of the *upper Tennessee,* so to speak, should be pressed at this very moment. The mayor and aldermen of Knoxville and the citizens at large should request their representatives in congress to get the secretary of war to instruct the engineers now surveying the site for the Charleston and Augusta Railroad to continue the survey over the Alleghany to some of the upper branches of the Tennessee River—French-Broad, etc., etc. I can do nothing more on this subject than to write you thus briefly. I propose also if I find time before the departure of the mail to write to one of the aldermen. I have also written a few hasty numbers over my old signature "Clinton" which are being published in the Charleston *Mercury,* calling the attention of the country to the general subject. I will send you the numbers. Mr. Pinckney, the talented editor, gives me every facility and enters heart and soul into the measure. He told me he exchanged papers with Mr. Heiskell and would re-publish any thing relating to this improvement in his paper and give its whole influence to its promotion. This city generally are aware of the advantages the proposed communication holds out to itself, as also of its advantages in a national point of view. East Tennessee should take care of herself and not sleep while others are acting. I send you also the number of the *Mercury* containing the account of the late celebration of the eighth January. As you will see the *official* account of our proceedings I am saved the trouble of many details I would otherwise have given you. Some few particulars relating to the only *representative* Tennessee had either at the table or in the city will, I presume, not be unacceptable to a small circle at Mecklenburg and a few others in town. The faculty and students of the medical college were invited to take, in the procession and in the church, the second rank—coming immediately behind the clergymen. The procession, you observe, was to have taken place at the exchange. I had been introduced to most of the managers and they put on me the duty of marshalling the medical class who were standing everywhere along Broad-Street. I had got several squads of them down to the exchange when a violent storm of rain put a stop to the whole. At three the guests assembled at the S. C. Lovely's hall in Meeting Street. . . .

In October of 1832, the Asheville Convention was held consisting of delegates from the Carolinas and Tennessee. Of this body Mitchell King was president. I prepared and presented the report from Tennessee.

I had, by the politeness of General Dunlap, a letter to Colonel Hayne of this city—one of General Jackson's aids at New-Orleans. After several *minor* introductions I was taken by him to the upper end of the hall and introduced to the president and vice presidents of the day, the intendant of the city, Chancellor Harper, all the judges, managers of the railroad, city council, etc., etc. (too tedious to mention in an advertisement like this) and invited to take a seat amongst them. Colonel Hayne mentioned to them that in addition to the improvement of my health I had another object in view. I then mentioned that the enterprise they had undertaken to Augusta was creditable to their public spirit, but that I viewed it as only the commencement of the grand scheme of connecting the Mississippi Valley with the Atlantic Ocean.

This topic, however, was soon lost in the all-absorbing subject of the anniversary. Our procession was very imposing and we were soon seated in the saloon of the city hall at an excellent dinner. You can imagine my situation, my emotion, my pride. *Tennessee was the burthen of the song* and I was the only Tennessean present. The toasts of Chancellor Harper and myself were perfectly accidental—that is, all was done without preconcert or arrangement, but that very circumstance gave it the greater effect. I had received so much attention from the faculty that I had intended to give—"The medical college of South Carolina etc." But when "The State of Tennessee" came out and was received with such cheers, not of the company only, but of the surrounding crowd who were admiring the effect of a very brilliant illumination of the city hall *I could keep my seat no longer.* You see what followed. I tell you I am proud of the part I acted on that very night, but can give no further particulars till I see you. If you see proper you may hand the *Mercury* to Heiskell. I must add one more particular; when "The President of the United States" was given it was not drunk, and some of the company called to the music to play the "Rogues March." Mr. Pinckney observed to me during the evening that Tennessee was now what Virginia always had been etc., etc. This identity of feeling and interest might be brought to bear with much advantage on the very subject so dear to me, and I wish you could act upon it at Knoxville immediately and efficiently. Colonel Hayne, to whom I had mentioned the subject, asked me to dine with him last Saturday. I, of course, accepted the invitation and found at his house the very men I should have wished to meet—Mr. Elliott, editor of the *Southern Review* and the reputed author of the article on "Internal Improvement," Colonel Huger, the gentleman who rescued La Fayette from the prison of Olmutz, Chancellor Harper, Mr. Aiken, a member of the railroad company, etc., and _____. Tell Mrs. Ramsey that when Mrs. Hayne was asked for a toast she gave in compliment, I believe, to me, "Absent friends"—and I thought at the time of drinking it of my own dear Margaret and other friends in Tennessee. Colonel Huger gave *"Our* Railroad." I gave "A continuation of *your* railroad to the Tennessee River." It was heartily drunk. I returned to No. 84 at half after nine, where I opened your letter of December 31, and one from Dr. McIntosh. Yours contained the melanchoy news of Mrs. Jackson's death. I sent the unpleasant intelligence with a note of condolence that evening to Colonel and Mrs. Hayne and next morning gave Conner the same extract which you see in the *Mercury*—the first intelligence of that unpleasant occurrence. . . .

On some other topics mentioned in your letter I wish I knew what to say. If my services can be of any advantage to my country she has a right to them. If others can do more I cheerfully comply. Consulting my habits and my pecuniary circumstances I should be very little induced to engage in politics. With the people be it. I wish the question could remain unagitated till I return. . . . I know it will be disposed of before that time and I suppose I will feel willing to accede to things as I may find them. I wish I could be less ambiguous in this matter than this but I cannot be. Let things take their course. I still calculate to be home, unless February is very cold, about the 20–25 of that month. I have not yet heard from Augusta whether or on what day the Tennessee stage leaves that place, so that I am unable to say on what day precisely I take shipping for Savannah. I shall make my departure from here correspond with accounts from Augusta. I always receive your letters the Saturday evening a week after you mail them (nine days) so that you can calculate accordingly. Let me hear from you at Augusta and Asheville, and here also as I can request Conner or the Postmaster to forward letters etc. by land to Augusta.

The subject had now become one of all pervading interest.[7] Through the newspapers it was pressed upon the consideration of both the West and the South. Early in 1835 experimental surveys were made of the intervening mountains. Charters were obtained and individual and state subscriptions were made. The Fourth of July, 1836, a convention from all the surrounding states assembled at Knoxville. Of this body General R. Y. Hayne was elected resident and Honorable Pryor Lea secretary. I was a member from Knox County and in conjunction with Judge William B. Reese and Mr. Lea was appointed to prepare an address on the subject for the people of all the states concerned. During the session of the convention a spirited debate arose between Mr. Cross or Dr. Daniel Drake, I believe, of Cincinnati and someone else as to the paternity of this great enterprise. It only amused me and my Tennessee and Carolina colleagues. Some of them asked me to assert my claims. I declined a conflict so ungraceful and puerile. An old friend of mine, Colonel Bogle from Blount County, spoke out from the gallery and ended the debate by declaring that the honor belonged to Tennessee and that he had heard me at his own house advocate in 1828, the policy of uniting the West and South by land communications. The subject was dropped.[8]

The charter of the L. C. &. C. R. R. Co. gave the privilege of banking

---

Mr. Henderson from Mecklenburg was here last week: friends all well. Cotton has fallen and he and Uncle J—of course were in the dumps. You will expect to hear something of my health. The weather is very cold at this time and has been so for a few days—20 degrees only above zero yesterday. Of course my head is a little constricted but not much, and when the weather becomes more moderate, as it is becoming so now, I know I will feel better. Otherwise I am improved—strength being greater and appetite tolerable. Tell Mrs. Ramsey that on her account, as expressed in her letter, I take care not to expose myself unnecessarily and adhere most scrupulously to her advice about study and fatigue. I hope on my account she will observe all the injunctions I laid upon her and the children. I hope they all will be preserved in safety and health. I need not tell you to give her my sincere love and affection, that if not expressed is always understood. Present me to all relations and friends. Tell Dr. McIntosh I received his esteemed letter, and the general—you must give him the respects of a friend who really wishes him all the success political and otherwise to which he aspires. Tell Margaret Mae that of course I cannot but write to her next week. Having another letter to write to Tennessee and one to Washington City I will be excused for haste.

Your brother truly,
J. G. M. Ramsey

[7] Preliminary meetings agitating the question of a railroad to Charleston were held in Knoxville in the summer of 1831. Cf., Knoxville *Register,* June 15, 22, July 13, and November 16, 1831. The Asheville Convention was held September 4–5, 1832. Eight delegates from four East Tennessee counties attended, with twenty delegates from eight counties of North Carolina.

[8] For a discussion of this convention and of the railroad movement of which it was a part, see Ulrich B. Phillips, *A History of Transportation in the Eastern Cotton Belt to 1860* (1908), 170, 182–184. See also S. J. Folmsbee, "The Beginning of the Railroad Movement in East Tennessee" in *Publications* of the East Tennessee Historical Society, No. 5. (1933).

to that company. The directors of the mother bank at Charleston elected
the board of directors of the branches. Unexpectedly to myself my name
headed the list as sent to me by Colonel Abraham Blanding. I called the
directors together. We met in the jeweler's store of Mr. Samuel Bell on
Gay Street. Mr. William Kennedy nominated me as president of the Knoxville branch. I was unanimously elected. The panic of 1837 caused all the
banks of the country to suspend specie payments. My branch continued to
pay specie all the time and never did suspend. Governor James K. Polk
in his message of this year made this statement officially.

But the panic so affected the stocks of the company that the great enterprise of going *directly across or rather under the Alleghanies* had to be for
the present abandoned and the parties concerned chose to run their road
around the mountains, via Augusta, Atlanta and Dalton, Georgia so as
to connect the Hiwassee Railroad ultimately with those improvements.
That work was pushed with energy until its funds were exhausted and its
credit ruined. All work upon it was suspended. It remained so for several
years. In 1842 a new board of directors was appointed to resuscitate if possible the now dead road and galvanise it into life. I was appointed one of
the *state* directors and attended its quarterly meetings regularly at Athens,
Tennessee. There were many delinquent stockholders and the state, liberal
as she was, had refused to make further payments until the individual
stockholders should make *pari passu* payments. The road was originally
intended to connect Calhoun and Loudon on the Tennessee and the Hiwassee rivers and the grading between these two points was considerably
advanced and made wide enough for two tracks. No charter had yet been
obtained from Georgia so as to connect with her state road from Atlanta
to Chattanooga. On my suggestion and perhaps on my motion our president was directed to proceed immediately to Milledgeville and obtain the
charter for that important link. It was further ordered that operations of
our company should be suspended on other portions of our road and be
confined to its southern extremity and thus make one section of it complete
and productive. Every mile thus constructed became a legitimate basis of
credit. Public confidence began to be gradually restored. But we had no
means with which to purchase the iron and equipment and another appeal was made to the liberality and enterprise of the legislature for additional aid to the finances of the company. The state had already contributed largely. These contributions had been expended and yet no portion of
the road was finished and could not become productive without further

appropriations. Without further aid all that had been expended would be valueless and lost. The legislature was unwilling to contribute upon the old plan but agreed to issue to the company state bonds to the amount of $350,000.00 to be expended by an agent to be appointed by the governor and who was required to give bond for a faithful performance of his trust —was restricted to a sale of the bonds not below par and the proceeds to be applied to the purchase of the rails, motive power, cars etc., etc. On the passage of this act I received a letter from Governor William Trousdale asking me to become the agent and to carry into effect all the provisions of the act which he inclosed to me. This appointment was wholly unexpected and unsolicited on my part. It involved a very delicate duty. Heretofore the sale of the bonds and the expenditures of the company had been confided to and made by the board of directors, nine, or half, of whom were appointed by the governor. Sales of the bonds under former boards had been made at ruinous sacrifices—some said as low as sixty cents in the dollar. Some of the provisions of the new act seemed to imply a distrust, not certainly of the integrity but as certainly of the financial ability and skill, of the board. I was one of them and on good terms not only of courtesy but of confidence in all my colleagues. The law gave the agent entire control of the whole $350,000.00—not only of the sale of the bonds but of the disbursement of their proceeds in purchase of the entire superstructure. Some of the board, considering that the act thus construed might seem to convey a reflection upon our predecessors, declined at first the acceptance of an appropriation with the restrictions of the bill for our relief and assistance. Some feeling was manifested. But the objections were withheld and the act accepted.

I hesitated before I could accept the agency offered to me by Governor Trousdale. I stood in a peculiarly delicate position in regard to my colleagues of the board. The duties devolving on me by the appointment were new, untried, and embarrassing. The responsibility was great. Tennessee bonds were everywhere much below par—in Philadelphia they were then selling at eighty per cent and declining. The whole progress of our work would be suspended without sales at one hundred. I frankly stated to the board my own construction of the provisions of the law and of the duties and responsibilities it imposed upon the agent; that as I had to give a penal bond, not to the board but to the State of Tennessee, in the sum of $700,000.00, I should if I accepted the agency keep the bonds and their proceeds strictly under my own control—subject neither to the draft of our treasurer nor to the appropriation by the directors. General Duff Green—our contractor for the whole of the road,—under the mistaken idea, shared with him and some of the directors, that *my* fund went into the company's treasury and formed a part of its assets, desired me to place in his hands so much of the proceeds of the bonds as he might wish to expend in the erection of iron works and a rolling mill to manufacture the rails. To this I replied emphatically in the negative—that was neither the spirit, much less the letter, of the law giving us the bonds. A member of the board said they could get it out of my hands by a writ of mandamus. I said if my construction of the act was questioned in court, any competent tribunal would sustain me. The thing was too plain to admit of a doubt. Another director inquired whether it was not the function of the president and chief engineer to select the rails, engines, chairs, etc., and purchase them? I replied frankly if I paid for them I would also purchase them. I would not agree to become the cashier neither of the company nor the state of Tennessee but I added, that if I assumed the duties contemplated by the appointment offered to me, I would of course consult with the engineer and president and avail myself of any assistance these officers could give me in selecting the articles needed, but that I would pay for nothing they purchased or ordered—if I paid I would also purchase.

With these strong convictions of the duties involved in the appointment I held it under consideration some time. I left Athens at the adjournment of the board—returned to Knoxville—detailed to my friends what had occurred at the meeting of the board and the different views between them and me. With not a solitary exception each one of my friends concurred in the construction I had given to the act and earnestly advised me not to disappoint public expectation by declining to accept the state agency. They assured me that I should not ask a single individual to go upon my bond as security. This assurance was faithfully realised. I never did ask one to go upon it. Whigs and Democrats, without distinction of parties, became my volunteer endorsers.[9]

Informing the governor that I had accepted the appointment his partiality had conferred upon me, I prepared at once to execute its duties. At the proper time I entered into bond, repaired to Nashville, procured the state bonds very neatly engraved on silk paper—each bond having

---

[9] For a description of the railroad legislation under which Dr. Ramsey was acting, see James Phelan, *History of Tennessee* (1888), 282 ff.

printed, on the same sheet, the law under which I acted, the great seal of the state of Tennessee, with the semi-annual coupons signed by A. R. Crozier, Comptroller etc., etc. They had been prepared under the direction of my brother, Colonel W. B. A. Ramsey, the secretary of state. Judge Alexander D. Keyes, the president, and Mr. Pritchard, the chief engineer of the company, joined me at Dalton, Georgia. I went with them via Atlanta, Augusta, Charleston, Wilmington, Weldon, etc. At each of these places I called upon Dr. _____, president of the state road, Judge J. P. King of the Georgia Railroad, my old friend H. W. Conner, Esquire, of the Charleston & Hamburg Railroad, General McRae of the W. & W. R. R. and consulted them in reference to my duties. Each of these gentlemen gave me a frank upon his road. From Mr. Conner I procured a letter of introduction to Honorable Eli Lawrence, president of the Bank of the State of New York. I had asked for one to an *honest* man in Wall Street. He replied he knew the very man I needed—one of old Hickory's custom house officers. His letter was laconic. These were its words. "This will introduce to you an *honest* Railroad Agent from Tennessee—my friend Doctor Ramsey. *Treat him well* and keep him from the jaws of the bears and bulls on Wall Street. Yours H. W. C." Arrived at New York I called on Mr. Lawrence—found him in his own room at the bank—handed him Mr. C.'s letter. I told him I was a green financier and without a friend in that city. He asked me to call on him often. He was a friend of Jackson and Polk and was always happy to see their countrymen and to serve them. I left with his cashier $100,000 of my bonds—showed one of them to Mr. Lawrence. He admired the execution of them and said they ought to sell well. I had brought with me the comptroller's report of the preceding year exhibiting the liabilities of the state of Tennessee (amounting then only to three millions) incurred for her banks and McAdamised roads soon to become productive, her population above a million. I pointed all this out to Mr. Lawrence and commented on the smallness of her debt compared with other states whose securities were then above par in New York, and especially Massachusetts and Maryland. I inquired how is it that Tennessee bonds are below par? He seemed interested in my remarks and proposed to go with me tomorrow to the Chamber of Commerce and try the market. I went with him accordingly the next day, taking with me one of my bonds and the comptroller's report. I was oppressed with the responsibility of the position I occupied. Tennessee securities twenty per cent below par. I was prohibited by law from selling below one hundred.

My road would not advance a step without I could realise that upon my bonds. Some one (W. A. Belmont, I believe) asked to see the one I held in my hand. I handed it to him. He praised the style of their execution and said that with the state seal upon them and their fine paper they looked like sterling bonds. I exhibited the comptroller's report and expatiated upon the resources of my state and her freedom from a large debt, etc., etc., etc.

This was a new issue of bonds from Tennessee and the one I offered as a specimen attracted a general attention and even admiration and my comptroller's report was carefully examined—especially the column of *liabilities* and assets. No state made a better exhibit. I did not fail to make the most of a comparison so advantageous to my proud Tennessee. The gentleman who had first asked to see the specimen I held in my hand was, as I learned afterwards, Mr. Belmont, the agent in America, of the Rothchilds or Barings or some European capitalists. He seemed particularly pleased with it and evidently wanted to invest. He inquired what I held them at? I replied nothing below par. He said Tennessee bonds are quoted this morning in Philadelphia at 80. I said my coupons are payable semiannually and in this city and at the Bank of the State of New York and nothing below par can purchase one of the bonds. I said this with emphasis and earnestly. He took it again into his hand and holding it up said "this is the prettiest bond in this market. I have seen none better in America but I have orders from across the water to make no investment in the securities of a *slave* state." I replied firmly "the sovereignty of Tennessee as represented by the signature of Governor Trousdale and her great seal of the state officially affixed is a sufficient guarantee alike of her good faith and her solvency." Good old Mr. Lawrence came at that moment to my relief and added "A state that has produced a Jackson and a Polk is a satisfactory guarantee to me." This nonplused Mr. Belmont who said in a subdued tone "Tennessee is a good state but my orders from across the water prohibit me from investing." When I left the Chamber of Commerce that P.M. my stocks had a decided upward tendency. The next day I visited most of the brokers on Wall Street and showed my bond and commented on the comptroller's report. I had yet made no railroad purchases and of course owed no money. I was therefore in a good condition to bide my time and make my negotiations deliberately for the equipment of my railroad.

Our engineer had found on Cliff Street a model of an approved rail and recommended its purchase. We were making the first bargain for any road in Tennessee and we were able to say therefore to parties offering to sell new equipment for our road that as we were the first Tennessee Company they ought to manufacture for us the best article and of the best material and at the lowest cost—as we were the fore-runners in our state purchasers, they should give us a good bargain as other connecting roads would see our patterns—hear the prices we paid and thus be induced to buy of them also. I made the most of this argument. At length *on the absolute condition that if I could effect a sale of my bonds* at par I would pay for the T-rail per American ton delivered at the mast at Charleston or Savannah at the rate of $22.00 in cash and $6.00 in stocks of the Company at par and $4.00 in the bonds of the Company equaling $32.00 per ton, we to pay the duties at the custom house—an extraordinary purchase certainly. The Englishman with whom I contracted, I believe, was a Mr. Radcliffe or some such name and a member of Parliament and being rather deaf—talking loud—I over-heard him say while I was in an adjoining room writing, "Is he a lawyer? He manages the thing very adroitly." Purchases were also made for engines from Norris at Philadelphia on very good terms but always on the express condition that I should effect sales of my bonds at par.

During these negotiations I was steadily pressing the bonds on the market but showed little anxiety to sell. I had no one directly interested in them but myself and I comparatively a stranger in New York. I left one of them on Mr. Lawrence's table for exhibition. The balance of them was in his vault. He encouraged me by the remark that when the capitalists returned from the watering places they would invest. One day I called on some of the brokers and remarked that I would leave the next day for Philadelphia as Tennessee stocks were better known there and I had found no disposition in New York to purchase. That evening a young man that I had seen before in Underwood's office near the Chamber of Commerce called at my room in the Irving House. He had heard that I was about leaving the city and had called to see me. I pointed to my trunk already packed and said as no one seemed disposed to take hold I must seek another market. I promised to be on Wall Street next morning. During that A.M. I was offered 104½ for $50,000 or less of my bonds. I went immediately to see Mr. Lawrence. He said he would advise me to let them go. I told him I needed then only $10,000 to pay the duties on the first cargo of rails and that by declining to sell $40,000 at the rate of 4½

premium I would run up my stocks. "You are not as green a financier
as you represented yourself to be. If you do not need the money yours is
the best policy." I had requested the broker to call in an hour at the Bank
of New York and we would close the transaction. He did so, but seemed
disappointed when I handed him but *ten* bonds. I deposited the money
and principal and premium with Mr. Lawrence. Next morning, I read in
the *Herald* that Dr. Ramsey, Agent of Tennessee, had declined the sale
of $40,000 Tennessee six per cents at 104½. After that I had no furthur
trouble in realising upon the bonds or in paying them out at selling rates
for cars, locomotives, chairs—or any equipment I wanted for the road.
My first sale I always believed was to Mr. Belmont but I did not see him
during the transaction.

I closed my agency after a perplexing administration of about two years
—settled my accounts with the treasuries of the state and of the Company
satisfactorily to both, even to a farthing. I never lost a dollar, lost a check
or missed a letter. I raised the stock of Tennessee to 104½—once to 106,
and purchased the equipment at more favorable rates than was ever done
before or since. I heard no more of a mandamus. I had the cooperation
and assistance of President Keyes and Chief Engineer Pritchard during
my whole administration. And I never heard that any one, Whig or
Democrat, friend or enemy, who spoke of it in any other terms than of
eulogy and approbation. Mr. Lawrence said I had financed better than he
could have done himself. Mr. Conner of Charleston who introduced me
to him said (and he was himself president of a railroad and a banker),
no other railroad had been equipped the same number of miles (from
Dalton to Loudon) for $350,000.00. And a few years afterwards when I
was leaving his city (after staying in it four months reading the proof
sheets of my *History of Tennessee*) paid me the graceful and delicate
compliment of calling his best locomotive "Dr. J. G. M. Ramsey" and
sent me in the train drawn by it, its first trip to Augusta—saying to me as
I left his depot "Doctor, you galvanised a dead road into life and equipped
it afterwards for $350,000.00." The first part of his complimentary remark
was more than I was entitled to. Judge Keyes, Judge Thomas C. Lyon,
Colonel W. B. A. Ramsey, Parson Sneed, Colonel J. H. Crozier, William
and T. I. Lenoir and Major John Jarnagin assisted in the galvanization he
alluded to and I cheerfully accord to them a full share of the credit of
doing it. If there is any merit in having equipped so many miles with so
little money I claim it is my own. I, *egome*—my very self, did it all.

Every enterprise, every corporation, has its own *secret* history. I mean by this not known to the world at large. This is true of the E.T. & G.R.R. Some of the proprietors of Loudon expected that place to be the eastern terminus of our road and that Knoxville would be drawn to and absorbed by it. I *knew* this to be true before the road was finished to that point. When I saw that everything necessary for its completion to Loudon was provided and that it would certainly be executed, I returned from one of our quarterly meetings and before going out to Mecklenburg, my country residence, I spent the night with my brother-in-law, Major Swan, in Knoxville. He was then the wealthiest man in town and owned more of its real estate than any other man in it. I told him all I knew of the intention of certain parties to arrest the progress of the railroad when it should reach the Tennessee River at Loudon. I unfolded to him all my own views on that subject and convinced him that if it stopped there his property in Knox county would depreciate to a tenth of its present value; if it were continued to Knoxville a corresponding appreciation of his property must ensue. I knew him to be a gentleman of enlightened liberality and public spirit as to steamboats and other enterprises but as to railroads I knew him to be, if not an opponent, certainly a sceptic as to their success in our interior country. I told him that the funds of our Company were exhausted and that if the road were to be constructed Knox county had to foot the bill—furnish the money or at least 90 per cent of its cost—the corner of Roane through which the road passsed barely pay the remaining 10 per cent. I told him further that he was the only man who could give the project sufficient impetus to carry it through. I gave him the estimates Mr. Pritchard had made of the money which must be bona-fide raised so as to entitle us to the state aid. I told him that without his cooperation the thing was already dead and I would abandon it and that if I could secure his assistance I had no doubt of success with other capitalists and property holders. We sat up till after midnight when I retired, remarking that in the morning, if you decline giving us your countenance and aid, I will go out home disappointed and despondent—if you concur we will go into town and put the ball in motion at once. I had succeeded. The Major told me next morning that he would cooperate earnestly. We went over accordingly, called a meeting of the town, invited the concurrence of the county and the country—and before three days the necessary subscription of stock was made, Colonel Sneed, Colonel G. W. Churchill, Major Swan and Colonel Crozier head-ing the list. Enough of stock was taken to secure state aid and the great policy (which I had originated in 1826 of reaching the Atlantic by railroad) was completed in 1858 and put Knoxville in connection with our South Atlantic seaports and through them with the commerce of the world.

CHAPTER III

Banking and Internal Improvements

But my devotion to this peculiar theory of our trade was not so intense or exclusive as to lead me to withhold my earnest cooperation with those who advocated other channels of commerce. The trade of Knoxville languished. The agriculture of East Tennessee continued unremunerative and many of the enterprising and skilful farmers were emigrating elsewhere. The general government had made appropriations to remove the obstructions in the Tennessee River, and the legislature of Tennessee, operating in the same spirit, organised a Board of River Commissioners and gave them the control of monies for the improvement of the streams of East Tennessee. Of these commissioners I was appointed one. We did the best we could with the means and powers with which we were invested—but as in most cases of river improvements our efforts and expenditures were almost worthless. I have almost forgotten the names of my colleagues in this board. Mozier of Jefferson County was one. They were all practical men—honest and patriotic citizens—but we effected very little.

A scheme was also projected to give East Tennessee the advantage of steamboat navigation as far at least up the river as Knoxville. This enterprise was inaugurated by my brother, W. B. A. Ramsey, Doctor James King, William Swan, James Kennedy, Dr. C. W. Crozier, and others,— all of Knox County. I took one share—my brother two—he was the largest stockholder and was commissioned by a unanimous vote of the share holders to repair to Cincinnati, Ohio, to purchase or build a boat of such form and tonnage as would best suit the navigation of our shoal rivers. Under his direction the steamboat *Knoxville* was built and brought around to the town for which it was named.[1] The difficulties under which he

[1] The columns of the Knoxville *Register* carried the account of the building and arrival of the *Knoxville*. Cf., issues of March 16, 23, April 13, May 4, 11, 25, June 29, November 16, December 7, 1831 and February 15, 1832.

At the dinner given by the citizens to Colonel W. B. A. Ramsey to celebrate the arrival of the *Knoxville*, Dr. Ramsey offered toasts to Dr. James King, president of the steamboat

33

effected the ascent at the Shoals, the Suck and Boiling Pot were almost incredible, and would have led one less enterprising and persevering to abandon the almost hopeless undertaking. *Labor vincit omnia* and by dint of contrivances innumerable and of indomitable energy and indefatigable perseverance he achieved success. On his arrival at Knoxville a vast throng of citizens and strangers assembled on the bank of the river and greeted the arrival with shouts of welcome and applause. Dr. King, one of the most active of the projectors of this nautical enterprise and at that time the mayor of Knoxville, welcomed Colonel Ramsey by a happy allusion to his return after his long absence—and congratulated him upon the success of his enterprise, and hailed the occasion as an auspicious era and as the commencement of a more prosperous commerce for East Tennessee. Colonel Ramsey, standing on the prow of his boat and surrounded by the crew and a few passengers, replied to the address of the mayor, and in a few words recapitulated the difficulties and dangers of the navigation of the river which he had ascended to that point. Other ceremonials and demonstrations followed. Immediate measures were taken to put the boat into the river trade. The result was as I had always believed. There was neither passengers nor freight to keep the *Knoxville* employed. When in port her expenses were greater than when under weigh. The stockholders rented her a while at a very low figure. In a few years they determined to sell her. The sale did not realise but about $90.00 to the share. Though the capital was nearly all lost still this failure and disappointment turned the attention of every one to *land communications* to the South, as the only scheme for the relief of our commerce. Nearly all the stockholders were then young and energetic and in a short time recuperated and forgot their losses. Our example was a caution to other adventures. The boat was sold to Major Swan, one of its first holders. He ran it a while without any adequate remuneration for his purchase money. The boiler and engine were converted into a saw-mill—the hull into, I believe, a wharf boat at Ross's landing (now Chattanooga) and this is the last I ever heard of the S. B. *Knoxville*.

There was an anecdote often told by Major Mynatt about this boat. Its occasion was the last meeting of the stockholders before selling her. Each member of the company was called on to give his opinion what was best

company, and to "Patriotism: Something else than party zeal or a selfish scramble for office." *Register,* May 11, 1831.

For internal improvements as an issue in Tennessee, see Stanley J. Folmsbee, *Sectionalism and Internal Improvements in Tennessee* (1939).

to be done with the *Knoxville*. One of them, old Mr. Shutterly, the senior stockholder, said, "Shentlemen (he was a Dutchman) there is but one way to do to save ourselves from further losses. Ever trip the d____d boat makes brings us in debt—every voyage she goes costs more than it comes to and my opinion is to run her up the river to the deep water at Dr. Ramsey's ferry and get some two inch augers and bore holes through her bottom planks—let in the water—sink her, and let her go to H____." Mr. S. was one of the few farmers who were willing to risk money to improve the commerce of the country and raise thus the price of its products. The river improvement scheme and this steamboat experiment were alike abortive and unsuccessful.[2]

After this slight digression from the main line of this autobiography I resume another topic of it. I have mentioned already that in November 1820 my venerated father died in the office to which he had then recently been appointed,—president of the branch of the new Bank of the State at Knoxville. His successor was W. E. Anderson. I was soon after appointed by the mother board to fill the vacancy occasioned by my father's death, and was annually appointed a director till its charter expired. When in 1835 the charter for the Louisville Cincinnati and Charleston Railroad and Banking Company was granted, a provision was made for a branch bank at Knoxville. A board of directors for this branch was elected by the mother bank at Charleston. Colonel Abraham Blanding, its president, enclosed to me a list of our branch board of directors. My name was placed at the head of this list. My colleagues were Robert King, Judge Reese, James Park, Esquire, Honorable J. H. Crozier, Colonel W. S. Howell, W. S. Kennedy, Samuel Bell, Mr. Pickett and others not now recollected. As chairman by courtesy, by usage it became my duty to call the gentlemen as named in the list together for the purpose of organization. We met by common consent in the jewelers shop of one of the directors, Mr. Samuel Bell. I presented and read the letter to me from President Blanding. No mention was made in that letter of any one for our president —nor any indication given of preference only that implied by the position of the names on the list sent to me. W. S. Kennedy, Esquire had, before we met, asked me if I would serve as president. I replied that if elected by a unanimous vote of the branch directors, I would. If not I would decline the position. He nominated me as president and the nomination was

---

[2] Dr. Ramsey here inserted the account of the East Tennessee Historical and Antiquarian Society which appears on pages 46–47.

unanimously confirmed. We then proceeded to elect our other bank officers—sent forward our cashier, D. A. Deaderick, Esquire, to Charleston for the funds with which to commence business. He went by stage—procured $100,000.00 as our capital and such instructions from the parent board as were demanded by our new position as bankers. Our progress met the entire approbation of the mother board and of the stockholders of the company. Our policy was to lend our issues generally to our Tennessee stock drovers—taking their bills payable at the principal banks of South Carolina and Georgia. These bills, as they matured, were collected, deposited to our credit, and constituted a fund equivalent to gold against which we could draw, and thus kept us fully supplied with gold, or issues equal to it, in all the southern marts. In this way we always protected our own circulation, and were rarely called on for specie as our check or drafts were always preferred by our customers to coin at our own counter. Thus we financed well and safely, and when that great crash and commercial convulsion occured in 1837 and forced banks North and South to suspend specie payments, no rush was made on our branch. President Blanding wrote to me that the principal bank had been forced to yield to the existing pressure and had suspended—suggesting to me that, without ordering us to suspend instanter, he would leave to the discretion of our directory when that suspension should take place. When I read this letter to my directors, one of them introduced a resolution to suspend at once. This member was Mr. Samuel Bell. I was in the chair and called Mr. Bell to my seat, and changing to the one occupied by him I proposed to amend his motion by striking out *at once* in his resolution, and adding the words after suspend *when ever the officers of this branch find it necessary and politic to do so*. My amendment was adopted—*nemini contradicenti*. The branch never did suspend, as mentioned on a preceding page.

A provision had been made in the original charter of the L. C. & C. R. R. that it should have the privilege of banking only upon the condition that the road should be built and that in the event of its suspension or failure then the banking privilege was to be withdrawn. Kentucky and Ohio had made inadequate provisions for that part of the road. The state of Tennessee and private stockholders had furnished the pro rata of her part of the great work. In North Carolina, where the heaviest part of the enterprise and the largest expenditures were requisite to tunnel the mountains and cross them, no state provision had been made, and that from individual resources was necessarily insufficient, it became evident the road could not be completed within the time specified in our charter. South Carolina, true to her state motto "Animis Opibusque Parati," stood now ready to execute her part of the work. But the existing commercial and financial embarrassments of the country had prostrated the resources of that state and of her people, and rendered all reasonable hope of achieving success at the present vain and illusory. Under these circumstances it became painfully evident that the great undertaking of constructing a railroad six hundred miles across a mountain country with the then available means of the states interested in it, must for the present be abandoned. The banking privilege was therefore necessarily rendered void. The branch bank at Knoxville was put in a train of liquidation. Our cashier was directed to wind it up and it ceased to be.

Under the existing state of the affairs of the company a meeting of the stockholders and of the general directory of the corporation took place in Columbia in December 1839. Kentucky failed to send a delegate. From Tennessee I alone attended—as the proxy of the state at large as well as of the individual stockholders. Only one, I believe, from North Carolina. South Carolina was fully and ably represented as usual. It was plainly seen that the charter had to be surrendered and the work abandoned as impracticable at the present time and with the present means.

But who ought to make the motion and propose to the meeting the dissolution of the company and the consequent abandonment of the work? From which of the states could such a proposition come most gracefully? We all hesitated. A sort of random discussion followed. South Carolina stood still ready to extend her aid. North Carolina could not, of course, be expected to provide her pro rata. I had always pledged to the Company that when the work was completed to our state line at Paint Rock, Tennessee would continue it at least to Knoxville,—which had been at my instance made a point on the road which should be reached. Tennessee had redeemed my pledge and had made legislative provision to take one-half of the stock necessary to complete it. Individual stockholders had made subscription for the other half, to be expended within her own bounds. I held in my hands a commission from Governor Polk as state proxy and was also the proxy of many of our private stockholders. Of course I could not be expected to move for a dissolution of the company. I had redeemed all the pledges I had ever made for Tennessee.

At the first convention on this general subject called at my instance in

1831 (I believe) and held at Asheville, North Carolina I had been placed by Honorable Mitchell King, the president of that body, at the head of the committee from Tennessee to report to the convention next morning. As its chairman I called my committee to meet at three o'clock P.M. at my room in Patton's Hotel. The committee consisted of General Alexander Anderson, my colleague from Knox County, and General A. E. Smith and Major William Robinson from Cocke County and Ellis from Sevier. This committee met at my room. I proposed to them to subdivide our duties and for each member to take his portion of it and to embody the different sub-divisions—(statistics—route—right of way etc., etc.) in our general report to the convention next morning at eight A.M. One of the committee after another excused himself by observing that the chairman had been devoting his time and attention for several years to the great subject and was familiar with it in all its details and each insisted that the whole report be prepared by the chairman and submitted to the committee for its consideration and adoption next morning. I begged again for the sub-division of the labor assigned us. I mentioned that we all had ridden several miles that morning on horseback in a hot September sun, that I was much fatigued and must ask them to assist me. The committee was inexorable and I had to submit. I directed the servants to bring up to my room a cup of tea as often as I rang for it. (Tea alone was my remedy for a distressing head-ache to which I was long subjected). At four P.M. I sat down to my work—wrote all night upon my report—finished it just as day dawned. Immediately after breakfast my committee came to my room. I read over to them the report, and asked them to suggest amendments, alterations, etc., etc. Major Robinson moved its adoption, and without dotting an i or crossing a t, his motion was unanimously concurred in. At nine A.M., the convention met in the court house. At the proper time reports were called for, and I presented that from the state of Tennessee. I had elaborated the whole theory of our trade, our distant markets, the inadequacy of our rivers for transporting our imports or exports, the unremunerative condition of our agriculture, and the poor requital of the husbandman's toil in Tennessee, and the hopelessness of any remedy for our embarrassed commerce but the construction of a land communication between the South Atlantic seaport and the navigable waters of the West. The last sentence of my report I can still recollect. In substance it was: "Standing on these heights (Asheville), in view alike of the plains and savannahs of the sunny South and of the fertile valleys and rich bottom lands of the rivers of the West, we pledge to the execution of this great work our mutual cooperation—our great resources—and our financial aid." The report was listened to with fixed attention and apparent approbation. It was soon after published with the proceedings of the Asheville Convention in Tennessee and the Carolinas. The pledge thus made was soon after redeemed by the legislature and the people of Tennessee. It was reaffirmed at the great railroad convention at Knoxville, July 4, 1836, of which I was a member from Knox County. And now, when this pledge had been met by the assured cooperation and aid of Tennessee, could I, as her representative at Columbia, propose to abandon my own bantling and extinguish the hope and blast, even for a time, the expectations of my countrymen? I would not. I could not. I did not.

But during the discussion I took the opportunity to say in substance that Tennessee had provided the means and was still willing to apply them to the construction of her part of this road so important and essential to all her interests. She is still prepared in good faith to cooperate fully with her sister states in the achievement of our original purpose. But, if any one of her co-states feels not inclined or forced to abandon it, Tennessee interposes no objection and is not unwilling to release such state from any implied obligation to persevere in the work at this financial crisis. As I took my seat I heard from several South Carolina members— "Good!—Graceful! Handsome! etc., etc." The question was thus, without any specific motion from any particular member, considered as settled and measures were adopted to wind up the L. C. & C. R. R. Co. No odium or blame was attached to any member or any state. The whole scheme was from the first too large and unwieldy to be effected by any one company. The work was too Herculean for 1839. It has been wisely assigned to other agencies since, and under different charters is at the present writing (March 1870) still likely to be accomplished to its original extent. Within the last year this writer came by steam cars from Knoxville almost to the North Carolina line—to Wolf Creek where in 1836 he met the engineer corps under General McNeill, engineer in chief of the L. C. & C. R. R., and on the identical track surveyed by them a railroad is being constructed up the French Broad as indicated in his report to the Asheville Convention a third of a century since, and he is yet not without hope that he may yet live to see the dream of his youth and the illusions of his manhood still carried out in their fullest extent. The Blue Ridge is now being tunneled, and his old scheme of connecting Charleston and Knoxville by railroad he *knows* will yet be realised.

This realization in one respect has come too late. Had that commercial connection been formed under Hayne and Blanding, an identity of interest between the South and West might have prevented the Revolution of 1860–1865. This was the main argument with the patriotic Hayne and King and others of the railroad convention of 1836. Statesmen could even then descry the coming storm on the political horizon. Hayne said to me: "Bind the South to the West by links of iron [meaning iron rails], give them a commercial identity, and thus prevent a political disintegration which paper constitutions and congressional restrictions etc., etc., are all unable to guard against."

I listened to him with respectful attention. I had never believed in the efficacy of a union of interest. That is something, it is true, but such a ligament as that is fragile at best and cannot overcome the antagonisms of race—of the type of civilization and the phases of society—nor the effects of climate and other physical causes. The people of our North and of our South have always been heterogenous, and have never been and cannot hereafter become homogeneous. They are essentially two peoples—as different in their civilization as the people of France and England. No one ruler—no one government—could be made to suit either country. In New England, as state agent I found by my intercourse, official and personal, with the highest and lowest of the citizens there I noticed a blind subserviency to others, to a fashionable public sentiment, whether in religion or politics, to the wealthy, to corporations to party, that we never knew in the South. They were less intelligent, less virtuous, less sensible of their personal rights and personal liberty, than even our unlettered and uncultivated common people. With a great deal of hauteur, and arrogance, and boastful effrontery, they are more selfish, illiberal and narrow than any people I ever saw. That high-souled honor, that strict regard to truth, probity, virtue, jealousy of liberty and personal self respect, that constitute the character of a Southern man, were all wanting in the Yankee and made him offensive and hateful to a Southern freeman. A Massachusetts manufacturer is a shrewd trader and has enterprise enough to make money. He will make an engine or a car and sell it well, but will always leave the impression upon his Southern customer that at heart he is a swindler. Interest makes him honest, not principle. The loss of a dollar wounds his feelings more than a stain upon his character. He has no lordly ambition to achieve any thing laudable and patriotic. His highest ambition is to become wealthy even by ignoble means. He is supercilious and ungenerous to his operatives and expects them to be servile to him and to become his slaves—his tools and a part of his machinery. It is unnecessary to trace the Yankee further (I do not say a New Englander)—nor to contrast him with the noble hearted Southron by a further delineation of Southern character. But although fixed in my belief of the antagonism between the two peoples I was not unwilling to allow General Hayne to make the most of his argument that our railroad would cement and unite such discordant elements. The future cannot hereafter (1870) make us one people. The disintegration against which Calhoun and Hayne then warned the South is now effected and is forever sealed by blood and must remain unalterable and eternal. We are essentially two people and the future will demonstrate the impossibility of uniting us under one government.

After my connection with the Southwestern railroad bank ceased in consequence of the dissolution of the L. C. & C. R. R. Co., I was elected a director of the branch of the Union Bank at Knoxville. Still later, the Bank of East Tennessee was purchased by Colonel W. M. Churchwell and some time after I was requested to become a member of his board of directors. I was then busily engaged on my second volume of my "Annals of Tennessee" and declined his invitation. After some months, he renewed his request, and I reluctantly consented to attend the weekly meetings of his board occasionally when such attendance should not interfere with my other pursuits, professional and literary. During the great revulsion and panic of 1857 that occurred about this time, the Bank of East Tennessee was forced to suspend, as did many other banks in the country. A meeting of the president and directors, resolving to meet in good faith all its liabilities, thought it advisable to place the bank in the hand of trustees. One of the board, Major Lyon, a good lawyer, was elected the trustee. He said he was not unwilling to accept the trust, provided the directors would associate me with him in its execution. At first I offered the reasons already given to become a director, as grounds of refusing to be a trustee. The trustee, known everywhere to be a gentleman of integrity, capacity, and character, assured me that if I would consent to accept the joint trusteeship with himself he would do the work and draw very little either upon my time or my assistance. Under this understanding, and thus assured, I consented to be associated thus with Major Lyon as trustee.

No two men ever accepted such a trust with purer motives, more disinterested intentions, or a more vigorous determination to wind up the bank fairly, honestly, legally, and equitably. At first our administration of the trust was, or seemed to be, perfectly satisfactory to the holders of its issues and it was believed if time was given the whole could be soon adjusted. But the holders became alarmed and sold the notes they held at a ruinous rate of depreciation. Combinations between speculators were formed, suits were instituted against the trustees and the assets of the bank were taken from the hands of the trustees and placed in the possession of the clerk and master, or of a receiver—I never knew which. Some of these suits are yet undecided. In the decree first decided by Chancellor Seth J. W. Lucky he said in substance that there was *no grounds in our administration of the trust that could impugn the honor or integrity of the trustees* of the bank. With this decree terminated my connection with the Bank of East Tennessee. I may incur pecuniary loss—perhaps have already incurred it. I will then be an innocent sufferer. But the character of the trustees is beyond the reach of malice, political spite, or defamation and low revenge. "Who steals my purse steals trash. But he who filches my good name steals not what enriches him—but makes me poor indeed." So sang some poet (Shakespeare I believe). Some vulgar tongue may have slandered him—some wicked defamer may have assailed his high reputation and his character—some envious falsifier may have maligned, and misrepresented, and vilified him. As to the trustees it is the viper trying to gnaw a file. Major Lyon, the chief, the acting trustee is now and was ever esteemed an honest man. He is now in an honored grave and beyond the reach of slander or defamation. As to his associate trustee, he still stands erect—proud. *Mens conscia recti* still sustains, has ever sustained him.

Besides this, he has lived to see his integrity established and vindicated by contemporaneous *testimony* that none can call in question. During all these transactions, and the groundless slander and abuse of the trustees published to the world in the Knoxville *Whig,* it was determined by the Bank of Tennessee to establish a branch at Knoxville. I was surprised one morning to receive by mail a letter from Colonel Johnson, then its president, containing a long list of names for the directory of the branch. I was not less surprised to see at the head of the list the name of *Dr. J. G. M.*

Ramsey. In the same letter he desired me to accept the presidency of the branch and to indicate my preference for twelve others on the list as my directors. Among the rest in the list, and in immediate propinquity to my own name, stood that of *Honorable T. C. Lyon.* My board was called together. I was nominated by Major Lyon as president. The motion was seconded by Honorable W. H. Sneed and I unanimously elected. I thanked the board for their unanimity in calling me to fill this important office, and gave my reasons for declining it. Colonel Crozier was then put in nomination and also unanimously elected. Under the circumstances, my election at the time as president of the new Branch Bank of Tennessee at Knoxville I have always considered as the highest compliment of my public life. To be selected for that responsible position by bankers, capitalists, business men of all parties, creeds, and professions, was a compliment not only to my financial ability but to my integrity and my private and public virtue. It was a *public endorsement of my whole character,* and has been universally so considered.

I considered it as the work of Divine Providence in behalf of two innocent and deserving citizens. The two trustees were both natives of Knox County, known to every citizen as gentlemen of the most elevated character and standing, who had their whole lives been in the public service, blameless and irreproachable, who had escaped all private or public censure. To defame such characters was the most desperate attempt of the most desperate defamer and slanderer who ever escaped the halter or the penitentiary. Instead of being made victims of the slander of the traducer, one of his own counsellors pronounced that "Lyon and Ramsey had been invulnerable—to slander or defamation." We may both have suffered pecuniarily, but the good character and integrity of each are established.

During the entire time of my administration of my Knoxville branch of the Bank of Tennessee, it retained the confidence of the people of the state and of their representatives as well as of the president and directors of the parent board. With Honorable Cave Johnson and his successor, Samuel A. Smith I believe, and especially of Colonel G. C. Torbett, I maintained the most friendly official and personal relations. In my own board no presiding officer ever met with a more harmonious directory. We were a unit and always cooperated heartily. I was elected unanimously at Nashville every year, and with equal unanimity was placed in the president's chair by the undiminished confidence and support of my local board. It consisted all the time of directors selected from both or all political parties. At the directors' table politics were eschewed entirely. *There,* at all times, prevailed unanimity and a spirit of cordial and official cooperation.

One morning my directors gave me an agreeable surprise. The occasion was this. Our new banking house was on the point of completion and ready to be formally surrendered by the contractors for our occupancy and use. The building committee invited us all to attend the ceremonial of inaugurating of what was then the finest banking house in East Tennessee—perhaps in the state. My cashier, Mr. M. B. McMahon, Esquire, who was also one of the building committee walked at my side, unlocked the door, and invited Mr. President and directors to walk in. We did so. From a point outside of the counter and railing in the large hall, Mr. McMahon said, "I have the pleasure of introducing you gentlemen," pointing to the rich ornamental work on the ceiling above our heads, "to General Jackson and Vice President H. L. White on the one side, and to President Polk and our own worthy president, Doctor Ramsey, here on the other." Then turning to myself he added "In choosing thus to associate you with the most illustrious and distinguished public men of Tennessee, whose pictures are before us, I take the opportunity to remark that we have made you the connecting link between the past and present of Tennessee and of the country. In one corner of the painting is the emblem of the patriotism and chivalry—General Andrew Jackson who was the first from the Volunteer State to occupy the presidential chair. In another the Honorable H. L. White, once our own townsman and neighbour—distinguished as the president of the *first* bank in Tennessee, as a jurist and statesman, and vice president of the United States. In another is the able and virtuous James Knox Polk, second president of the United States from Tennessee, and distinguished for every public and private virtue. In the other corner we have placed yourself, and beg to assure you that in so doing we have desired to offer you in a permanent form some token of our official confidence and our high personal regard." In my reply I returned my acknowledgements for the official and personal compliments they had just paid me. I had known well and intimately all three of those associated with me on the canvas or painting. The two eldest had been my father's friends and co-pioneers in the infancy of Tennessee: That "I had received them all as guests and friends in my own house: I esteemed them living and now venerated their memory when dead, and that you Gentlemen could not have conferred upon me a higher private or public compliment or have given me a more agreeable surprise than the graceful civility thus unexpectedly offered me."

The clock struck our hour, and I said "The directors will please come to order by retiring to their room and entering upon our day's business." After the discounts were finished, we discounted other things than accommodation paper—real transactions and bills of exchange. No president ever had an abler, or more conscientious board of directors during the time I administered the financial affairs of the Knoxville branch of the Bank of Tennessee. That time embraced from the period its first establishment in 1858, as has been heretofore narrated, down to the invasion of East Tennessee by the Federal army under Burnside. Its further history will be resumed on a future page.[3]

---

[3] See Chapter VII.

CHAPTER IV

Intellectual Improvements

I had further agencies in the internal improvement of Tennessee—material moral and intellectual. In 1829 when General Richard G. Dunlap represented Knox County the system of common schools was inaugurated by the legislature. I became a school commissioner for Knox County. I set on foot also the formation of the East Tennessee Historical and Antiquarian Society. Chancellor William Brown Reese became its president—Professor Stephen A. Foster, vice president. I was elected Perpetual Corresponding Secretary (and am, of course, still in office unless an honorable [because a compulsory] exile since September 1863 disqualifies me for the position). Honorable J. H. Crozier was recording secretary and some one else treasurer. At the death of Mr. Foster, our vice president, Reverend T. W. Humes was elected his successor.

The most flattering compliment or literary civility I ever received was at the semicentennial celebration of the founding of Knoxville 1842. Our society was toasted by Honorable T. C. Lyon, following his sentiment with some remarks. Cheers followed. When silence was restored, I noticed the eyes of the company were directed alternately to me as secretary and to Chancellor Reese as president. I bowed to him at the other end of the table, intimating to him to respond. He bowed very gracefully to me—seeming to waive the question of precedence. These courtesies between the two officers of the E. T. H. & A. Society were reciprocated several times until I, determined not to disregard official propriety—much more the presumed preferences of the company—arose to my feet, exclaimed, clapping my hands at the same time, "My president, Chancellor Reese! A speech from President Reese. A speech!" "Reese! Reese! Reese!" resounded from every one in the hall. The president acquiesced in the unanimous demand of the guests. A speech followed and such a speech—from such a speaker and such a president! I may not here attempt to present to the readers of this autobiographical sketch. This writer can only here allude to the compliment paid by the speaker to his secretary for his official

46

zeal, industry, and devotion in collecting, preserving and perpetuating much of the early history of Tennessee and the West that otherwise would have been lost. In the conclusion of these prefatory remarks he said "Your speaker has the titular distinction of president of the E. T. H. & A. Society. Our able and faithful perpetual secretary has done and still does all the work. Doctor Ramsey constitutes himself the E. T. H. & A. Society. He is *the society* and as his modesty declines the response to Major Lyon's toast I shall attempt it." His speech was well received and clamorously applauded. It must be here omitted. But it is due to the memory of Judge Reese to add that when the first conception of the society entered my mind he was the first to whisper the words of encouragement in my ear and cooperated cordially in promoting the objects of our association.

Our friendship was early formed, 1820. It was never for a moment interrupted. It was life long. The great republic of letters knows nothing of the factions and estrangements and animosities of different states and political parties. I was *ab initio* a Democrat of the Jeffersonian school—a believer in that theory of government which makes the states really sovereigns—the creators of the union and not its subjects—and that in this sovereignty the states could at their option nullify unconstitutional acts of congress—or secede from the union whenever such usurpation of power by the central government should render such secession proper or necessary—that the states as states possessed as reserved rights, the power to judge of the infraction of these rights as well as the mode and measure of redress. These were my youthful political sentiments in 1820—They were my political creed in my manhood—in 1840—and the deliberate convictions of my old age in 1870. On the other hand I knew they were not the political views of my friend Judge Reese. I voted for him for congress in 1823? perhaps 1825. He never was a Federalist, much less an abolitionist or a consolidationist. He was a virtuous man and a patriot. I loved and admired him. We were bosom friends. Politics after our midlife were a forbidden subject. We travelled in company to the North in the same conveyances—the same cars—in the same ships—he as a Whig delegate to Philadelphia, I as a Democratic delegate to the Baltimore convention when Cass was nominated as the successor of Mr. Polk. Still I did not vote for the successful candidate (Cass) but stood up and threw three ballots for a better man and a real Democrat and statesman Levy Woodbury.[1]

---

[1] Dr. Ramsey's historical interests had already brought him in contact with Lyman Copeland Draper, a young historian whose interests in Tennessee and the pioneers of the "old Border" coincided with Dr. Ramsey's antiquarian interests. Draper resided in Baltimore in

During this exciting period and that long journey Judge Reese never mentioned politics once to me nor I once to him. Yet we visited the departments—private families—and learned societies together—worshiped in the same churches—dined with the same friends. Politics, as before remarked, was a forbidden subject. We both agreed to disagree. This cordiality continued to his death. He had frequently been my guest at Mecklenburg. I heard of his declining health with apprehension. For I knew that the sword (an over worked intellect) must necessarily soon cut through the scabbard and put him among the Immortals in Heaven. I saw him often. Less frequently than I wished for his mental activity seemed only to be stimulated into greater action by his increasing bodily debility. Even the day before his death we conversed together on his favorite topics: Homer Longinus, Belles Lettres, Horace and Virgil etc., etc., and I had to admonish him that talking so much, and especially his evident intellectual exertions, would exhaust his diminished strength. He acquiesced in the propriety of my admonition and quit the subject of our conversation. On retiring from his chamber I said *Vale*. He promptly replied *Vale tu quoque*. I never saw him afterwards.

On my way home I told Colonel Sneed and others of the older members of the bar that the chancellor could not survive many hours. He died soon after. On this occasion the bar met and adopted the usual resolutions of respect and condolence. Strange to say, and unexpectedly to myself certainly, the bar requested me to draw up the biographical sketch which next day was published with their proceedings. This unusual compliment to me I endeavored to decline much as the duty was agreeable to my private inclinations and genial to my personal regard of this genuine Christian gentleman, accomplished scholar and erudite and profound jurist. I felt assured he would, had he survived me, have done a similar sad duty for me.

1848, and was as ardent a Democrat as Dr. Ramsey. Just before leaving for the convention, Dr. Ramsey wrote to Draper, April 4, 1848, sending him a copy of a "Boon Inscription" and an account of the frontier battle of Point Pleasant. "I shall be in your place about the twenty-second," he added. "My being a delegate to the National Democratic Convention. There I hope to see you to assist me by your friendly suggestions about publishers, engravers, books, etc., etc. Will you be in Baltimore about that time? I go on after the convention rises to Philadelphia and the eastern cities. Inter nos, who are your candidates for president and vice-president?"

The meeting of the two historians marked the beginning of a life-long friendship between them. Dr. Ramsey's letters to Lyman Draper on historical and political and personal matters are preserved in the Draper and Wisconsin Historical Society Correspondence in the library of the State Historical Society of Wisconsin. These manuscripts are hereafter referred to as "Draper Correspondence." Draper's collections on historical subjects, to which Dr. Ramsey contributed many informative notes, are cited as "Draper Manuscripts."

To resume the thread of this sketch of the agency the writer has had in the improvement of Tennessee. I have already mentioned my appointment as school commissioner. The system did not work well. The poor, for whose children principally the legislative assistance had been provided, refused to send their children for the reason that they could not dress them equal to the *quality*. So they called all those who could pay for the schooling of their children and wished and intended to educate them. Thus the kind intention of the Tennessee legislature proved abortive. I failed—all my colleagues failed—to overcome this prejudice. The gratuity of the state benefited only those who did not need it.[2]

---

[2] In 1852 Lyman Draper migrated to Wisconsin where, in 1854 he reorganized the State Historical Society and became its corresponding secretary. In 1857 he was elected state superintendent of public instruction. Dr. Ramsey followed his career with interest, and was especially impressed by a voluminous and exhaustive school report which Draper issued late in 1858. "It should be in every school district in the United States . . ." he told Draper. "Here in Tennessee, we need it especially as our school system is an admitted failure, and it will do much to turn our further and future efforts in behalf of education into the proper channel." Draper Correspondence, April 16, 1859.

Inspired by Draper's example, and stimulated by a second report, Dr. Ramsey wrote again, January 17, 1860.

"Your report for 1858 you had previously sent me, and during the canvass of last summer (eschewing for the nonce all other topics) I and a few friends of educational reform here made it primary essential and paramount with the hope of effecting something salutary in the Tennessee system of common schools. We effected nothing of importance. I lent your report to several school teachers and others with the hope of securing their influence and cooperation in directing the attention of the *aspirants* for office to a remodeling our educational system and of improving, if not perfecting, it. It was all a vain and nugatory effort. Our present system is not only a failure but a positive injury. We had better schools, better teachers, more pupils fifty years ago when I was at school than now when money (sixty or eighty cents per pupil) is furnished by the state, and the teacher is appointed by functionaries here called school commissioners. Decidedly better in 1806–10 than 1860. *Self-reliance* then prompted the better men in every neighborhood to associate together, build a school house, employ a good teacher; while now, this association of the better class is nullified by the masses usurping the power of electing commissioners in each civil district for the reason that they will disburse the patronage to someone related or who will teach *cheaper* than someone else. I see no motion in our legislature to act on the subject. My advice has been given either to amend our school law or to throw the fund into that of internal improvement or the general treasury of the state. Still, I do not believe that the cause is absolutely and hopelessly dead. It needs your reforming head and hand and if you had not interdicted the use of your name in this behalf, I would have prepared a concise and forcible article for the "Nashville Union" setting forth your agency in the educational reform and system of Wisconsin and prompting by letters to my friends in the legislature to invite you to the seat of government to concoct and carry out every possible improvement in our very defective system. And, I reply to you this early to suggest to you to visit Nashville this winter—the Legislature may not adjourn before March or April—where, if I can, I will meet you and if I cannot do that, I can arrange a very cordial welcome for you. I think there is no difficulty in the way. Your elaborate and excellent Report of 1858 will introduce you at once most favorably, secure to you the architecture of a new system of which yourself shall be the designer and the architect. Do adopt the suggestion. I could urge it on account of the youth of my great state, your own fame and character beside other considerations scarcely less important—our milder climate, political condition, etc. Besides, although I harbour no revenge myself, nor cultivate or incite it in you or others, still you ought to shake the dust of Wisconsin off your shoes and leave them to their own fanaticism. I know it was no official delinquency of your own that beat you. It was nothing but that wanton spirit of free-soil-ism—alias anti-democratic prejudice—that elected your successor. (I had not heard it before and could have scarcely believed it

But in another way I tried to advance the cause of literature around me. I set on foot, and succeeded in organising near my residence, Mecklenburg Academy. We appointed seven leading men of our neighborhood its trustees. I gave the ground and more than half the money necessary for a frame building thirty-six by eighteen feet—a brick chimney at each end. It was plastered, glazed, and well finished. I gave also the privilege of fuel in perpetuity. I was appointed secretary to the board of trustees.

possible if I had not heard it from yourself.) Let them rip—if disunion follows, the North is the guilty cause of the unwelcome catastrophe. Answer this far of my letter early.

"I am greatly obliged by the report of your historical society. It will be a model for mine not far off, but on a smaller scale. We need you in Tennessee, too, to aid our historical efforts only scarcely begun. By the way, let me inquire what delays the publication of your life-long labours? Do let it come out before I go home. You need not like me be deterred by pecuniary considerations. If you would get Benson J. Lossing to illustrate it—(*alamode* his *Pictorial Field Book of the Revolution*) and interest him in the publication (stereotyped) you will sell ten thousand a year for ten years. I mean what I say. I know your subject and the manner of treating them. In the whole West and Southwest you will find a substantial patronage and much elsewhere. Print. The public is eager for it and you can't live always (only through your works). I made no money, you will several fortunes. Why I would give the price of one volume to see even the sketch of General (Doctor) William Fleming of Virginia, my aunt's father. So of every other reader or student. Besides this, let us claim you as a Tennessee author and if you will bestow and leave your unpublished collection of manuscripts to any but your legatees let me plead with you for Tennessee—come and take charge of her educational interests and her historical associations. Write me early, also, on this subject too. (If I get an opportunity I will send copies of your school reports to Governor Harris and other friends at Nashville. This is not interdicted by your letter and if you come south will facilitate the views and intentions of your friends in Tennessee.

"One word for me and mine if you are not already too much wearied to hear it. I and my good wife are yet well and active (—five children yet at home. Our eldest daughter, the widow of Colonel Breck once of St. Paul, Minnesota, two younger daughters and two sons). Our eldest son, General J. C. Ramsey, practices law in Knoxville, is U. S. District Attorney and was defeated for Congress last August. Our next is settled near us farming, our third on a tramp to Texas and two daughters married to two learned physicians in Knox and Boone —convenient to us. Our life, hereafter, is of course down-hill, and although much binds us to earth and time, we are looking out for a better country, even a heavenly. There, I hope to meet you. . . .

"P. S. Knoxville is now accessible to all the world by our railroads. If you come by Washington, twenty-eight hours will bring you here on your way to Nashville or Mississippi— Make our house your home at least a week or two."

On February 6, 1860, Dr. Ramsey wrote again to Draper. Draper had been defeated for reelection as school superintendent, and Dr. Ramsey had begun to take steps to induce him to migrate to Tennessee. "When I returned home from the bank Saturday afternoon," he wrote, "I found your esteemed favor of the 25th of January on my table. I then read over your first letter, and reflecting on both of them, determined to exercise the discretion you gave me on the matter and first wrote marked *private* to Governor Isham G. Harris—calling his attention to the defects and palpable failure of our common school system:—that it was unsatisfactory to those who administered the law, (I had been commissioner myself twenty or thirty years ago) and had disappointed public expectation; that I had studiously endeavoured to supply or correct those defects: had despaired of improving much less perfecting the system; had read your able and luminous reports as superintendent etc;—and had requested you to send him copies of them and expressed the hope that he had received and read them; that just such a man as you was now needed at Nashville to indoctrinate our legislature in effecting an educational reform in Tennessee; and that the chairman of the school committees in both branches of our legislature ought, by all means, to confer with you on the subject before attempting to inaugurate a new system—and that I believed if they or the governor, himself, would telegraph you at Madison, Wisconsin, you might be induced to pay a flying visit to

The Reverend A. Penland, pastor of the Presbyterian Church Lebanon, became the first principal of our academy. His school soon became so large that we had to appoint an assistant tutor. Several classical scholars were educated there—some of whom became instructors—and members of the learned professions. The academy continued in existence up to the time of Burnside's invasion of the country.

I became early in life one of the trustees of Hamden Sydney Academy in Knoxville. I was made chairman of its board of trustees. During the late war our buildings and grounds were used by the soldiery of both armies and much damaged. I do not know whether it has been resuscitated.

Nashville; that you were not now in the school service of Wisconsin,—the avalanche of fanaticism there having superseded you in November in a vote of 123,000 by less than 3,000 —showing by your heavy vote over your comrades on the Democratic ticket that your official services had been appreciated beyond the party question;—that tho I was not able to say that you would consent to come to Tennessee and take charge of educational matters here, yet I believed you could be induced to do so if prospects of permanent usefulness should be held out to you; that, if he did not himself know you, ex-Governor W. B. Campbell, General W. S. M. of Lebanon and Dr. Reese and Colonel A. W. Putnam of Nashville could endorse you—but that your Reports were sufficient endorsements—Jared Sparks, George Bancroft, Benson J. Lossing, Henry Barnard, Henry S. Randall and I had done so.

"This is a hasty outline of my letter to Governor Harris. I wrote, at the same time an article of the same purport for the Union and American—omitting any allusion to your race in that Black Republican state but taking the same view of the defects of our present educational system and suggesting the same course to be pursued in making it more perfect and effective, requesting the editor, Burck, to withhold my name and Post Office (as that identifies the writer).

"These two long papers I wrote Saturday night. This morning I wrote to A. W. Putnam, suggesting the need we had of your services in remodeling our system,—covering the same ground of the other papers, but asking him to confer with Campbell and M. at Lebanon and Dr. Reese and other friends in Tennessee to get the chairman or the Governor to try and get you to come and inaugurate a reform here. These letters and the communication for the Union and American were all sent by today's mail. Tomorrow I will write to our three members—to whom I had mentioned during their careers and showed your report first sent me. On them I will urge the necessity of having you present in Nashville to try and modify and improve our system. On this subject I know they (although of the opposition) will listen to me attentively.

"I do not know that all this will get the legislature to move a peg. The whole thing being a failure hitherto, the subject has become unpopular and distasteful to timid members. Still, I am not easily discouraged. In 1831, a member of Congress from this district said I was a mono-maniac on railroads but I persisted and my whole plan, then ideal and problematical, has been fully realized. Indeed, so anxious and solicitous am I of success, that if it becomes necessary, I will go to Nashville and try to do something. My bank duties may call me there before long. Let me hope to meet you there if the thing goes further. I want you in Tennessee for a scarcely less important purpose. You will see in the Union and American that I did not use any extra laudation of you as you admonished me I should not.

"P. S. No time was to be lost if this Legislature will do anything and as I am pressed with other duties, excuse this galloping epistle. I did better with my letters to Nashville. Write me again and I will omit nothing."

Two weeks later, on Washington's birthday, Dr. Ramsey wrote again. His personal misfortunes probably account for the failure of this last effort to do something for the improvement of the common schools of Tennessee.

"Since I wrote you last, Doctor Dickson, the husband of my second daughter, ceased to breathe. He died of tubercular consumption—lingered several months, but sank rapidly the

About 1822, or soon after my father's death, I was elected to fill the vacancy occasioned by his death, in the board of trustees of Blount College—since the University of East Tennessee. Not long after my election to this position I chose to resign it. Differing with the majority of my colleagues on the board on what I considered a vital question, the minority consisting of Major W. B. Lenoir, Major Arthur Crozier, myself, and perhaps others tendered our resignations. President David A. Sherman refused to accept mine and invited me to withdraw my resignation. Reminding him of the usage of the British ministry on such occasions, I replied that the majority must in future bear the whole responsibility for their own policy.

Several years after this I was elected trustee of Washington College near Jonesboro, Tennessee. I had received from its faculty previously my second degree of Master of Arts, and being an alumnus of that oldest literary institution west of the Alleghanies I could not decline the literary civility implied by my election as a trustee. It was nearly one hundred miles from Mecklenburg, my private residence, and I rarely attended the meetings of its board of trustees. Its grounds were classic and historical— I had graduated there. Its halls were venerable from their age, and illustrious from the character, and services, and patriotism, and worth, and public and private virtue of its founder and President, Reverend Samuel Doak, D.D. He had planted it in the wilderness during the Revolutionary War. He had watched over it during its infancy—its precocious manhood, and before his death had witnessed its expansion and maturity. Like the monks of the Middle Ages, he had kept alive and burning the fire of a genuine and profound literature. The germ of his own planting on the distant frontier of what is now Tennessee, had blossomed under his own culture—had matured and borne fruit. Longinus on the sublime Horace's Art of Poetry, The *Bucolics* of Virgil, the *Metamorphoses* of

---

last few days; died calmly, easily, trusting in the merits of our Saviour and Redeemer, with the Christian's hope and the Christian's courage.

"I snatch a minute to say that I have not seen my communication in the *Weekly Union and American,* nor have I heard from Governor Harris nor any other correspondent at Nashville. I cannot account for it and deem it right to inform you. The whole subject, as I before told you, has become distasteful to our people and our legislators,—but this furnishes the stronger reason why you should have been invited.

"I am confined to my room by a bruised and sprained ankle from falling in a dark night a week ago, into a deep gully while walking up the inclined plain to the depot at Athens. It would have been more in consonance with my past pursuits and my earlier aspirations for distinction and usefulness in railroad enterprises, if I had been smashed up between or under the cars. But to have stumbled into a miserable ditch—an achievement which any Negro could have performed as gracefully as I did—cashiers me for life. Excuse me. I only wished to say that I cannot account for the silence of my correspondents."

Ovid, the orations of Demosthenes and Cicero were studied and read aloud under the ancient trees around Dr. Doak's Log College, as Martin Academy was first called. The primitive forest that had once resounded with the scream of the panther, the howling of the wolf, and the terrific war-whoop of the Cherokee were now vocal with classical literature and the young men in every cabin in which they boarded around what had become Washington College were engaged in the study of Latin, Greek, and Hebrew languages. Such was the transmutation accomplished by the energy and learning of President Doak. His trustees, the patrons of learning every where, appreciated his genius, his attainments and his worth. His students idolised him, and some few years after his resignation of the presidency and his removal to Bethel a number of them waited upon him at Tusculum and requested him to sit for his likeness before an eminent artist. He negatived the request at first, but an excellent picture of the now superannuated and venerable patriot divine and scholar was at length obtained. It was left by the artist in the office of Dr. Samuel Blair Cunningham in Jonesboro, a favorite alumnus of Washington College. There I first saw it. Attending next day a meeting of the trustees in the new college edifice just then erected, I proposed a resolution "That the secretary of this board apply for and receive from Dr. Cunningham the picture of Dr. Doak now in his possession and that as a token of our respect and in veneration of the memory of the first president and founder of this college, his picture be framed and removed to the library room of Washington College and be perpetually preserved as the most valuable of its archives." My resolution was carried by acclamation, and afterwards carried into effect. It is a very accurate likeness—less finished and artistic perhaps than was due to the subject of it. But Dr. Doak was remarkable for the primitive simplicity of his character, and it may not be inconsistent with true taste that the painting should be inartistic, inexpensive, and inartificial likewise. I had been Dr. Doak's favorite student and he was proud of my attainments under his instruction. My father had once been a worshiper under his pastorate at Salem. They had both been *revolters* and members of the Franklin government (from 1784 to 1788). They were co-pioneers on Holston and Nollichucky: both were Calvinists, both Presbyterians of the strictest sort. They were warm personal and political friends. It was thus peculiarly proper and becoming that I should be the one to introduce the resolution I offered before the board of trustees. I felt it to be an act of almost *filial* piety and veneration. During my exile from Tennessee some unknown friend sent to my son, General J. Crozier Ramsey, at Knoxville a photograph of Dr. Doak taken from the picture of him in the college library with the request that it be presented to me. In March 1869, when I visited Knoxville the first time after my exile (September 1863), I found the photograph in my son's office. It would have graced my parlor or library at Mecklenburg, burned by the vandals under Burnside September 1863, but I was now houseless and homeless and an exile—a stranger in a strange land. My son, to whom the picture had been sent, was now in a soldier's grave in Gray Cemetery near Knoxville, and I left it in the hands of my wife's brother, Honorable J. H. Crozier, of that city.

When the news arrived at Knoxville in 1830 of the death of President Doak, I called together the alumni of Washington College within my reach. At that meeting I offered the customary resolutions of respect to the memory and veneration for the services and virtues of one so erudite and useful and illustrious as our deceased teacher, Dr. Doak. The names of members of the meeting which I can now call to mind were, beside myself, Hugh Brown, J. H. Cowan, S. D. Jacobs and my brother, W. B. A. Ramsey. On the motion of Hugh Brown I was appointed to prepare a suitable memoir of the deceased. This grateful duty I performed. It was afterwards published. The proceedings of our meeting will be found published in the Knoxville *Register* of that day [3]—of which Mr. Brown was co-editor with F. S. Heiskell, Esquire.

After the resignation of his presidency of Washington College, Dr. Doak removed to Bethel and there started Tusculum School which he intended as a preparatory department for the college he had left, and which was now under the presidency of his oldest son, Reverend S. W. Doak, M.D. Students flocked to his school. Here with his son Reverend S. W. Doak, who was vice president when I graduated at Washington, Dr. Doak continued to teach with great acceptance till his death. His son, S. W. D., continued the school. It was called at first Tusculum Academy. It progressed well and was finally incorporated by the legislature as Tusculum College. I was elected one of its trustees and sometimes I attended the meetings of its board, especially at commencements. Two of my sons, J. C. Ramsey and W. Wilberforce Ramsey, received their education there, and their brothers, R. M. and J. G. McKnitt, also attended there several

---

[3] Knoxville *Register*, December 29, 1830. The news account attributes the resolutions adopted by the meeting to Colonel W. B. A. Ramsey.

sessions. This college was seventy-five miles from my residence and, therefore, I could not give much of my attention and care. Governor, afterwards President, Johnson was one of my associates in the board.

I received, at several periods of my life, honorary membership in many of the literary and scientific societies in America.[4] The one of which I was specially proud was from the Medical College of South Carolina—secured to me, as I believe, from my successful treatment of a case of dropsy in the chest in Charleston, South Carolina—which I had been invited to see and to treat while on a visit to that city for my health and professional improvement in the winter of 1829–1830.[5] Another literary distinction which I also valued high was honorary membership in the Ethnological Society of New York and still another from the historical society of the state of Georgia—*cum multis aliis* too numerous to mention here. These, with my diplomas, certificates of honorary membership, commissions, etc., etc. from the civil authorities, were, with my family, considered as my chief treasures, my idols. And when I was driven into exile, they—my wife and daughters—rescued them from the incendiarism of the enemy, while much—nearly every thing else of intrinsically more value, were left to the vandalism of Burnside and his thieves, robbers, and house burners. The ladies of my house in my absence saved them from the fire. All fame to them for this regard to my preferences and taste!

I had the honor of a correspondence with the elite and distinguished every where whether in church or state—with A. Jackson, Calhoun, Polk, Mitchell King, Professor Dickson, Dr. and Judge Frost, Reverend H. S. Foote, D.D., President Davis, all railroad presidents,—the scientific generally—Democratic leaders and editors everywhere. Beside my private correspondence, copies of my addresses, essays, contributions to the literary, political, secular, and religious journals of my times. All my historical and antiquarian manuscripts—some of them containing the substance of my second volume of the *History of Tennessee:* viz. from 1800 to the end

---

[4] Upon his election as an honorary member of the State Historical Society of Wisconsin, Dr. Ramsey wrote Corresponding Secretary Lyman Draper: "I beg . . . to assure the members that it will afford me great pleasure to contribute in some humble degree at least to the promotion of the objects and wishes of the association." He ordered his publishers to send his *Annals of Tennessee* to the Wisconsin society. "It will be a pleasure to me hereafter to contribute autographs and other historical matter to your collection." Draper Correspondence, March 23, 1854.

This was a reciprocal honor. A decade before, September 3, 1844, Dr. Ramsey had informed Draper that he had been elected an honorary member of the East Tennessee Historical and Antiquarian Society. *Ibid.*

[5] The Knoxville *Register,* April 13, 1831 reported that the Medical College of South Carolina had conferred an honorary M.D. degree on Dr. Ramsey on March 18.

of Polk's administration—unpublished biographies of the leading master spirits of their day in Tennessee and elsewhere, all these being in my office and study adjoining my dwelling house fell victims to the flames. These were themselves a pretty complete history of my own times and a perfect history of my participation in them. My library—medical, miscellaneous, (and especially that which I principally valued) historical and literary, I had for many years been collecting from Europe and America, and which was, I believe, the best in the western states—was stolen, destroyed, or burned. I saw some of my books in a book store on Gay Street, Knoxville, but did not care to claim them. I left them to bear evidence of some one's atrocious dishonesty. I hope not the booksellers.

CHAPTER V

The Annals of Tennessee: Letters of a Historian

Draper Manuscripts [1] 6 XX 12

Mecklenburg
September 20, 1845

My Dear Sir

Your kind and valuable favors of February 19 and of August 11 were received by due course of mail and I write now more to acknowledge their receipt than to reply to them. I would feel it necessary to make a long minute apology for so long delay in doing so and to ask you to forgive the apparent incivility—more, the absolute neglect—did I not recollect that you were in some degree acquainted with the incessant demands my business (chiefly professional) has upon my time. I intended to answer your letters in detail, and carefully and put off from week to week the business of replying to them, hoping every week to have a little more leisure. And now at the end of nearly seven months I can only excuse myself by the reflection that in that time I have not had *one leisure hour* —and especially since your last favor came to hand I have not set at my desk five minutes at a time unless when writing prescriptions. After I left the bank I found it necessary to *nurse* my practice a little which I necessarily had to some extent relinquished while financing. I advertised accordingly, and I have been overwhelmed with its duties ever since. And just now is our sickly season and I scarcely eat one regular meal at home or abroad—and some days do not even see all of my own family. Under these circumstances it would be injustice to you to myself, to the truth and accuracy of history to attempt to answer your inquiries etc., etc. But I will not lose the opportunity of telling you that *I will write to you* (I hope

---

[1] Dr. Ramsey made but the most casual reference to his *Annals of Tennessee* in his Autobiography. That the work consumed much of his time and thought, however, is evident from the letters given in this chapter. Dr. Ramsey wrote frequently to his fellow historian, Lyman C. Draper, and they exchanged information and material. The letters in this chapter are from the Draper manuscripts in the library of the State Historical Society of Wisconsin. The cryptic symbols at the beginning of each letter refer to the library's classification of the material. Those labeled "XX" are the "Tennessee Papers," "C" are "Boone manuscripts."

some time soon) on the several topics of your letters [and] give you all the information upon them in my possession. It will not be of much importance or value to you but what ever I have will be very cheerfully communicated.

Do accept my thanks for your kindness, and do me the justice to believe that I duly appreciate it, and excuse me, I beg you, once more for any delay that may occur before I may find time to reciprocate your favors in kind. My family is well and myself better than usual. While all around me are sick I am constantly able to make visits to the extent of twenty or thirty miles daily.

Yours Respectfully and Sincerely

J. G. M. Ramsey

P. S. I cannot omit to add how much we are pleased in Tennessee to feel ourselves again restored to the Republican family. Polk's administration is very popular. My "Annals" will come down to its close.   *J. G. M. R.*

Draper Manuscripts 6 XX 25

Mecklenburg
October 26, 1846

I have a proposition to make to you to which I invite your deliberate attention. I have in my possession *nearly all* the materials necessary for the (first volume of) History of Tennessee. The mass is so large, and the labor of arranging it for publication so Herculean that I advance so slow in its performance as to lead me sometimes to despair of accomplishing it till the shades of the evening of life shall begin to darken around me. My cares increase and my public and private duties multiply so as to leave me too little leisure to devote to a work that ought to be so well done as to reflect credit on myself—and upon my native State.

The proposition then I have to make to you in confidence is that we put our capital together, form a partnership in the work, and finish it at once. The proposition is a novel one to me. It is doubtless so to you. Still I see no insuperable obstacle. Let me hear in reply your opinion. Excuse me again for neglecting my last promise. I have a valid excuse. Not one hour of perfect leisure have I seen in the last year.

Draper Manuscripts 17 C 12

January 17, 1848

Yours of January 6 was received by last mail. I hasten to say in answer that the only narrative I can find (and I believe the only one I have) on the campaign to Point Pleasant, alias the Kanawha campaign, is one from Robert Campbell. You say "I recollect your reading to me some notes of Colonel John Sawyers about Point Pleasant Battle" etc., etc. As I read to you probably I accompanied it with some remarks or recollections of my own in which Colonel Sawyers' agency in that battle and victory was incidentally mentioned. Certain it is that after a pretty general search I cannot find any narrative from or of him except an excellent one relating to Kings Mountain. While therefore an amanuensis is copying from Campbell's narrative the part of it relating to the engagement, as being most relevant probably to your object, I add to it what I have heard from authentic sources.

The battle had continued all day with no decisive effect—certainly none assuring even ultimate victory to the whites. The night was approaching and it was evident that without a desperate assault made at once upon a defense from which the Indians were making their deadliest fire, the conflict would not be terminated in daylight and that in that event the result might be disastrous. Col. Sawyers (not then an officer, but a volunteer under Captain Evan Shelby from what is now Tennessee, then North Carolina) had observed all day that Cornstalk and his best warriors were giving a most destructive fire from a temporary breastwork to which, when driven from other points, they always rallied and from which they renewed the assault and prolonged the conflict, proposed to the commanding officer to lead an attack upon this strong position of the enemy and capture it. The suggestion was approved, and acted on. Sawyers, with less than eighty men who followed him, drove out the Indians and decided the fortunes of the day. I suppose your notes on the incidents, dates, etc., of that campaign are full. It would give me pleasure to add to them.

I have a facsimile of an inscription upon a tree still standing in Washington County—not far from Boon's Creek. N. Gammon, Esquire of Jonesboro Tennessee kindly procured it for me. It is about twenty inches by fifteen in tolerably plain letters yet.

D. Boon

cilled <u>A. Bar</u>   on

Tree

in the

year

1760.

This date is earlier by some years than that usually given as the time at which he first crossed the Alleghenies. I have no doubt of the authenticity of this singular memorial of the great western pioneer and adventurer. Tradition points out close by this tree his camp—a natural one made by rocks and in the center of what is known to have been fine hunting ground. I am trying to get an engraving or plate made of this inscription. Will send you a copy.

I am glad to hear you speak so favorably of your success in procuring matter for George Rogers Clarke. When I had the pleasure of seeing you here did I show you what the Blount MSS say of him? Write me and if I have anything you have not I will send it at once. I recollect that he mentions him with enthusiasm. Thank you for inquiring at Richmond for the Seviers, Robertsons, etc. Carter's settlement was believed to be in Virginia and I had hoped to find in her archives something about the temporary government that the first settlers adopted previous to the Revolution.

The preceding part of this narrative refers to the organization of the army—the wilderness it had to pass through, roads, mountains, supplies, etc., and not being very important is here omitted.

"At the levels of Green Briar, it was judged, that the necessary supply of provisions was not obtained. Colonel Christy and his division were ordered to remain till they could make up the desired amount and then to follow the main body. The whole amounted to fifteen hundred men, under the command of General Andrew Lewis. The object of this expedition was to burn up the Indian towns on the Ohio and its tributaries, and compel the Indians to sue for peace. The main body advanced to the fork of land included by the rivers Ohio and _____ and took station on this level, guarded on both sides by the rivers, which were too wide for the enemy to shoot across. Here they lay in waiting for Christy, with his supply of provisions to join them.

The country was full of game, and individuals were permitted, at their personal hazard to rove in its pursuit. On the tenth of October nearly by daybreak, two men had advanced a mile from the camp, and ascending a piece of ground, at its first rise from the river bottom, when they were suddenly met, and fired upon by the Indians. One of them was killed. The other succeeded to run back to the camp. A regiment was quickly ordered to advance. It did so in two lines. The Indians met them in a numerous body, fired and shouted to the charge. The first line of our men was driven back to the second, and this stood and begun the fight. The second regiment was ordered to support it, and then the third, which made up the whole army present, except the guard, which remained with the general camp. The battle lasted with various fortune till dark, when the fires on both sides gradually ceased. The Indians drew off with what dead they could throw into the river. And our men kept possession of the field.

Our men fought to great disadvantage through the day. The Indians, at the first of the action, possessed themselves of a natural breastwork consisting of a bank, ten feet high, of a winter rivulet running into the Kanawha, but at this season of the year dry. From this position they fought with security. For the British commander Lewis took not the precaution to send a party of Americans to ply their rifles from the heights behind. Had this been done, little chance would have remained of an action so long continued, and so deadly to the ranks of the American soldiers. He remained in camp at no other risk of personal safety, than what might arise in the event of a total defeat of his troops. His brother Charles Lewis fell bravely in the first onset of the battle. The Indians here were estimated at one thousand and our own men numbered about the same. The loss of the Americans was _____

In the meantime a runner had gone from the main body to meet Colonel Christy, and apprize him of the presence and attack of the Indians. Receiving this intelligence he left his baggage and cattle unprotected, and by a rapid march, arrived at headquarters late at night. Fortunately the Indians had no notice of his baggage, and left it unmolested. The next day he returned, collected his provisions, and brought them to the camp. Our troops now rested, made a block-house for their sick and wounded men and proceeded eighty miles to Scioto river. Governor Dunmore in the meantime, advanced with an equal army to Fort Duquesne, now Pittsburgh, descended the Ohio, made peace with the Indians, and thus opportunity saved them from the havoc of our men. Hostility was growing between the British and Americans, and it was policy for the former to keep peace with the Indians. When our troops returned to Kanawha, they were disbanded. And in groups of five or six, as they could best agree with one another, retraced their path, at immense hazard, privations and toil, through this desolate wilderness.

The pay of a common soldier was a quarter of a dollar; that of the commissary a dollar more. This payment was made in specie. End of Mr. C's narrative.

I shall have a broken link in my annals if I cannot supply it in Virginia. Pray keep the subject in mind and if even a ray of light dawns upon it let me hear from you. I thank you for the list you have enclosed me of new works. I shall order some of them. I add something daily to the material of my work but am sorry to tell you that other pursuits have still so much engrossed me that I have done very little on the work itself. And worse, my notes, papers, etc., are exactly in such a condition that if Providence should in his wisdom cut short my life, the *full* history of Tennessee will never be written. This reflection sometimes makes me feel unhappy. The president kindly gave me an appointment and I would have accepted and gone to Mexico but that I would have had to drop my pen for a few years at least, and perhaps forever.

Our Society did receive some of the papers of the Maryland Historical Society. Its first volume of transactions will be interesting.

My family reciprocates your remembrance of us. When will you visit the West? Excuse my haste and if I ever appear—what I am sensible I never am—not punctual or tardy on my answers ascribe it, I beg you, to no unneighborly feeling or disesteem of your *realized* correspondence and believe me ever yours gratefully.

Draper Manuscripts 17 C 13

September 18, 1851

I was glad to learn your whereabouts and your welfare by yours of July 29 which I found on my table on returning from one of my rambles. I have so much to do lately with locomotives that my movements have become erratic and ubiquitous. Am seldom long enough at home to write any but business (railroad) letters. Hereafter I will be more stationary.

Facts are so stubborn that we cannot, even when we would, alter or accommodate *dates*. It is so with my Boon inscription. I can't make 1 out of the 0. No way I can fix it. I could easier make 9 out of the last figure in the date by supposing the lower part of it to be obliterated by the growth of the bark and the progress of time. And that date 1769 would well correspond with the first settlement of other pioneers of Tennessee on our upper tributaries. What do your contemporaneous narratives do in support of that reading? Tell me. Also how does 1760 correspond with the true period of Boon's nativity? (for I notice accounts differ on this subject). I have not yet had it facsimilied. The state of hostility at that time between the Indians and Carolina and Virginia has not much in it. The country on the Watauga was never in the occupancy of the Chero— but was a hunting ground common to Cherokees, Shawnees, traders, and hunters, Spanish, French and American—and Boon cared for neither. That place was not one hundred miles from the border settlements— head of Yadkin and Kanawha.

I am progressing so well as to contemplate the issue of my volume (at Charleston) in 1852 and but for my agency in the service of Tennessee would have printed this year. That agency will absorb me less hereafter and will cease altogether, I hope, in six months. What takes you to Cincinnati? Hang them free-soilers—let them publish for the Mormons and abolitionists. No *Union* loving author should go there.

The Historical Society at Nashville had a hasty accouchement, breathed once after it got into its nurse's lap, gave a convulsive gasp to let its aunts and its cousins know that it had vitality enough to squeal, gave a wild stare upon its seniors, and suddenly swooned away. Some of the doctors say expired. I hear nothing of it since. Don't you observe that *Commerce* chokes the growth of any such infants? It does not furnish the pabulum by which science and literature are nourished. A wealthy merchant here the other day asked me what would be the price of my volume? "I want," said he, "to get one if the price is not too high—put me down for one anyhow." I replied, "If you want to act your part *gracefully,* take at least fifty—a free Negro if he could read will take one." I want no such patrons. Let my book rot first on the shelves. He represents the commerce of the country. Yankeedom is taking a vigorous growth everywhere.

Excuse this irrelevancy. Call to see us on your way West. We should compare notes. Let me hear from you soon and often.

P. S. What do you think of engravings in such a work as mine? Whom would you recommend? Will woodcuts detract from the value of my volume? Such as you see in *Howe's Virginia.*

Draper Manuscripts 6 XX 31

November 4, 1851

I have lately visited in person all the Franklin counties. Amongst other places of interest which I examined was the "Long Island" and the battle ground near it. I can't understand it satisfactorily. You once told me you had found an official account of the Island Flats battle in an old file of newspapers for 1776. Can you favor me with your notes and accounts of it? Especially its exact *date?* Is there in your possession anything essential about *Donelson's* voyage omitted in his journal?

I am progressing well and without saying one word as to the *manner* of my book I can promise you in advance much really new and interesting.

Draper Manuscripts 6 XX 32

January 30, 1852

Yours of January 5 is before me—received two mails back (probably detained by ice) and found me absorbed in the closing up of disbursements to the amount of $343,216.50 leaving me yet to disburse $11,437.67 before I am through my agency for state expenditures on E. T. & G. R. R. I mention figures to excuse myself for even a day's delay in replying. Money is out of my mind now and I can write *ad libitum*. If you sent me official account of Long Island Flat battle it miscarried and I am sorry to trouble you for another. It will still be in time. Your date of that affair, July 20, 1776, conflicts, as you observe, with Haywood—and (I add if you do not correct me) with me too. You will find in Howe's *Virginia* (*Washington County*. I have lent the volume and cannot therefore cite the page) that in a small attack near Abingdon, Virginia, July 4, 1776, William Cresswell was killed there and his ashes repose in the graveyard —indicated by a stone with his name and this date. Now I have known his son Andrew Cresswell all my life and he has told me frequently that his father William Cresswell was in the battle of the flats—that he was the man who accused one of the captains (who is in my notes nameless) of cowardice—that the said captain, after he reached the fort, became very brave and wished to vindicate his honor by a fight with W. Cresswell

when he, Cresswell, struck him with his gun, etc. My narrator, Andrew
Cresswell was the best authority I could ask for and I suspect *July* 20 is a
mistake for *June* 20. How is it? Do put me right if I am wrong. Other circumstances favor the earlier date. After the Long Island affair the Indians
went up Clinch and fell upon the settlements north of Black's station and
the fourteen days would about be required to reach there July 4 when
William Cresswell was killed. This investigation will cost you some
trouble, but the date is important and I beg you to look into it. Does the
official account you allude to mention the day? The date of the affair
between Tipton and Sevier is erroneously given by Haywood and others
as February 3. It was the last day of February 1788 of which I have full
proof. My work is unlike those you mention and does not go by counties.
The annals of Tennessee in exact chronological order. I had not intended
many plates or cuts and no profiles or portraits. Will be obliged for the
name of a good and cheap engraver in wood. Must I see him to give the
outline of say King's Mountain, Knoxville as it was in 1791, and Nashville in 1783 or 4, and such places? Could one be induced to go to my
publishers, say Charleston? Again. Whether I have plates etc. or not, I
intend to accompany or have inserted in my book at least three maps;
1770, 1780 and 1790 and perhaps 1800—showing the progressive settlement up to that time. How will I get that done and by whom? Can that
be done without an interview with the engraver? or the cerographer?
Morse? These will add greatly to the interest and value of my several
decades. I have not a single number of the (Nashville) "Museum." I
have not seen Peck's Boone—Howe's Great West, nor Parkman.

One word on politics. Chaos reigns in our party—not so much in Tennessee as in the Union throughout. No one of the present more prominent
aspirants can be nominated and if he were has not availability enough to
be elected. Butler possibly might be, but even his chance is questionable.
I am for him and so is Tennessee. But it will be at Baltimore in June as
it was in 1844. The convention will not harmonize but will have to take
up a *new* man. That is Trousdale. Mark what I say. I said this in 1843
and that Polk would *be the nominee.*

When you go West again come by me. You cannot believe how such
a visit would please and help me. I have mentioned you in my *Annals.*
Come this spring and let me show you some of my chapters. I have an
invaluable and interesting work. I mean to say nothing by this of the
manner of it—but the material. Excuse haste—as I am interrupted by an

unexpected call since I began. My family reciprocates your civilities. We celebrated the eighth by giving away another daughter. This one to T. H. Dickson, M.D., late of Charleston S. C. Write me if I can return any of your historical favors, and believe me.

Draper Manuscripts 6 XX 34

February 20, 1852

I cannot express my obligations for your last favor—favors rather. The official account of the Island Flat battle is the very thing I needed. That as given by Haywood and others is not satisfactory. The date of it, July twentieth, is undoubtedly correct. Still you will not wonder at my skepticism when I tell you that I *knew* Cresswell was in the battle and as the inscription on his tomb says he was killed July fourth. I was hesitating how the dates could be reconciled. Your solution of the difficulty is doubtless correct—that the error is on the tombstone which is easily accounted for. It was put down from memory, or perhaps tradition. I will make the official account you sent me the basis of my pages about it. I feel relieved by knowing it is correct. I have not Force's work, and may not soon have an opportunity to examine it, and will therefore be greatly obliged if you will send me as you kindly intimate the documents about the origin of the Cherokee outbreak. I am sorry to impose so much trouble on you. Perhaps a sketch of them and dates would suffice (I have the evidence, etc., of the course Captain John Stuart and Cameron adopted to incite the Cherokees against the whites. Is that *Henry* Stuart?) I would like though, very much to have the letter of Henry Stuart to the frontier people—a copy of which was sent to Watauga—and will thank you for it. By a singular piece of good luck I have the original reply of Colonel William Preston to the Watauga Committee dated June 3, 1776. He promises them lead and powder and gives an order on Colonel Callaway at Fort Chiswell for them and acknowledges receipt of the deposition of Bryan (much the same as that of Janett Williams). If it would be at all desirable to you to have it let me know and I will forward you a copy. I observe what you say of Captain Gist. Let me copy for your eye just here a few lines (and if you desire it I will hereafter send you the whole) from the "Instructions to Colonel William Christian commander-in-chief of the forces on the expedition against the Cherokees" . . . : "you must insist on their . . .

and giving up to justice all persons amongst them [the Cherokees] who have been concerned in bringing on the present war—particularly Stewart, Cammeron, and *Gist,* and all others who have committed murders and robberies on the frontier." Do you say *he* joined Christian?

I am daily expecting Wheeler's volume. I have corresponded with him since '48. Will I get anything from it? Your letters always give me something valuable. I am relieved by seeing William Cocke signed to that official report. *He* wrote Haywood's account of the battle and I had heard of his conduct there as rather disparaging him. But he fought so well afterwards in South Carolina and in the Creek war of 1814 that I was and still am unwilling to believe he faltered. He would scarcely have been allowed a participation in officially communicating the report with Thompson and Shelby if he had not behaved well. Still Cresswell told him differently at Heatons the same day. I cannot get you to say whether *illustrations* would become my book. I have somehow got the impression that they are considered as an essential appendage to works of no solid and genuine merit, but that books of sterling value are not expected to have them. Am I correct? I want no one to buy me merely for the *pictures.* Maps are a different thing, and some of my pages are almost unintelligible without them—especially my account of the settlement of the county south of French Broad and Holston and west of Big Pigeon. I saw Orr last year in New York. He seemed to think that I would have to get an artist first to daguerreotype for me or something of the kind and he could then engrave the battlegrounds, court houses, etc.

You can hardly get me into politics this fight. I want to be not on the pensioned but retired list. Our Democratic State Convention will not agree to it though, as they on the eighth of January assigned me again the position of chairman of the central committee—a place they have imposed on me since 1839. I must leave it to the younger Democrats to do the labor. I will be one of the council. I do not think Mr. Cass has much chance for the nomination and less for success if he should be the nominee. He is not available, was once badly beaten and is no stronger now. He is not new nor fresh enough for a good leader. His strength is amongst the politicians and that is defeat itself. The masses north, south, east and west are not for him. They are against him. Your New York friend and correspondent I think is greatly mistaken. In all this I speak only for myself and not for Tennessee. Polk's friends here are not for anyone specially but I think our platform will be the doctrines of 1798. State sovereignty, state rights, anti-consolidation, strict adherence to the constitution. If Mr. Cass would plant himself manfully on this platform we may go for him but not otherwise. I still believe all the old set should be dropped—Douglas and Houston, too, and either Trousdale, Butler or some new man put on the track. Kossuthism is a weight no one can carry south of Pennsylvania and Ohio, and no one can get along without some help from that quarter.

I will be careful in the allusions I make to you in my book to mention your intended publications on Tennessee, her pioneers, and the Southwest in general. Be as specific on the subjects, plan, etc., in your next letter to me as you choose and I will make the reference accordingly.

I am sorry you postpone your visit to us till steam will unite Knoxville and Cincinnati. We will both be old men before that time. Knoxville will soon be a terminus on a railroad and I hope the facility of reaching it will some day soon give me the pleasure of welcoming you at our home. My family and myself will be always pleased to see you.

P. S. I placed the date 1799 at the head of my pages yesterday. You see I am almost through—my first volume terminating with that year.

Draper Manuscripts 6 XX 35

March 18, 1852

Yours of March third reached me a mail or two since. I reply before I file it away and in its order. Am greatly obliged for the whole of it. The letters from Stuart to Gage I had seen and commented on. Your remarks on them however are new and of course useful. I had also the depositions of Aaron Smith and David Shettise. But the letter of Henry Stuart and the deposition of Nathan Read *are entirely new* and are the very things I needed. I cannot tell you how much you have obliged me by sending them.

I knock under about Gist. I have no alterations or erasures though, to make about him as I had used none of the *censuses* made by Preston and other narrators in my possession to his disparagement. Preston, May 1775, classes him amongst "our worst enemies." Lane imputes "most of the mischief" to him. I have no need to assail or criminate him. Now you have got him vindicated by Evan Shelby and Russell. I feel disposed rather to mention him favorably as some of the same name were the pioneers and soldiers of upper East Tennessee.

Martin's Campaign of '81. I know no authority for this but Haywood. He gives it in February. This is hardly probable, though as he confines the expedition to "between Little Tennessee and Tellico" it is possible a short excursion that far may have been made by him. Not one of *my* narratives mentions Martin or his excursion then. I said hardly probable because as late as January fourth Sevier, Arthur Campbell, and Major Martin (as agent) held a conference with the Cherokees at Coyata in their nation stipulating that they should meet early in the spring and form a treaty (see Campbell's letter to Governor Jefferson) out of which grew the treaty. Commissioners appointed by General Greene (see Johnson's life of Greene). But Sevier had two campaigns very much alike as to the amount of men and their results. Both pursued the same route, both had battle on Boyd's Creek. All my narratives agree in this—the captains were different and prisoners taken different—number of killed nearly the same. One in 1779—the other in November and December 1780 and part of January '81 just after his return from King's Mountain. Indeed, as the army returned from there as soon as it had crossed Catawba and the prisoners were safe, Sevier sent one of his captains (Russell) direct home across the mountain from an apprehension that in the absence of so many men and guns from the settlement the Indians would break out and destroy them. Russell retained his command as then organized and the moment Sevier reached home he went forward at the head of Russell's company and a few others, had his hard battle at Boyd's Creek and there waited for Colonel A. Campbell to come on with supplies and reinforcements—and then went as far south as to see Cypress swamps and long-leafed pines—Oustinalla and Coosa. It could not have been William Campbell that is mentioned as being at Patrick Henry in '81—as he was then with his regiment with or marching to General Stevens' command preparatory to Guilford Court House battle.

It is very hard to make all these narratives in books and manuscript dovetail. I am trying to be accurate and minute. I have got Wheeler and have read it. As to Franklin he gives nothing new. I wonder at this the more as many materials were in his reach at Raleigh. It gives me the more room though and I have taken it.

You say you will draw on me and with interest too when you get to the Tennessee pioneers. I will be ready for your drafts, especially when my first volume is off my hands. There is a good deal of material which I cannot insert. It would make my volume too clumsy. My figures were 1799 not 79. If the latter I would give up and quit, as everything nearly follows that date. Still with all that progress I am still busy. I wish to *locate* some facts—particularly in Cumberland—examine some old maps, get more information about distances from point to point, etc. You see in the *Whig Review* the massacre and captivity of Brown. I had that narrative six years ago, verbatim and literatim as far as it is accurate. You have much about *General* Martin of West Tennessee. I am promised the narrative of a *Martin*. I suppose the same. Has it much general Tennessee history in it? I won't let Sevier's own letters go out of my hands till I hear from you what will be of most service to your work.

Draper Manuscripts 6 XX 39

April 15, 1852

Yours of March 28 is received. I have persisted in writing to you for the purpose specially of getting you to be more specific (as you promised in your second letter that you would be but which you have failed to do) as to the *announcement* I might make in reference to your forthcoming publications.[2] Twice I have referred to you gracefully for information and connection of dates received from you. If I could serve you by stimulating public expectation and avidity to read you by a less general reference, a more specific enumeration of the subjects of the work you are preparing, it would give me a most real pleasure. Think of it and if you think proper send it before I go to press. (October 1852.)

I say this before it is forgotten or omitted in what follows. In not a single narrative out of the hundreds I have read and have on hand in manuscript have I received the slightest allusion to Martin's separate expedition of 1781. Haywood alone mentions it. I have therefore omitted it, though I occasionally adopt him as authority in other cases. I have an

---

[2] Even as Dr. Ramsey was finishing his *Annals,* his correspondent, Draper, who was looking for employment, wrote his old friend, former Congressman William B. Campbell, asking about a rumored legislative appropriation for a historian for Tennessee. Draper had heard of the appropriation from Colonel A. W. Putnam of Nashville. Campbell corrected the impression that the legislature had appropriated a thousand dollars for the purpose, but promised his influence to secure the appointment of Draper to any such subsidized task. "I think you would be able to produce a work far superior to any that could be prepared by Doctor Ramsey," said Campbell, while Colonel Putnam's contemplated work on Sevier would "be little less than a eulogy . . . with a great deal of romance and old Womanish traditions." William B. Campbell to Draper, March 23, 1852. Draper Manuscripts 6 XX 36.

official letter from Martin to Sevier giving an account of a short expedition which he carried on north of Clinch and in which on his return he diverged south nearly to *Chota*. He saw no enemy and of course did nothing.

But—Were the expeditions of 1779 and of 1780–81 the same? I have been perplexed with the coincidences that occur in each, but have greater perplexities when I assume that they are identical and the same affairs. All my narratives agree with Haywood on page 61 that Walton and Tipton commanded with him, etc., in 1779 and I can find nothing to conflict with that. There I have the military records or official proceedings of the officers called November 20, 1780, in which after enumerating the officers such as were to go immediately on the requisition of General Davidson across the mountain, and such as were to go on the "present expedition to rendezvous at Jonesboro on the 30th instant." The names of Walton and Tipton are not mentioned in the latter. My narratives harmonize in giving the battle on the same creek (Boyd's)—though not at the same place, but ambuscaded in the same way. Captain Elliott of Sullivan was the only man killed in 1780: nobody in 1779. Different captains and actors in the several parts of the expedition are given in each set of narratives and the two campaigns pretty well made out though not perfectly satisfactory. The case is very similar to Grant's and Williamson's invasions from South Carolina. They passed over the same war trace, were fought at the same point and ambuscaded in the same fortress precisely though carrying on separate campaigns and at different periods. The Big Island Sevier's or Buckingham's was the point of defense for the Cherokees—They told Christian in 1776 that he should not pass French Broad and assembled in the same island one thousand strong to resist him. They continued to be tenacious of the same policy of defending it as the key to their territory, and adhered to the illusive hope of doing so even after 1781. I still believe there were two campaigns, 1779 and 1780–81, but will examine further and scrutinize the evidence closely. I ought to say that my narratives are from the most reliable men, some of them officers in both.

Draper Manuscripts 6 XX 41

May 29, 1852

I appreciate very highly your favor of eighteenth instant and still more highly your strict regard to historical accuracy. We agree fully that Martin took no campaign in February 1781. There is no authority for it but Haywood—nor that Isaac Shelby accompanied the expedition of *November* '80 and January 1781. I have the Shelby papers and there is no mention of that service by him. (I say *November*—because I have the proceedings of the officers who projected it. Will copy it and enclose to you herein). The testimony you address is more than sufficient to counterbalance that of Haywood and narratives in my possession going to prove *two* campaigns and *two* battles on Boyd's Creek. Like that of Gist and Pearson as cited by you they must have taken 1779 for 1780. I am nearly satisfied that it is so, though some of my narratives have the battle at Cedar Spring, others the Blue Spring—one three miles from mouth of the Creek, the other near its source. Still I think you are right.

As to Colonel Putnam. I think he ought to let you bring out the biography of Sevier—and at the time *you* may think best. What I will say of Sevier ought to satisfy Colonel Putnam till your Clark and Boone are out. As to what Putnam can give you it will be meager and some of it *tradition* only. His father-in-law, the late Colonel G. W. Sevier, son of John Sevier, gave me his father's papers.[3] As I was later in going to press than Colonel Putnam thought right, he has asked for the papers which will be given up to the Tennessee Historical Society soon as low down as 1800. Those after that period I will next spring copy or extract from and afterwards give them up too. As to any influence I could exert in getting him to give you up his proposed work to you I fear it would be small— still if you request it, I will do so cheerfully and promptly (write me). He cannot hurt you much if he should go to press before you. He writes badly and has little patience or industry in collecting anything. Still he ought to be induced to give up to you what he has collected. As a Tennesseean proud alike of Sevier and Robertson I have a sincere wish that you may be their biographer. I think my book will aid you as to both.

I see General Joseph Martin was appointed by North Carolina agent to the Cherokees and was required to keep a journal of all he did and saw and furnish it to that government. Do you know where his journal is?

I sympathize in your feelings at the death of your friend and patron. I know how afflicting and overwhelming is the intelligence of the death of a friend and kinsman in a distant land. I may have told you before that I and my family have had our share of that almost intolerable suffering. We lost our most promising son W. Wilberforce A. Ramsey more

---

[3] See below, note 5.

than a year since in California. He was not only richly endowed and well educated but was amiable, moral, honorable, enterprising, affectionate, dutiful, and, we believe, pious. He was the favorite of the whole connection and *our* idol. God in His wisdom, perhaps in His mercy, has taken him. I feel it to be so. God help us! Write me if I can ever serve you. If you go to Mobile take us in your way. . . .[4]

[P. S.] The proceedings of the court martial are unimportant only as to date. Sevier was president. It was held November 20. Majors Robertson (Chas. I suppose) Tipton; Walton, adjutant; McNabb, Nelson, Brown, Williams, Newman, Trimble, Patterson, Bean, Jonakin captains. Nave, lieutenant; Roane, ensign. Captains Bowyer and Gibson, with their companies were ordered to march and join General Davidson, Captains Brown and Stinson for present expedition to rendezvous on thirtieth instant at Jonesboro.

Draper manuscripts 6 XX 43

Charleston, South Carolina
January 14, 1853

Your favor of November 10 addressed to my home at Mecklenburg reached there in due course of mail, but in the absence of my son upon his circuit has been allowed to remain there till his return to Knoxville last week. He immediately enclosed it and it is this moment read and contents noticed. I wrote you at Leverington, Philadelphia County Pennsylvania which I hope you received, though I have been surprised at the delay. Not hearing from you I have occasionally through the progress of my *forms* credited to you the information you have been so kind as to furnish. I am now on Franklin (1787) and cannot recollect whether my sheets have any further reference to you or not but if they do not I will endeavor to make a suitable notice of your forthcoming work or works —for they are legion.

I have been here six weeks and am not yet quite half through my first volume—hope it will be out in one month more. The second will not go

---

[4] Peter A. Remsen, Draper's patron with whom he made his home, died in Mobile, Alabama, April 16, 1852. Draper's subsequent search for employment led him to Madison, Wisconsin in the following October.

to press for a year to come. The first comes to 1800. The second to 1836 or perhaps 1848. The great object was to get what was early, obscure and unknown, into a less perishable—much of it old and almost illegible letters and documents—form before I should die. Others can do what remains undone. Much of what I had no one could arrange but myself, and I am rejoiced that my labor in reading proof is half over. My health is poor or I would promise another volume next year. I rejoice with you at Pierce's election though Tennessee's position I both regret and repudiate.

Pray indicate how a copy of my work will reach you. I will have great pleasure in forwarding it to you. When you see it you will judge how much of benefit it may be to your larger enterprises. I have excluded one-third of what I brought from my study with me so as to compress my volume into a volume of 750 or 800 pages octavo. I am making a neat volume without plates—except King's Mountain. I think you advised that as the best taste.

I have written you in haste. The compositors give me two forms a day sometimes and I am too anxious to reply by this mail to your long un-answered letter to write more fully. After February 15 I expect to be on my way home. In the meantime I will be glad to hear from you as soon as this reaches you.

P. S.—If my Book has one fault greater than another it is the minutiae and details of Sevier. It reads too much like a biography of him rather than the history of Tennessee. But his life is the history of East Tennessee as Robertson's is of Middle.

What ought my volume to sell for?

Draper manuscripts 6 XX 44

Mecklenburg, Tennessee
April 14, 1853

Yours of March 17 reached me today. Before this I hope you have received my volume by mail. You were the first nearly on the list I left with my printer to be furnished of those first out of the bindery. For fear it has miscarried I will order another from my Philadelphia house. You *must* have it—not that I consider it so *invaluable,* but I want to hear your opinion of my *first born*. Here it is well received and sells well. The press in Carolina and Georgia notices it most favorably and that of Tennessee most complimentarily. The first three boxes are nearly sold. Two more arrived today, and others are on their way to Nashville and other points.

I am glad to hear of your progress and shall await your issue impatiently. In my preface I say you will be out next year—having been thus informed from Nashville.

The press calls on me for another volume—the first ending with the last century. The material is on hand and some progress made, but I have made no positive pledge.

"Smith's Review of East Tennessee" I never saw nor heard of before I met it in your letter. It was certainly not a volume. I never heard of such a magazine or pamphlet. I regret that I can give you no account of it. "Life as it is" is the only thing besides Haywood which has seen the light in the way of a book in East Tennessee—and that is not worth sending to you.

P. S. I do little in politics but I must take time to say that Tennessee must be revolutionized this year. Pierce is adding to our strength. Look out for a victory in August.

Draper Manuscripts 6 XX 46

May 27, 1853

Your favor of the fifth instant is this moment received. I am somewhat surprised that the copy of my book which I ordered the publishers to send you by mail had not reached you. Should it not come let me hear it. You must see my bantling and examine its features and write me what you think of my first-born and tell me how to do better the next time. Thus far it is a favorite, especially with its Tennessee kin and its Carolina ancestors.[5] Its cousins in the west I hope will not be ashamed of it.

---

[5] Colonel A. W. Putnam's and T. J. Campbell's reactions were not wholly favorable. They each assured Draper that the field of Tennessee history had not been closed by Dr. Ramsey's work.

"Smith's Review of East Tennessee—map—1842." I collected everything since 1823. Can mind nothing of it. It must be either Nat. Smith—entry taker for our Hiwassee District—perhaps his report to legislature of townships and sections—or William Smith, a Yankee schoolmaster who *may have* made a geological map of East Tennessee. I will inquire further, but

---

Draper Manuscripts 6 XX 45

Nashville, Tennessee
May 4th, 1853

L. C. Draper, Esquire

Dear Sir,

I have for months awaited a letter from you, and indulged the hope that you would give encouragement to us of a *visit*.

Dr. Ramsey's "Annals of Tennessee" is a volume of some six hundred pages, published in Charleston, South Carolina.

But one copy has been received here—by his brother, Colonel W. B. A. Ramsey, secretary of state. I had but twenty minutes perusal of it. I think it a great mistake to have published by a house and in a place from which very little notoriety and influence can go forth to aid sales. I doubt not that one of the known and large publishing houses North could have brought it out and secured sales of ten to one that will now result.

I was pleased with the dedication and introduction, and hope to find pleasure in perusal of contents.

At his request, I sent to Charleston a daguerreotype of General Sevier's portrait to be engraved for the *Annals,* but he says it was received too late, to his regret; I am sorry too.

He has *not yet* returned me General Sevier's papers. I wrote him again last Monday.

The Watauga government makes a considerable chapter in the *Annals.* I had not the opportunity of reading it through but conclude it to be not as interesting and anomalous as is the "Provisional Government of the Judges or Triers at Nashborough," now in my possession, and which I wish you to avail yourself of fully, tho' I cannot send the volume out of the state.

Will you write me again whether there is any probability of your visiting Nashville; and how you will have manuscripts and papers that can be spared sent you hence.

I expect to go North before end of this month and be absent about two months.

Very respectfully,
A. W. Putnam

Draper Manuscripts 6 XX 53

Nashville, August 11th, '53

L. C. Draper
Madison, Wisconsin

My Dear Sir,

I returned from the North a few days since and have today read your favors of 17*th*, 21*st* May. I had only finished the perusal when I met Dr. Robertson who immediately pulled from his pocket your letter to him under date of 20th June . . . I had to say several things to pacify him: He is not pleased at what he considers the prospect of publication of the life of his father—(in his own lifetime,)—thinks or fears that you are more ambitious and engrossed in collecting manuscripts, etc., than in preparing and writing history. . . . I mention this *entre nos,*—believing you will make due allowance for the inevitability of age: His impatience is not unnatural, nor unusual—but after Dr. Ramsey's measure of time,—'tis too soon to murmur, though anxiety be ever so great. . . .

Colonel Joseph Brown *was alive* last May when I left home, and I believe is yet alive, notwithstanding Dr. Ramsey's book. That narrative received through hands of General Zollicoffer, is about the only communication for which he gives credit to others and in saying

I despair of finding anything historical or scientific. My "second volume"
—I have not promised it yet. I have the material, but must rest till my first
is out of the way a little. This far it sells well and I am impatiently waiting now for further arrivals. The binder has been unable to keep me supplied with it. Charleston is not New York as to pushing work off by telegraph.

Your *Boon* (so Daniel spelled it in 1760 on my beech tree) I hope to see
in 1853. You will find little in the *Annals* to assist you there, but when
you come to Sevier my book makes him its hero. Indeed, his life is Tennessee history itself. He is not only in every chapter, but every page. (By
the way—it is proposed to celebrate next seventh of October at King's
Mountain by Virginia, South and North Carolina and Tennessee. If it
takes place I will arrange an invitation to you to attend. Will you come?)

You ask for specialties as to cost of my volume. I give them for your
own eye. The edition is 5,000—printing, including composition, paper,
press work, everything but binding—about $3,000. Binding according to
the style—cloth, leather, fancy—from 22½ per copy to 50 cents. Leather is
the most demanded in Tennessee even at the higher price. A few fancy
copies only are wanted—say five per cent of the whole edition. I published on my own account without the promise of a single subscriber. I
failed to say engraving my continental bills of credit by North Carolina,

---

that the narrative "is now first published," he proved that *Mecklenburg* does not receive "all
the papers and magazines and books that are published"—and so, in some other instances I
could name. . . .

   Dr. Ramsey promised me when I was at his house, and since then by letter, to send me
the papers of General Sevier—that I might have them bound with those I have; but he has
not replied to my two last letters asking for them and in his Book ventures to say "he found
them in an old house in Knoxville!" *I* selected them 20 years ago when at Locust Shade,
Colonel Sevier's residence in Overton, and he shewd me *very little* more than those I had
furnished, and *on* which were many of *my endorsements* of contents made 20 years
before. . . .

Putnam

Draper Manuscripts 6 XX 56

Athens, Tennessee, 7 September, 1853

Lyman C. Draper
Madison, Wisconsin

My Dear Sir,
   To comply with your request will be to me a very grateful work, and I have already set
about to get up the information you desire. I feel that Dr. Ramsey's work has not done justice
to the memory of Colonel Outlaw, as he was one of the leading spirits of his day, and did
much I am sure for his country at the time when that country needed the service of all her
sons. . . .

Very Respectfully
Thomas J. Campbell

the surrender at King's Mountain and the map of Cumberland and Franklin cost me above $300.00. My retail price is $3.00 cloth, 3.50 leather, 4.00 fancy. Book agents and booksellers have very high commissions for selling—such is the invariable custom of the trade—from twenty-five to fifty per cent. Otherwise the thing pays well. The first edition should never be stereotyped. An author sees many things—arrangement, words, sentences —which he desires to change after he sees it printed which in manuscript the most practical and critical eye passes over unobserved. My next edition I will stereotype and can sell lower. The Nashville Historical Society is doing nothing valuable as I hear, ours ditto. Money, railroads, towns, politics exclude science and especially history. I do not know where Mrs. Ellet resides. She writes me from Nashville, Baltimore and New York. She is a peripatetic and a cosmopolite, I think. I do not consider her very scrupulous or exact as to dates and facts. This is not *gallant* and I say it to no one else.

I am well, but a heavy domestic bereavement, which I know I must have mentiond to you at the time of its occurrence,—the death in California of my excellent son Wilberforce—weighs like an incubus on my heart. I shall meet him in heaven. The first proceeds of my sales I am devoting to the rebuilding of our (old) church. The second will be in removing his remains to our burial ground near it. His injunction written in poetry in a camp on his tour through the wilderness still rings in my ears. The end of every verse is "Oh carry me back—oh carry me back! To Mecklenburg once More!" Write me often and especially let me know whether my book has reached you.

Draper Manuscripts 6 XX 47

June 6, 1853

Your favor of the seventeenth ultimo is to hand. I am glad to hear that my volume reached you. Under the apprehension that it had miscarried I ordered you a second copy. If the supernumerary makes its appearance hand it over at your discretion to some reading emigrant from Tennessee —to the editor of some Wisconsin journal or to your state or other library. I am glad to have had an analytic reader. I hear every day "your book has mighty pretty reading in it—or it is very interesting—or contains new and valuable matter." This is some commendation, but when Mr. Draper says I have done my state a good service; have done it "in a manner really creditable to myself," and that the arrangement of the work meets your approval, etc., I feel and appreciate the compliment.

To your inquiries, I say, page 66. Second visit of Dr. Walker to Kentucky is given on authority of Marshall, page 39 at that date. I prosecute the inquiry *now* no further but it is my impression that there is further authorities to this point besides the Boon inscription which is at least something in its favor.

Page 69. I give in support of the account, as given by Haywood, of Boon's 1764 trip the oral narrative of Mr. W. S. Callaway to me last November. He had from the lips of his ancestor that he was at the side of Boon when he made that noted declaration. I do not recollect that W. S. Callaway mentioned the date. That is given from Haywood, page 35. He was his companion and kinsman.

Page 109. In reference to *John* Boon being associated with Robertson in negotiating, etc., I conceive Haywood to be authority most ample and reliable. Robertson was his associate and neighbor and can scarcely be supposed to say John when it should be Daniel, but I have sought for and have, I believe, no further evidence than Haywood to whom I refer my reader on page 109. I think it satisfactory.

Page 109 and 139. I suppose all I showed you on the subject of Sevier's being from Williamsburg was the letter in manuscripts of an old settler informing his correspondent that "a portly youngish looking gentleman had come from Williamsburg named Sevier and had brought encouraging accounts to the frontiers." One of my narratives too, I believe that of Mr. George Hufacre, mentions his return from Williamsburg. Thither probably he had gone for supplies before the Cherokee outbreak in 1776. Dunmore commissioned him, I believe, in 1774 and he was probably if never a resident, occasionally a visitant, there. I have often heard my father Colonel F. A. Ramsey, deceased, in accounting for Sevier's urbanity, explain it by supposing he had seen good society at Williamsburg. He was exceedingly urbane, and, when he chose to be, genteel and accomplished. The inference—it is something more—that Sevier had been at Williamsburg is therefore legitimate.

Page 234. *The Shelby Papers*—copied nearly entire by Haywood in his history on page 59 and one-half of 60, and resumed at bottom of page 63 and continuing to every part of our participation in the Revolution. These I have still preserved though most of my manuscripts were destroyed at Charleston when I came out of press. I have not alluded to Shelby's Pamphlet on King's Mountain. I had only a newspaper with part of it in it. Where do I say that *John* Sevier was in the battles of the Kanawha I have no positive proof that he was or was not. Some accounts, printed and written, say that Captain Shelby's company had in it the Robertsons and *Seviers*. It may be possible that some of the latter besides Valentine junior was there and it is not improbable that John Sevier was there in some other company, as he is not mentioned in the printed list of Captain E. Shelby's men—but being commissioned that year, by Dunmore—as Haywood gives it—he may have been under Sevier, Fleming or Christian. On my page 261 I don't say John *Sevier* flashed his maiden sword. Valentine was also a leader, though the reader might infer none but John was meant. I have already said that my evidence does not enable me to say he was or was not. I have heard that Colonel Joseph Brown is dead. How or when I know not. I hope he is still living. He is a remarkable man and will figure in the future *Annals of Tennessee*. On the authority of Willie Blount's papers, who knew Ore and Montgomery and Jackson like a book, I state that the latter was at Nickajack. You say Kendall confirms it and that Jackson himself so said also. It must be so. Nothing could have kept him out of just such a frolic. It was his element. When did you see a fish jump upon dry land and stay there when a single almost involuntary effort would place him in a lake? If Jackson said so to you, he was there and no mistake. Blount is too candid and truthful to have volunteered his statement that he was and his comment about his presence. My whole paragraph on page 614–15 is from Blount. I know nothing further of Samuel Newell than I say of him, nor of his descendants. I pass his old Station on Boyd's Creek every few days and will inquire further. His wife was a Montgomery. He was a good Presbyterian, a Franklin captain and a brave man. I know nothing further of Captain William Bean. General Kennedy lived and died near Greeneville. I have all his papers. Nothing of Colonel Roddye—John Anderson. Colonel Clark died above me on Pigeon. I got all his papers and recollections. The same of Colonel Samuel Wier—whose descendants are here and in Missouri. Colonel Kelly and Colonel Hubbard Do. of Outlaw. You have a bad record in American State Papers. Major Robert King has left nothing. You say Haywood is in error about Henry Scaggins, and that it should be Skaggs. That may be. Haywood is not always right, though there *was* a pioneer Skaggs.

You wish to hear of my sales. This far very good, exceeding the supply of the binder. I have not a dozen unsold in Knoxville. This happy state of things may not last long, though I hope it may. The press reviews and notices me favorably, and calls for another volume. I must replenish my purse and rest a little before I say yes. I wrote you something on this subject a week or two since and need not enlarge now. I wish to realize at least cost this summer and then I can bear delay most patiently. If the public will let me off I prefer repose in future. Since 1820 I have not known one day's absolute quiet, rest, and leisure. I wonder in this hurly burly—this tumult of life—this constant and unremitted devotion to business, to the world, and to time—I have not wholly forgotten my Creator and my duties and service to him. Help me to praise him for even a small spark of love to him and for the feeble wish to serve him better.

P. S. I have here a receipt from the sheriff of _____ County Virginia for the taxes of Valentine Xavier. If you want it or a copy of it let me have the pleasure of sending it to you.

Draper Manuscripts 6 XX 57

September 9, 1853

Your favor of fifth ultimo was duly received. When I tell you that in one day of last week I visited patients in four counties, you will not consider me very negligent in replying to it. I have not time or patience just now to look over a whole shelf full of old letters to find McGaughey's (I believe) letter about Sevier's arrival from Williamsburg—nor is it necessary. I missed the line which informed his correspondent, my grandfather in Pennsylvania, that a portly stranger the name of Sevier is just in from Williamsburg and brought encouraging news about help, supplies or something of that kind. It was written about the time of the Cherokee outbreak of 1776 and mentioned that there was such danger that some talked of leaving the settlements. As I have heretofore said Sevier may not have been a resident of Williamsburg but an employee only of the Virginia authorities.

Willie Blount was the most *minute* man I ever knew—was Jackson's most intimate friend, knew all *his* neighbors and died surrounded by them—could not have been mistaken and he says not only that he was at Nickajack but *planned* the attack. I have no doubt of it. The *force* of that campaign consisted of so many separate detachments from such remote sections that it was impossible for any to know all that were there and thus even those who knew J. so well afterwards might believe and say that he was not there. I believe he was and such is the general though not universal belief. Still, as the French say, "ne importe." The Shelby papers are at your service, but every word *verbatim et literatim* is in Haywood, not one line omitted—but not credited as you will see. So also of the Museum. All is exactly copied in Haywood. It is communicated by someone— Demumbrane, I suppose, or Mansco. Both are, however, at your service. If you still want to see them please indicate the channel by which they will reach you and they shall be sent. Please return them. I have inquired for the descendants of Samuel Newell, Charles Robertson, Roddye, Hubbard, Kelly, Crawford and King—without learning of their present residence. Colonel Kennedy's grandson is a respectable citizen of Greene County and had furnished to me all his papers. Colonel Wier's widow gave me twenty years since all his papers. His surviving son Pleasant M. Wier emigrated soon after to Missouri. P.O. not known.

Your expectations have been gloriously realized. Andrew Johnson is our governor. Tennessee is revolutionized. The Maine liquor law will never be a statute in any state two years. That is a hard saying for a Progressive Democrat and a friend of temperance who has never drunk in his life of fifty-six years to make—but mark the result. A law to prevent covetousness or adultery though sustained by Divine sanction could not be enacted or enforced. Much less a law to regulate men's diet, drink, etc. The only corrective of intemperance is the propagation of the religion of Jesus Christ, the spread of His Blessed Gospel, and the influence of His example and spirit. The Lord Help us to imitate Him in all His immutable perfections. . . .

P. S. The folding leaves me an unoccupied line. Be very careful at Cincinnati in your stipulations with your publishers. The *et ceteras* are to be carefully investigated or you will be wronged and deceived. Even in Charleston I got once or twice into the hands of Northern screws. Take care. I don't mean my publishers, Walker and James, but engravers and binders and packers.

CHAPTER VI

Industrial Necessities of the South

(Private)

Mecklenburg near Knoxville, Tennessee
April, 1858

L. W. Spratt, Esquire
Charleston, South Carolina
My Dear Sir,

In the proceedings of the last Southern Convention[1] I see that "Dr. Ramsey of Tennessee" is placed upon the committee of which you are chairman. Gentlemen of the same name and of the same title are residents of Tennessee and I have no means of ascertaining that I am the Dr. Ramsey intended. But having heretofore thought much on the subject and written some newspaper paragraphs on several branches of it, I venture to presume that I am associated with your committee and under that presumption I append below some suggestions on the question assigned to you. You will find them rather crude and immethodical, not suitable in their present shape to form any part of the well digested report you will make to the Montgomery Convention, but showing in a brief and desultory manner by a general outline my long-cherished views on this most important subject, and enabling you thus to see how far a Tennessee member of the committee concurs with its chairman (for I cannot expect to go to Montgomery and confer with you personally.)

---

[1] Throughout the eighteen-fifties Southern Commercial Conventions met annually in various cities of the South. For the most part they were concerned with achieving the economic independence of the South, encouraging direct trade with Europe, promoting a Southern railroad to the Pacific, and furthering Southern education in matters economic. The Montgomery Convention of 1858, however, fell into the hands of politicians and its discussions became a forum for the "fire-eating" brand of Southern extremists. Cf., H. Wender, *Southern Commercial Conventions, 1837–1859* (1930).

The letters which comprise this chapter were copied by Dr. Ramsey and attached to his autobiography, but with a note declaring "The letters marked *Private* from number 1 to 7 addressed to Mr. Spratt, Chairman, etc., are not to be published, but preserved as *speculations* of my own and not as part of this Autobiography."

First then, and very briefly, let me say that everyone familiar with the climate, soil, productions, and geographical position of the South cannot fail to have observed two great and primary "Industrial Necessities" of the Southern States. These are, first: The want of a direct communication between our section and the great centers of population, commerce and wealth in the other hemisphere and especially in Europe. I cannot amplify on this point and will specify but a single detail (and that only because it has not been heretofore sufficiently estimated or considered). Up to 1765–1775 European immigrants came to the Southern colonies *direct* through the Chesapeake and South Atlantic harbors. Through these channels arrived the very best elements that go in to constitute society—industry, enterprise, thrift, self reliance, intelligence, high-toned moral sentiment, public and private virtue, character, learning, subordination, regard for order and law, etc., etc. Each neighborhood enriched by immigrants of this character became at once the nucleus of communities of the same stamp—perfectly conservative and with no tendency in it to radicalism. (Look at the expansion and growth of Maryland and all south of it.) The Revolution succeeded. By its results indirectly the channel of immigration was changed. The bottoms that carried off our products and brought in our imports gave new facilities for the introduction of another description of European immigrants—with indeed some virtue, intelligence and wealth, but with a large mixture of pauperism, vice and crime. The facilities above alluded to increased every year and the North was inundated and has continued to be over-flown with a flood of immigrants made up generally of the unworthy, the plebian, and the poor. These readily supplied the place of servants in the cities and laborers and operatives on the farms and in the manufactories of the Eastern and Northern states. Manumission enactments followed—not that slaves were not wanted but because the labor of the dependent German and the hardy Irishman was cheaper than that of the Negro. Thus supplied with a good substitute for his slave, the Northern owner sold him South if he was young or emancipated him if worn out or worthless. Interest and policy, not benevolence or justice, originated the enactments abolishing slavery where it has been abolished.

The certainty of finding employment and receiving comparatively good wages in the North stimulated immigration into that section and, gradually but constantly, the voting population has so far increased as to give at length a certain and absolute majority in congress to the free states and in the same proportion to diminish the political strength and importance of the slave states in the legislation of the government. I need not mention the effects of this upon our section. We have become hewers of wood and drawers of water. We are dependent and are becoming every day more so. Dependent upon them as our carriers, our manufacturers, our law-makers, our authors even. How shall this state of things be corrected? I mention a single method of at least mitigating the evil if it may not restore our original equality: Form a direct communication between the South Atlantic seaports and the markets of the world. Export directly in our own ships our own products to these markets and import in like manner all that we consume or wish or need from abroad. Give us commercial independence. Restore to Charleston what she had in 1765 and distribute to her rival southern harbors their fair proportion of the increased business since that time.

The subject will be continued in my next.

J. G. M. *Ramsey*

Free J. G. M. Ramsey, P. M.
Mecklenburg, Tennessee

(Private)
Letter 2.

[Mecklenburg, Tennessee]
[n. d.]

L. W. Spratt, Esquire

Dear Sir:

In my last I mentioned the want of a direct communication between our section and the markets of the world as one of the "Industrial Necessities" of the South. I cannot here dilate further on that point, but hasten at once to another—equally important and more obvious, second, the want of labor.

The area of the slave states is in round numbers 856,000 square miles. Of these it is believed 500,000 are arable while only 150,000 are now under cultivation, leaving 350,000 square miles unproductive and valueless. The productions of the acres by this estimate now under culture amount to $_____ annually. Were the one-fourth of that still remaining uncleared, now placed under culture similarly remunerative, there would be added to the existing amount of pecuniary profits the vast sum of $_____. This difference between the present profits of agriculture in the Southern States and that which would result were the whole of its arable land in use, is greatly increased by taking into the computation other sources of wealth which would spring up from the large cities, the multiplied manufactories, the extended commerce, increased population, etc., etc., which are consequent. I may not dilate here, nor can I delay upon the *inadequacy* of the *natural increase* of our Negro laborers to supply the present and growing want of labor in the South. That inadequacy will not be questioned. It is admitted by all who look into the subject. It is axiomatic and I hasten to consider the question *how the deficiency of labor in the South can be best supplied?*

I alluded in a former letter to the exhaustless supply of laborers in our Northern States by the immigration into them of European laborers. The cheapness of the passage and the frequency of voyages to the North Atlantic seaports have secured to them almost a monopoly of the immigration into the United States. The early construction of the Erie Canal and more recently of railroad communication with the interior and the great North West has increased that monopoly and may perpetuate it even after a more direct channel of intercourse shall have been established between Europe and the South. Besides, the adaptation of the soil, climate, etc., of the North to the modes of tillage to which Europeans are accustomed (the cereals, etc., and not cotton) the free soil infatuation which deludes equally the native and foreign laborer, the reputed greater fertility of soil, and the mistaken opinion of a wider and more perfect immunity from disease, will all continue to confine immigration to its present channels—the northern and middle states. But were it even otherwise it can easily be shown that the plantation states cannot advantageously employ European laborers. These cannot fell a forest, open and subdue a wilderness, erect a cabin, control a mule, nor cultivate and gather southern products, however well soever some of them may inclose a prairie with a ditch and cultivate the products of the North. They have no knowledge of the axe, none of southern husbandry in general. Besides a foreigner of the Caucasian family, being of course unacclimated, must in all portions of the South undergo a *seasoning* and in many places be exposed to and become the victim of malarian diseases. Besides all this, the European laborer feels in the more southern states dissociated from society around him, becomes discontented, sometimes insubordinate and vicious, seldom amalgamates with his neighbors or becomes identified fully with southern communities—and goes off to the more congenial free states.

As the South then cannot depend upon this source of supply for the deficient labor of our section the question still remains how shall that deficiency be supplied?

In the consideration of this question I go at once *in medias res* and remark that the South can depend on *African* labor and on the African laborer *alone*. The climate suits him and he suits the climate. Miasma affects him as little as it does the alligator or the crane of the everglades of Florida. Paludal exhalations are to him harmless and inoperative and heat and other atmospheric influences which would enervate and destroy an Innishillen dragoon or a phlegmatic Hollander only add to the comfort and increase the efficiency and health of the African laborer. Further, the *description* or kind of labor in the South is just such precisely as is suited to the genius and intellectual capacity of the African under the general direction of the white man. With no mental training—with no tedious process of indoctrination—his instincts alone are almost sufficient to teach the Negro the duties of a field hand. A Negro is at home and happy in the field.

J. G. M. Ramsey

(Private)
Letter 3.

April 15, 1858

Having in my last attempted to show that African labor and that alone can supply *the* great "industrial necessity of the South" it remains for me to inquire how far that can be obtained. I have already asserted that the natural increase of our slaves is inadequate to the needed supply of African labor. It is true that under our benignant system of slavery, under our temperate climate and almost tropical sun, with a plentiful supply of wholesome food, with an entire absence of care or other mental inquietude either for today or the morrow, our Negroes increase beyond the ratio of any part of the population of the world. But vast, certain and rapid as is this multiplication of that race, it can be easily demonstrated that the sections of the South now most densely populated with Negroes are most inadequately supplied with slave labor. What then must be the deficiency in that almost immeasurable area yet to be cleared, yet to be occupied, yet to be settled especially in the extreme south and southwest? This deficiency can be supplied only by fresh importations of native Africans. This, I am aware, opens up to our investigation not only the whole question of slavery as it exists at present in the United States but also involves the right and also the expediency of reviving and legalizing the slave-trade. Now, as I profess to be sound in my morals and orthodox in my system of ethics, I propose to examine this question in several of its phases and will endeavor to show briefly that it is humane, benevolent, scriptural, Christian, patriotic, and perhaps politic and expedient. Each of these positions will not be argued separately and alone nor in the exact order in which I have characterized them. I will condense the argument to the shortest limits possible and may, if leisure permits, answer and refute some objections.

(It may be necessary to premise that where slavery is mentioned I mean African slavery—the relation of the Caucasian master to the Negro slave.)

The relation of (any) master and (any) servant is an accompaniment of, and inseparable from, the least progress in civilization. The relation becomes only the more intense and perfect as civilization advances. In the simplest form of the savage state there may possibly exist an almost perfect equality. Physical strength, age, superior skill in the chase or in war soon introduce artificial distinction and the original equality that marks the most primitive and simple form of an uncivilized or barbarous tribe begins imperceptibly to disappear. Someone becomes, if not in name certainly in reality, superior. His wigwam is less rudely constructed, his costume of furs is perhaps neater, his war-plume is made of the feathers of the eagle or some rare bird. His bow is better polished, his quiver holds more arrows. He kills, of course, more game. He holds his position in the assault upon or in the pursuit of the enemy longer than those who yesterday were his compeers and equals.

The equality of that tribe exists no longer. There is an *artificial* condition of things beginning to form which continues to grow till someone, if he be not called and acknowledged a chieftain, arrogates to himself a superiority. He strives to maintain, enlarge and enforce it. He becomes the head of his tribe, has authority, gives law, and has his prerogatives and privileges and rights sanctioned by his co-savages. Equality no longer exists there. So on an American frontier the hunter and pastoral stages of society at first recognize no inequality. Socially they are all equals. One has larger flocks—or is a better hunter and accumulates more peltries. One achieves a greater exploit with his rifle or his trap, or penetrates deeper into the pathless wilderness. Incipient distinctions are already being formed in these stages of society.

Again, squatters going from older communities to a distant and unbroken forest find themselves suddenly in a state of (apparent) equality in wealth, character, position, social and political. At first they recognize no superiority, no inequality. Each head of his family is supreme, is a sovereign. He is the compeer of every other head of a family, and no one in that community is admitted to be his superior. All live alike in the same primitive simplicity, working for and waiting upon themselves. The picture is soon changed. Someone becomes so rich as to employ the daughter of a poorer countryman to wash or scrub for his wife, or an indigent boy or a sojourner to black his boots or do other menial services for him at his table or on his farm. In either case wages are paid for services of a menial kind rendered. Menial service is rendered for money given to requite it. In that community of squatters servitude is already established as an institution or element. The employer is, *quoad hoc,* the master; the employee, *quoad hoc,* is the servant.

This form of servitude, however simple in the squatter state of society, soon becomes a more distinct feature as civilization progresses to the agricultural, the manufacturing and commercial phases of social and political organization. In its chrysalis state it bears the mildness almost of the parental relation and continues to maintain nearly that character throughout the purely agricultural state. After that the transition is more rapid till it ends, in the manufacturing and commercial states, in the absolute and despotic authority of the employer and the dependence and subserviency of the employee.

(Private)
Letter 4.

April 16, 1858

In my last I mentioned that *servitude* is a necessity of society and in some form or other is an accompaniment of and inseparable from civilization. In support of that position I found it to exist in all the phases of society from the savage state to the highest point of human progress and refinement. It follows that the condition of perfect *equality* exists nowhere, and the hypotheses that rest upon such an idea are necessarily Utopian and absurd. Indeed, variety and inequality are stamped upon every work of the great Creator. It is so in the material universe: "One star differeth from another in glory." "One is made for honor another for dishonor." Compare the brilliant autumnal sunsets of East Tennessee with the murky atmosphere of Labrador, or the genial influences of your South Carolina skies with the bleak and churlish temperature of an Icelandic winter, or the barren and unproductive deserts of Africa with the rich alluvium of our Mississippi bottoms;—the trees of the forest, the flora of the valleys and the products of the farm and garden, the beasts of the field and the fowls of the air. The rational creation the *genus homo* itself bears, too, the impress of the same variety and inequality, in their physical, moral and intellectual manifestations and developments. Compare the idiotic features of the Hottentot with the contour of the cultivated European, the forehead and eye of the educated Irishman with the lusterless stare and vacant countenance of the Asiatic drone, the genius and brilliancy of Newton and Fulton with the dullness and stupidity of the aboriginal American. Inequality exists everywhere. It is one of God's laws extending throughout inanimate, animate, irrational, rational, and probably the angelic, seraphic, cherubic and the purely spiritual creation. Nothing of all this will be denied. But the inferences, legitimate and irresistible though they be, are questioned and denied and the objector is ready to ask for the *warrant,* the authority, the source of the *power,* the *legality* of thus using the inferior *genera* of creation to promote the growth, enlargement and progress of the superior *genera.* Let the objector reflect that it is by a fixed law of nature and by the necessary operation of natural causes that the rich mould of the hillside gradually disappears from its primary location and is as gradually removed to the valley below to enrich and fertilize it. *Nature* itself takes from that "which hath and giveth to that which hath not." Let him reflect that the monarch of the forest derives its growth and aliment and vigor from the decay and decomposition of the inferior and weaker co-vegetables which surround him. His wide-spreading branches shut out the rays of the sun, his deep running tubers absorb the nutriment and cut off the supplies of every plant covered by his shade. Let him reflect that the smaller animals, by a necessity of nature, constitute the necessary food of the larger—that it is a fixed law of nature that the "big fishes eat up the little ones." I ask where is the *warrant* for this? Carry the argument further. It is a fixed law of political economy that the effect of human progress, advancement, civilization, if you will, is to make the rich richer, and of necessity the poor poorer, the influential more powerful and the indolent and ignorant still more insignificant and inferior in society and the world. The canebreak and the prairie have little dissimilarity and inequality in their products. That uniformity is soon lost and is succeeded by the magnolia, the palmetto and the majestic oak.

Will the objector still ask for the *warrant* for this transmutation? If he rejects the great law of nature stamped on all creation let him reflect on another law—the command of the great Creator himself to man viz; to *subdue* and *cultivate the earth*. Here is the great scriptural warrant and authority to progress, to civilize, to subdue, to govern, to elevate, to refine. And as a corollary to use the inferior creation (races) and make it subservient to this high purpose and end. Now I shall not enter into the physiological argument of the inferiority of the races of men. I am content here to say that the Negro is below the white race in his physical, moral and intellectual nature; that no one is more conscious of this inferiority than the Negro himself; no one more sensible of this superiority than the Caucasian. It is an innate sentiment, irradicable and self evident, perfectly compatible with reason, justice, Scripture, right and in no sense incompatible to, but rather in entire accordance with, the dictates of humanity and the kindest feelings of our nature.

(Private)
Letter 5.

April 23, 1858

The pressure of other engagements has left me no leisure till this morning to continue the remarks I wish to make in further illustration and support of African slavery. I believe I have already sufficiently touched upon *servitude* as a condition and relation of life inseparable from even a low form of civilization. *Slavery* is the same relation differing only in the degree of its intensity, or most perfect form, and in these remarks I confine it to the enslavement of the Negro race alone.

This race, it is known, is remarkable for its improvidence, indolence, submissiveness to the superior race, adaptation to labor under a tropical sun, its capacity to resist malarian influences, its apathy, its barbarism (in some places its cannibalism), and its general disinclination to or incapacity for civilization and culture. The country inhabited by and most congenial to it is the barren deserts and sandy wastes of tropical Africa. From this barrenness of the soil, the heat of a vertical sun, and the natural indolence

of the natives, the means of subsistence are inadequate to the support of
its inhabitants. This inadequacy becomes the more considerable from the
prolific character of many of the tribes. The females become mothers in
their thirteenth year. Hence the race multiplies in a ratio unknown to the
temperate and more polar regions. The means of subsistence being insufficient to support the rapidly increasing population, and the deficit
not being supplied by commerce (of which there is none), the natives
resort of necessity to war to obtain more food and to diminish the
consumers of food. These wars are necessarily *predatory* and *internecine*.
The victors, of course, kill (or eat) the prisoners—otherwise the victorious
would become the vanquished tribe. If a captive or subdued enemy were
to be fed, as in the case of civilized warfare, the difficulty which originated
the war would be only augmented by success and victory. Hence their
prisoners are doomed to death. The same fate awaits, even in the time
of peace, the aged, the infirm, the helpless infant. All these, in seasons of
scarcity, are drowned, burned or left to starve in the desert. A ship arrives
on the coast laden with rice and other supplies of food. Will anyone deny
that to exchange that cargo for a doomed captive, for an infirm and unfortunate native, for a helpless and starving family of young Negroes is
human, is benevolent, is legal, Christian? The great law of love is to do
to others as we would that others should *ceteris paribus* do to us. The
sixth commandment is, "Thou shalt not kill." This divine command requires "all lawful endeavors to preserve our own life and the life of
others." It also forbids "the taking away of our own or our neighbors' life
or whatsoever tendeth thereunto." Without arguing the question further
as a question of morals I appeal to every New England Puritan to answer
my question truthfully and with candor.

Again, were a mart for the sale of Negro prisoners—the starving im-
becile and the helpless children—established by law or the rules of legitimate traffic on the border of every African tribe where this unfortunate
description of Negroes could be exchanged for such a supply of the necessaries of even savage life as would prevent the cruel necessity of internecine warfare among themselves would it not promote and advance the
great cause of humanity, diminish the general amount of human sufferings, preserve human life, add to the comfort and advance the progress
of the African race? Again, the Negro in his own country is not only a
slave but his master is a barbarian and a savage, a pagan and an idolater
—sometimes a cannibal. I cannot here enlarge upon this idea, nor com-

pare the relation of the Caucasian master (owner is the better word) enlightened, humane, refined, Christian—with the submissive, docile, patient
Negro slave conscious of his own inferiority and proud of being owned
and governed by a superior. I may not consume your time here to mention the patriarchal character of slavery as it exists in the United States,
the *higher* civilization which it has produced (which, it must be admitted,
it *alone* can produce) the high souled, manly, honorable, chivalric tone
of feeling and conduct which it instigates and confirms. These are so
obvious as to be generally admitted by the intelligent and candid even
of our Northern fellow citizens; but I may mention that, paradoxical as
it may seem to them, there is found among slaveholders a greater jealousy
of liberty, a keener sense of right, a more intense feeling of independence
than elsewhere. The master spirits of the Revolution South were all slaveholders while their truest allies and compeers North—Hancock, Warren,
Otis (John) Adams, and others—held the Negro in bondage (so I have
heard).

(Private)
Letter 6.

April 29, 1858

I have thus hastily and with little method given you my own views on
the two great industrial necessities of the South, and in doing so have
necessarily gone into the subject of servitude as an invariable accompaniment of progress or civilization, and of that form of it which is called
slavery, and especially African Slavery as it exists in the Southern section
of the United States. In the course of my remarks I had to defend the
morality of the institution, its tendency not only to improve but to elevate, refine and enoble society and to foster a lofty spirit of freedom and
independence. I could have enlarged on these several topics. I could have
compared society as it now exists in the free states with what it was previous to the abolition of slavery north of Mason and Dixon's line. I could
have compared the present state of society in the South and in the North,
the morality and obedience to law in the one section with the venality,
corruption, discontent and insubordination in the other. The country,
its condition, and its institutions between Florida and the British posses-
sions north of us I have traveled over and observed closely. I have *analyzed*
them and am prepared to say that in many, almost all, of its aspects society

is better, morality purer, civilization higher and more general, and government more stable in the South and Southwest than in the Eastern and Middle States. Indeed the tenure by which property, character, life, is held in the older section of the free states is much less secure and inviolable than in the slave states. Were it not for the safety-valve, which emigration to the far west furnishes to the densely populated free states, the great centers of population North, would every year explode and be revolutionized. I could have compared the anarchy and crime and decay of the present United States of Mexico with the condition of things in that delightful country while slavery existed in it. I could have compared the system of peonage, the delusion of the equality and amalgamation of the races, the inefficient government, the declining commerce, the neglected agriculture of the present Mexico with those existing when the proud Castilian was master and his plebians were slaves. I could compare Jamaica with Cuba and Brazil. But time and leisure do not permit me and it remains to look briefly into the question of the *expediency* of reviving and legalizing the African slave trade. I have heretofore admitted that such a policy was humane, benevolent, lawful and patriotic—to Africa especially and to the cause of civilization generally. But is the policy expedient at this time for the South? That is the question.

I conceal from no one my deep conviction that the days of our present Union are nearly numbered. Apart from the slavery issue there are other elements at work which, at an early day, must produce a dismemberment. Our people will never again be a unit. The antagonism is too strong, the estrangement is too deep seated to be reconciled or healed. We are essentially two people—we are not only not homogeneous but we have become radically heterogeneous. The high toned New-England spirit has degenerated into a clanish feeling of profound Yankeeism. Our passions, our tastes, our character, our vices even, are different and dissimilar. Our interests conflict. We are no longer one family. The masses of the North are venal, corrupt, covetous, mean and selfish. The proud Cavalier spirit of the South and of the slaveholder, the virtue and integrity of the Huguenot, the probity and honor of the Presbyterian not only remain but have grown and become intensified. They tincture the whole surface of Southern society. I repeat the North and the South are heterogeneous. We are essentially two people. Could the vivacious, free thinking Frenchman and the steady and deliberate Englishman harmonize five years under one government? Even were France and England not separated by the British Channel? They could not. A spontaneous outbreak or a bloody revolution would disrupt any political bands that might be contrived to combine elements so incompatible and incongenial. It is so with our people, North and South. We are destined to a separation. Sooner or later it must take place. It is inevitable. Shall the separation be peaceful? I hope it may. I almost think it will. The South must keep herself in the *right*. Let aggression go still further, let a wrong against southern rights and against the guarantees of the constitution be not only premeditated but enacted and realized, a zone of states—certainly all south of Tennessee,— will throw off all allegiance to a broken union and regard for a violated constitution. These will become at once the nucleus of a Southern Confederacy around which from time to time other co-states, perhaps not at first co-terminous states, will upon the principle of elective affinity cluster, gradually, but of necessity certainly, and the government is separated peaceably and safely to the South and to her institutions.

The bearing of these remarks upon the question before us will be seen in the next letter.

(Private)
Letter 7.

April 29, 1858

If, as I said in my last, the dissolution of the union is inevitable, it becomes the more necessary that the new confederation (association of states rather) should be careful to place themselves in the right—not only with her confederates or associates but with the world at large. Unfortunately for the South, the slave trade is in conflict with the *sentiment of the world*. Treaties, enactments, practice, have almost universally made this traffic not only illegal but odious—in some instances piratical. Now in all past time on all other subjects the *sentiment of the world* has not only been radically *wrong* but is now admitted to be so. The sentiment of the world was opposed to the preaching of Noah—eight only of its innumerable inhabitants believing that he was a preacher of righteousness or that his prophecy of a coming deluge would be realized. The sentiment of the world at large favored polytheism while the worship of the one true God was confined to the descendants of Abraham. The sentiment of the world was opposed to Christ, his kingdom and his religion, while he and twelve apostles alone propagated the true faith. Even at this day the sentiment of the world is against the Christian religion and its author. The sentiment of the Christian world is against Protestantism and the majority of Christendom is yet in favor of papacy and the pope. The sentiment of the Protestant world is opposed to the Calvinian system. The sentiment of the world, if not in favor of monarchical, is certainly opposed to republican government.

And yet which of us now denies the Noachic deluge, or avows a polytheistic worship, or pronounces the religion of Christ a delusion, or declares the Reformation wrong, or that the system of Calvin was unscriptural, or advocates the opinion that the people have not the right of self-government? What member of any Christian denomination is willing to surrender his private judgment merely because the sentiment of the world is not in consonance with it? I argue, therefore, that merely because Great Britain has changed her policy as to the slave trade and with some other governments now pronounces that piracy which was once considered legitimate traffic, the rest of the world must not be precluded from this gainful commerce—advantageous alike to the buyer and seller—promotive, too, of the great cause of humanity, and essential to the paramount object of civilization and Christianity. Still it may be expedient to wait for a further development of the great change which is every day manifesting itself in the public mind on this great question. Since we of the south have spoken out upon the subject, have defended the relation of master and slave as a Scriptural and Christian institution, defensible alike by the laws of God, the interests of society, the policy of nations, and by the sanctions of an enlightened conscience, the slave traffic has lost with the candid and considerate most of its odium. Popular clamor has ceased its reproaches and popular prejudice is every day yielding to the persuasive voice of reason and common sense. This is very apparent. Fanaticism, it is true, is *pari passu* stimulated to a more phrensied excess and a wilder extravagance. But the reaction from these very excesses will be overwhelming and decisive. The free soil and equality notions of the North will sooner or later end in agrarianism, radicalism, and the prostration of all law. Licentiousness will then follow with anarchy and ruin. I read in vain past history and the present signs of the times if this be not true.

Further. The present demand for Negro labor in the South and Southwest is so great that the present holders have a great vested right in that species of property and monopolize and engross its productiveness and its value. It may therefore not be expedient at once to destroy that monopoly. Such a policy might disaffect our best friends and our most stead-fast auxiliaries. Wealth is timid and almost sometimes selfish. We had better not shock too suddenly those whose slaves are their only property. *Festina lente* is a good motto.

But lastly, on the supposition that the separation of the Union will be one of force and violence, it may be both inexpedient and unwise to pre-cipitate the revival of the slave trade before that affair is finally settled. Once separated and independent, the southern states may give such form and vitality to their own government, such features to their own insti-tutions, and such exterior sanctions to their own policy as their principles and their convictions of what is right and necessary may dictate. It may be necessary to delay for a few years the renewal of the slave traffic with-out shocking too suddenly the prejudices or the judgment of the border states, slave or free. At this time Tennessee, I do not believe, would sanc-tion it. With further enlightenment she would. At this time southern Indiana and Illinois would oppose it. Let things remain a few years as they are and by elective affinity these would belong to the new Confed-eration and, in a few years after, they and other border states would sanction the importation of slaves.

From these hasty and undigested remarks you will be able to decide how far I concur in the report you will offer at Montgomery. No part of what I have written can be incorporated in it. I have written *currente calamo* and amid frequent interruptions. Take it only for what you may think it is worth. When you have read these letters over, or such part of them as is pertinent, please fold in a safe envelope and hand them to some one of the Knoxville delegates whom I will request to bring them to me. In the meantime I will be glad to hear from you either before or after the tenth.

CHAPTER VII

A Confederate Banker

As being part of my public or financial life I may as well right here mention another theater on which it became my unexpected duty to act upon a somewhat similar pursuit.[1]

In the meantime many of the southern states had seceded from the government of the United States and had set up the Southern Confederacy.[2] Tennessee had in effect done the same thing. I early saw, and

---

[1] See last sentence of Chapter III.

[2] On April 16, 1859 Dr. Ramsey darkly predicted the course of coming events as he asked Lyman Draper, "What will become of the Democratic Party? And of our loved country? All is gone. The free states will elect in 1860. The union is then dissolved virtually and soon after will be so in form. All north of the Potomac, certainly of the Hudson, will be one mass of isms and will never after act with even the Northwest, much less the South. There can never indeed be enough homogeneousness to keep the two sections together. We are now more hetereogeneous than France and England and can no longer be a united people." (Draper Correspondence)

Returning to the subject on May 10, 1859, he wrote Draper, "I cannot answer your questions about our Democratic Party, only to say someone else than Seward must be president or the constitution and the union will be lost. I do not believe that Douglas can beat him—nor anyone else."

Then, January 14, 1861, he wrote again. "A year has passed since I last heard from you. What changes that year has brought with it. Our union dismembered, our people estranged from each other, war threatened, anarchy probable with all its attendant evils. Even moderate and steady Tennessee in convention and on the point of resuming her delegated powers and setting up for herself. I believe it is full time for separation. If there is so little regard even for the whims and caprices, to say nothing of the rights, of the two sections, that even an unmeaning verbal concession cannot be extorted from the Black Republicans, it is demonstration that we are two peoples and cannot live together in peace. The South will never submit to the rule of a despotic majority and coercion is unauthorized, inexpedient, and wrong."

A month later, he wrote again—but it was a letter counseling his friend to moderation, and giving some intimate glimpses of his own life. Dr. Ramsey had no inkling of the future that was in store for him.

Draper Correspondence

February 12, 1861

"My Dear Sir,

"Your valued favor of January 26 accompanied by your state historical society's volume was received in due time for which I am greatly obliged. Is it possible I have not heretofore presented to your library a copy of my "Tennessee"? For fear I may have been so neglectful as to have failed to do so I now append an order on Keith & Woods, St. Louis, Missouri for it. Please present it at your earliest convenience. Even if you have a copy, a duplicate will be worth its room on your shelves.

"In a previous letter you mention an *interruption* to your usual good health—(for I will not allow myself to apprehend that it is anything more)—and ask me what you shall do for it? Don't medicate. Study, think, write less. Cultivate the social principle more. Old age

indeed had predicted in a series of letters addressed to the Montgomery Convention some years before, what must be the result if the partial legislation of Congress and the meddlesome and fanatical spirit of the Northern legislatures and people were not curbed, so as to preserve the union and the constitution intact and inviolable, and I had therefore entered into the support of the southern cause with every energy of mind, soul, and body.[3]

(excuse me, I know you are not old) requires calm, quiet inaction, the *otio cum dignitate* dignified leisure, with a few intelligent friends of appreciative tastes and preferences. I do not mean to tell you to be idle. That is worse than too much labor, but we are no longer young men and cannot longer endure the heat and burden of the day. Travel is good for you, come further south—come at least to Tennessee this summer—and luxuriate among our plain people and enjoy our primitive modes of civilization. If a visit south should give you or be followed by an intermittent—it will only be the better for revolutionizing your whole biliary and digestive systems and rejuvenating you. At your age I underwent that process and have been better ever since. Diversify your pursuits. Do nothing that is a *task*. I advise from *experience*. I care no longer for wealth. Subsistence is enough. Money is of no use to our children and we know it is of no value to ourselves. Look at the forests and the prairies around us. They toil not neither do they spin etc. I *select* my patients, take only such as I choose to, ride to town three or four times a week, supervise the bank of the state (of which I am just reelected president by a unanimous vote), meet a few literary friends, confer benefits where I can, have all my cares out of doors, sleep like a child, cultivate the domestic and social virtues, have but one enemy that I know of in the world and I have the satisfaction of believing that he hates me only for my virtues. I live yet as an old frontiersman, leaving off his use of whisky and reading by pine light. I take a glass of cold milk and a warm piece of hoe cake just as I go to bed etc. I tell you all these minutiae for the purpose of encouraging you not to allow yourself to be laid on the shelf till the *magnum opus* of your life, your border history, shall have been completed and published. (Just here let me advise you not to publish yourself. At any time this would be wrong—and at this revolutionary period will be, must be, ruinous. I have only saved myself and will publish no more.) For years to come our political troubles will not be settled. The executive patronage of the general governor has corrupted and will continue to seduce so many of the politicians of all the Northern States and such men as John Bell and Andrew Johnson of Tennessee in the Southern that the conflict will be interminable. The Southern Confederacy (a fixed fact) will soon exhibit the superior virtue and civilization that spring from slave institutions and the providence and authority of God demonstrate their wisdom and necessity. Tennessee, you see, is conservative and tardy, but when her time comes will secede too. Her leaders though cannot resist the seduction of Lincoln's patronage.

Truly yours
J. G. M. Ramsey"

[3] The following two paragraphs, penciled in Dr. Ramsey's handwriting, were pinned to the manuscript at this point. They bore the date "October 18, 1876."
"1876
1819

57 years ago last August 1 I gave my *first* vote for General William Carroll for governor of Tennessee against his then competitor, a Federalist though a good man and a patriot. Ever since, at every biennial election in Tennessee and every presidential and congressional election, I have steadfastly adhered to the same political faith and have in every instance always voted for a Democratic candidate and supported the Democratic party.
"My allegiance has always been, as I considered as due, first to my native Tennessee and second and through her to the United States. This double allegiance I have never renounced, but have held it inviolable and supreme. But when the voice of Tennessee was uttered in declaration of her states rights I obeyed that voice which absolved me from any allegiance to the union which had violated the constitution under which Tennessee was admitted as one of the parties to the compact forming the federal union. I always held with Jefferson that each *state* possessed the right not only to decide for herself *when* the constitution was

A bank convention was considered essential for the regulation of the general finances of the South. Official business called me to Nashville. While there, the subject of the convention of all southern banks at Richmond, Virginia was agitated, though not formally introduced in the convention then called by the parent board at the state capital. Colonel Torbett, the president, and myself concurred in the policy then agitated by the Confederate press of holding the convention of bankers at the Southern capital. Others of my presidential colleagues concurred with us. My own board of directors, on my return from Nashville, proposed that I should attend at Richmond as a delegate.

We met there accordingly on Monday after the day of the first Battle of Manassas. I arrived the day of the battle at four P.M. Telegrams were constantly arriving of the progress of the conflict. I had promised General Vaughn—then Colonel J. C. Vaughn—(whose regiment I had attended while at Knoxville as surgeon, and who had taken to the field the soldiery of my neighborhood and of East Tennessee) that if any of his men should be wounded to telegraph for me and that as soon as steam could take me I would be at his side. As soon, therefore, after I got out of the cars I hastened to the office of the secretary of war—heard that many were wounded and probably needed my professional assistance. To the secretary I was an entire stranger. President Davis, to whom I was well known, was down at Manassas: Mr. Albert Taylor Bledsoe, who was the only officer of the war department whom I could get to see, said the cars were full and declined, very courteously though, to give us the transportation ticket I asked for. I returned disappointed and vexed to the Spotswood House, joined Colonel Torbett there and passed an anxious, sleepless night. I found in the house my good and patriotic neighbor and friend, John Mason Boyd, M.D., just arrived from Knoxville. I told him how solicitous I was to go to the field of carnage and do something for our wounded. He was no less anxious, too, to go to their relief. Next morning we both went early to the war office, saw Mr. Bledsoe again, and met again a cold and unwelcome negative. Dr. Boyd remained longer importuning most earnestly. I knew Mr. Memminger intimately several years before, as a most enlightened and efficient advocate of our old railroad enterprise. He was now secretary of the Confederate States treasury. I entered his office, told him I had unsuccessfully

violated but also the further right to judge of the mode and measure of redress. Then as one of her native born freemen I approved of secession and thus became a Confederate— Call me Rebel if you will."

applied for passports to our camp, and begged him to go with me then to promote my wishes at the war department, or to give me himself the needed order for transportation. He said that could not be done, but that if I would wait a few minutes he would go with and introduce me to Mr. L. Pope Walker, the secretary of war. We found Dr. Boyd still there, but still unsuccessful. Not finding the secretary in his office, Mr. Memminger wrote and handed me a hurried note introducing his two friends, Doctors Boyd and Ramsey, and urging him to send us forward. It was without avail. A short time after, Dr. Boyd's application succeeded. I went up and entered the bank convention. Our deliberations were ended satisfactorily. I returned home, carrying with me some of the trophies of victory won by the valor of my countrymen, but disappointed that I had not been granted the privilege of being on the field of their glory.

This hasty interview with the secretary of the Confederate treasury served to renew the acquaintance we had formed several years before in Charleston, Columbia, Knoxville, and elsewhere while engaged in our railroad enterprises. But I had become still further known to him in the following way. Some of my friends in and around Knoxville, knowing my extreme Southern preferences, and my states rights orthodoxy and my constancy to principle, chose of their own free will to act thus in my behalf. I think it was early in the spring of 1861 (certainly before Tennessee had seceded and therefore before she had any representative in the Confederate States Congress), my personal friend Judge W. S. Swan, never a favorite political friend, as I had often voted against him, got up a memorial or petition to the Montgomery or Richmond authorities asking that I should be considered by them as a *quasi member* of congress at least till Tennessee, by the action of her people, would make provision for a regular and legitimate representation in the new government. The petition was carried around town, and signed irrespective of the Democratic and Whig parties. It was shown to me and I can still recollect the names of some of the memorialists, viz. Honorable W. H. Sneed, a former congressman from the Knoxville District, and a Whig; Judge Swan, a Whig; Honorable J. H. Crozier, also former congressman, and also a Whig; General J. A. Mabry, a Whig; M. B. McMahon, Esquire, an old line Democrat, and others. On seeing the petition and inspecting the names of the petitioners I expressed myself as agreeably surprised. The metamorphosis I could scarcely understand *"novas frondes miratur, non suas."* They were all gentlemen and patriots, and I felt and appreciated the high compliment they were offering me personally and politically, and still I could not conceal my surprise nor withhold the natural inquiry: "Gentlemen, what platform do you expect me to occupy?" They replied without one exception: "The Platform on which you have always stood since 1821—the platform of the South." I replied, in continuation: "By the blood of the Alexanders, and by the hallowed memoirs of Old Mecklenburg, I go for states rights, Southern rights, Southern independence. This is, and shall be, my platform."

The memorial thus signed was at once forwarded to the seat of government. A few days after, Judge Swan brought to my office the response. It was from President Davis. In that he said some complimentary words, and assured the memorialists that Dr. Ramsey would be most cordially received, and for the present would be considered as a *quasi member* of the Confederate States Congress. Thereafter, my correspondence with Mr. Davis and two members of his cabinet was constant, cordial, and confidential—sometimes advisory and commendatory, but oftener condemnatory of some of the measures of the administration; especially in reference to his military policy in Tennessee. I could wish that in some unexpected manner my official letters may have been preserved and that they might yet see the light.[4] In one of them I said: This Southern Confederacy must never become a failure—that were to not only ruin the South but to blight the best hopes of man of human improvement and of freedom everywhere. And to prevent this failure I advised a commercial treaty with France—giving to that power the entire monopoly of our cotton trade for a term of years, and receiving in turn her friendly recognition and the guaranty of our independence of the United States. If this advice had been adopted *Illium fuit* never would have been said of our Confederacy. (Some of these letters I may hereafter refer to as

---

[4] A number of Dr. Ramsey's letters to President Jefferson Davis are found in the *Official Records of the Union and Confederate Armies in the War of the Rebellion.* As early as November 4, 1861, Dr. Ramsey warned Davis that the enemy planned to invade East Tennessee through passes in Fentress and adjacent counties in a region filled with unionists. He suggested bringing General Arnold Elzey from the Potomac with Colonel Vaughn's regiment to guard the passes. Such action would discourage the malcontents, frighten the enemy in Kentucky, and "incite" the spirit of volunteering—"which I am humiliated to say is very low." Cf., *Official Records,* series 1, vol. 4, 511–512. See also, for other correspondence, *Ibid.,* p. 540; vol. 7, pp. 721–722; and vol. 50, part 2, pp. 267–8. In April 1864, after Longstreet had withdrawn from East Tennessee, Dr. Ramsey wrote Davis urging that storehouses of supplies for the families of East Tennessee soldiers be established on the border of East Tennessee. The unionist leaders, notably "Parson" W. G. Brownlow and Horace Maynard were successfully appealing in the North for funds to relieve the suffering of unionists in the region. *Ibid.,* series 1, vol. 50, part 2, pp. 655–656. Dr. Ramsey's letters regarding foreign aid to the Confederacy are not preserved.

these recollections may call them to mind.) In 1862, July 17, I received from Honorable C. G. Memminger, secretary of the treasury of Confederate States, his letter of July 9th, informing me that I was appointed *Depositary* under the act of April 15, 1862, increasing the number of depositaries.

At the time this letter of appointment from Mr. Memminger was received, I occupied the position of president of the branch of the Bank of Tennessee at Knoxville. On this account I felt it necessary to say in reply to Mr. Memminger that perhaps there might be an incompatibility in one and the same person holding the two offices, and if so to consider my letter as declining to receive the appointment he had given me of Confederate States depositary. In his second letter he said there was no incompatibility but rather a peculiar fitness in the two offices being filled by the same individual. I accordingly forwarded my official bond and entered on my new official duties. I found them to be exceedingly onerous and responsible. I did not know that I was allowed an assistant, a deputy or a clerk, and continued to discharge all the duties myself—often devoting the entire day and sometimes part of the night to their full discharge. One day Colonel C. Powell, a large merchant, came in the P.M. to my office, and finding me perfectly absorbed in official duties, told me he never saw me on the streets, nor at leisure in my room; that there was not a regimental quartermaster in Knoxville who had not one, two, or three assistants on a salary. I had not inquired on the subject, but began sensibly to feel that I was overworking myself and intruding occasionally upon the time and convenience of the cashier of the bank of which I was still president. Upon my application to him, the secretary promptly gave me authority to appoint such assistants as I found necessary. To know the extent of my labors and cares it is only necessary here to say that from 1862 to April 1865 I disbursed between forty-two and forty-three million of dollars for the Confederate States treasury, and though I had in that interim made seven or eight hegiras and hair-breadth escapes, I never lost one dollar of my funds. Up to November 25, 1862 I had no clerk.

Early in 1863 I was appointed Confederate States tax collector for Tennessee. After holding it some time, I found its duties would call me much of my time from Knoxville, and I declined it.

December 30, 1862 I was called to Atlanta on detective business with Colonel G. W. Lee there. Either on that occasion, or one similar to it, as I passed through Dalton, Georgia, the sound of cannon was heard in

the direction of Chattanooga. Rumors of an invasion of that place and
other points in East Tennessee had been in circulation before I left Knoxville, and I determined to go down to Chattanooga to decide for myself
whether it might not be wise to return and take the assets, both of my
branch and depositary, elsewhere. Accordingly, I got on the train which
went cautiously nearly to the depot in Chattanooga. Old Dr. _____
of Cleveland was also on the train with me. On nearing the Crutchfield
house, Governor Isham G. Harris came to us, and said: "What has
brought you *old* men to this post of danger?" We replied that we
both knew that he would *seek* the post of danger, and as he was not
invulnerable, we desired to be on hand and render our professional assistance to him and his comrades if wounded. He gave us an account
of the attack by cannon from an eminence across the river, which he
pointed out—informing us that there was little injury suffered, and that
the enemy had retired with some loss. Fragments of shells were lying
upon the streets—one of which had fallen near to my gallant friend,
Major Washington Morgan. He held some of the fragments in his hand
and gave them to me to put in my cabinet.

Hearing that my chief, President Torbett, was in town, I went to seek
him and found him and the entire Bank of Tennessee corpse in a small
house up a dark alley, down towards the river, with arms in their hands,
keeping watch over the treasures of the principal bank and the branches
in Middle and West Tennessee. John A. Fisher, H. L. Claibourne, and
other officers of the bank were all there. From them I received instructions and advice, of which I afterwards availed myself in the removal
of my branch assets and our future policy generally. The principal thing
he, Colonel Torbett, said was: "as *inter arma silent legis* your board and
you must be a law to yourselves. Our duty is to take care of the money
of the people of Tennessee, and to keep it safe and out of the hands of
the enemy." They concurred with me in the belief that the present repulse
of the assault on Chattanooga would make it unnecessary for me to return
then to my branch. I accordingly took the train for Atlanta. Finding
Colonel G. W. Lee, he empowered my son, Colonel F. A. Ramsey, then
a member of W. C. Kain's Artillery Company, to apply to General
_____ for a sufficient guard to penetrate as far into the enemy's lines
as Putnam County and arrest _____, _____, _____ known as counterfeiters of Confederate currency. An account of this dangerous but

partly successful achievement will hereafter be given under *Services of F. A. Ramsey.*

While at Atlanta, I also saw Colonel William W. Clayton, cashier of the railroad bank of Georgia and made arrangements with him for the safe keeping of our metallic capital, and other assets, such as had been or should hereafter be placed in his vaults. I found him to be patriotic and obliging. On my return, a large remittance of issues had been made to my depository from Richmond, and had to be sent to Tullahoma under an escort or guard. This on the 12 February 1863 I sent forward under charge of my son, J. G. McKnitt Ramsey, also a member of Captain W. C. Kain's Artillery. His services will hereafter be more fully given.

CHAPTER VIII

First Raid on East Tennessee

1863: Known generally as Sanders Raid, Friday, 19th June. Early this morning, being casually on a visit to my daughter, Henrietta Rutledge Lenoir, at Lenoir, Roane County, Tennessee I was awaked by William Lenoir, Esquire, knocking at my room door and informing me that the enemy late last night was at Kingston, about twelve miles off. Dressing myself and coming downstairs, I found my daughter preparing to accompany me as far as Concord on my return to Knoxville. I dissuaded her from it, mentioning to her the intelligence I had just received that the Yankees were at Kingston and might soon be there on their way to Knoxville, which was evidently their point of attack. Acting under this impression, I did not wait for the passenger train, but a freight train coming in view soon after, I got on it and, arriving at Knoxville, saw on the platform Major Richard C. Jackson, the then Superintendent of the E. T. & G. R. R. I went near to him and told him what news I bore. Just then a telegram from Loudon, via Augusta, Lynchburg, etc. (our own wires being cut), informed us that the enemy was between Kingston and Loudon, and would probably attack Knoxville within twenty-four hours. I immediately determined to remove the state and Confederate assets in my hands beyond their reach. I went into town, found Dr. Strong, my cashier, asked him to empty the vault (our specie was in Atlanta) of all its contents, box them up, and have all ready for the eastern train of the Virginia Road. I found my son, McKnitt, of W. C. Kain's Artillery, stationed there to assist Dr. Strong in packing up our assets—to send word also out to my family at Mecklenburg what would detain me from home that evening. After a short conference with some of the directors, I hurried down to the Bell House, the headquarters of the then commanding general. I inquired for him. He had not yet come to his office, but entered it soon after hurriedly and excited. I applied for transportation, my passports, and a guard to protect my treasures. He directed his adjutants to give them at once, observing at the same time that I could not get out of Knoxville too soon. He authorized me to select my own guard. I replied: "As you will be attacked today or tomorrow, I am unwilling to diminish the force necessary for the defense of the place." I therefore selectd from among the noncombatants, Colonel Jacob Miller, of Hawkins County, and president of our Rogersville branch, but then casually at Knoxville; Honorable West H. Humphreys of Confederate States court, Reverend Archibald Alexander Doak and one or two other gentlemen of known character. I gave them orders not to be seen about the bank that day. Outside of the bank and its officers, no one knew my intentions. For I knew there were citizens around me, unfriendly to the South, and willing to betray our cause. The train was to start eastward at three P.M., and an army wagon or ambulance was to be in our back lot at three to receive our boxes. To my son, McKnitt, this duty had been assigned. At about ten A.M., I was surprised to see the general commanding, escorted by his lifeguard under Captain Wallace, pass by the bank where I was—en route, as I learned afterwards, to Clinch River sixteen miles from town.

Except the brave citizens of Knoxville itself and a few from the country, Captain Kain's Artillery Company and a small force under Colonel J. J. Finley from Florida, there was no force adequate to the defense of the metropolis of East Tennessee. This small volunteer force though was put under drill by Captain Pleasant M. McClung, and the whole under command of the gallant Colonel R. C. Trigg of Virginia.

There had been some unexpected delay in starting the train. A little before sundown, the last of my boxes was contrived aboard, and I and my guard with it. Someone rode up and said aloud that the advance of the enemy was then at Armstrong's, about two miles below town. The whistle sounded, but for want of steam did not get far and backed a little. During this short stoppage some horsemen started off at full speed north over the commons, and disappeared at once in the adjoining woods. I was afterwards told that one of them was _____ Coker, and that he had been seen all day hanging about the depot and the train I was on, and was evidently in communication with a part of the enemy's cavalry then encamping in the neighborhood of Colonel Scott's old mill. This is probably true, as I heard after my return to Knoxville that just after our train passed the house of Hannibal Love, these horsemen arrived there —disappointed that they failed to intercept or prevent our escape with my assets and those of others entrusted to my care and left in our vault. The train went rapidly to McMillan's Station, ten or twelve miles from

Knoxville, where it met the descending train. While taking in a supply
of water and wood, Judge Humphreys and myself went aboard the Virginia train. I inquired what troops these were and who was the commanding officer? They replied they were part of the regiment of Colonel
Trigg of Virginia who was now in Knoxville. I then inquired who here
was in chief command? An officer came forward whom I informed that
twenty-four hours before the enemy was within thirty miles from Knoxville, and will meet you there. Judge Humphreys, when the officer expressed doubts on the subject, told him who I was, and that I was then
taking away to a place of safety the Confederate and state assets as I
believed the place would be assaulted at once. The officer gave orders
to the men to load. (On another page what followed with these soldiers
will be again mentioned.) I took my assets to Abingdon, Virginia (as
I could find no vault in Jonesboro or Greeneville), and, leaving them in
the custody of the Confederate States depository there, I took the down
train to Knoxville. Colonel W. P. Sanders, after his repulse at Knoxville,
had passed rapidly up the country destroying the bridges and burning the
track at several places as far up as Mossy Creek, when he crossed the
Holston and fell back into Kentucky. Our returning train could get no
further than a little east of New Market. The country was full of disaffected citizens, seduced from their hiding places by the presence of an
armed Federal force. Many of them spoke out in favor of the old flag:
others affected neutrality, and seemed relieved at the absence of the invaders. I and one of my guards walked several miles down the railroad,
tried everywhere to hire or borrow means of conveyance home. At last
someone, more loyal to the South than his neighbors, was also bold enough
to lend me two horses, and I, in passing from Strawberry Plains with
Mr. Doak, saw and conversed with several men of well-known Union
proclivities, and we were neither insulted nor molested. Some of them
asked whose horses we were riding. I told them who had been so kind
as to lend them to us. I returned them to the owner and heard afterwards
that they were stolen.

As I approached my own residence, several of my neighbors told me
they had seen my wife and daughters pass their houses a day or two
before in carriages and wagons and some Negroes and then passing again
homeward. On arriving at home, I learned from my family that the day
I left on the train for Abingdon a military court (not a court martial)

of the Confederate States had come out there to avoid the invaders, and that next morning, hearing the cannonading at Knoxville, they wished to put further space than four miles between themselves and danger, advised and insisted on Mrs. Ramsey to put her daughters and her most valuable effects into the carriage and buggy and an ox wagon and escape in the direction of McBee's ferry, and there take the train eastward. At first she refused to do so. They told her that the enemy would take and hold the city, and that she would be far safer and less annoyed on the way than at home. Their importunity prevailed over her own good judgment, and the cavalcade had progressed into the very jaws of death or captivity when it met a motley group of scared women and frightened children fleeing from the fight at Fort _____ and the burning of the village and the bridge at Strawberry Plains. The firing was then heard, and soon after the smoke of the incendiaries admonished my ladies that they had gone far enough in that direction, and they turned their faces homeward.

In this confusion, the military court, the advisers and at the time the natural guardians, protectors, and guides of my family, disappeared and I never heard from them afterwards. Not so with the pious, and venerable, and reverend, Methodist Divine Reverend _____ Cross, D.D. of Nashville, Tennessee. He had become a guest at Mecklenburg the day before this Hegira to the Plains. He stayed close by my family, was attentive to their wants and comfort, cheered them in their exposures, and acted as the gentleman—the Christian and the chaplain. My brave wife— heroic as Julius Caesar, and her three daughters, also—never really consented to go away from their home, and only yielded to what she considered military necessity, and to proper and becoming subordination to authority. The exposure and fatigue of the journey of twenty-six miles in hot weather, and some trivial losses at home, were all disregarded when I unexpectedly arrived safe and sound with my good guard and chaplain, Reverend A. A. Doak, at my home.

The next day early, I reported to the board at the bank what I had done, and also wrote more fully than I had time to do at Abingdon in a second letter to Mr. Memminger. The directors approved of my conduct and the secretary expressed his official approbation and communicated to me the thanks of the government for the zeal, energy, and vigilance I had showed for the public interest.

After I had got on the freight train early that morning, as mentioned on a preceding page, my daughter, Mrs. Lenoir, after bidding me an affectionate adieu, walked through the passage to the back door and looking along the road towards Kingston saw a cavalry force riding rapidly towards her gate. Supposing them to be Confederates retiring before the invading Federal forces she inquired artlessly: "Are you escaping from the Yankees?" One of them, perhaps Colonel R. K. Byrd, who knew her, replied, "We are the Yankees themselves." They then rode forward opposite to the house, dismounted and entered the store and post office across the great road. The safe had been unlocked that morning and the key was still in its door. Knowing where the money was kept, she walked deliberately across to the store. Wearing a garden or sunbonnet she was not recognized by many of the horsemen as Mrs. Lenoir, and was allowed to pass along among them unknown and unmolested. She went directly to the safe, took out of its open shelves large parcels of money, placed them in the bend of her arm, and taking several hanks of yarn from an open bale of it lying beside and near to the safe she quietly and deliberately passed out of the store—into and through the house and deposited the unseen treasure under a hedge in the garden. She was neither insulted nor otherwise molested. I have always believed that Colonel Sanders was a Southerner and a gentleman, and that Colonel Byrd was one also. Though the atrocities committed the same day at Dr. Baker's and higher up the country a day or two afterwards gave a different complexion to the character and conduct of these officers, still at Lenoir's their behavior was soldierly delicate, politic and gentlemanly. It savored of honor, chivalry, and elevated virtue that once distinguished the profession of arms. Mrs. Lenoir always spoke candidly of the good behavior and honorable conduct of these raiders, and of some others who afterwards made their headquarters at her house and acted as gentlemen, while she never failed to inflict upon those who acted differently her heaviest censure and sternest rebuke.

I may add here a short account of Colonel W. F. Sanders assault on Knoxville, June 20th, 1863, as I received it from others—not being, as already stated, present at the affair.

The evening I left, some of Sanders' cavalry bivouacked near to Knoxville and some small arms were, during the night, discharged into the suburbs without effect. Next morning their horsemen were seen around town and especially on its north side beyond the depots. At _____ A.M., they erected a battery and planted some small cannon and commenced firing on the town. I have already said that General Simon Bolivar Buckner had, on the A.M. of the nineteenth, gone with his lifeguard in the direction of Clinch, and that Kain's Artillery, parts of two regiments from Florida under command of Colonel Finley and the local militia and volunteers of Knoxville constituted the whole Confederate force. The Federal batteries were advancing nearer to our lines, and giving protection to their cavalry behind them in the woods—unseen from Summit Hill, and their real number unknown. Their bugles indicated a considerable force as ready to make an immediate assault. The regiment from Virginia which I had met and spoken to the evening before on the train at McMillan's had, in the meantime, arrived at the fair grounds near town and reported to their commander, Colonel Trigg, now within the city and in chief command. Early in the day, Colonel Trigg inquired for someone most familiar with the localities between the fair grounds and the east end of Knoxville; as by that route he wished his regiment to approach the town and join the forces in it. Someone mentioned my son, J. G. McKnitt Ramsey of the artillery stationed then on the heights of East Knoxville, and R. Jarnagin, also, as being very familiar with the grounds. To him Colonel Trigg assigned the duty of bringing in to his aid the regiment at the fair grounds. McKnitt, in passing out of our lines on this duty, went by the battery on the height and told the artillerist not to fire on the Virginia troops when coming in view, under the belief they were the enemy's advance to the assault. The officer at the battery had left his position for a minute, without giving the precautionary notice to his substitute not to fire. At the first sight of the Virginia regiment, as it appeared coming out of the woods on the hill beyond General Mabry's house, the artillerist, mistaking it for the enemy's advance, was in the act of applying the match to his gun when he was told in a loud voice by the Captain "not to fire—it was Trigg's regiment." If that gun had been fired, loaded as it was with grape, confusion must have ensued, and Knoxville might have been captured and destroyed. Fortunately, the arrival of this reinforcement was seen and noticed by the assailants. Their assault was feeble and badly executed. Their bugles sounded a retreat, and they were soon in a rapid march against the defenseless post of Strawberry Plains. Little harm was done at Knoxville. The enemy did not even enter into any part of the town proper, but paraded in the woods adjoining it on the north. We lost one gallant officer, Captain Pleasant Miller Mc-Clung. He was fearlessly exposing his person in going from point to point wherever the danger was greatest, encouraging the men to repel assault whenever attempted most seriously. It was said he fell by the last cannon ball fired before the enemy withdrew. He was a brave man, a patriot, and an excellent citizen.

A few of the enemy's shot took effect in the houses, fences, etc., of the town. A ball of grape struck the side of Judge Humphreys' window. His room and office were in the upper story of the branch Bank of Tennessee. A spent cannonball entered the coal house of the bank but no other injury was inflicted.

So soon as the injuries to the railroad between Knoxville and Morris-town were repaired, my cashier, Dr. Strong, and my son McKnitt went to Abingdon and brought back safely to Knoxville both the state and Confederate assets.

CHAPTER IX

Buckner's Trap

Thus it had been demonstrated that East Tennessee was most vulnerable to the predatory attacks of the enemy marching through Kentucky. It had become evident, too, that a large number, perhaps a majority, of our citizens were so disaffected to the Southern cause as to be only waiting for a suitable opportunity to abandon it and declare for the old government. No pronunciamento to this effect had yet been made public, but I had received information from sources I could not question that if East Tennessee should be invaded by a respectable force, that would be considered as the signal for the rally of such of our military as were concealing themselves in the woods and mountain fastnesses and of the return to their homes of the thousands of them who had fled to Kentucky. I sought an early opportunity of an interview with General Simon B. Buckner at his office and of making such representations to him of the perilous condition of our section of the Confederacy as might awaken his zeal, stimulate his vigilance, and prompt his earnest efforts in our protection and defense. I went so far as to say that if the invaders were not met and repulsed at the three gaps between us and Kentucky all the trenches he was then digging around Knoxville, and all the fortifications he was erecting there and at other points of the country, were not only valueless and inefficient as defenses, but that these works of our soldiery was so much work done for our invaders. I said further to him, while looking at the maps and drawings before us, that ten thousand men properly distributed along the Cumberland chain could prevent any invasion by an army with artillery and other stores. That nature had made East Tennessee impregnable, not certainly to such a raid as the recent one under Sanders but to one which would expect after invading to overcome and hold the country, and which could only secure that object by bringing with them not only their field and besieging artillery but carry with them at the same all their military supplies and their means of subsistence. I went further, and said to him earnestly that if our line of communication through East Tennessee were once tapped successfully the Confederacy would be bisected and our cause hopelessly lost. I failed to get even the serious attention of General Buckner. He said with some levity—and more vanity—"if the enemy succeed in getting across the Cumberland heights we will then have them in a trap just where we would like to have them." I said to him I was too much his senior to let such a puerility be a becoming reply to argument and legitimate inference and truth. This much I had already written, but at greater length and more earnestly, to the president and some of his cabinet, and told them plainly that if East Tennessee were abandoned now (July and August) 1863 the Confederacy was already lost. To these earnest remonstrances I received a reply that the country should never be abandoned and every effort be continued to hold and defend it. At this time I was a state director of the East Tennessee and Georgia Railroad, and conferring one day with one of its principal officers was informed that an order had been received to dismantle its principal workshops and fall back with them south of the Tennessee River and perhaps south of the Hiwassee. This was only a few days after the *official* assurance from Richmond had reached me. I made one more earnest protest against this fatal policy and prepared as best I could for subsequent events, disasters.

I had informed General Buckner's adjutant that I wished to be informed of the time he would evacuate Knoxville, as the secretary of the treasury had left it to my own discretion what disposition to make of my office and my Confederate States assets and that the authorities of the state of Tennessee, the mother bank and my own board had given me the same discretion as to the branch bank at Knoxville. Some days after this, being at his headquarters at the Bell House, I heard the General had gone and his staff all seemed rather busy and confused packing up for a hasty departure. I returned to the bank and told my cashier, Strong, and clerk, Faxon, that the time had arrived: that my official duties were primary, and that I was determined to take my office and assets in the direction of Richmond, leave them in a place of safety, and return to Knoxville, and, if necessary, fall back with the army wherever it might go. Before leaving town for my residence, I went into the office of J. L. Moses, Esquire, near to the bank, and telling him what were my purposes, requested him to take charge of three closely packed leather trunks which were in the counting room of my office at Mecklenburg—where he would also find my historical and other manuscripts, collections of antiquities, my correspondence, etc., etc. These all I requested him to take care of and preserve. He promised to do so. He was, I believe, an honorary member of the E. T. H. & A. Society, fond of letters, and I believed my trustworthy friend. On my return home the same evening I sent for my neighbor, Dr. Anderson, and asked him to take care of and preserve my shop, medicine shop, furniture, medical library, and my ledger and book accounts. He also promised to do so. My son, Francis Alexander Ramsey, was that night at home. I requested my ladies to prepare in a few days to move out of our house, taking with them such things as they might consider most valuable and necessary for their comfort and to stay a few days with our daughter, Mrs. Dickson, till a comfortable house could be rented and occupied temporarily by them. I left it to themselves and to contingencies that might thereafter arise whether to return to our house, remain in town, or join me wherever I might float to in exile. I sent a servant after a son, Arthur Crozier Ramsey, who was a student of perhaps sixteen then at school in Jefferson County under Mr. Wilson. I went to town early next morning, got passports and transportation again, and took my depository to Abingdon. Not knowing when I could see them again, I left them in the hands of the depository there, wrote also to Mr. Memminger to that effect, and I and my guard again on the same evening got on the train on my return home. All went on well till we reached a point below Morristown. Some emissaries, as was believed, from the invading Federal army had during the night fired the crossties in several places and thus rendered the road impassable till repaired. I was glad to hear the Holston bridge was still safe. I accompanied a small squad of railroad section hands down the road before the train, removing obstructions and extinguishing the fires at several points. After a delay in all probably six or eight hours we met at New Market, I believe, a long train filled with refugees from Knoxville. From them I learned that General Ambrose E. Burnside expected to reach Knoxville the next day. Colonel Sneed, Colonel Crozier, and others were aboard. Not they, but others, attempted to persuade me not to go further. I had determined to follow the army and hastened forward. We were several hours behind time and my son Robert M. Ramsey, who had been half the day waiting for me at the depot, had given me out. But he had not left town a mile when our whistle announced the approach of the car in which I was. It was now after sunset. The depot was deserted, not a single person could I see on the street. I went right to the bank—met there my son, General Ramsey, Dr. Strong, and two or three of the directors. On inquiry I found that all our books and paper money were already boxed up and ready for the transportation wagons promised to us by Major Glover, the quartermaster. My advice was renewed, to load up that night, taking aboard General Ramsey's trunks and Judge Humphreys' official papers and himself, cross the river and go in the direction of Maryville. I told them I would go by home, say farewell to my family, cross the French Broad, and by private roads which I knew well overtake them before they reached Maryville.

At this very moment my son Robert came to the bank door with a led horse for me. With him I returned home. J. Crozier Ramsey could not then accompany us. His trunk and papers he wished to put aboard of our bank wagon. I found my family all well, a little uneasy about me, and also about our little "Benjamin" who, on his return from school, was compelled to pass through some of the least loyal neighborhoods in East Tennessee. (Loyal to the Confederate States, I mean.) My good wife put her ring on my finger. I never felt before that I was really leaving home. She preserved her equanimity well, regretted that as I had no way to carry a trunk she could put me up so small an outfit from my wardrobe. She filled a large carpetbag with my clothes, and I was ready to start before day. I had gone to bed but not to sleep. For all night long people from Knoxville, in wagons, on horseback, and on foot were constantly passing my ferry—some we suspected to join the invading enemy, others we knew to avoid him. My son, Colonel F. A. Ramsey, mounted and armed, accompanied me. General Ramsey and Captain Ramsey remained behind to give their advice and assistance to their mother and sisters, who expected that to be the last day they would remain in their own house. I had left home for Abingdon on the twenty-fifth of August. I had gone there and returned home and now on the twenty-eighth [?] of August, 1863 I was on my horse, and bade adieu to my family, to Mecklenburg— to my home in youth and the home of my old age. We left rather before daylight. After crossing the French Broad we took a near road through the country over which I had often ridden night and day. We fell into the Maryville road at the nearest point. There we met Mr. Corley *walking to* Knoxville. I sent by him a renewal of my request to I. L. Moses, Esquire about preserving my manuscripts. I never heard that the message was received. We overtook, about noon, Major Glover's whole cavalcade, our wagon, etc., etc. My party was at the hotel. Dr. Strong and Judge Humphreys were reclining on the floors perfectly exhausted. Here I was told some unwelcome news about the route before us—that it was infested, as it had been all summer, by a set of free-booters under command of Captain Duncan and others on Piney. I thought our best policy would be to push directly ahead, so as not to give time for intelligence to reach the country that Knoxville was evacuated. I made this suggestion to Major Glover and he put our wagon trains immediately in motion. Late at night we made our camp at Malcolm's, a confirmed and bigoted union man. The encampment was formed near the water and beyond his house. I came back on foot and asked leave for three of us to sleep in his house and, Judge Humphreys, Dr. Strong and myself were very comfortably entertained, but none of us let him know that Knoxville had been left an easy prey to the invaders. Next day, in fording Tennessee near Morganton, some of the vehicles were upset and some mules drowned. My son hastened to the ferry above, and, seeing the boat on the opposite bank, and being an expert water-man, jumped into a canoe, crossed the river, and brought back the boat. The craft was sufficiently capacious to carry the hospital stores (under charge of my brother, Dr. Frank A. Ramsey, Medical Director in Chief of East Tennessee) and also of the *army chest* under Dr. Strong and myself. As we passed over the stream the owner, Mr. Tipton I believe, who seemed to know the value of a part of our cargo, warned us to go by Madisonville as it was unsafe and dangerous to go to our destination Loudon, by the way of Piney. Judge Humphreys, overhearing this, asked me to request Major Glover to send an express through to Loudon for a guard. When we reached the bank a paymaster from Virginia was found ready to go to Loudon for a guard to meet us at Piney. He started off in a gallop, leaving a verbal request from me to Buckner to furnish a guard. (I learned afterwards from the paymaster—perhaps his name was Clarke—that near Piney he was met by the marauding party under Duncan, was arrested, robbed of his money, $6000.00, clothes, watch, horse, boots, everything, and to conceal their robbery most effectually the party made him go a private road in towards Louisville. It was in this way they happened not to be on our road so as to intercept or molest us. We arrived safely at Loudon. But a guard had to be kept over our effects, as camp followers were all around that place. Next morning was the Sabbath, and there being no train towards Athens, we put our boxes into a strong car and placed a guard around it.

At dinner that day General Buckner bowed to me. As his intention was next day to fall back south of Hiwassee I inquired nothing about the *trap* he had set at Knoxville in which to catch the Yankee invaders. He seemed anxious to keep his own army out of the trap. I suppose, however, he was acting in obedience to superior officers, Bragg, or Davis, or both. I never knew. The policy was a fatal one to us as I had always said.

The bridge across the Tennessee was to be burned the next day. It had, ever since its erection, been one of my idols (—strange that inanimate things ever should become the objects of our idolatry) and I wished to ride over it once more so as to see my amiable and beloved daughter, Mrs. Henrietta Rutledge Lenoir, and her two interesting boys, James Ramsey Lenoir and William B. Lenoir. After dinner, therefore, Colonel F. A. Ramsey and myself got the countersign, crossed the river on the bridge, and rode up to Lenoir's, and spent the afternoon with our relations there. A detachment of the Confederate troops was still there. The quiet and stillness of that holy day I had never seen disturbed there before. Everything around the place was noise, profanity, intemperance, and tumult. Mrs. Lenoir was herself sad, disconsolate, uneasy about the situation and exposure of the family at Mecklenburg,—their exposure there at Lenoirs. She had acted the lady and the heroine when Sanders and his raiders passed her house on the morning of the 19th of June of the present year. She had often told me of all the details of the raiders there. . . .[1]

But on the occasion of this last Sunday visit she seemed dejected and sad, feeling an ominous presentiment of future disaster and overwhelming bereavement. She did not say this in words but I plainly discerned that she apprehended and felt it. Bidding her and her children a sorrowful adieu, and leaving with her a message for her mother and sisters at home, we mounted and returned rapidly to Loudon.[2] We were the last Confederates that passed that bridge. Next morning, by direction of General Buckner, the whole wooden structure was fired and destroyed.

The hotel at Loudon was of course crowded—the room in which I slept was full of officers. After the lights were extinguished I heard one of them reciting the story of his wrongs. I found him to be the paymaster of the

---

[1] See above, Chapter VIII, page 110.

[2] The next day, August 31, 1863, Dr. Ramsey received a pass. On the back was a pledge of loyalty which he filled in with a personal description:

"Residence, Knox Co. Tenn. Age, 66
Hair, Dark and gray. Eyes, Dark
Occupation, Physician
Height, 5-11 Beard, Dark and gray
Complexion, Dark

"I, Dr. J. G. M. Ramsey, above described, hereby pledge my loyalty to the Confederate States.

"Loudon Aug 31 1863"

Virginia regiment, Clarke, I believe, or at least the one who was entrusted with $6000.00 for its use and who was robbed of everything he had when going as courier to Loudon for a guard. He was giving the details of the whole affair. The bushwhackers halted him, demanded his money first,—afterwards leading him off into an obscure path where no one passed they prepared to hang him, and had a halter made for the purpose, and were on the point of putting it around his neck when one of the banditti said: "Boys we have had pretty good picking out of him already. Let us strip him to his stockings and turn him loose." The leader gave his consent. The prisoner was released with the injunction to go in an opposite course—straight towards the Tennessee River. On his way he found some Confederates who supplied him with a few clothes and brought him to Loudon with them.

At this place also we were overtaken by others from Knoxville. Amongst these were my two sons, General J. Crozier Ramsey and Captain Robert M. Ramsey. From these we learned that the former had remained in town till his trunk and his papers were securely stowed away in Dr. Strong's money-wagon, and saw that wagon start in the boat across the river: that he then, nearly at midnight, took the road to my ferry and came to the house, Riverside, of his sister, Mrs. Dickson. Finding no one at home and everything deserted he rode down to the ferry and hallooed for the ferryman across the river, but failed to awaken him. Hitching his horse on the bank he laid down amongst the weeds beside him, fell asleep, but not long after was aroused by the arrival of a crowd of refugees escaping from town and going towards Dandridge. Day had not yet dawned, but soon the ferryman was heard putting some horsemen across to the south side of French Broad (probably Colonel F. A. Ramsey and myself). He and others were soon after taken across the Holston. He acquiesced in the advice I had given to my family for them all to remove the most portable and valuable of our effects over to Riverside with Mrs. Dickson. His brother, Robert M. Ramsey, and himself remained half the day putting this plan into effect and then bidding a farewell to their mother and sisters. Amidst these gloomy surroundings they crossed the French Broad and, striking the road leading towards Louisville, fell in with Colonel James White Humes, sick and exhausted, unable to travel. They assisted him and got him at last to the house of Talbot Cox at Louisville, where the weary, sick, and exhausted refugees were hospitably entertained. Reaching Loudon Sunday at night they gave me the last information I was to receive directly from my family and from Knoxville. They were at Riverside and comfortable, buoyant and determined as ever. The last rumor at Knoxville was that Burnside was camped at Beaver Creek eight or ten miles from town, and that his army would in a few hours be in undisputed possession of that important strategic position—controlling the river and the two railroads connecting at Knoxville.

Our bank effects were put on some platform cars, under the care of Dr. Strong, destined for the vault of the branch at Athens. I remained with the troops on horseback part of the time, but occasionally on the train—open flats. As we left Loudon and saw the blazing bridge, Captain Kain said: *"Sic transit gloria mundi.* Dr. Ramsey, we will never see our homes again."* Less despondent than he, I said; "I will yet return with the army and try to recapture Knoxville," though I concurred with the Captain in condemning and ridiculing the silly policy of Buckner in laying this *trap* to catch the Yankees in.

At Sweetwater I met J. T. Lenoir Esquire, Reverend _____ Sneed, my cousin and once my classmate, Colonel R. A. Ramsey, all of that place. On seeing the latter I said, *"Nos patriae fines and dulcia linguimus arva."* He was a good Latinist, and knowing the fertile bottoms I had left, he repeated with emphasis, *"Dulcia arva, dulcia arva."* He was one of the most amiable, inoffensive, public-spirited, moderate and pious men I ever knew—but having two or three gallant sons in the Confederate service, he became a doomed man. I understood afterwards that when the enemy under, I believe, Sherman invaded his section he was arrested late in the P.M. and hurried off in the night in inclement weather to Kingston to answer for his *disloyalty. Loyalty*—true to one's own country, own people, own home! May I and mine ever be thus considered *disloyal!*

At the same place, too, I met my old neighbor, Captain James Campbell of Knox County—an aged gentleman, one of General Jackson's soldiers in 1814, and a peaceable, quiet citizen—a noncombatant from his age and infirmity. The loyal in his neighborhood, many of whom had subsisted on his bounty and his profusion, gave him notice that if he did not abandon his home and quit the country his house and mills should be burned. As threatened, these loyalists did burn his mills. When I saw him at Sweetwater the old veteran looked feeble, disconsolate and careworn, but he was afterwards permitted to return to his home. He still survives. (1870).

With Parson Sneed I had been many years familiarly acquainted as one of the directors of the East Tennessee and Georgia Railroad. He was benignant, kind, and exemplary in all the relations of life—a skillful and industrious farmer, a very humane and indulgent master. None more so. His Negro cabins were models of cleanliness and comfort. The rations for his slaves were furnished without stint and were substantially the same eaten at his own table. In sickness and in health, the care and supervision of their humane owners were never withheld. This care extended to their moral training and culture, and especially of the young—not only bought with his money but born in his house and treated with paternal kindness. When opportunities offered for public worship—not only in his own (Baptist) church but in all others which they might prefer—his slaves were permitted, often required, to attend. He furnishing in many instances the facilities of such attendance. Withal Parson Sneed was a conscientious and unwavering Whig, Union Man, and utterly opposed both to the policy and the doctrine of secession, states' rights, etc., etc. Two months after this when I was on the return march with the army to recapture Knoxville, I was informed that when the Federal army reached Mr. Sneed's neighborhood under, I believe, Sherman—certainly some Federal general—the reverend and venerable slaveholder Sneed was unceremoniously driven from his house. Each Negro family was then called up and directed to load, each one of them, a wagon belonging to the plantation with the amount of grain, meal, flour, meat, etc., etc., such furniture, bedding, clothing,—even books—as each Negro chose to claim and appropriate as his or her own. This they were required to do, and forced to do by the threats of the gang perpetrating this outrage: that if it were not done these effects should be burned or otherwise destroyed. Some of the Negroes were unwilling to leave their old master and old mistress, or the old place where they had lived happily and contented all their lives. Finally the ox teams (the horses were claimed by the conquerors) were put to the wagons and driven some to one place and some to another. Dissatisfied with their new homes and their new condition, some of the Negroes came back furtively to Parson Sneed's, desiring to remain with him. These were rearrested, taken away again to their new bondage, and threatened by their captors and new friends that if they returned to their former masters the severest punishment should be inflicted on them. Afterwards I was told in Atlanta, Georgia, that in one case, that of a house-servant of Mrs. Sneed, a cook or a nurse, she insisted on going back to her old mistress and did effect that object. She was by military authority forced again to leave her and go back to (I believe) Receville. She absconded again, and though dissuaded from it by Mrs. Sneed, insisted on it as her right and duty to live at the old place and in the employment and care of her former owners, her natural protectors and guardians. Force was resorted to to prevent her third return, and from the effect of injuries inflicted by that force the poor but faithful Negress died when almost in sight of her master's gate. While I vouch for the substantial truth of all I have said before, I do not assert that the tragic finale of this incident is true. For the credit of the Federal officers who commanded in the South and for sake of those humanitarians of the North who presume to claim a higher civilization and a more humane form of servitude than the slaveholding South has exhibited in all our past, let it be hoped that the oppression, injustice, and cruelty of the Yankee army in Tennessee in the fall of 1863, as here detailed, have been exaggerated. It was told to this writer just as above stated.

The command of General Buckner continued to fall back. I reached Athens with it. Dr. Strong had our bank and its assets safe in a good vault. But there were various rumors among the officials: One was today that Burnside was in pursuit of us enroute by Maryville, McGhee's ferry, and Madisonville, determined to capture us and our stores. Tomorrow it was that the Federal troops deflecting around Chattanooga would dash against the Western and Atlantic Railroad at Dalton or above and cut off our retreat by that channel. Mr. T. A. Cleage, the cashier of the Athens branch, thought this latter policy the more probable and feasible, and acting on this belief packed the more valuable and least ponderous of his assets in a United States mail bag, and being very familiar with a lateral and nearer route through the Ocoee district placed his mail bag on a mule and on horseback himself led his mule through safely. He tapped the W. & A. Road beyond Dalton, perhaps at Calhoun. With us he left part of his treasure, and having carefully concealed his branch books in a place where they were never found, the keys were handed to us. I could ascertain nothing positive about the movement of the enemy and was at some loss to decide what my own should be. Very early next morning an officer with his aides rode up to Bridge's Hotel and, without alighting from his saddle, conferred for a minute with his comrades. Someone told me the officer was General Forrest. I had never seen him, but knowing him to be a matter-of-fact man and a reliable officer I walked over to him and ascertained the way was still clear behind us, and inquired how long could he promise that the enemy should not intercept our passage on the railroad via Dalton? He hesitated a minute, but on learning who I was and the reason why I had asked this apparently impertinent question, he asked me how long time I wanted? I told him twenty-four hours. He replied, "I guarantee that and longer." His squadron had come up, his bugles sounded, and they dashed down the road towards Charleston. I told the proper officer what I had learned from General Forrest, asked for my passports and my transportation ticket, removed our effects to the car, and after some delay the train was in motion. At Cleveland we heard a renewal of the rumor that the Federal troops would intercept us at Red Clay or Varnells, and the train passed those places cautiously. We arrived after dark at Dalton, but owing to some cause we missed the connection. We kept guard all night but were not disturbed.

Next day we reached Atlanta. I deposited our branch monies with Mr. Clayton of the railroad bank, with whom Mr. McMahon and myself had already deposited our specie and our more available state issues. Colonel Clayton politely invited Dr. Strong and myself to use his office temporarily for the transaction of our official business. I wrote to the secretary of the treasury where I was—had informed him before where my depository was (at Abingdon)—and that I awaited his pleasure and commands. In answer he told me that as there would probably be large army disbursements made in Georgia that he would send to me by express my office at Abingdon, under the impression that I could find a suitable building in Atlanta for my depository. After this I changed my boarding house, which was nearly a mile in the northern suburbs of Atlanta, to Major Good's, not far from the First Presbyterian Church.

The town, its hotels, its private houses, were all full of refugees from Louisiana, Florida, Alabama, Arkansas, and especially from Tennessee. Major Good's was always crowded with the *elite* of Nashville, Memphis, Knoxville, and the more interior towns. Here the Knoxville (Atlanta) *Register* was again set up by Mr. J. A. Sperry, its former editor. His office was the constant rendezvous of (especially) East Tennessee refugees and army officers. Sperry and others made me write editorials and contributions for his columns. I became his army correspondent when I was in camps or hospitals as I always volunteered to be. Indeed I was usefully employed. I was actively and constantly employed. I was surrounded by my own countrymen, Tennesseans and Tennessee patriots and refugees from Tennessee.

An invalid son, General J. Crozier Ramsey, was for a while in Atlanta with me. He had been as Aide to General J. C. Vaughn, much exposed in the trenches at Vicksburg. On one occasion a beautifully finished flag, made and presented to the brigade by my now deceased daughter, Charlotte Barton Ramsey, was placed by him on a battery in an exposed position on the Southern defences and outworks. It became a target for the enemy's artillery. A desperate effort was made to prevent its capture. The effort was successful and the flag of Miss Ramsey, though tattered and torn, was after almost superhuman efforts and heroic enterprise preserved. He brought it home with him in his trunk when, after the surrender of Vicksburg July 4, 1863 he with Vaughn's brigade was paroled. He never recovered his health after undergoing that dreadful siege. He had lumbago, rheumatism, and general debility. Being a paroled prisoner he could not till exchanged, again bear arms. He fell back with our army from Knoxville to Atlanta, hoping every day to hear of his exchange when he might again buckle on his sword and do battle for his country, its rights, and its honor. Hope deferred maketh the heart sick. He stayed near me as long as he could in our exiled state at Atlanta. Helping me, comforting me, obeying me like a dutiful son, encouraging me under trials almost without a parallel, solacing me under bereavement, soothing me in adversity, rejoicing with me when the cloud of sorrow was blown over, sympathizing with me when its darkest tints overshadowed my path, and was always the first to discern and point out to me the silver lining around the blackest cloud. He was always pleasant, never discontented, ever cheerful and radiant with hope. He was our first born son—perhaps was too much the idol of his parents and our family. At Atlanta we could hear nothing of his mother, his sisters. He was anxious for their safety and their comfort and determined to get nearer to them. Where we were then and were likely to be thereafter, the distance between us was steadily increasing. He determined that it was best for us all that he should leave Georgia, go around to Bristol or some point lower down in East Tennessee, where, being nearer to his old home, he might possibly hear something from his mother and sisters. Of course I interposed no objections, but at once gave my assent to his plans and the day was set for his early departure.

CHAPTER X

Captain Robert M. Ramsey

My autobiography will of course embrace sketches of the public services of all my sons and indeed the more important incidents in the life of my entire family. And here I introduce to the reader's attention my son Captain Robert M. Ramsey of the Confederate States Navy, and principal courier and scout of General Longstreet, General Wheeler, and other commanders. He was our fourth son. After his preparatory education, acquired under the preceptorship of Reverend Thomas Davis and Reverend N. A. Penland, both at different periods holding for a time the pastorate of our church (Lebanon) and the position of principal in Mecklenburg Academy near us and on my own land, he was sent to Tusculum College—still under the presidency of Reverend S. W. Doak, D.D. His proficiency was respectable, but mixing from his boyhood with the gallant soldiery of the Volunteer State who had performed such adventures and achieved the remarkable conquest of Mexico, he could not relish the tamer pursuits of literature and science, and inheriting all the martial spirit of his late grandfather, Captain John Crozier, "had heard of war and longed to follow to the field some warlike chief." His taste, even when a boy, was for wild adventure and romantic daring. His youthful sports were all of this kind. Agile and strong, no one of his years could beat him in a foot race, throw him on his back in a wrestling match, dive deeper, or swim a wider river. At sixteen he was admitted to be the best marksman and the best and most graceful horseman in Knox County. While at Tusculum, a fellow student, in attempting to swim across the Chucky, a most rapid river, was heard to hollo for help and was seen to sink the first time. Robert denuded himself instanter, dashed into the river, swam nearly to the further shore and caught his friend in the moment of sinking the third and last time, and thus rescued him from a watery grave. This was pronounced to be a great feat not only of manhood but of devoted constancy to a friend and of unselfish generosity to a fellow student.

Another instance of his fearlessness occurred a year after. I witnessed it myself. On the opposite side of the Holston from my residence lived a tenant of my own, Henry Payne, his wife, and three small children. During the remarkable freshet of 18___ the river had surrounded his house and of course cut off all chance of escape. I had admonished him all the P.M. that he ought to effect his escape to the hills as before morning his cabin and his family might be swept off. He persisted in saying that the river would soon attain its greatest height and refused to leave. Night came on. The river continued to rise and about ten o'clock P.M. he was heard to exclaim, "For God's sake, come over and take us out of this water." The night was dark, tempestuous and cold. The river was covered with floating masses of timber and the wrecks of bridges, barns, mills and other buildings. Even in daylight it would have been dangerous and rash to attempt the crossing. My three sons Alexander, Robert, and McKnitt were all at home with us that dreadful night. The wind was directly down the river and from the north. This increased the hazard and the danger of the attempted rescue. But I could plainly see that the young men were determined to make the desperate attempt. The river had not been crossed for twenty-four hours even in a canoe. They thought the only plan which promised either to be safe or effectual was to take the horse boat, and taking two other good Negro water-men and extemporizing an extra oar, they prepared to leave the shore. They insisted that I should not go with them. I replied that some caution was necessary and as they were all incautious I ought to go along. Finding my purpose unchangeable they reluctantly acquiesced. Leaving the lights burning in the dormitories nearest to the east bank of the river, we embarked and passing over the garden and the adjoining cornfields and bayou, now all submerged, we had little difficulty in ascending the river nearly half a mile opposite the lower end of Boyd's Island. "All hands to your oars," and we stemmed the impetuous stream. I held the steering oar and kept the boat in the direction of Payne's house. By almost superhuman efforts the prow rested against the open door of Payne's house. Robert sprang into it with the cable in his hand and secured the boat, while the others with their setting poles shoved off the floating timbers. We found the porch of the house already gone, the gates and outbuildings had preceded it. A brick chimney thus far had protected the house but that was almost on the point of floating too. Seeing the emergency did not allow a minute's delay, I walked to the end of the boat nearest the door. I looked in. Payne had piled up some rocks in the fireplace on which to keep light and fire. The water was more than a foot deep on the floor—had not yet reached the beds, though a few inches more would have covered them. The underside of the wood was already in the water and the fire would in a few minutes more have been wholly extinguished. Payne and his wife were setting around the fireplace, holding the children on their knees, their feet placed on the rounds of the chairs to keep them dry. I exclaimed, "Payne, throw the children into the boat, such of your bedding as is dry, and then some fire chunks, and come in yourselves." This was the work of a minute, and with all aboard we struck into the cornfield west of the house, struck the high lands beyond it, and at length reached Riverside—a house then unoccupied. There we put out our cargo, five living beings and two beds. From this point we could see the lighted windows across the Holston. I steered the boat nearly half a mile across Mrs. Dickson's orchard and bottoms in the direction of the island again when the poles were dropped, the oars resumed, and by dint of hard and skillful pulling and steering we at length got among the top branches of a large sycamore tree standing at low-water mark near the ferry landing. It was now the dawn of day and we were able to appreciate the danger and exposure we underwent in this perilous night voyage. There were islands several hundred yards long of floating drift and timber passing almost continuously with the rapid current which not even in daylight we would have been willing again to encounter. One of these islands of driftwood we once did strike, but energetically disengaging our boat from it we reached the shade trees around my office and got out safely into the porch around it.

Many instances like these of adventure and enterprise I could here give. But there is one other I may not omit. When a full grown man Robert sought the wilds of Texas. On his journey he met another traveler. At Galveston, the latter was taken sick with yellow fever. He importuned my son not to leave him there to die. To remain with his friend was to expose himself to the deadly infection, but he assured him that he would not leave him. He stayed with him till he was able again to resume his journey. This I always considered as the true moral sublime of friendship, humanity, and heroism.

In 1860 the question of secession was agitated in the South and had reached Tennessee. My sons all declared at once for the South. Robert, after South Carolina seceded, wished to go at once to the defense of the Palmetto State. I suggested that Tennessee would, I believed, soon join her southern co-states and that he might then have a theater on which to exercise and gratify his patriotic ambition. This seemed to quiet for a time his longing for the field. In March of 1861 he told me he believed our state would not go out and that he had determined to go to Fort Sumter. He met in Knoxville Captain A. M. Wallace, then recruiting troops for the State of Georgia. It was arranged that volunteers from Tennessee, though still in the union, should be embodied and organized for the Southern service. Robert got, I believe, seventeen to join him. He went over to Maryville where Captain Wallace then was and tendered his men. Returning and crossing Little River at night he reached our home. Taking affectionate leave of us, he intended to leave upon the first train. But at this time it was by some deemed *treasonable* to avow adherence to the Southern cause or sympathy for the Southern Confederacy. It was soon whispered around Knoxville that some officials were watching around the depot ready to arrest any belligerents that might be enrolled for the Confederate States service. It was even said that warrants had been issued and were then in the pockets of officers to prevent the departure of such as were then contemplating revolution or any change in the government. Robert and his men knew one another but wore no badge or uniform to distinguish to what service each belonged. The day fixed for their departure arrived. Groups of young men could be seen standing around the corners of the streets talking earnestly about something not known to everyone. Captain Wallace was at his hotel. I went there to see him. Many of the young men occasionally called there too. Yet nothing was definitely known. A good deal was suspected and even hinted aloud. The friends of the South, then vastly in the minority in town, at length began to assemble in and near General Ramsey's office on Gay Street. From this point they marched noiselessly in the direction of the depot. Some of them I know were armed. Arrived at the train not yet ready to start, we entered the cars. Some of us stood on the platform: Others remained within, not fearing so much the threatened arrest, certainly, as the disappointment of their cherished hope of seeing the field. I could plainly see where in that large crowd the virtue, intelligence, and patriotism of the country stood. Almost every countenance was radiant with approbation. A scowl, an averted eye, and ominous shaking of the head I could see here and there. There was no cheering, no indignant feeling uttered by any. A kind leave-taking followed. The officer believed to have warrants in his pocket was the last to come forward and say farewell. He did this very cordially to Robert. "I wish you well, but when we meet it will be on opposite sides." "All right," Robert replied. He shook my hand too, cordially. We had always been friends, and there is no cleverer man than Colonel W. P. Crippen, and said, "Not you going, too." "Only to Lenoir's," I added, "to give the boys some good advice." At Lenoir's, I bade my gallant young countrymen adieu. At Atlanta they learned that the affair in Charleston harbor was already over. They joined the regiment of Colonel J. H. Williams, were sent to Fort Pulaski, thence to Tybee Island, where they remained till ordered forward to the First Manassas. When I arrived at the Spotswood House, Richmond, Virginia the following summer and was entering my name on the register I discovered upon it the name of Captain A. M. Wallace and hastened to his room. He told me Robert and his comrades were behind him and would probably be there that night. It was partly for this reason I was so anxious that if Colonel Williams' regiment was sent forward there next morning I might go to Manassas with it. But the battle was over and another destination was assigned him.

After my return from the bank convention at Richmond I received from Mr. Memminger a dispatch inquiring for the whereabouts of my son Robert. I gave it to him. He shortly afterwards received in camp a commission from President Davis appointing him lieutenant in the Confederate States Navy, giving him a furlough of several days before he would be required to go into active service. He repaired immediately to the seat of government, got his uniform and his sword, and came to us at Mecklenburg. The considerate kindness of allowing him a short furlough suggested the probability that he owed his promotion to my good friend Mr. Memminger, though I had met the secretary of the navy at Mr. Davis' reception on the occasion of the adjournment of the bank delegates as heretofore mentioned. . . .

At the expiration of his furlough he received orders to join his captain * and associate lieutenants at Pensacola. Thither he repaired with all possible promptitude, and discharged, besides the duties of his immediate command, others not less important or onerous, between Pensacola, Mobile, and New Orleans. He was afterwards sent to Norfolk, was present when that place was evacuated, went then to _____, and finally went to the defense of Richmond—being at Drewry's Bluff when the attack on that place was so signally repulsed. He acted as one of the sharpshooters there. The accuracy and efficiency of his aim were loudly applauded. The Federal

---

* Captain Simms I believe.

navy was compelled to abandon the James as the channel of assault and Richmond was for the time secure.

The battle of Malvern Hill was going on almost simultaneously with that of Drewry's Bluff, and at the close of the latter, several young officers of the Confederate navy asked for and obtained leave of absence for a day to go into the fight at the former place. The leave was granted. They rode rapidly in the direction of the guns, and finding the headquarters of General [T. J. Jackson?], who commanded on that occasion, asked for "a place in the picture." The post of danger was assigned to them. The conflict was prolonged far into the night, was resumed again early next morning. The lieutenants' leave of absence had expired. The battle raged without intermission. New forces were brought into the fight but the enemy were at length repulsed and driven from the field. Until the battle was decided, the young men had never once thought of the Bluff—nor their orders to return to their commands after one day's absence on leave. It was unsoldierly to leave before the victory was won. At the time they had achieved it—the commander-in-chief had barely announced the result—the young men turned the heads of their horses in the direction of the Bluff, and not taking time to give them their oats or take any refreshment themselves they were galloping off to their cantonment. Arrived there they were mortified to learn that their captain had them arrested for *absence without leave.* This was technically true. But in such a case Napoleon would have promoted them on the field. Andrew Jackson would have said gracefully, "Young gentlemen, you have nobly won your spurs and other epaulettes—Lieutenant, you are a Captain. Lieutenant, you have won the command of a battalion. Lieutenant, I put you at the head of a regiment—your commissions to bear date from yesterday morning." These illustrious chieftains would have said, "You did right in standing by your colors, leave or no leave of absence. The rule is never to leave your field of duty while the battle is undecided." The young men pleaded their excuse, but pleaded in vain. They resigned their commissions at once and retired to the ranks. History, honor, posterity, will sustain their manly conduct.

Lieutenant Ramsey returned from Virginia to Tennessee at the time General Kirby Smith was inaugurating his celebrated campaign to the Ohio River. He was invited to join the command. He gladly accepted the invitation. He had frequently crossed the Cumberland Mountains and had gone as far as Richmond, Kentucky, where his sister lived who had married Colonel Daniel Breck, Jr., the son of Honorable D. Breck, M.C. from that district. This service exactly suited the genius and taste of Captain Ramsey. The theater on which he was now to act was congenial to all his tastes and preferences. He was born insensible to fear. He loved adventure and courted danger: withal he was an expert rider, an experienced woodsman. His unerring and trusty rifle never deceived him. He was General Smith's chief courier and scout.

General Smith was at this time organizing his campaign to Kentucky. His headquarters were at Knoxville. I saw him every day. He called with Mrs. Smith to see my family. We were on good terms. He asked for the whereabouts of my sons Robert and Alexander. They accompanied him on his march. If to any two men under his command, the success of *his* invasion is indebted, it was to them. Especially the grand affair near and at Richmond owes its great result to their minute knowledge of its localities, and so of other places. They were with him in his dash upon Lexington. They procured supplies for his army, of subsistence, clothing and leather. This latter they obtained in large quantities at the eminent hazard of life in _____. General Braxton Bragg had now the whole command in Kentucky and when Smith, in thirty-six hours more, would have been battering down Cincinnati, Bragg gave orders for an inglorious retreat. The former had the Queen City of the West within his easy grasp: the latter made him relinquish it and thus extinguish the hope and paralize the efforts of all Kentucky then preparing to espouse our cause. In conducting this retreat the aid of my two sons was again called in requisition. By Robert's skill and experience and energy the trains were safely brought over the big hill seventeen miles this side of Richmond. Without pursuit, and with but little comparative loss, the whole was brought safely back to Knoxville. Without the delay of more than a day Bragg went forward to Richmond, Virginia, explained away to the credulous and confiding Davis the *errors* he had plainly committed—*blunders* I will not call them—changed the whole program of Confederate action, disaffected in a tender point our true ally, Kentucky, and thus remotely but certainly ruined the Confederate cause.

After returning home Robert was sent to Cumberland Gap to superintend the erection of further defenses at that important but now vulnerable pass. His chief passed the highest eulogy upon him when he said to me that without his skillful and energetic assistance the magazine and other works would not have been built. The tortuous and serpentine road up the mountain he obviated by his contrivance of steering the hind wheels of a wagon to one side while the tongue of his wagon was directed to the other. An army engineer from West Point would not have thought of this simple contrivance, with which every East Tennessee boat builder is familiar and has seen often used in bringing gunwales more than a hundred feet long and four or five feet wide over the most crooked and zigzag roads. Without doubt, common sense is more indispensable in the affairs of life than much dignified with the name of sense though acquired from books or from the schools.

My son Robert remained with Bragg's army and was in several engagements with the enemy. Many of the incidents of Joseph Wheeler's cavalry to which he belonged have escaped my recollections. One only of these will be here given. Wheeler, with his command of some thousand horsemen crossed the Tennessee at Kelly's Ferry and struck for the rear of the Federal army with the hope of diverting their attention from further conquest in Georgia. The command made several raids in Middle Tennessee, cutting off supply trains, tearing up the railroads and bridges and capturing several small Federal detachments. When not met by not less than two to one, Wheeler's men were in every case the victors. Returning from one of these successful raids, the detachment to which my son Robert belonged encountered a Federal force which quadrupled ours. Striking it near its center, the detachment was surrounded and captured. Robert, and his boy Wesley among the rest, were made prisoners. Riding near to one of his officers Robert disclosed to the officer that he had determined to effect his escape. The officer remonstrated against the attempt as suicidal, on account of the small number and unarmed condition of the Confederate prisoners as well as the large armed force that now surrounded and guarded them. Robert repeated his purpose as taken; the officer persisted in dissuading him from the mad attempt. They were all riding in a very long lane and just then they came in view of the encampment of the Federal army nearly a mile distant. Realizing that every rod he advanced nearer to that army only diminished his chance of possible escape, he saw on the fence on his left hand a panel one rail lower than the rest. He reined up his horse to it, put his spurs into his flanks. He leaped over it at a bound, and was turned by the fearless rider in the direction of a distant clump of cedar trees. As he dashed across the field several shots were fired at him. Like a Comanche rider the moment he had jumped the fence he threw his whole weight on his left stirrup and clasping the horn of his saddle in his right hand and clinging as close as he could to the left side of his horse, little of his own body was exposed to the fire of a great number of muskets fired at him. Several shots nearly spent struck the right side of his saddle; a few reached his horse and his clothes had some bullet holes made in them. He reached the clump of cedars in safety. His sword arm had been slightly paralyzed in the morning when he was captured by the stroke of a heavy saber in the hands of a Federal light-horseman. This was the only personal injury he received during the war. Being the chief scout of General Wheeler, he knew all that commander's movements, promulgated or concealed in his own bosom. And knowing the point at which he would aim to be that night, he joined his camp next morning before day. The boy Wesley, a prisoner too, riding far behind his young master in the rear, had heard the firing at the escaped prisoner without knowing though who he was. He told afterwards that no one of the enemy's cavalry could get over the fence till their riders dismounted and laid down the rails and that they made no pursuit after crossing the fence. The horse, the efficient cause of Robert's escape, was the best I ever saw. He was a stately and magnificent black, with a flowing mane and tail,—gentle and docile ordinarily but in a combat and amid the clangor of arms seemed to be instinct with ambition and rage—vaulted high and loftily, leaped a fence, a wall, a ditch, a ravine, was impetuous and foremost in a charge and when the enemy's bugle sounded a retreat, so eager was he in the hot pursuit that on some occasions his rider could scarce escape another capture. He will be mentioned again.

Wesley continued with the captors till they bivouacked at night. Then, learning from the other prisoners that it was his young master who had effected his escape, determined to escape also: mounted his mule, dashed by the sentinels at night, took the direction of the Tennessee River, got on Wheeler's track and overtook his command just as the last company was crossing the river. He brought off his booty, a large army sack filled with officers' best clothing and uniform, revolvers, etc. His sack had not been opened at the encampment. It and its contents had been captured at McMinnville.

CHAPTER XI

Other Sons and a Cousin

With Captain Ramsey was associated on this same service during this daring invasion of Kentucky an elder brother, Colonel Francis Alexander Ramsey. Like his grandfather of the same name, he entered in his nineteenth year upon his public life. Before he completed his studies in East Tennessee University he joined a company of adventurers to go overland from Knoxville, Tennessee, to San Francisco, California. He drove the first wagon out of the encampment a mile north of town.

An older brother, W. Wilberforce Alexander Ramsey, was his messmate and companion on the whole route. Wilberforce had the stamp of genius on his face, was exceedingly intellectual and fond of study. He had graduated with distinction in East Tennessee University and had obtained license to practice law in his native district and had entered on his circuit duties. But the *auri sacra fames* had bewildered most of his countrymen and seduced them from the tamer pursuits of ordinary life. At this moment the company was being organized to penetrate the vast interior of the Great West—cross the Rocky Mountains and thus reach the shore of the Pacific Ocean. It was not the belittling love of money nor the hope of acquiring a thing so little and insignificant that led Wilberforce from a society he could so well enjoy and adorn, from his books, his studies and his profession of which he was so proud and of which he would have become an ornament and a pillar. No. His ambition was loftier. It was to cultivate science, to study nature in its primitive simplicity, to investigate ethnology, philology, the flora of the interior, its climate, soil, products, and resources. He was very fond of antiquarian and historical researches and devoted to the acquisition of knowledge. Mental culture, mental discipline,—in short, intellectuation—this was his forte, his ambition, his purpose, his idol.

The journal which he kept and which has survived the exposures of his long and perilous expedition over mountain and desert and wilderness and, alas too, the life of its writer, is the evidence of what is here said by a fond father of the endowments and attainments of a favorite son. His fondness of the Muses is evidenced by an ode, since published, written in the depth of a boundless wilderness by his campfire with no other book near him than his Bible, a present from his beloved and idolized mother. Besides the mental traits thus enumerated Wilberforce, too, possessed and developed in good proportion the physical attributes—courage, endurance, enterprise, manhood and self-reliance not always found in a nature so ethereal and sublimated.

Such were the two brothers en route to California. The one was the *sua vitur in modo*—the other *fortitu in re*. The one eager in the pursuit and capture of the buffalo on the plains or the hostile Comanche lurking in the Nevada fastnesses, the other talking to the padre in Latin at his ranch or investigating the features and language of the inoffensive and quiet Pernos in their lodges or wigwams.

The route of the adventurous explorers was by St. Louis and Independence, Missouri, and from the latter by the usual trading path to Santa Fe and Albuquerque where the company wintered. Leaving their winter camp, in the spring they struck across the continent, came to the Colorado (of the Pacific). Some exorbitant Yankees had established and claimed a ferry across this stream and demanded the unreasonable toll of $____ for crossing. The company, resisting the exaction, built a boat a little below the Yankee ferry. My two sons were not only good water-men but at my own boat landing at Mecklenburg had learned the whole plan of boatbuilding and of calking and launching the craft. Under their direction the boat was soon finished. They tore up their shirts to answer for caulking, no supply of hemp nor cotton being within their reach. My sons took command of the boat and put across that river not only their own company but gave transportation to a vast number of Mexicans, peons, Indians, who during their stay on the bank had accumulated around their encampment.

I will not stop here to tell the usual incidents of surprises, resistance, escapes, hardship, hunting, exploits, scarcity of water, of fuel and of food occuring in so long, so dangerous and so difficult a route. Many of them are narrated in Wilberforce's journal with his remarks upon the physical history of the interior of this great American desert and wilderness, his account of the traditions, language, religion of the aboriginal tribes, etc. The company at length arrived at Los Angeles on the Pacific, each man having in his knapsack only a teacup full of bean-meal procured from the Indians by exchange of some worn-out shoes and clothes.

From Los Angeles the adventurers, after a short rest, distributed themselves to different points on the slope of the Pacific. My sons and a few others stopped at a place known there as Volcano Diggings. A small river was turned from its old channel. The excavation required for this purpose was laborious and exhausting in the extreme. Poor Wilberforce sank under it. The dreadful winter at Albuquerque and the unparalled sufferings of their terrible tramp to Los Angeles had brought on an imposthume of the lungs, a predisposition to which he had inherited from his father. (He had my flat chest, my complexion, my hair, especially my eyes, my voice even, my contour—my whole physical, intellectual and moral nature.) He sank quietly to his grave in peace with his God and his fellow men. He was the first man buried in a coffin at Volcano Diggings, California. Strange to say, poor Wilberforce had a Christian burial in these wilds. A Presbyterian minister, Reverend Davidson, originally from Mecklenburg County, North Carolina, performed for him the last funeral rites. He was, if I had a favorite, my favorite son, my child of promise and of hope. (See my *History of Tennessee,* page 498, footnote.)

My son, F. Alexander Ramsey, was also taken sick in California and determined to return back to us. The sad information of the death of our son was, soon after its occurrence, communicated in a friendly letter from Captain J. C. Vaughn, one of the California adventurers. At the time this letter came to Knoxville I was absent and on my way to a meeting of the E. T. &. G. R. R. at Athens. My son Crozier opened the letter, and seeing its contents dispatched a messenger after me. I was at Philadelphia, Tennessee when the messenger overtook me there at night and in bed. I knew his voice and that his night mission portended no good. I returned with him to Knoxville. My son Crozier had thoughtfully withheld the mournful intelligence from others. He rode out with me home when I had to communicate the distressing news. Our anxiety was now turned to the return of our other son, Alexander. He might arrive any day at New Orleans sick, destitute, and without friends in that strange city. I wrote by mail, I telegraphed, I watched the papers for marine intelligence. At last I found under the head of "Arrivals from California" among other names that of Francis Alexander Ramsey. Supposing that he would come up the Cumberland rather than the Tennessee River, I took the stage to Nashville and telegraphed to different points, but heard nothing. Almost in despair I took the stage back to Knoxville. At the supper house in Kingston Dr. McNutt, once a medical student of mine, came in and gave me the agree-

"Swan Pond," near Knoxville, now undergoing restoration by the Association for the Preservation of Tennessee Antiquities to become a state historic shrine. Built by Colonel Francis Alexander Ramsey in 1797. The Childhood home of Dr. J. G. M. Ramsey. Thompson photo.

able information that he had a few days before seen Alexander on board
the steamboat bound to Knoxville and that he was sick. Next day, on arriving home, I found him there. But how changed! *Diarrhoea Mexicana*
and a long voyage by two seas and the rivers had almost ruined his excellent constitution. His native air, the comforts of home, and the care we all
could give him soon resuscitated him and restored his health. A vacancy
just then occurred of colonel in our regiment. The recital of his adventures, his exploits, his dangers, gave him great popularity and consideration with the military and he was elected to the position of colonel of the
regiment.

In the meantime my son-in-law, Colonel Breck, had become interested
in a large landed property high up on the Kentucky River, and wishing
to improve and develop it by the erection of machinery invited my son,
Alexander, to become his active partner. This he did. Under his direction
a mountain was tunneled and one of the forks of the Kentucky River
diverted through it. The mills proved to be valuable, furnishing to Frankfort and other places vast quantities of plank and lumber transported in
rafts down the river. Sometime after, he returned to Tennessee, and becoming acquainted with Miss Presley of South Carolina went there and
married her. I gave him the property sometimes known as Swan Pond,
more recently as the Stone-house. . . .[1]

As before stated I gave as his patrimony to my son Colonel F. A. Ramsey Swan Pond which had been the home of his grandfather of the same
name and title. He occupied and improved it for a few years, and the war
coming on, he took his wife and children to South Carolina, returned
to Tennessee and entered upon the active duties of a soldier's life. He
joined Captain Kain's Artillery, went to Chattanooga, bore a gallant part
in the affair at Bridgeport, followed his captain in the campaign he carried
across the Sequatchee and Walden and Cumberland Mountains. From
these towering heights their cannon resounded one day from one eminence, the next day from another, perplexing and confusing the enemy
by their rapid change of place and giving rise in this way to the report
that the mountains were filled with rebels, and causing thus a precipitate
retreat of the enemy back from the Tennessee towards their main army. In

[1] The description of Swan Pond, which Dr. Ramsey inserted here, appears as footnote 5
in Chapter I.

one of these excursions Kain aimed at (perhaps Winchester) where Andrew Johnson had an appointment to speak for the Union. The artillery expected to disperse the crowd and hoped to capture the speaker. A countryman passing along, and too good a Confederate to attend such a speaking, informed the captain that a large body of Federal troops was near the place appointed, for the protection of Mr. Johnson. But for this opportune information our one hundred artillerists would have fallen victims to the vastly superior forces of the enemy. Next morning Kain was beyond their reach thundering his cannon at the head of Elk River. During the whole time of his absence on this *secret* service not a word could be heard of him and his men, and when they emerged from the woods on Embree and made their appearance at Kingston it was as if they had risen from the dead. Everyone believed they had been captured or destroyed.

In some cave of these mountain solitudes my son hid in the night enough of artillery stores to have furnished a long campaign. He knows where they are. I take it to be near the head of Sequatchee. Captain W. C. Kain promised me an account of this daring campaign, but I have not yet received it. It deserves a place in history. His small force and his artillery artfully roaring forth its thunders from every hill top in that mountain region drove back thousands of the Federal forces and thus delayed for one year the assault upon and capture of Chattanooga.

The artillery was left again at Loudon and more formidable defences erected near it. It was at this time, I believe, that I procured the detail of my son Alexander to go as a detective after the counterfeiters in Putnam county—an account of which has already been given.

This may be the most proper place to introduce to the reader another of my sons,—the junior of his brother, Robert, last mentioned. J. G. McKnitt Ramsey had also been a member of the class in Tusculum College but had not completed his studies when the portentous clouds of war began to hang over our South and Tennessee. From his youth he had been a pattern of sobriety, industry, patient attention to business, always and under all circumstances reliable and efficient. He had assisted me in my shop, compounding my medicine and keeping my books, in my absence and on distant rides prescribing to my patients—often curing them. He also assisted me supervising my farms, my ferry, and my business generally. Essentially practical, he had little of the visionary and enthusiast. He was fond of good society and indulged his taste for it. With all, at home and abroad, he was the favorite. When it became necessary, he aided me in my financial duties in the Bank of Tennessee, as well as in my Confederate States depository, often acting for me as a teller. After the war commenced I had him detailed to transport my monies from one point to another as army exigencies required. He was thus qualified for almost any of the duties of life, in peace or in war. He never made an error of a figure and his count was invariably correct and accurate. His health was less vigorous than some of his other brothers. He first went into camp at Chattanooga (Anglice, the River of Death), he contracted malarial disease and soon became quite sick and was allowed to return home. During his convalescence he was often detailed to light but responsible duties elsewhere. At length, the service demanding it, he was assigned the duty of commander of the steamer *Jas. Glover,* and was constantly on that boat which transported supplies of subsistence, army stores, etc., from the mouth of French Broad to all points below on the Holston, the Tennessee, Clinch, Hiwassee and Ococe rivers. Some of these points were exposed to sudden incursions of the enemy. . . .

At an earlier page it has been mentioned that I was at Atlanta. One P.M. a telegram was sent me. It found me near Mr. Clayton's bank. (It is here appended.) The operator by mistake, or in the hurry and confusion of the battle raging near him, had put the wrong name to the telegram. It should have been Abner Baker Crozier instead of A. B. C. Ramsey. At first I thought it was my son Robert, who was dangerously wounded, and acted accordingly. I went at once and applied for transportation to the provost marshall. Seeing me in citizen's clothing the clerk said I could not get transportation. I replied I must have transportation. My son was wounded at Chickamauga and had telegraphed for me: that I was a civil officer of the Confederate States and that as a surgeon of its armies I was needed on the field. He refused the second time. I asked for his chief. He pointed to him. I went to him and, presenting my telegram, asked him to read it. He did so and wrote for me this special permission: indorsing it on the telegram, and observing kindly to me that one would help the other wherever I went. It was almost night when I got on the train. There was no light in the car but I recognized the voice of many sympathising friends on board. Arrived at Dalton, I heard the passenger train would go no further. I found a lumber train on the point of leaving, laden with material to rebuild a bridge burned the day before. I took a seat on top of the timbers but was directed to get off. I appealed to the sympathies and humanity of the conductor. I and a few others were permitted to remain on the train. We at length reached the burnt bridge. Of course we could go no further by rail. I inquired the moment we stopped for someone who could direct me the road to Mr. Corry's where, according to my telegram, the wounded soldier lay. Mr. Inman, an acquaintance formerly of Dandridge, Tennessee, spoke from the surrounding crowd that he would pass his gate and would be glad to be my pilot. I followed him on foot across the country and through the wood. Coming at length to Catoosa Church where yesterday had been a battle I saw dead horses, broken cavalry wagons, and artillery fragments laying scattered all around. The killed and wounded had been removed before I reached the place.

I went on to Mr. Corry's gate and saw from it my son Robert walking near the house and some other Confederate soldiers standing around it. I went up to where Robert was. He had not yet seen me and I exclaimed, "Why Robert! I heard you had been wounded." "No," said he, and manifesting some emotion added, "It was Cousin Robert Crozier, and he has just died." A cousin of my own in the neighborhood, William Baxter Ramsey, came in and promised to go and procure a coffin. I asked Mrs. Corry to allow us to dig the grave for the gallant soldier who had just expired, in the family burying ground and not at the church yard of Catoosa —where we would be exposed to the enemy's cavalry near and around us. She immediately granted me that permission. On entering the inclosure of this private cemetery the first gravestone I read: "Sacred to the Memory of Mrs. Elizabeth Ramsey, Wife of Reverend S. G. Ramsey," etc., etc. On other gravestones I read similar inscriptions *in memoriam* of other members of the family of my cousin Colonel R. A. Ramsey, formerly of Catoosa. Mrs. Corry was his neice and granddaughter of Major Lenoir, father of my own son-in-law. From the moment I read these inscriptions I felt relieved that the remains of my nephew would be interred amongst the ashes of my own kindred and in a Christian cemetery. Here they were interred by moonlight in a quiet forest. Poor Robert Crozier! He was buried by his comrades in arms without the usual military ceremonies. We were in hearing of the enemy's camp and it was thought to be best not to make such a demonstration. We returned in sadness to the house. But soon the comrades were seated around the fire, running bullets, burnishing their revolvers and their sabers so as to be prepared for another fight tomorrow. Around this fire I heard from the comrades of Lieutenant Crozier the details of the service he had seen and especially those of the conflict in which he lost his life. From these on my return to Atlanta I prepared the obituary notice here inserted as cut from the columns of Sperry's Atlanta *Register*.[2]

I also wrote to the parents of the deceased an account of the sad event. They were then at some hospital of which Dr. Crozier was surgeon. (Perhaps Cassville, Georgia.) In my letter of condolence I alluded to, as the assuasive of their grief, the fact that he was buried in a private Christian graveyard and surrounded by kindred and pious dead.

Early the morning after this interment, my son Robert took me over to the burnt bridge and at once joined his comrades already in their saddles across Chickamauga. Each of them seemed determined to avenge the death of their brave and patriotic lieutenant.

Arrived at the burnt bridge, I saw ambulances coming in with the wounded from battlefields near and around it. I at once determined to remain there and render what surgical aid one man could do. I extemporised a wayside hospital by using for that purpose the woodshed there, now empty. I had straw hauled in from the adjoining farms and the place made as comfortable otherwise as the circumstances around me permitted. There was not a single table, not a single chair, in my improvised hospital. The

---

[2]   OBITUARY

Died Tuesday morning, September 22d [1863], of the effects of wounds received on the nineteenth, Lieutenant R. C. Crozier, elder son of Doctor C. W. Crozier, of Knoxville, Tenn., in the twenty-fifth year of his age.

The deceased joined the Provisional Army of the Confederate States as early as May, 1861, in the company of Captain Paxton's Knoxville Guards, Colonel Cummings' Regiment—was in nearly all of the battles in Kentucky, viz: Wild Cat, Fishing Creek, Richmond, Lexington, Sommerset. In the latter he was taken prisoner and remained in captivity in Camp Chase and Fort Delaware several weeks. As soon as exchanged he went immediately again into active service under Captain Deven's Company D, Colonel Ashby's Second Tennessee Regiment, General Scott's Brigade of Cavalry. After the evacuation of East Tennessee this company fell down towards Chattanooga, and under command of First Lieutenant J. F. McMahon has been in constant and successful skirmishes all around General Bragg's army. On Saturday, the nineteenth, this company was the advance of General Scott's command, and six of them, viz: Lieutenant Crozier, R. M. Ramsey, Jas. Legg, _____ Beeler, and _____ Ford, and _____ _____, being in front came upon the advance of the enemy drawn up in line in force of more than one hundred. Not waiting for the rear to come up, these six, dismounting from their horses, waded a creek, which skirted the field occupied by the Yankees, and ascending its bank fired rapidly on the enemy's line. It is known that nine of them were killed and several others wounded. The enemy in falling back to the woods on the opposite side of the field continued to fire, killing Mr. Ford on the spot and inflicting a fatal wound on Lieutenant Crozier, who was carried off the field by one of his comrades a short distance. . . .

number of the sick and wounded was constantly increasing, arriving some in wagons, ox carts, buggies, ambulances,—some on horseback, some on foot. Some very seriously wounded, in danger from hemorrhage, from comminuted fracture, from lacerated as well as incised wounds; some almost dead from complicated injuries of the joints. Some suffering from tetanus, some moribund from exhaustion and neglect—a sleepless night and the constant jolting of their vehicle over a stony and uneven road in the night. To add to present difficulties and embarrassments I found there were only two assistant surgeons in the camp, and these furnished very poorly with imperfect instruments and a most inadequate supply of medical stores. Fortunately a full supply of whiskey, brandy, wine, and especially coffee had been captured from the enemy the day before and had been brought to the burnt bridge. Many of the wounded must have died in a short time without this opportune capture of cordials and stimulants. I gave my attention first to those in most imminent danger, leaving for a time those whose wounds were more manageable and excited least apprehension on the part of the surgeons and inflicted least pain on the part of the sufferer. I soon found that the three surgeons were breaking down from the constant stooping posture we necessarily had to take, and the labors we had to perform. I telegraphed for more surgical and medical assistants to all points within my reach. Dr. Pride and Dr. _____ were sent to me. Soon after, other professional reinforcements came also to our relief. We placed wagon bodies on their side under shade trees, and spreading blankets over the inequalities of the surface of the exterior of a wagon bed, we began to operate with less fatigue to the surgeon and in some cases with less pain to poor patient. We were in railroad communication with the towns above us in Georgia—Ringold, Dalton, Calhoun, Cassville, etc., etc. And as soon as a carload of the wounded had passed through the hands of the surgeons they were placed upon the open flat cars and sent elsewhere. An assistant surgeon generally went on each flat. A bucket or canteen of water was placed within reach of every wounded or sick soldier. Augur holes in the gunwales of the flat were arranged so as to receive a bush or a limb of a shady tree so as to protect the patient from the incessant glare of a September sun and often in that oppressive weather the travel was confined to the evenings and night.

To avoid miasmatic diseases to which surgeons alike with others were exposed anywhere near the Chickamauga (Anglice, "The Stream of Death"), whose paludal exhalations are always productive of febrile disease, we found it necessary to remove our wayside hospital to more healthy stations higher up the country. Dr. Pride—a victim to professional zeal and humanity—amongst the surgeons. Let me here bear witness to his patriotism, his skill, his constancy under the fatiguing pressure of that extraordinary service, under extraordinary exposure to malaria, to discomfort, to perpetual mental and physical labor. I saw it all daily and on one occasion, when taking charge of a platform car filled with wounded men for Atlanta, admonished him how susceptible a physician practicing on the heights around Maryville would be to disease under the poisonous atmospheric influences of the deadly Chickamagua. He had a chill next day and apprehensive of the issue took the cars for Macon where he died. I prepared a suitable obituary of the deceased which was published in Sperry's paper and which I hoped to find and append hereto.

My other son F. A. Ramsey remained with Bragg's army watching the movements of the enemy and for a suitable opportunity to join any Confederate forces that might be organized to return to East Tennessee and recover Knoxville. Crozier was at Atlanta and McKnitt was now at Bristol; Alexander and Robert around the enemy's camps in the neighborhood of Chattanooga—all of them burning with an ardent desire, common to them, to me, and all my East Tennessee co-refugees to expel the invaders and rescue our families from the domination of our enemies. This began to be talked of as the policy of the administration. I urged it by letters to President Davis. The recovery of East Tennessee was the only hope of preventing the bisection of the Confederacy—an event which, as all knew, it could not survive.

CHAPTER XII

Longstreet in Knoxville

I myself divided my time between my offices in Atlanta and my cheer-fully self-assumed duties in the camps and hospitals. These latter had now become better arranged and systematised. Once or twice in every week I went down the road looking after the sick and wounded. At Atlanta we put on foot a subscription paper to procure such supplies of clothing, sub-sistence, medicines, etc., as could not be found in or near the camps. This application was responded to promptly and liberally by the Atlanta people themselves and by the munificent bounty of the patriotic and wealthy now concentrated in and around that metropolis of the up-country of Georgia. One of these was William Lenoir of Lenoir, Tennessee. He gave us $1,000. We had committees and subcommittees of relief. Of these I and Dr. B. R. Strong were chiefs and no two men in the South were more faithful or indefatigable. I accidentally preserved . . . the certificate of our appoint-ment, signed John W. Duncan, Esquire, and dated November 19, 1863. With this in my pocket I went everywhere and was everywhere recog-nized and respected. If I could only have heard from my dear family at Knoxville the time thus spent in kindnesses to the suffering soldiers would have been the happiest of my life.

On one of these excursions I was at Marietta. We established a hospital there. Sitting up at night and receiving from the ambulances the wounded as they were sent in from the battle of _____ I found Governor Neill S. Brown in attendance. I had to use him as assistant surgeon. The functions of this new position he discharged well and skillfully. Next morn-ing, I met Mr. Bruce Deery, formerly of Sullivan County. He informed me that my residence and out buildings at Mecklenburg had been robbed and burned by the enemy under Burnside. I thought little of the loss of property. But the apprehension that my library, my manuscripts, my un-published second volume of the *History of Tennessee,* my correspondence, my museum etc. were also taken or burned did give me a bitter pang— none could be more bitter. Property I could replace or live without it. But this loss was irreparable. None but myself could fully appreciate and realize it. But still I received from all friends the sincerest and heartfelt sympathy and condolence. When I met them they alluded to it with the utmost delicacy and respect to my feelings. One of them, Mr. William Lenoir, came right up to me and seeing me without a watch, pulled off his own and hung it around my neck and insisted that I should take and wear it. I did so. He is a frugal and economical gentleman but he gives like a prince. I have since learned that William Lenoir and brothers suffered from similar atrocities during the war more than $100,000.

As early as December 27, 1862 I had applied for and received from General Kirby Smith a ticket of transportation at large. This I always carried with me and it is strange that, exposed as it was to use, exposure and accident that it is still here and preserved so well. It was an *introduction* to me everywhere, at all times, among friends or in the midst of strangers. It is marked for this page.[1] Such relics and antiquities of our first Rebellion were once valued and sought for by the historian and the curious all over our country. Our Southern people and their successors will regard with no less veneration, those of the Rebellion of 1860-61.

It had been intimated to me from a rather official source that General Buckner's favorite idea of getting the enemy into his trap at Knoxville and of thus capturing the invaders, was not the puerility I had conceived it to be as represented on another page and as pronounced by me to that general

---

[1]   H'D. Q'RS. DEP'T. EAST TENN.
                                    Knoxville, Decr. 27th 1862
   All officers and guards will permit Dr. J. G. M. Ramsey to pass in this Department—or beyond it especially between Knoxville and Atlanta, Ga.
                         By Commd. of
                         Lt.-Gen. E. Kirby Smith,
                              H. L. Clay,
                                 A. O. G.
Transportation furnished in Kind from Atlanta Ga to Charleston Tenn., and return. Sept. 3, 1863.
                              Jno. Trizzell
                              Cap't and A Q M
Transportation furnished in Kind from Abingdon Va to Knoxville Tenn June 22d. 1863
                              Wm Rodefer
                              A. Q. M.   T. A. C. S.
T_____ furnished in Kind to Chickamauga and Return
                              Jno. Trizzell
                              A. Q. M.
   Approved
       Brig Genl. Davis, Comdg Post
       Jno. B. Major
       A. D. G.

himself. It was understood that the enemy around Chattanooga were going into winter quarters and that after ravaging the fine country from
Knoxville to the Hiwassee, the Federal forces that invaded East Tennessee
under Burnside had called in their detachments and were concentrating
them at Philadelphia, Loudon, Lenoir's and Knoxville. Mixing a good deal
with army officers and more frequently with the common soldiery, I ascertained that the sentiment was universally in favor of the enterprise and
I left Atlanta so as to go to the extremest eastern encampment, then
Cleveland. Here I met General Vaughn and two colonels (names not
recollected). I had engineered the whole country and was familiar with
every route leading to the enemy's camp and was able therefore to assist
the military in forming plans for the future. One was to avoid Athens,
cross Tennessee at Tamottlee ford not far from McGhee's Ferry, pursue
the Nobb road in Blount and Sevier and get to the Confederate camp east
of Knoxville wherever that might be and then act according to circumstances. I knew the whole route and proposed to General Vaughn to be his
pilot. Another more feasible plan was to surprise the enemy, then understood to be in some force at Philadelphia under _____.

We had repaired the railroad as far as the Hiwassee River and our lines
reached that stream at several points. The cars had not yet gone that far.
But scouts reported the west side of the river as free from a Federal soldier
but that the Unionists were lurking around all through the country. I
wished to go on the first car to reoccupy the country and reach Charleston.
I did so. A small guard attended the train. We moved cautiously and
slowly. Soon after starting I heard a colored man aboard tell another that
he was trying to get to Knoxville and was this far on his way there. I took
the opportunity of writing on the cars a note to my wife, being careful to
say nothing more than I should. I beckoned to the Negro to come to my
seat. I found him to be a brickmason who knew me. He said he had
worked at Lenoir's steam furnace. I asked him to carry my note and leave
it at Lenoir's. The honest fellow seemed to understand his duties and
promised me to execute them faithfully. My wife told me a few weeks
afterwards that the letter in pencil was skillfully delivered to herself and
that the bearer to whom I had intrusted it told her he had seen me in person and had left me at Charleston. The first and only intelligence she had
received from me or our sons after I left home. The cars returned immediately to Cleveland. General Vaughn had the day before gone down from
Cleveland to a military council below and reported progress. It was un-

satisfactory, at least to one like myself uninitiated. There was too much of West Point in it. Too much delay. Sevier, Jackson, Vaughn—any selfmade commander—would have *struck* two or three weeks sooner than Bragg's order to Longstreet indicated his "on to Knoxville."

I returned to Atlanta and resumed other duties: spending part of my time at Dalton and intermediate points.

In the meantime the projected campaign began to assume shape and proportions and General Carter L. Stevenson (I believe) came forward with some forces. I had been several times as far as Sweetwater and was there when the successful dash was made at Philadelphia. But an order came recalling Stevenson (if it was he) and investing General James Longstreet with the command. The troops were ordered back from Sweetwater and other regiments and brigades substituted in their place. This caused a delay of another two weeks. It was fatal. We never recovered from it. Stevenson, if he had gone on as at first arranged, would have recaptured Knoxville and possibly have saved the Confederacy. Though I considered it lost from the permission of Buckner to give up East Tennessee.

After the rear of Longstreet had passed Loudon most of the refugees from Knoxville followed more leisurely. At Cleveland I first heard of the return of Wheeler's cavalry and of the probability of his passing through that place. My son Robert, his chief scout, rode up to the depot, and I there first learned where he had been the last month or two. I had left him at the burnt bridge in Georgia, heard of his crossing at Kelly's Ferry with Wheeler but got no intelligence of him till this interview. He still had his boy Wesley with him. Robert went on hastily to join Longstreet and left us refugees at Cleveland waiting the next train to take us to Loudon. The cars reached that place at sundown and could go no further. The bridge there had been burned, and the pontoons there had been removed or destroyed. My ladies were six miles across the river at Lenoir's. I procured a horse, got my passports from General Vaughn, post commander, to pass to Lenoir's by way of the ferry. The ferry man told me that Colonel Robert K. Byrd's cavalry had been in that neighborhood that day. I really hesitated what to do. Colonel Stanfield was the only one with me and we both concluded that it might be worse tomorrow, and therefore we went on. A little out of Loudon we began to notice, although it was dark, the villas of encampments on each side of the road now deserted by the Yankees. We met or saw but one man and he on horseback. He did not speak nor did we. Arrived at Lenoir's late at night I walked quietly in. I rapped at the parlor door quietly. I heard our daughter, Sue, exclaim, "La! that is Pa. I know the way he knocks." Everything around the house was quiet as death. The morning of the preceeding day the enemy had been driven from their large encampment at Lenoir's and had hastily and in great disorder fallen back on Knoxville hotly pursued by the Confederates—my sons and Judge Reynolds among the number. These three, with their Enfields and their revolvers, had passed their comrades in the pursuit and taking an advantageous position at a favorable point near Campbell's Station, fired deliberately upon the retreating foe and captured several batteries and wagons laden with military stores and supplies. As I went up a few days after I could still see evidences of the panic which had hastened the precipitate flight of the enemy. The pursuit was continued till the invaders found protection behind their fortifications in Knoxville.[2]

I was in error when I said on page 124 that I bade farewell to my son Crozier at Atlanta and that he went from there round to Bristol. That had been our intention. But at Augusta where Dr. Strong, my cashier, was then staying with his sister, Mrs. T. W. Fleming, of that city he heard by telegraph that the "on to Knoxville march to Knoxville" had begun, he and Dr. Strong came on after me and joined us at Loudon. Procuring a cavalry horse at that place from General Vaughn, now commander of the post there, I went up towards Knoxville. At Lenoir's, as it was now late in November and the weather was becoming cold, I replenished as best I could my wardrobe, borrowing an antique overcoat. Tying my hand valise to one end of a rope halter and a carpetsack to the other I flung them across my saddle, bade my family a long adieu, and mounted.

What was best to do with my dear little Arthur we could not determine. His brothers were all in the Confederate army. He was not yet seventeen but he had an irrepressible desire to join them and share their fate. And yet it was hard for one so affectionate and devoted to his mother and sisters to leave them and go into our camps. As I left the house I saw him walking up on the railroad alone. I knew the conflict that was going on in his manly bosom between inclination and duty. His step was elastic and he bore himself like a soldier and a patriot as he was. His mother and sisters never saw him afterwards. I passed him again on the railroad track— I deflected from it on the dirt road.

---

[2] The account of the evacuation of Mecklenburg and the migrations of his family, which Dr. Ramsey gave here, has been placed at the beginning of the following chapter.

At Campbell's Station the house was pointed out to me in a field where the enemy's sharpshooters had made an obstinate resistance and which they held until the small party before mentioned; viz., Honorable R. B. Reynolds, Robert and Alexander Ramsey, by their accurate and incessant fire succeeded in driving them out. They found in it and captured thirty guns loaded and in good condition for use. The pursuit of the routed enemy was quickened. At Loveville they tried to make another stand but our sharpshooters coming up, their battery was soon unmanned and they hastened to get behind their entrenchments around Knoxville. It is the universal opinion, not only of the assailants but of those who were in town when the retreating foe, now panic-stricken and defeated, arrived in it, that if the pursuit had been vigorously followed up Knoxville would have fallen without a siege. I have since conversed with some of the beseiged who assured me that while the Federal troops were entering town the conviction was general that if the Confederates made an assault that night resistance would be hopeless. Next morning, the army of Longstreet delayed so long in their encampment at Loveville that time was thus given to make preparation for defense. Had Andrew Jackson led our army it would not have suspended pursuit, but would have assaulted and entered the town before it halted. Indeed, the capital error of this commander was his tardiness—the fault of fat men generally, and especially of the phlegmatic and apathetic. He lost two weeks nearly when he was substituted for Stevenson (I am not certain now of his name, tho I was present at Sweetwater when the order for the fatal substitution was received).[3] Then he was too slow again in crossing at Loudon, too slow when he camped at Browder's, and when the sentinels of the two armies were almost in contact he should have continued his march a mile or two further and struck their encampment at Lenoir's where the enemy were allowed to decamp the whole night. Jackson would have at least ascertained that they were breaking up camp—if he had not sent a large detachment around by the old Kingston road and intercepted the retreating foe at Campbell's Station and thus having them between two fires, two Confederate forces, captured them before reaching Knoxville. Longstreet should not have camped at Loveville. He should have made one day's work of it and gone into Knoxville before he paused an hour. It

[3] Dr. Ramsey's memory was correct. Major General Carter L. Stevenson engaged in movements and skirmishes near Sweetwater, October 17–27, 1863. He reported to Longstreet November 12, 1862. *Official Records of the Union and Confederate Armies in the War of the Rebellion*, series 1, vol. 31, part 1, pp. 6–8.

is *well known* that the enemy expected his attack the same night and they have since admitted that if the assault had been then made it would have been necessarily successful.

Late at night of the same day I had left Lenoir's (and gone down to Loudon and returned by the former place), I reached General Longstreet's headquarters—the house of Judge R. B. Reynolds. I sought an interview with him. His aides were in a room downstairs. One of them enquired from me something about the surrounding localities, and especially *above* Knoxville. I was a stranger to all the gentlemen present, but believe my interrogator was Major J. W. Fairfax of General Longstreet's staff. I told them who I was, where I had lived forty years, that I had been in every house within fifteen miles of my office. He then brought out a map or diagram of the adjoining country. On this map French Broad River was not laid down at all and something was said about having cut off the enemy's supplies by placing a cavalry force between Knoxville and the fertile grounds upon Little River, and that they would thus be able to starve the Knoxville garrison into a surrender. I took the map and laying it on the table, expatiated at some length on its inaccuracies and especially its omissions, and with my pencil delineated the French Broad and its tributaries Chucky, the Pigeons, etc., mentioned the vast resources of subsistence, corn, meat, etc., for sixty miles above town. On inquiring whether there had been any forces placed at its mouth, my own residence, so as to control these supplies reaching the enemy, what was my surprise to hear that his forces did not reach beyond the north bank of the Holston and that the channel of the French Broad had all the time been open and unobstructed and accessible to the crafts and boats and supply trains of the enemy in town or their allies and friends above. One of the aides carried the map with my additions and corrections immediately upstairs to the commander-in-chief. While this aide was gone I was further questioned about supplies coming out of the French Broad: Would they be sufficient to keep the enemy from starving, etc., etc.? I replied that five days of open water communication would be sufficient to throw into Knoxville supplies for six months. After a few minutes Major Fairfax returned to the room and said the general wished to see me at his room and conducted me up. I repeated to him all I had said to his aides below stairs, and, with some confident emphasis: "If you wished or intended to cut off the enemy's supplies a cannon loaded with grapeshot and a few sharpshooters placed on the bluff above the fork of the rivers near my old residence would prevent a bushel of corn from coming into Knox-ville." With these and similar remarks I left him.

Next day the camp was in motion. It was rumored all day that the policy of starving out the enemy was abandoned and a falling back in the direction of Virginia was about to take its place. I met the general during the day once or twice and that night remained still at his head-quarters in Reynolds' house. After I had gone to bed someone tapped at my door. I knew the voice to be that of my son Robert. I had seen him and his three other brothers all day in camp and could not conjecture the cause of his thus coming to me at night. Ascertaining that there was no one in the room but me, he replied almost in a whisper to the inquiry; "What has brought you here at midnight?" that General Longstreet had sent a courier to his camp four miles off at Crawford's with a command for him to appear at once at his headquarters. That he had done so. That his mule and horse were now being shod at the army blacksmith shop near by, that his duty required him to reach Clinch River before day, that he had procured a Yankee army coat and—I guessed the rest. I said, "Rob-ert, it is a most dangerous but a most important service you have under-taken. Have you money enough? Here, take my pocketbook and take out what you wish." The room was perfectly dark. He stirred up the coals, took out as much money as he desired, returned the pocketbook to me in bed, bade me adieu, and left the room. Next morning I met Colonel Stanfield, a pilot and pro tem. aide of General Longstreet. He told me that General Longstreet had asked him to find and send to his headquar-ters the best man in the army for a secret but very dangerous service. That he had selected my son for that purpose and that I might not see Captain Ramsey for several days. Perhaps never, thought I. During the day I joined General Longstreet on horseback and mentioned to him the dan-gerous mission he had assigned to Robert my son. He said "I am pleased that he told it to you. But I have every confidence in his success. Wheeler said to me I could not have found a better man." During our further ride he said to me, "I wish to send to Bristol Gap one of my staff who is slightly wounded though convalescent today. I will send him in an ambulance with a guard. Major Wallace and some of his subs will ac-company him though there is no surgeon with the company, and I hope you can go along. They are along somewhere behind." I had ascertained already that the siege was raised and the besieging army was already in motion for Virginia, and all hopes of retaking Knoxville were doomed

to be disappointed. I therefore assented at once to this opportune method
of returning via Bristol to my offices and hospitals at Atlanta. I saw my
son Alexander, and told him to communicate to his mother at Lenoir's
this plan, and rode on past Colonel Scott's old place till we were out of
reach of the enemy's shells and waited there till Captain _____'s ambulance and the guard overtook us. That night we stopped at Roseberry's
Creek at McMillan's. He had been an old patron of mine—only six miles
from my old home. He sympathized very sincerely in the loss of my property and the separation from my family and he added that he knew everybody wished me well and hoped for my speedy return to my old practice.
I felt though deeply anxious and uneasy about Robert and his youngest
brother Arthur. I knew the youth and inexperience of the latter and the
reckless intrepidity of the former. Everyone in camp had a new exploit
of his to narrate to me—one of which only will I here mention. During
the siege he took a few of Wheeler's men, crossed the Holston through
Lyons Island, went through the country to the Maryville road, overtook
a supply train with a heavy cavalry guard, captured and dispersed the
whole of them, and pursued the frightened guard till in sight of town.
Near Dr. Rogers' he lost his favorite charger but captured if possible a
better one, and returned the same evening to camp.

Leaving McMillan's early next morning some of us reached Mrs. Shannon's that night, the others of the company staying at another house. Mrs.
Shannon was a loyal Southern lady and drew a strong contrast between
the Confederate and the Federal troops. The next night we lodged at
_____ and crossing Lick Creek at Guthries' old bridge reached
Greeneville at three P.M. It was the Sabbath and wore the stillness and
silence of death. As we rode through the streets Colonel Arnold came
riding by in a gallop. Some bushwhackers had that morning killed some
Confederates and he was hastening in pursuit of them. Our guard primed
anew and we went on to Henderson's Mill where some days before there
had been a battle between General John S. Williams, our commander, and
Colonel John W. Foster of the Federal army.[4] In this engagement as
usual the enemy's forces vastly outnumbered ours. McKnitt, my son, acted
on this occasion with the infantry. Being overpowered after a gallant fight
in which the enemy was several times beaten back, our foot was likely

---

[4] The engagement at Henderson's Mill was on October 11, 1863. See *Official Records*,
series 1, vol. 30, part 2, pp. 590, 641. Dr. Ramsey left blank spaces for the names of the
opposing commanders.

to be captured in the streets of Greeneville, McKnitt, observing a comrade passing him rapidly, asked him to take him up behind him on his horse. He refused to do so. McKnitt turned abruptly down a cross street accidently—rather providentially—came near to another Confederate escaping on his horse from the unequal combat who took him on his horse and both made their escape. It was afterwards known that the first one who had refused to lend McKnitt his assistance in this hour of extreme necessity was himself captured.

The retreat was continued orderly and with skill to Henderson's Mill. There a stand was made and one of the most gallant affairs of the war took place. I walked over the battleground with Mr. Henderson who witnessed the whole of it from his house and gave me many of its details: three of my sons participated in it. They had been known to him when students at Tusculum and he seemed to be really proud of the achievements of the Knoxville boys. While at this place Reverend John Doak came in and sat an hour or two. He had been hunted all over the country like a wolf—had been in this fight—showed the pluck of the Old Covenanters of Scotland—and having no peace or security at home he sought safety in the army and could find it only there. The Union sentiment was nowhere more acrimonious or intolerant than in some parts of Greene County.

Our caravan went the next night to Caruther's in Washington County. We heard of the lawlessness of the bushwhackers near our route but were not molested. The next night we reached Bristol. I turned over the horse I had received from General Vaughn at Loudon to the Confederate States quartermaster at Bristol and took his receipt for it.

I left Colonel ———— nearly well at Bristol. The same night I took the train for Atlanta. I was, however, so fatigued that when I got to Liberty, Virginia, I could go no further. I had been on horseback incessantly and continuously from Loudon to Bristol that I chose to spend a day with my wife's brother Colonel J. H. Crozier, Colonel Sneed and their families and other refugees there from Knoxville. Much refreshed by one day's rest—the first I had of *real* rest since leaving Atlanta—I took the next day's train for that place. Arrived there I found all right as to my offices. The enemy had, however, been steadily but slowly advancing into Georgia. Frequent skirmishes, almost battles in some instances, took place daily. Our hospitals were constantly being replenished by new *recruits* from the armies below. I resumed my old routine professional duties in the camps and the hospitals. East Tennessee wounded soldiers that heard of me in Atlanta preferred to be near me. Captain William L. Scott, my nephew from Memphis, and two of the Humes thus came to Atlanta. I got them private boarding and furnished them other facilities. If a soldier from Tennessee died I attended him to his grave, dropped a tear to his memory and for his absent friends at home. I wrote his obituary. If one recovered or escaped death, or achieved a heroic act, it was communicated to Sperry's paper so as thus by accident to reach the anxious mother at home. A roommate of ours was paid to act the part of a *deserter,* go into his old neighborhood, deliver some letters to our friends, learn their whereabout and their condition, desert again and join us bringing us the latest news. He made the trip successfully. Another attempted the same experiment, was captured and his letters exposed. He had none of mine.

General Ramsey had fallen back with Longstreet to Bristol. The Confederate treasury issues had been counterfeited. A law was passed to have all the issues of a certain description and denomination funded in eight per cent Confederate bonds. The depositary was authorized in cases where there were no bonds on hand, to give certificates to the holders of these issues which should entitle the owner of the certificates to bonds in the future. The army and the people in East Tennessee had no depositary who could afford this facility. These all came to my son Crozier and requested him to write to Mr. Memminger, the secretary of the treasury, and to me also to come to Bristol and open my office there or lower down —Jonesboro or Greeneville if practicable. Mr. Memminger replied that the season was exceedingly inclement, that I was too old for such a service, but that he would telegraph to me at Atlanta the public wants and wishes on the matter but would leave it entirely to my own preference whether to go to Tennessee or remain at Atlanta. He wrote this to me, but rather dissuaded me from the undertaking. I had this same duty to perform daily in my office. But Mr. T. A. Cleage, my faithful and obliging assistant, at my request agreed to perform all the duties of my office during my absence to Tennessee. I telegraphed to my son Crozier to inform General Anderson and others who had requested this service that I would start that day from Atlanta and reach Jonesboro as soon as steam could carry me there. When the train reached Bristol at night, I found McKnitt sick and in bed, and he told me that his brothers were all below at Jonesboro. I went down next morning to Jonesboro where Crozier, Alexander, Robert and Arthur were all waiting my arrival. An office had been procured for my use. I entered it, received thousands of dollars of Confederate States issues, signed and delivered the necessary certificates and was getting properly in gear when the advance of Longstreet's army entered town and were falling back towards Virginia. This put a stop to further funding there at Jonesboro. My sons put my papers and money hastily back into my trunk, went with me to the car, carrying my trunk for me and threw it upon the platform, assisted me onto it just as the last whistle gave notice to start. My poor little Arthur had sat near me all the time I was in Jonesboro—contributed in every way he could to my comfort. Their rations were scanty and poor but he divided with me. He had determined to join a new company then being formed by Captain A. L. Gammon of Jonesboro made up of the younger sons of the first gentlemen, the elite of the country. I had at no time advised him to do so but I could not but commend his chivalrous patriotism. I put some money into his hands, bade him farewell expressing the hope that I would meet him in a few days in Bristol where I intended again to open my office. Vain hope—illusive dream—blasted expectation! I never saw him afterwards!

I reached Bristol after dark. I had a trunk full of uncancelled Confederate issues. The night was dark. Some acquaintance assisted me in carrying my trunk to my son's sickroom. I passed through crowds of strangers. I found McKnitt better but still in bed. I whispered in his ear to keep his eye upon the trunk I had put under his bed while I should go to Colonel Anderson's, an old friend not far off. Captain Kain went with me, and made my case known. He was commander of the post. He told Colonel Anderson I would need a secure office tomorrow, a bedroom and a plate at his table, that I was a Confederate States depositary and that the public service required all these facilities—nothing more, nothing less. Colonel Anderson replied his house was already overcrowded as were all in town with guests but that he would do everything he could. I returned to McKnitt's room, slept there that night. He was still better next morning. I got him detailed to assist me in my office. After breakfast I moved my trunk to Colonel Anderson's store. He had sold out. He had a good desk, good stationery, kept a good table, had a kind family. I had a good bed and was already well prepared for funding and issuing certificates. The soldiers and others would have overpowered me with official duties but Crozier and McKnitt assisted me through the day and Colonel Anderson himself at night. Thus usefully employed I might have been happy. But the recollection of the condition of the family at Lenoir's, of my sons in the army—and especially of our Benjamin, not yet 18—these made me often uneasy. Alexander and Arthur had not yet joined me at Bristol. I heard the reason afterwards and was proud of it.

One morning, Robert, whom I had not seen since he left my room at General Longstreet's headquarters and entered upon the hazardous duty assigned him by that officer, rode up to my office door and inquired for me. He had not time then to give me the details of his adventure towards Kentucky. He was with his company then on another scout. He looked well and defiant, had another fine horse and well equipped. He spoke with me a few minutes. I asked him to take care of Arthur.

After cancelling the large amount of money I had received at Jonesboro and at Bristol and had forwarded it to Richmond I took the train and again returned to Atlanta. I could barely reach that place after such fatigue, labor and exposure as I had undergone. I was perfectly prostrated in body and mind. But unwilling that any rumor even should be circulated of my illness and thus reach any of my family, I went down every day to my office and to the principal hotels so as to appear to be well. But I really passed through a lingering attack of typhoid fever. Dr. O'Keiff occasionally called to see me and I sometimes went with him to the hospitals when really unable to perform that service. An excursion to Stone Mountain, a picnic, etc., etc., was gotten up and by the kindness of R. M. Lowry and Mrs. Markam I was invited to go along. I did so and from that time I began to improve and "Richard was himself again."

I boarded near to and often attended public service at the First Presbyterian Church in Atlanta. I became, soon after arriving there in September '63, acquainted with its pastor, Reverend Dr. Wilson. Nearly all of the Tennessee refugees attended his church and through the politeness of the Messrs. Inman a number of pews were set apart for our occupancy.[5]

---

[5] On a loose page in his manuscript Autobiography, Dr. Ramsey inserted the following account:

Tutor ne ultra cupidam

Thursday September 3, 1863

McLaughlin, the boss of the Confederate States shoe shop at Knoxville in charge of thirty of his hands, refugees that were escaping from the Yankees, found his cars left at Sweetwater unattached to any engine and that their cargoes, work-hands, cars and all would fall into the hands and be captured by the enemy. Captain Seidemore suggested that instead of steam, the agency of the muscles of his stalwart men be employed so as to avoid capture. The names of these men I wish to preserve as worthy of historical mention. They follow: From Alabama, S. C. Anderson, Jack Harlington, John Hilderson and _____ Bishop. From Georgia, Charles Gray, James White, J. W. Prince, Jarvis Ethridge, W. W. Burgett, W. R.

General Austell of the Bank of Fulton offered me his counting room vault and safe. These were a great convenience to my Depositary business.

Thomas, U. J. Bush, S. H. Taylor, John Price, William Dunnington, Stonewall Jackson, William Walls and R. H. Tucker. From Tennessee, James Derberry, C. A. Mitchell and ———— Page. From Kentucky, ———— Myers. From Florida, Pynem Allen, Moses Buchanan, and John Benguard. From North Carolina, R. H. Holland, D. M. Morrison, Fuller Norton, A. J. Yonce, Wilbern Swift, C. S. Nichols, and from Virginia, D. D. Burnett. At Sweetwater and all along the railroad the citizens hollowed out that the enemy were upon them and urged them to obey the discretionary order to burn cargoes and cars which were now twenty miles within the enemy's lines. The first day they came to Facility (General Reagan's). At this time Byrd's command was within two miles of them. Second day to Athens. Third met an engine, which soon extricated the sons of St. Crispin from the dilemma in which they were placed. I saw them afterwards in Atlanta with a good shop. They had pulled and pushed the cars in all twenty-two miles. It was a daring exploit, heroically performed.

CHAPTER XIII

Rebel Ladies

I will not attempt to describe [my] first interview with my family since the commencement of my exile in August.[1] I was now with them at the house of my son-in-law Dr. B. B. Lenoir. But how altered that house, how changed his interesting family. Lenoir's is a principal and important station and depot on the E. T. & G. R. R. twenty miles below Knoxville. In some respects it is the most valuable property in Tennessee or the West. It contains between two and three thousand acres of land, much of it island and river bottom. Upon it have been erected a cotton spinning factory, planing machines, mills and other large improvements of several kinds. When I last saw it before there were in its barns, cribs, meathouses, any extent of these supplies necessary for the subsistence of an army. The cellars were filled with groceries of all kinds. The forests on the property were scarcely excelled anywhere for their extent or their value. These extended to and embraced the dwelling house and the outbuildings. The outstanding crop in August before promised a yield of _____.

About September 1, the enemy came and took whatever of supplies they chose to of all kinds. They exhausted the smokehouse and cellar of all the necessaries of life, cut down the forests as they pleased, and erected in their fertile fields villas of cabins for their soldiers. They took possession of Dr. Lenoir's office and established in it their headquarters for General James M. Shackleford first and then General Edward Ferrero and General William B. Hazen, General Robert B. Potter. Two brigades were generally camped on the place. The officers' tents were pitched in the yard and gardens around the house. Everything was appropriated by the invaders and used as they pleased. The family consisted of three brothers, all loyal to the South. Dr. Lenoir's wife was my beloved daughter, Henrietta Rutledge. I have already mentioned her heroism and loyalty

---

[1] Dr. Ramsey inserted the account on the following pages immediately after he related his first meeting with his family late in 1863. See above, page 148.

at the Sanders raid. Their children were three. The eldest J. Ramsey Lenoir, named for me, the most interesting and manly little boy I ever saw and so pronounced to be by everyone who met him on the cars, on the streets, at the Springs or in the house. He was precocious, beautiful, intellectual, amiable, dutiful, gentle. His two brothers were younger, and of course less attractive and less interesting. They were idols in the family and amongst the whole connection.

Soon after the arrival of the Federal forces at Lenoir's, Dr. Lenoir himself was arrested and held in prison as a hostage for some frivolous cause not now recollected. He was sent to the jail in Knoxville. His children were taken sick shortly before his arrest. No cause was assigned for this cruel and arbitrary arrest and imprisonment.

At Lenoir's Mrs. Ramsey gave me a minute account of her own movements after I left home August 28. On that day, as I had advised, the family vacated the house taking with them the most portable and valuable of her effects. They went with these to our daughter across the Holston, Mrs. Dickson at Riverside. Late at night our carriage driver, Levy, returned home and bringing with him our youngest son, our "Benjamin," who had been absent at school in Jefferson County. A day or two after this our son, Arthur Crozier, not yet sixteen, went with his sister to town for the purpose of renting a house there. It stood near the intersection of Clinch and Water Streets and not far from Scott's Mills. There they settled. But the Federal cavalry were turned into that and Mrs. Kennedy's adjoining lot and as their tents were pitched in the latter they soon found that the annoyances were so great as to make it necessary to leave it at the end of their first month. One evening at tea a servant came to the door to say that Mrs. Pryor, an old neighbor, had just returned from a visit of mercy to the jail and that she had there seen Dr. Lenoir a prisoner, and that she had been requested by Dr. Lenoir to give this information to my family. Mrs. Breck, a widowed daughter and living in the family, went immediately to the jail taking with her the cook and a supply of refreshments. Dr. Lenoir told her he had been in jail several days and had not yet learned for what offense. Nor had he heard from his family, then sick. When leaving the jail, Mrs. Breck was requested to ask General Samuel P. Carter, the Federal post commandant, what was his offense and to give him the opportunity to communicate with his sick family. She called next morning at the General's headquarters. He treated her with the courtesy becoming a chivalrous soldier and in a short time after Dr. Lenoir was released and never did know the cause of his arrest. Returning home his children had relapsed. Two of them died with pneumonia complicated with diphtheria. They died in one night. Two Yankee surgeons were called in and showed some attention and sympathy to the afflicted family and especially to the heartbroken mother who had lost an eldest and a favorite son. But during all this time no opportunity could be had for the grandmother and the other females of the family to visit or hear from poor disconsolate Henrietta. Her grief consumed her and she never afterwards smiled.

Mrs. Ramsey quit her rented house and moved to and occupied a part of the house of her brother, Dr. C. W. Crozier. He was in the army and his two daughters were with him in Georgia. Of his sons one was killed in the fight as already mentioned. Another was under Wheeler. His wife and two younger children were still at their home in Knoxville and with them in the same house were living my wife, our two daughters, and our youngest son Arthur. He became rather a favorite with the Federal officers and as he was approaching the military age they often tried to seduce him from his southern convictions and sympathies. "Little Secesh" for so they called him "join our flag. The rebellion will soon be put down and the rebels either killed or hung." These seductive and menacing remarks were all lost. The true little patriot heard but laughed at them and as will be seen hereafter he lived and died loyal to the Southern cause.

Soon after going into Dr. Crozier's house our daughter Sue was attacked with fever. Her convalescence was slow. Dr. Lenoir was called to see her and he advised that she should be removed to Lenoir's as a more healthy place. According to this advice and invitation my ladies were taken to Lenoir's. Sue soon recovered. It was a merciful Providence that sent this sickness and thus caused the removal of my family out of Knoxville. Had it have been otherwise they would have had to undergo the discomforts and dangers of the siege. The house they occupied was the most exposed of any points in town. During the siege the house was first robbed and then burned and to make a full wreck of our property everything that had been saved from the burning at Mecklenburg was stolen or burned at Dr. Crozier's.

Early in April 1864, I received a telegram from my son Crozier at Bristol. "My sister Sue has just arrived by Flag of Truce, sent out for disloyal *acts*. What shall I do with her." I answered "Take her to Colonel Anderson's. I leave in the cars today and will soon join her." I got on the train and found her at Liberty, Virginia in the house of her uncle Honorable J. H. Crozier. My first inquiries were of course about my wife and daughters at Lenoir's from whom I had not heard since my last interview with them the preceding December at that place, when leaving them for the headquarters of Longstreet. She told me that they had received a single pencil note from me at Jonesboro, that my daughter Mrs. Lenoir was in bad health, and that for that reason Mrs. Ramsey and Mrs. Breck had the *indulgence* granted to them of watching by her bedside and waiting the result of her protracted sickness and her approaching confinement. But that her own banishment had been early determined on—perhaps to the North, perhaps to the South—she knew not which till a short time before she left Knoxville when as a matter of grace she was allowed the favor of being sent out by flag of truce to the mountains of Virginia. Not to Atlanta, Georgia where I was, but to the Confederate lines wherever that might be—with probably no acquaintance or friend within her reach. The departure of the flag of truce had been anticipated a day or two and she being twenty miles below Knoxville the truce train had started before she got there. All her co-exile lady friends had left the previous day and not one of her own sex was present to accompany her in her lonely exile from her native place and her banishment to a land of strangers. She therefore went out again to her sister's, Mrs. Dickson's, at Riverside. Late that afternoon some soldiers came out there for her. She refused to go with them at that late hour and requested that a suitable conveyance should be sent for her the next day. The soldiers replied that their orders were to bring her to town that night. She told them again she would not go. Mrs. Dickson also refused to let her go. They replied if she did not go they would place a guard around the house and hold her a prisoner.

Next morning Mrs. Dickson accompanied Sue to town, Captain Boyd kindly furnishing his carriage to them for that purpose. Sue's trunk had been packed at Lenoir's in the presence of Colonel James S. Jaquess, post commander at that place, and had been left at F. A. R. Scott's while she went out to her sister's. Major Gratz, pro-tem provost martial in the absence of General Carter, went to Mr. Scott's, asked for the trunk, and finding that Sue had the key, proceeded with other keys to open and search it for contraband goods or treasonable documents, Confederate conspiracies, etc., etc., that a noncombatant—a lady in her teens—could be

imagined to have concealed in her trunk. But his patriotic vigilance and
his soldierly zeal in detecting treason, stratagem, and spoils were doomed
to an inglorious failure. Miss Sue had not any plans of attack upon Loyal
Knoxville; no projected campaigns by her gallant Confederate countrymen against the Federal hosts now in their undisputed possession. Not
even the evidence of an apprehended raid on the part of her five brothers
against the Federal bulwarks around town—no complicity between the
modern Joan of Arc at the head of a dashing scout of bushwhackers could
the chivalrous and faithful Detective Major Gratz make known or dis-
cover. His return from Mr. Scott's house to his headquarters elicited no
congratulatory peans, no éclat, no promotion. The trunk escaped con-
fiscation or robbery, and was allowed to go on the train. But Sue found
not a single female upon it. Seeing this, Mrs. Dickson, as at present the
natural and only guardian of her youngest sister, volunteered to go with
her. At Bulls Gap the train stopped, the road being not yet repaired beyond that point. All the means of conveyance had been exhausted in transporting the passengers of the preceding day. Mr. Walker, a merchant
of Knoxville, happened to be there and proposed to Mrs. Dickson that
if she wished to return home he would take charge of her little sister and
if he could find a conveyance would carry her on to where the two flags
of truce would meet. Mr. Walker could find no conveyance. This came
to the knowledge of General (perhaps only Major Cox) Jacob D. Cox of
the Federal army and when he heard the artless tale of the Little Rebel
now an exile he very politely directed that his own ambulance should be
brought up and offered to Mr. Walker. When I heard this incident of
Susan's trip to the Confederate lines I immediately inquired what state
General Cox was from. That is still unknown to me. But the act was
so kind, courteous, polite and gentlemanly that I risk little in claiming
him as from the South. This allowed Mrs. Dickson to return the same
day to her home and also enabled Mr. Walker to hand over his protegee
to the officer having the charge of the Confederate flag of truce.

Sue here described her feelings of relief and joy when she met the Confederate troops—the men in grey. For several weeks she had seen only
Yankee uniforms, Federal troops, Federal officers, the United States flag.
Yankee Doodle had been in sight and hearing ever since I had bidden
her farewell at Lenoir's. No Confederate had she since seen, only occasionally a Confederate prisoner or wounded soldier passing on the train
to a hospital or a northern prison. When her name was announced, "Little

Rebel, Little Rebel," was vociferously shouted. She met several Confederate officers who knew her and her history. She inquired for me and for her brothers in the army. At last the truce arrived at Bristol. She had never before been out of Tennessee—never before been at Bristol. But when the train stopped there, what was her inexpressible joy and surprise to see on one side her brother J. G. McKnitt Ramsey and on the other her oldest brother J. Crozier Ramsey. The latter, as has been before stated, immediately telegraphed to me at Atlanta this joyous announcement. Mrs. Anderson, wife of Colonel Anderson, whose guest I had been while funding the Confederate States issues a short time before, hearing of her arrival at the depot, hastened there, took her to her hospitable and genteel house, and acted the part of a mother to her while she stayed there. A day or two afterward her uncle, Honorable J. H. Crozier, telegraphed for her to come to Liberty, Virginia where, as before stated, I soon after joined her.

She told me that her Ma and her sister, Mrs. Breck, were still at Lenoir's standing around the sickbed of her sister Mrs. Lenoir—and that it was hoped she would soon be better but that the place was almost in a state of siege from the armies of General Ferrero and General Hazen camped near and around it. And that from the hateful sight of these enemies and spoilers of the South constantly in her view and that from the heavy domestic bereavement occasioned by the death of her two interesting boys her heart had been pierced and broken by an irremedicable wound. I knew her sensitive nature too well to unite with her in the expression of the hope that poor Henrietta could recover. She told me further that so soon as they could leave her, Mrs. Ramsey and Mrs. Breck had obtained permission to follow her to Dixie.

This much of Sue's narrative I heard before we all retired to bed. Next morning I inquired the reason why she had been sent out before the rest of my family and what was meant by that part of my dispatch from her brother Crozier that said for *disloyal acts?* "What disloyal act can you, a girl of sixteen, have perpetrated—surrounded as you were by two army corps of the United States?" I knew that like all others of her age she was more than earnest, she was enthusiastic for the Southern cause. When Tennessee seceded her father and her brothers approved of and endorsed her secession and took an early and a bold stand to maintain and promote it. One of them had gone into Campbell County and had at Jacksboro bearded the lion in his den, appealing in a public harangue at the courthouse to the patriotism and manhood of the young men of that mountain country to join the standard he had planted there for recruits for the Southern Confederacy. Half a dozen bullies had attempted to intimidate him by threats of personal violence. He finished his speech and brought home with him several volunteers, recruits to a Confederate company he was raising. So also of four of her brothers. At the earliest possible period of the rebellion each of them volunteered and went at once to the field.

Another sister of Susan, two years older, of similar patriotic impulses, no less susceptible, alike earnest and enthusiastic,—Charlotte Barton Ramsey, our fourth daughter—was the first to devote the beauty and fashion of Knoxville to the southern cause, the first to sing and play Dixie and to inspire her hearers with a passion for the sunny South. Well can I recollect that when the clansmen of her native East Tennessee began to pass Mecklenburg in small groups, then in organized companies and still later in regiments, how gracefully and modestly she stood in our front veranda waving to the proud soldiery as they passed the beautiful flag of her own making. And also the impressive scene at the Knoxville depot when at the head of the elite ladies of the city and country Colonel Duncan (?) on the arrival of his valiant regiment of Kentuckians in his *On to Richmond* was received with deafening plaudits amidst a shower of bouquets thrown upon the cars by the young ladies. The compliment was so cordially and gracefully bestowed that Colonel Duncan (?) in his reply to the speech of welcome from Honorable J. H. Crozier noticed it handsomely. He said: "These soldiers from the *'dark and bloody'* grounds of Kentucky, on their way to the rescue and protection of their mother state, Virginia, have passed through the beautiful capital of the Volunteer State —our sister, Tennessee—through the young city of Chattanooga and the intermediate towns and villages, and have everywhere been received with the greetings of your patriotic people. But here at the ancient capital of Tennessee, the style and tone of our reception exceed our expectation and merit." Then bowing to the long line of young ladies standing on the platform near him, he continued, "Animated by your smiles, cheered by your welcome—and especially by the graceful and tasteful manner of its bestowal—I return to you young ladies of Knoxville the grateful acknowledgments of my regiment, and pledge you in advance their devotion to the South and their fidelity to our young Confederacy."

But it was not alone in these friendly greetings and joyous manifestations of regard that Miss Charlotte exhibited her kindness for the soldiers of the South. On the return of her brother McKnitt from the sickly camps on the Chickamauga she heard from him a detail of the sufferings and wants of the sick and wounded in the hospitals. As far as she could she contributed to their comfort and relief: and when her own supplies were exhausted she determined to appeal for assistance to others. On an inclement day in March of 1863 she and her sister Susan went on horseback through her own neighborhood and above it into Sevier County on a mission of humanity and mercy. Their success was remarkable. They obtained supplies even from unexpected quarters: The families of Union citizens contributed their full proportion. One of them, Wesley Hufacre, Esquire, told me he was unable to resist the fascinating appeal and the bewitching earnestness of my daughter. But alas! That earnestness was fatal to my poor Charlotte. The fatigue and exposure of that long ride—twenty or thirty miles over rough roads and on a bleak and cheerless day of early spring brought on a typhus fever. The dutiful daughter, the affectionate sister, the patriotic and humane girl, the humble Christian bade adieu to Earth and went to Heaven. Her pastor, Doctor Curry, wrote a beautiful tribute to her memory. No one of her age was more highly esteemed, none more cordially loved. The chasm made in our family was irreparable.

This apparent digression from the thread on which I had entered of Sue's banishment, has been made for the purpose of presenting one of the *antecedents* that made that measure necessary in the belligerent operations of the Federal authorities in Tennessee. She had made Confederate flags. She had floated them in the grounds at Mecklenburg, and on the verandas of her father's domicile. It was even said that with a girlish fondness for having something of her own she kept a flag of diminutive size folded away in her trunk. Be this as it may, it was mentioned at headquarters as evidence of the most enormous disloyalty and rebellion against the best government the world ever saw. It was further said that after the beautiful home at Mecklenburg was first robbed and then burned and when everything owned by her family had been confiscated, stolen, and destroyed and they had become quiet unpretending occupants of a rented house in Knoxville, they preferred to visit and to be visited by such of the citizens as would sympathize in their misfortunes and adversity and if necessary relieve their wants. It was even hinted at, if not openly charged, that this Presbyterian family actually preferred the ministrations and the society of their old pastor, Reverend W. A. Harrison, until he was silenced by the military authorities—then under command of Major General Burnside—and after that humble and pious divine had been banished from his home and his pastorate, that this rebel family transferred their membership to the Second Presbyterian Church in which an old acquaintance, a friend, Reverend J. H. Martin officiated: and that in these churches they actually sat near to, and recognized and exchanged friendly and Christian salutations with the mothers and daughters of Southern men. These treasonable acts I do not pretend to palliate or deny. I was not there to witness them and I am not unwilling to admit the entire truth of these several charges and specifications. Women in all ages have been true to their faith, their modes of worship and their God. And I cheerfully admit that the history of our Scotch Irish ancestors exhibited centuries since a similar constancy to their creed, a similar devotion to the rights of conscience and of liberty, and similar acts of disloyalty and rebellion against tyranny, oppression and wrong. But in doing thus they burned no houses over the heads of noncombatants, stole no one's books, no one's plate, no one's property. With these examples before them it is highly probable that the ladies of my desolated household did all these atrocious acts of treason alleged against them.

But it was further intimated that these rebel ladies declined the attentions of United States officials then at Knoxville and that this was proof of disloyalty. This is also very probable and I admit it. Southern ladies are proverbially aristocratic in their social relations and especially with strangers. They are aristocratic in the true meaning of the word Aristocracy—the few, the best. Of the aristocrats there is more than one kind. In their vocabulary, the first is the aristocracy of Birth, of family. They can never be brought to believe that because an individual has had a grandfather or an ancestry of elevated character, unquestioned integrity, high-souled honor, stainless reputation, etc., that he is thus placed on a level with the son of a thief, a defamer or a blackguard. A second kind of aristocracy, and which Southern ladies esteem highly, is the aristocracy of *Virtue*. A love of truth, probity, sincerity, candor, justice, humanity, honor, and public and private virtue—these confer on the individual possessing them a title of nobility which even the disciples of Black Republicanism would be unwilling avowedly to discard or openly to invalidate. And if to these attributes is added a becoming deference to age, to character, to position, to sex, and to private worth the possessor is deservedly esteemed the superior of the ignoble, the supercilious, the vulgar, the rude, the selfish upstart and pretender.

A third kind of aristocracy is that of Intellect. This forms the grand distinction between the rational and irrational creation. A well cultivated intellect, a well disciplined mind, well balanced thinking powers, the ability to investigate, to discriminate, to analyze, to sublimate, to elucidate, to philosophize, to generalize—this ability gives to the individual possessing it a genuine claim to true nobility. His superiority *quoad hoc* is admitted and unquestioned and *pro tanto* he is one of the *Oi Aristoi*. When to this are added the first and second kinds of aristocracy—that of family and of Virtue we have the truest noblesse of any land.

But there is yet a fourth kind of aristocracy—that of Wealth. In America this is too often considered the primary class of nobility. In Europe it is otherwise. Inherited wealth in most instances is the result of ancestral worth, station and endowment. In America, and especially in the late United States, it is often the result of accident or good fortune, as we call it. Now wealth acquired by honest industry and diligent and skillful application to business in the honorable and lawful pursuits of life is not illaudable. It is rather praiseworthy in the possessor of it—especially if he be generous in his public and private benefactions, unselfish and liberal in his charities, a patron of learning and science and the material improvement of the country and a philanthropist and benefactor of his race. But wealth acquired by fraud, extortion or usury, by ignoble and dishonorable trickery and intrigue, or shrewdness in driving a bargain, or a low flung meanness or duplicity—these debase the possessor and stamp him as ignoble and really belittle him. Such wealth makes the owner purse-proud, arrogant, supercilious and pretentious, intolerant and overbearing to the poorer classes, sycophantic or envious to those superior to them in rank or public esteem. Their aspirations, if such men can aspire, are low and vulgar. They belong to the pseudoaristocracy, the class known as the shabby-genteel and the upstart. If in times of political turmoil and revolution they attain to preferment or official station they become bogus-aristocrats. Their honors sit awkwardly upon them and their assumed consequence not only belittles but degrades them.

But it was further stated that the Southern ladies at Knoxville declined persistently the attentions of Federal officers. This allegation did not assume the dignity of a *charge* of disloyalty. Coming as it did to the ears of the United States army officers through the chambermaids around the hotels and boarding houses, it was considered by the genteel and refined as puerile and ridiculous and in the army phrase specifications were in no case brought forward or urged. Still there was abundant and satisfactory proof offered every day that the statement was founded in truth. The conduct of the Southern ladies needs no justification or apology. In the days of chivalry to be a soldier was to be a gentleman. In more modern times a British officer is necessarily and of course a gentleman. In the army of Washington from that great chieftain down to his lieutenants all were gentlemen. In the Mexican War, Scott and Taylor and Pierce and Pillow would have felt unworthy of their epaulettes and of an association with gentlemen if they had connived at or tolerated even in a subordinate officer a discourtesy to a lady or the infliction of a private wrong upon a noncombatant. The rules that regulate and govern the conduct of men of honor always exclude such an offender from good society. True chivalry would pronounce him infamous and the army code denounces such conduct unofficer-like if not unsoldierly.

It will not be denied that in the late war against the South, the Federal army too often discarded these high-souled and manly virtues. No disavowal has been made, no disavowal can in truth be made of intentional and palpable insult and discourtesy to ladies and of acknowledged injustice, violence, outrage and cruelty to the aged, the infirm, the helpless noncombatants. Instances are not wanting, where *loyal* families became victims of the heartless rapacity and oppression that too often left an indelible stain upon the military reputation of Federal officers while invading the South. It is said that Napoleon, when the French army invaded Russia, cashiered any subaltern of his who should supply his commissariat from the resources of the Russian peasantry without ample compensation for it in French ducats. It was with the same honorable and humane spirit likewise that he bore himself to the nobility of Russia. If they remained unarmed on their estates, their rights of person and of property were always respected. There was no incendiarism, no robbery, no perpetration of a private wrong. The serfs even were as secure in their huts as were the grandees and noblemen in their palaces. There was no intrusion upon the privacy of the domicile, no burning of libraries, no wanton destruction of works of art, science or taste, no profanation of churches,—no pilfering of trunks, bureaus,—and family escritoires, no searchings for concealed treasures, no stealing of jewelry or personal ornaments of women. Such was the Emperor Napoleon. The Kossacks said he should be called the French Czar.

In the invasion of Mexico, Scott and Taylor were alike observant of the usages of honorable and civilized warfare. From Reseca, Monterey and Vera Cruz to the halls of the Montezumas in the city of Mexico the rights of all private and unarmed Mexicans were respected. Along the track of our armies the padre (priest) was unmolested. His sacerdotal garments gave him the amplest protection from insult or aggression by the civilized and chivalrous invaders. He was allowed to carry the host or present the crucifix to the wounded Mexican and to perform the rites of absolution or of sepulture to a deceased Catholic without restraint or intimidation on the part of the victors. The shepherdess on the heights of Cerro Gordo with her crozier and her voice guarded her sheep and never lost a lamb of her flock by the rapacity of a hungry American soldier. The peon brought the fruits from his vintage to the bivouac of the soldiery of the United States, was liberally compensated for his welcome refreshments and left the camp with the impression that although "inter arma silent leges" was an axiom of war yet even in the midst of belligerent operations inseparable from an invasion of his country the laws of honor and humanity are never silent, but that the American soldier or commander is still a gentleman and not a stranger to the laws of chivalry and civilized warfare.

Nor are we without illustrious instances in the history of the short-lived Confederate States of the prevalence of these lofty sentiments and this enlightened and liberal policy both in the cabinet and in the field. I give but a single instance in each of these departments. On the arrest of Honorable T. A. R. Nelson by the Confederate authorities, he was taken to Richmond—not as a prisoner or with any of the appliances of a humiliating captivity upon him but in a public passenger car—with no armed guard around him, either on the train or in the hotels. He was allowed to select his own lodgings and his own companions and to go in and out at his own pleasure. He had been one of the most able, most constant, and influential advocates of the union in the whole South; one of the most devout worshippers of the old flag in Tennessee. When before President Davis no concessions were required, no penitential confessions, no degrading pledges of allegiance were extorted or even called for. He was known to be a gentleman of personal honor and political virtue. Under these circumstances what did President Davis do? He was magnanimous as well as brave and patriotic. To this writer he telegraphed—"Your letter received. I have released Mr. Nelson on his personal parole of honor. Jeff. Davis, President, etc."

Again. In his celebrated invasion of Pennsylvania by General Lee that officer acted the part of a model of chivalry and of knightly bearing. He invaded like a prince and where he conquered, he conquered like a benign angel of mercy. His orders were not to disturb a noncombatant, inflict no avoidable injury upon the inoffensive. "Private property must be respected. Rations, subsistence and forage must be paid for." A Confederate brigadier told me this was the substance of his orders. If on the field of battle he was a desolating tornado or the consuming fire on a prairie yet when the bloody conflict was over or when he was on the march he appeared calm as a summer evening, gentle as a woman and sympathizing as a friend. Ulcerated by the wrongs to his noble wife at Arlington or by the outrageous atrocities committed against his own Virginia or by the vandalism perpetrated against the South everywhere, it might have been supposed that his proud spirit would prompt him to retaliate— the low revenge, the malignant hate, the mean pilferings of the enemy— and thus imitate the example of Burnside, of Sherman and of Butler. But Lee could not let himself down to a level so degraded. His standard of heroism was higher. He preserved to the last his self-respect by carrying out his regard for the principles and laws of honorable warfare.

It is not deemed necessary or proper here to carry further the contrast between the North and the South. Or to institute a comparison further between the armies of the two sections. It is enough here to state that the type, the style, of Southern civilization is essentially and radically different from the Northern,—not only different but antagonistic both in form and in substance. Which of the two has the most valid claim to superiority in my estimation, the reader of these pages will be at no loss to decide. Truth and candor impel me to this opinion, and the judgment of posterity and future history as well as the past will sustain its correctness.

But to recur again to the narrative of Sue as given to me at Liberty, Virginia. On one occasion, while my family were still keeping house in Knoxville, a subaltern of General Burnside came to the door and rudely commanded one of our slaves, Mrs. Ramsey's cook, a favorite servant, to go with him—her services being required elsewhere. The Negress refused to go. The subaltern rebuked her folly for preferring to live as the slave of rebels when she was really free. She replied that she liked to stay where she was with her old mistress and said again she would not leave her. He went away declaring that he would take her with him by force tomorrow. Mrs. Ramsey, accompanied by Sue, called immediately at the office of General Carter, the commandant of the post, and requested his interference in her behalf in this matter. General Carter received the ladies very courteously and at once gave Mrs. Ramsey a note to General George L. Hartsuff in whose department such matters were placed. General Hartsuff very readily gave orders for Mrs. Ramsey to retain her cook and a further order and a guard of soldiers to reclaim a horse stolen from the plantation. The horse was a gift to Sue by her now absent father and on that account the more highly prized by her. The cook was retained but the horse was never found.

The courtesy and politeness of these officers were duly appreciated by my family and whenever either of them asked for permission to go to the country, it was in no case withheld by these gentlemen. They as far as possible mitigated the severity and misfortune of war as suffered by this lonely and desolated family.

Soon after this the torch of the incendiary was applied to the beautiful old family mansion at Mecklenburg and everything the proprietor owned there was destroyed or stolen. Next morning the strongest union men of town and country came forward offering their sympathy and assistance. Such indignation was publicly expressed upon the streets and in more private circles that even General Burnside felt constrained to notice and punish the outrage. The ostensible perpetrator of the arson was actually drummed out of camp and run back to Michigan and thus escaped further military service in the grand army of Burnside then engaged in the patriotic duty of coercing one of the sovereign states of the Union which had chosen to secede from it. Everyone who witnessed the infliction of this idle military ceremonial laughed at the inadequacy of the punishment to the enormity of the crime. Even union men of Knoxville mentioned to the commanding general that his lenity would be considered as a premium for desertion and that the penalty for incendiarism was the coveted privilege of retiring from the United States army and of thus ingloriously deserting the old flag. The burning of a Southern patriot's house and making a gentleman's family homeless and houseless was rewarded by allow-

ing the convict quietly to retire to private life with all his laurels fresh
upon his brow. The truth was Burnside inflicted no punishment at all
upon the criminal. He tolerated the crime and offered thus a premium
for the repetition of it. Such were the indignant remarks of Doctor Ramsey's union friends all over the state. He was everywhere known as a
public benefactor. He had spent nearly the whole of his long life in the
service and in the material improvement of his native Tennessee. No one
had been more active, no one more successful in promoting the physical
improvement of the country. In private morals, in public virtue, and in
patriotic spirit no one, as all admit, was his superior. His private benefactions were upon the same scale with his public services. It became thus
necessary to appease the general indignation against the commanding general for his misplaced lenity and indulgence to the miserable Michigander
who had committed this outrage against the code and usages of honorable
warfare: and a Knoxville journal the day after the culprit was subjected
to the *condign* punishment of being drummed out of the United States
army said with a flourish how promptly sentence had been pronounced
and executed upon the offender, and then, as if apologizing for its severity,
added that Dr. Ramsey was a very *bad* man. In the vocabulary of the times
a very bad man meant a citizen very loyal to the Southern Confederacy
and very consistent and persistent in his support of the Southern cause.
That was all true and he here pleads guilty to the charge. And it is his
present boast and glory in 1870 to say that he, his whole family—sons,
wife and daughters and his whole connection—were and always have been
loyal to Tennessee, loyal to the South, loyal to their section, loyal to their
country, and loyal to liberty and to the right of self-government; and if
Mr. Burnside or any of his incendiaries suppose that by the infliction of
a private injury, in a way so pusilanimous and little, they could curb or
repress that *loyalty,* they have very much underrated the weight and dignity of Southern character and underestimated the genuine impulses of
Southern patriotism. I said this publicly a year ago on the streets of Knoxville near the Lamar House on the arrival there of ex-president Johnson
and I record it here—

> "I never bowed the knee
> "To any Power but that which made me free."

If this is *Treason,* the oppressor and the tyrant of 1865–1870 can make
the most of it.

The true history of this arson is this. The miserable private from Michigan is not, was not, responsible for the enormity of the outrage. It was traced at the time to a higher source. Why was Doctor Ramsey selected over a thousand other secession and disloyal citizens as a fitter victim of Federal revenge and malevolent hate? If he were a *bad* man, if he were a *worse* man than any other of the Southern gentlemen in East Tennessee or at Knoxville, why was *Mecklenburg* the *first,* the *only* object of destruction under the military administration of the illustrious invader? The proprietor was unknown to the commanding general, still less known to the poor private—the instrument of his unmanly revenge and the miserable tool of his lawless ferocity and his acknowledged violation of the well-known rules and regulations of honorable warfare. Trace out the secret history of the whole infernal infamy of the low revenge and private and personal hate. Look especially at the *special time* at which the incendiary arrived at Knoxville from Cincinnati. Learn that the very day after his arrival he was known to inquire for the road to Dr. Ramsey's house—how to find it, how it was known from other houses across the river, and consider the intensity of his purpose to burn *it* and *it only*—and that, too, against the earnest remonstrances of Union men around him and the extreme villainy of the whole matter, including the inadequacy of his punishment can be explained and easily understood. The poor wretch had been bribed at Cincinnati to execute a certain purpose of a malignant prompter.[2] Defamation and abuse, scurrility and falsehood had signally failed to affect the well-earned reputation of Dr. Ramsey wherever he was known and among gentlemen everywhere: and where the tongue of slander had failed to injure his good name, the torch of the bribed incendiary had been effectual in destroying his property. A viper had been

---

[2] The reference, of course, is to "Parson" William Ganaway Brownlow, editor of the Knoxville *Whig,* who was in exile in Cincinnati before Burnside entered Knoxville. Brownlow seemed to have an especial animosity to J. Crozier Ramsey, who was, in his opinion "but a few degrees removed from an idiot. He is the nephew of the Croziers and the son of one of the directors of this villainous bank, against whom I instituted and recovered an important suit, exposing the *father,* the *uncle,* and the entire Democratic swindle." W. G. Brownlow, *Sketches of the Rise, Progress, and Decline of Secession* ("Parson Brownlow's Book"), 290. Young Ramsey was, said Brownlow further, a "*corrupt scoundrel* and most unprincipaled knave (p. 295) who attempted to "get up a company of volunteers, but was never able to muster more than *thirty* men; and, being detected in drawing rations and clothing for sixty-five, he was, under General Zollicoffer's reign at Knoxville, drummed out of the service (p. 302). The irate "Parson" dismissed Dr. Ramsey as "the vain old historian of Tennessee, against whom I brought and sustained a suit for a nefarious *bank-swindle,* and to avoid the damages of which, the old rebel has put his property out of his hands, making this corrupt son the trustee!" (p. 301.) In December 1861, Dr. Ramsey protested to Jefferson Davis against the release of Brownlow from prison. *Official Records,* series 1, vol. 7, pp. 743–744.

twenty years gnawing at a file, with no other effect than to smear its surface with a harmless venom. An adder blinded by its own virus, had attempted to bite a diamond. Its fetid saliva and its poisonous breath, failed signally to lessen its value or bedim its brilliancy. A signal judgment of Heaven made the slanderer voiceless.—

An instrumentality scarcely less base or ignoble, though less wicked and nefarious than defamation, was now necessary to punish the disloyalty of Dr. Ramsey and his patriotic family. A bribe offered to a venal private in the army of the enemy, was the miserable resort of the profession of arms once considered honorable, or of an individual presumed to be pious. That instrumentality was successful. Private property was destroyed and Burnside is entitled to the glory of this great martial achievement. And while he boasts of these laurels thus ingloriously won, thus infamously claimed and thus indecently worn, it will be the pride and glory and boast of the proprietor of Mecklenburg that he was the earliest victim in East Tennessee of Federal aggression and outrage and when asked for his jewels he will be able defiantly and proudly to point to the *ashes* of his old home. To be thus designated as the *earliest victim* will be to him glory enough for one lifetime—glory as perennial and eternal as the infamy of him who inflicted the wrong.

Few were found even in Knoxville, the headquarters of the Federal army and the central point of Unionism in East Tennessee, who justified the destruction of private property and the disregard of private and of individual rights, inaugurated by Burnside after the retirement of the Southern army. As the evacuation had been made without a conflict or the firing of a gun, a generous enemy would have taken possession of the town quietly and without the air of an indecent triumph on the part of the victors. The invaders had met with no resistance. Their conduct afterwards should have been signalized by a magnanimous spirit of courtesy, toleration and forbearance, and especially to ladies and noncombatants. A Southern general under similar circumstances would have made no humiliating exactions, permitted no discourtesy, nor especially would he have given his official sanction to an infraction of the rules and observances of good society nor the amenities or pleasant charities of life. Chivalry forbids such infraction as unbecoming a gentleman and unworthy of an officer. But at Knoxville Might made Right. An order was issued making it a criminal offense for any of the inhabitants to go at large who had not taken their oath of allegiance—forbidding any such the privilege of purchasing or selling anything, even subsistence and clothing, prohibiting the ministers of our holy religion from the exercise of their sacred calling, even the duty of visiting a sick parishioner or the performance of the funeral service at his grave or of offering consolation to his bereaved family. Mrs. E. the patriotic wife of a Confederate absentee, was arrested, charged with the grave offense of purchasing something she needed under the *permit* of a loyal lady who was so kind as to offer it to her for that purpose. There were men on the streets brave and loyal enough to watch Southern ladies, dog them to the stores, notice and report their purchases to the military authorities who in the omnipotence of their inquisitorial power threatened them with transportation North if the dignity of their law-martial was again trampled on or thus ruthlessly violated by these unprotected and defenseless females. Nor was this watching and dogging confined to the mercantile operations of the rebel ladies. Many a treasonable conspiracy was drummed up and conjecturely established by some of these self-constituted detectives. "I saw old Mr. G. actually whispering something in the ear of Miss S. as they came out of church Sunday," said one of these vigilant patriots and loyal lickspittles Monday morning early to the provost marshal. "You ought to double your sentinels and increase your guards. Something wrong is hatching. They are both disloyal and especially that little girl. She is poison and ought to be sent out. Her brothers were in the Fork last Friday and may be here tonight." "Never mind that Little Rebel. I will attend to her case," replied the official as the detective left the office. These remarks were overheard by two female friends of Mrs. E. as they retired after a fruitless intercession for her release.

In the absence of General Carter from his post as provost marshal, another assumed his responsible duties. His mantle fell upon a Foreigner, Major _____. He wore United States epaulettes, held a commission in the United States army, and of course was presumed to be a gentleman. Another detective soon reported to him that he had seen the rebellious Miss Sue actually leave the pavement and step into the mud near the curb stone rather than walk under the Union flag hanging over it. This intensely wicked and superlatively disloyal act—very pardonable as a piece of girlish prudery, and would have been so considered by General Carter himself—was by the detectives magnified into the very quintescence of disloyalty and rebellion and thus reported by them to the acting provost marshal who in the exuberance of his superior love of country, and his greater vigilance over the *liberty* he was here to protect and defend against the machinations and intrigues of the *natives*—men women and children "to the manor born"—he pronounced it a punishable offense and worthy of banishment or even of transportation North. The crime was so heinous, the guilt so well established, that the patriotic wrath of the pro tem provost could be appeased only by the infliction of the aforementioned punishment. A crisis was at hand, a renewal of the rebellion in Tennessee was apprehended. One rebel girl, if not in arms, was yet unsubdued and defiant. *Fiat justitia—ruat celum.* Thus thought the autocratic provost pro tem at Knoxville—the successor of the polite and chivalrous Carter.

Some time after the defiant refusal of Sue to walk under the flag of a country hostile to her own, as was her wont, in passing from Lenoir's to Riverside the residence of her sister, Mrs. Dickson, she went into General Carter's office to procure from that officer the necessary passport. She inquired for General Carter and was told that he was still absent. She then mentioned the object of her call. Major Gratz [3] inquired for her name. Learning this he signed the passport and pointed her attention to the printed oath of allegiance upon it. He rather rudely added, "You must sign that oath," handing her the pen. She refused to sign the oath and threw the pen upon the counter remarking at the same time that General Carter had never in granting her a passport exacted from her an oath to renounce her allegiance to the Southern Confederacy in whose service her father and her five brothers were then engaged. The major then said something about the duty of loyalty. She replied, "I am loyal but my loyalty is only to the South. I will not sign that oath." "Then you shall not leave town." He was evidently excited and more irascible and passionate than gentlemen usually allow themselves to be, even in the exercise of an unpleasant official duty to a lady. His voice was tremulous with an unmanly anger as he charged her as she retired from the office, "You must stay in town. You sha'n't go to the country."

On the street Sue found her sister's carriage waiting for her and she was soon on the road to Riverside. The driver had filled the same position for my family his whole life that he was now occupying for my two daughters. Though faithful to us, he was now loyal to our enemies and was thus entitled to the passport he always carried in his pocket. It was late and very cold. As the carriage approached the *lines* the sentinel on

---

[3] Dr. Ramsey crossed out the Major's name here and in the next paragraphs. No Major Gratz can be identified among the Union forces in East Tennessee at this time.

duty left his fire which he had kindled under a tree some distance from the road and started towards the carriage. The driver, not knowing that he was conniving at disloyalty, drew his own passport from his pocket and displaying it with a flourish exclaimed, *"All Right,"* and was permitted to pass by without further examination. They soon after arrived at Mrs. Dickson's but in a few minutes some Federal soldiers rode up to the gate and inquired for Sue and told her they had orders to take her a prisoner to Knoxville. She replied that she would not go, it was too late, the roads were too muddy, and the weather too inclement and that if Major Gratz wanted to see her he must send a carriage for her tomorrow. The soldiers persisted in demanding her immediate return. Sue still refused to go that night. Mrs. Dickson then declared that her little sister should not go with them. Then said they, "We will place a guard around the house and hold her a prisoner 'till a courier should be dispatched to town and receive the provost marshal's further orders."

It appears that this energetic and superlatively vigilant officer, baffled in his patriotic and magnanimous purpose of keeping a little rebel girl a prisoner of war within his strong fortifications, had achieved the great military feat of not only discovering the escape of a noncombatant prisoner but had also achieved the further glory and renown of promptly sending a sufficient armed force to make pursuit, to find, and to capture and hold as a prisoner one rebellious lady who was bold enough to say to him in his office "I owe allegiance only to Tennessee and the Southern Confederacy." What might have been the result of this daring pursuit and successful capture of Miss Sue, had the gallant originator of the enterprise—the commander in chief Major Gratz—been personally present, military strategists have not yet agreed. It has been suggested by some of the wisest and most experienced of them that if the soldiery besieging the house, instead of occupying the kitchen near it and receiving from Mrs. Dickson's a more liberal supply of provisions than they were accustomed to in the Federal camps, had built their campfires on or near the path to the spring they might have deprived the two ladies and the children and servants belonging to the house, of all practicable access to water and thus compelled a surrender, or at least dictate to the besieged honorable terms of capitulation. But that dignitary, having delegated to some subaltern the command of the pursuing troops, wisely remained in town. The escape of his prisoner from his entrenchments gave immediate rise to fabulous reports that Miss Sue intended to excite afresh the rebellious

spirit of her countrymen, rally around her standard the clansmen of Old
Mecklenburg, build pontoons across the Holston, march at their head a
second Joan of Arc, besiege Knoxville and capture Gratz. These fabulous
reports received confirmation, from the information sent regularly to his
headquarters every morning by some of his detectives. The substance of
their reports was that they had actually heard with their own ears the
night after the escape of Miss Sue, several of her classmates, associates and
co-rebels singing Dixie—out-aloud too, with the candles burning and the
window curtains up at that. "I tell you Major, these Dixie girls have got
some good news and I believe Longstreet will be here tomorrow. All
these disloyal secesh women must be sent out of our lines and the sooner
this is done the better." Such rumors and alarms compelled the Major to
acquiesce in what had now become the general public sentiment—the
expulsion of Miss Sue from the Federal Lines.

This determination brings our narrative back to the besieged house at
Riverside. Things remained out there in *statu quo ante-bellum*. A kind of
armistice had obtained there for some time. The besieging party had made
no approaches on the old castle, no entrenchments had been made, no batteries had been erected. Both camps were quiet; Mrs. Dickson furnishing
the best of rations to the besiegers and allowing them to stay in her
kitchen. The assailants in the meantime cutting her wood and laying it
quietly on her porch ready for use and bringing water from the spring.
Nothing indicated a renewal of hostilities. If war existed around Riverside
it was a civilized warfare. One of the privates was heard to say he was
tired of this war against women. They could do no harm anyhow, and
they should be allowed to go and come when and where they pleased. Indeed, if all that was said and done by the besieging party, had been reported to the provost headquarters some of the loyal soldiers of the United
States army would have been arrested for disloyalty to the Union and
certainly to Major Gratz. The thing had become ridiculous and some of
the officers clamored for a cessation of existing hostilities. But who should
propose the terms of capitulation? Miss Sue could concede nothing. She
was a rebel. She was a true Confederate. She loved and bowed down before the Southern flag and a compulsory oath of allegiance could not
modify or change that allegiance. She persisted therefore in her refusal to
take it. But the question was settled by the arrival of another functionary
at Riverside who proposed that the prisoner should go out of the Federal
lines tomorrow under flag of truce and thereafter remain in Dixie, and

that if Mrs. Ramsey, her mother, and Mrs. Breck, her widowed sister, chose to accompany her the privilege should be granted them to do so. Miss Sue replied that she could not go tomorrow. Her trunks and her wardrobe were then at Lenoir's and, using the imperative instead of the subjunctive mood, "I must have time to prepare for my long-wished-for exile to Dixie and my expatriation from Tennessee, my native home. As to my mother and sister, they are now watching around the sickbed of my dying sister at Lenoir's. You must consult them. They will decide for themselves. But as for me, if I can tear myself from my poor sister Henrietta and our dear mother and sister, I go cheerfully to Dixie. Banishment, expatriation, exile have no terrors for me. I suffer them cheerfully and can bear them patiently." Thus spake this brave girl, calm, defiant and graceful. The terms were accepted. A passport and transportation to Lenoir's were politely furnished and at her earliest convenience she hastened thither. Soon after arriving there a telegram from Knoxville was sent to her that the flag of truce train would leave there the next day and that she was required to come up on that morning's train. Her mother replied that Sue was not yet ready with her wardrobe. Her trunk was not yet packed. This explains to the reader the delay, as heretofore mentioned, which caused her to be a few days too late for the flag of truce. In the whole conduct of the military in these preparatory movements there was an appearance of indecent haste, but my ladies went at once to work in executing their part of the program.

Encamped around and near to Lenoir's was a large Federal force. Of this Colonel James F. Jaquess acted as provost marshal. Before packing her trunk Sue requested that officer to come over to inspect the packing and to see that no contraband of war went into her trunk. He was very polite and gentlemanly and said he would cheerfully obey her request but that he supposed the trunk would be again examined by Major Gratz, provost at Knoxville. This name when first mentioned elicited from Sue some reminiscences and remarks neither pleasant nor excessively charitable to the Knoxville subaltern, although not one unlady-like word escaped her lips. It might have been conjectured, though, from the words and motions of the speaker that she entertained no very exalted appreciation of the refinement, courtesy, culture or high breeding of the epauletted provost. To her remarks upon the character of a real gentleman Colonel Jaquess replied "Miss Sue when your wrath gets up to the boiling point just pour it out all on me. I can bear it. I know how to speak to ladies.

But let me advise you never to speak to these Dutch. They have no conception what a genuine lady is. Pour out your wrath on my head. I have been always accustomed to ladies. I understand them, and know how to speak to them. But, never talk to these Dutch." True to the instincts of a gentleman of refined feelings and of delicate sentiment, Colonel Jaquess during this conversation and the packing of the trunks never once turned his face in that direction nor once averted it from the fire around which they were seated. Though requested to see if anything there was contraband of war, he simply replied, "Miss Sue, a lady is never to be watched." As he retired from the hall, Colonel Jaquess took the young rebel kindly by the hand and bade her a polite and affectionate farewell. My ladies all appreciated his kindly manner, his sympathizing demeanor to them. As already said, at Knoxville another provost marshal—true too, to his own instincts—violated the lock of Sue's trunk, scrutinized its contents closely, and roughly replacing them put the United States seal upon it and left surlily. I never saw Colonel Jaquess but I infer his mother was a lady and he has conferred honor upon that lady by this exhibition of her method of training her son.

The narrative of Sue's varied experiences in Tennessee as thus given to me in detail, the morning after we met at Liberty, Virginia, had failed to convince me that she had perpetrated so disloyal an act as to justify her expatriation. After dinner, therefore, I said, "Sue was there nothing more disloyal in your conduct in Tennessee than that you played and sang Dixie, declined the attentions offered you by Federal officers, refused to walk under the Federal flag, or sign the oath of allegiance to a government hostile to your own? I concede this was all *disloyal* to the United States if your state had not previously absolved all allegiance on the part of every one of her citizens, even girls and boys, due to the old union. Was there not something more atrocious that you had done thus to provoke the resentment of the military authorities by which you were surrounded at Knoxville, Lenoir's and Riverside?" She replied, "Pa, I have no disposition to conceal from you anything which I have done. I confess I always did dislike the Yankees. They are so different from our Southern people. The New England gentlemen that used to visit you at Mecklenburg, such as Dr. Coffin, Dr. Strong, Mr. Sherman, Mr. Cornelius, and others of that kind, were erudite, eloquent, polite and even refined— gentlemen of taste, culture and weight of character, unselfish, generous, liberal, patriotic and public spirited—but I never considered them as Yankees but as countrymen of our own and entitled to regard and esteem. Even for my tutoresses from the North I never cherished any respect. Many of them were not ladies. After the war began, what had been prejudice once became intensified into hatred and hostility. A blue coat and a [Illeg.] I detested as enemies of enlightened liberty and as the tools of tyrants and usurpers. Under the influence of these feelings I participated in an affair of which I make this recital," handing to me a paper headed the *Lost Rifle*. It is appended on the next page.

CHAPTER XIV

The Lost Rifle

The Confederate army under General Longstreet had three days before passed Lenoir's where I was temporarily residing with a near relative. Hourly intelligence reached us of the progress of the siege of Knoxville and of the position of Bragg's command at Chattanooga. I had a few days before bidden adieu to my father and four brothers who were now in the besieging camp. The issue I knew was doubtful. No one who has not experienced it can conceive the anxiety and apprehension I felt when a courier announced that Bragg had been defeated and that the siege of Knoxville was raised. I believed as a necessary consequence that East Tennessee must be the second time evacuated and we, the ladies of our household, would be again left within the Federal lines. It was a cold and bleak December evening and everything outside the house comported well with the cheerless and gloomy condition of our public affairs. The sad news just communicated confirmed our worst apprehensions. The house was in great confusion, all full of excitement, blasted hope and withered expectation. I was standing in the front door. It gave some relief to my sad heart to look from that point upon the scattered artillery and the abandoned camp left by the Federal troops upon the advance of our own

Indulging a moment in this reverie I saw several Confederate soldiers approaching the house, through the wintry storm that was then falling, at a very slow pace. One of them seemed to be helpless and exhausted and was supported by his comrades. At once I supposed him to be one of our soldiers wounded in the fight. One of his comrades asked me if they could get a room for his friend who was very sick and almost at the point of death. His last chill seemed already on him and he could evidently go no further. Though the house was then full and crowded with the wounded yet my sister (whose it was) said, "Yes. He must stay." We did everything possible under existing circumstances for his comfort, hoping that he might be able in a short time to join his brigade before the Yankees should occupy the place and take him prisoner. When morning came he was no better, had high fever and severe headache. He united with his comrades in the request that he should be allowed to remain with us while they for fear of being captured should hasten to the Confederate camp. To this my sister and I replied affirmatively, assuring them that the poor soldier should be cared for and that we would ourselves wait upon him. The comrades hastily withdrew and we entered the sick man's room that his comrades had left. I imagined that I saw a tear of sorrow glistening in his eye [but comforted] [1] him with the assurance that the Yankees should not know that he was there. He told [me what] matter troubled him. It was his rifle which had his name engraved on it and had been presented to him by his commanding general and that he would rather lose anything else than that. He had carried it through so many battles that he was miserable when he thought the Yankees would get it. I promised to hide it from them. The next night after all had retired and no servants being around to watch or report I took the gun out of the house and fortunately finding a brick loose near the basement window slipped the favorite gun through the opening, believing that it would take one sharper even than one of Burnside's bummers to find it, went into his room and told him the place of its concealment, with which he seemed to be much pleased and considered his rifle safe. The soldier, sick as he was, we put into an unoccupied room of an outbuilding on the premises and stealthily and in private administered to his wants. He remained weak and helpless for many days but at length began to improve, was in better spirits, and was able at length to come into our parlor after dark and take tea with us. During the day he was not allowed to leave his hiding place. In some way, we never knew how, on one occasion a prying Yankee found his way into our little rebel's room. He told me afterwards that he got quick into his bed, groaned as if he were almost dying, and the Yankee believing him to be very sick stayed but a few minutes in the room and said nothing about arresting him. We expected him to have reported the discovery to headquarters and that it was full time now to make further arrangements for the escape of our prisoner beyond the Federal lines.

The plan was this. . . . We . . . had to get a neighbor four miles up the river to bring his canoe and take the recovered soldier over to the south side. The neighbor came. We appointed the night, the hour, and the place

---

[1] In several places on this and the succeeding pages the manuscript is mutilated. Bracketed words are the editor's guesses. In other instances the extent of mutilation defies any attempt at reconstruction.

of meeting. Previous to his departure we contrived to disguise him so that if he should be seen by Union men or Federal soldiers his Confederate grey should not betray him. For this purpose I went to the attic of the house, found some clothes that had not been worn for a quarter of a century and selected a coat of the olden style commonly called "claw hammer." It had been worn by a gentleman six feet high. Our Confederate was scarcely five feet—we called him the Little Rebel Palmetto and really he was so for when the coat was put upon him it nearly reached the floor. *His own* papers were sewed into some part of the coat least likely to be seen if he should be searched. He was furnished with money both Confederate and Federal and the necessary provision for his long and exceedingly hazardous journey. All these arrangements being perfected the night for his departure came. There was no moon but the stars shone brightly and he could see to travel very well. The hour of twelve at which he was to be at the river bank was near at hand. He bade us a sorrowful and affectionate farewell, promising that when he reached Dixie he would write to our friends there of his escape and of our welfare.

Some time after he left my sister and I went out to lock up his room, etc. What was our surprise to see our rebel at his door and asked what could have brought him back? He seemed embarrassed, but stammered out that he had come back for the picture of his sister which he had left. We thought it was for the picture of another and perhaps as dear person. After taking a second leave we wished him a pleasant journey. Another Confederate accompanied him from the neighborhood. He was better acquainted with the road. Here for the present I will leave our soldier and resume his story again.

The day after Guffin left three Yankee soldiers again came into the house searching for a Rebel soldier! Oh how we all rejoiced that he had escaped! As usual they stole a great many articles they had no use for. Amongst them was a beautiful Confederate overcoat left there by some of our officers. One of them put it on, marched all through the house, singing, talking and abusing the Rebels, and said he was delighted to hear of Rebel property being taken and burned. I remarked that our house had been burned. He said, "Oh, that was glorious! glorious!" I told him I too was glad. That I had rather it was burned than [that] him and all the other [enemies] of the country to be [in it]. While I am now writing I feel just as I [did] then—so very angry that had it been [possible] I would have killed him. Seeing [him so de]termined to keep the articles he had

[I] said little to him. In a few days Lenoir's [was occupied] again by the enemy. Several briga[des] encamped there for the winter. The headquarters [of General] Hazen were near the dwelling house. . . . One day I saw from my window several soldiers standing in the yard and seeming to be much interested looking at and examining something. I ascertained it to be the rifle of poor Guffin which I thought I had successfully hidden under the house. I believe a Yankee can see through a brick wall if there was anything to steal. How else could he have known it was there I could never imagine. I at once went to General Hazen who, by the way, I must say was a gentleman. I told him the gun was mine and desired him to give it to me. He replied as the soldier had not taken it out of the house, it was not stolen and he could not make him give it up, but that if I could buy it or get it from him in any way I could have it as long as he commanded there. There was an old Federal musket in the house and this I exchanged for Guffin's rifle which I kept as long as I remained in the Federal lines. . . .

Months had elapsed. The scene is changed from abandoned and desolated East Tennessee to the Sunny South; from bleak and cheerless winter, blue coats and Federal rule to the bright summer, the Confederate grey and the ardent patriotism of the Old North State. I had been banished from my native home, had said farewell to a never-to-be-forgotten sister then confined to a sickbed from which she never arose till she awoke in a better world—in Heaven. A girl yet in my teens, I had been sent out of the Federal lines for *disloyal acts* and under flag of truce was brought out to Dixie. Seated in the veranda of Colonel Anderson's house in C. one pleasant May morning whom should I see enter the gate but the proud Palmetto soldier, Guffin whom I had last seen at Lenoir, Tennessee, on the night of his fortunate escape from captivity and possibly death. I received him almost like a brother risen from the grave. I was electrified by the narrative he gave me in full detail of his [journey] through the mountains, the dangers he encountered, his fortunate deliverances, and of his eventual arrival at his home in Abbeville, South Carolina. I was much interested when he told me that through all the storms and rains and the mountain streams which he had encountered on his wanderings the picture which he had so nearly [forgotten] came through safe and intact. On the other hand he seemed to be no less interested in the recital I gave him [of my release] from Yankee thraldom in my beloved [Tennessee] and [my] expatriation to Bristol first and then to Liberty. . . .

He inquired [with] affection and solicitude for my mother and sisters whose kindness had assisted and whose sympathy had [cheered] him during his sickness and confinement at Lenoir's. He shed a tear of sorrow when he heard that my sister Henrietta, his hostess and benefactress, had never recovered her health and spirits after the sudden death of two promising boys but that though she bore the spoliations of the enemy and the privations of property without concern and without a murmur and with heroic fortitude, yet the wound of the heart was deep and incurable and she had pined away and died from its infliction. I told him, too, of the exile of my mother and another sister whose sudden departure from Lenoir's had been hastened by the sad letter of a brother in prison at Camp Morton that he had been captured at the disastrous battle of Piedmont, and that he left on the field our youngest brother—a noble boy of eighteen —dangerously wounded by a cannon ball. My aged mother after remitting money to Camp Morton hurried from Lenoir accompanied by her eldest daughter and came by flag of truce to Bristol, hoping to reach Piedmont in time to nurse her wounded son. They had scarcely reached the Confederate lines when some officers whom we had known in Tennessee disclosed to her the painful and unwelcome information that after the amputation of his leg poor Arthur had died of lockjaw. Guffin heard it all with interest but with deep sorrow. After a suitable pause he inquired, anxiously for his rifle left with us at Lenoir's. I gave him the history of its discovery and of its re-purchase and that when I was sent out of the Federal lines I had entrusted the valued treasure to the care of a true woman and it was safe. Hearing this the eyes of the brave Palmetto regained their usual luster and fire, his countenance brightened, the car-whistle sounded, the soldier told me farewell, and left for the army of Virginia, and I saw him no more.

CHAPTER XV

Misfortunes and Bereavements

We listened to this interesting narrative with the liveliest satisfaction. I told Sue that while there was nothing to condemn in all her conduct, she might well be proud of the *overt act* itself as while it proved her disloyalty to the Union her kindness to Guffin had also demonstrated her loyalty to humanity, to womanly feelings and to her Southern sympathies. She added one further item to her narrative of the siege and capitulation at Riverside. Before the passport to Lenoir's for her trunk could be signed by the *parvenu* at Knoxville it was required that some loyalist should guarantee her good conduct for the interim between her release and her expatriation. Who should be the guarantee? Mrs. Dickson, her sister,— a lone widow, with her two little boys, unprotected and dependent—had been told that if she did not take the necessary oath of allegiance, the fate of her house and property should be the same as that of her father's across the river and in ashes. Anticipating the same vandalism in her own case she had been induced to take the oath and thus become loyal. She volunteered and became the guarantee for Sue's good behavior. Mrs. Dickson had taken the oath under duress and doubtless with many mental reservations. Her sympathies remained unchanged, and were always what they ought to be. She was the only member of my family that was ever reduced to the humiliating necessity of renouncing allegiance to the South. Had she persisted in declining the oath her military tyrants exacted from her, the widow and the fatherless would soon have been made like ourselves houseless and homeless. Sue told us further that after the Yankees had made the discovery that a Confederate soldier had been concealed at Lenoir's, new precautions were adopted against the recurrence of similar acts of disloyalty. Additional guards were appointed, the sentinels were duplicated and a more rigid surveillance established over the rebel family at Lenoir's. This will account for the detective policy set on foot on her arrival at Knoxville and the rigid siege of Riverside. The vigilance and energy and skill of the provost pro tem at headquarters were

187

unannounced, and unrewarded. No promotion of the gallant principal in the affair took place. The ridiculous farce became a subject of merriment even to the invaders. No censure was ever insinuated against the Little Rebel. Her conduct was universally commended. And she herself was gratified in what she had most desired, her banishment to Dixie. This was the more gratifying also to myself as Mrs. Ramsey sent me word by her that as soon as their duties to Henrietta would permit her she and Mrs. Breck would seek a similar refuge in the Sunny South. Under the hope that this would soon take place we all at Liberty concluded that Sue should remain there with the kind exiled family of her uncle Colonel Crozier with the promise on my part of re-joining at an early day this hospitable home of Tennessee refugees.

Accordingly the next day I took the train for Atlanta and was soon absorbed by my financial and professional duties there. The enemy had made daily advances in the direction of this important metropolitan city of central interior Georgia. I wrote, therefore, to Mr. Memminger for further instructions to govern my movements in case of the siege or capture of that place. He replied that he had no instructions to give me on that subject but that he surrendered to me the entire control of my depository. I had an interview with General _____ and got from him the assurance that he would give me due notice if he would find it necessary to evacuate the city. In my correspondence with the secretary of the treasury I suggested two branches of policy, each necessary for the success of our cause. One of these was to enact a law making the Confederate issues everywhere a legal tender. The other to grant to France the entire monopoly of our cotton trade for _____ years upon conditions of the recognition by that power of the Southern Confederacy and of a full alliance with us for that purpose. Several large cotton planters from the South then at Atlanta assisted me in the elaboration and defense of this policy and joined in the application for its immediate adoption.

The General Assembly of the Presbyterian Church of the Confederate States met in May, 1864, at Charlotte, Mecklenburg County, North Carolina. My venerated pastor Reverend W. A. Harrison was with me at Atlanta and suggested that though his Presbytery (Knoxville), *flagranti bello,* could not convene and for that reason had given him no credentials as a commissioner to that ecclesiastical body he wished to attend its session at Charlotte. He asked me to accompany him. I did so. Tennessee had not a single representative duly authorized and commissioned. But I met several of my old clerical friends and associates in early life. The moderator, Reverend J. A. Lyon, D.D., was educated in my Alma Mater, and had often been my guest at home, and had married the daughter of my brother-in-law, Mr. Deadrick of Knoxville. My new pastor at Atlanta, Reverend _____ Wilson, D.D., was elected the successor of Dr. Lyon. I had often mentioned to my home pastor, Mr. Harrison, the extent of Presbyterianism in North Carolina and the size of their congregations, number of communicants, etc., etc., and he wished to see and preach to one of the seven old churches (not of Asia) but of Mecklenburg. We went up by rail on Saturday afternoon to my grandfather's old church, Hopewell.

One of the earliest ecclesiastical organizations in the southern colonies, Hopewell was more than one hundred years old. Hopewell and Sugar Creek constituted in the olden time one pastorate. Of the former my grandfather, John McKnitt Alexander, Esquire, was the founder and the oldest ruling elder and his elder brother, Hezekiah Alexander, Esquire, exercised the same functions in Sugar Creek. It was in the midst of these two then infant and frontier churches that the fire of liberty and of independence broke forth into a flame May 20, 1775. Besides the two Alexanders already mentioned four others—Abraham, Adam, Charles and Ezra —were all members of the Mecklenburg Convention. John McKnitt Alexander was the secretary. We passed the old oak tree under the boughs of which these early Whigs of the Revolution deliberated, keeping their proceedings as secret even from their wives. The charge of *disloyalty* is no new thing in our family. It began in 1775, was repeated in 1785 during the Franklin revolt, was persisted in 1860. May right, liberty, and conscience continue to be the title of nobility to all my posterity as they have been to our ancestry. Incendiarism is also no new thing in my family. Loyalists burned the house and destroyed the papers of J. McKnitt Alexander during the Revolution. Loyalists burned the house and destroyed the papers and other property of his grandson J. G. Mc. Ramsey in 1863,—a common calamity, a common patent of nobility and a common infamy to an ignoble loyalty. The next day at Hopewell I showed Mr. Harrison the graves of my ancestors and told him if I died out of Tennessee I wished my remains to be interred in the same sacred cemetery. Though not related to me he was sensibly impressed with our solemn surroundings. New-made graves of the Confederate soldiers brought home for interment, the occupants of nearly every pew in mourning, the sad aspect of our public affairs all tended to desecularize the mind, and prepare the audience for public worship. The pastor in charge, Reverend S. C. Pharr, invited the Tennessee divine and the exiles' refugee-in-attendance, Reverend W. A. Harrison, my excellent pastor, to occupy the pulpit for the entire day. He is always eloquent and impressive. But on that occasion he exceeded himself. I lived afterwards two or three years in the same neighborhood and had frequent opportunities of hearing high commendation bestowed upon this pulpit effort of Mr. Harrison.

That night we spent in the house of a kinsman in the neighborhood. His son, Captain Francis Ramsey Alexander of the Confederate army, had come home from Petersburgh on a short furlough and charged with the sad duty of bringing home for interment the remains of an officer in his command. That duty performed, the next morning had been appointed as the time of his departure to the tented field. Of course, his return to the army threw a deep gloom over the socialities of the evening. I observed with pleasure the dutiful and filial demeanor of Captain Alexander to those he left behind and especially to his aged mother and his affectionate sisters. He was very tall and graceful and bore a very martial appearance. He spoke little and in a subdued tone. Seated between his mother and a sister and on the same sofa he manifested to them all the soothing attentions and affection of the son and brother, and not withstanding the presence of the two strangers who witnessed the sorrowful scene he reclined his head alternately on the shoulder of each. At family worship his deep toned bass was tremulous and sometimes scarcely audible from the tenderness and emotion which he vainly endeavored to conceal. He politely lighted Mr. Harrison and myself to our room and as the captain retired from it I remarked that the scene we had witnessed below was ominous and that our gallant young friend had a presentiment that next morning's interview would be the last he would have on earth with his family. We witnessed the sorrowful parting at the depot as we took the train next morning for the army of Virginia. The railroad between Greensboro North Carolina and Danville, Virginia was not yet completed and we had to walk thirteen miles—the length of this incompleted hiatus. At our bivouac at night Captain Alexander politely and kindly spread his India-rubber blanket for my comfort and protection from the damp earth on the

roadside, assisted in carrying my baggage and gave me such other attentions as I could have only expected from a considerate son. At Danville
we separated.

He had told me that he had the presentiment that he would fall in his
next battle. This turned out to be, alas, too true. Arriving at his camp just
at the moment to make the night assault on the entrenchments of the
enemy, he gallantly took the head of his company and led the assault.
Cheering his Mecklenburg men forward he received a fatal wound in the
breast and died soon after. His remains were carried back to Hopewell
and there interred. I saw his sword afterwards. It was the sword worn by
his patriotic ancestor General William Davidson who fell February first,
1781 at Cowans Ford, and has since been formally presented by the relatives and friends of Captain Alexander to the faculty and trustees of Davidson College, Mecklenburg County, North Carolina. Of this institution of
learning Captain Alexander was an alumnus and had he survived he
would have reflected high honor upon his Alma Mater. The sword of the
ancestor who fell fighting in the Revolutionary war in defense of American independence in 1781 was worn by the youthful descendant who fell
in defense of Southern independence in 1864. It has been the property of
two southern officers alike gallant and patriotic. Amongst the archives of
Davidson College, this relic, well representing the enlarged patriotism and
the heroic virtue of old Mecklenburg, cannot be too carefully preserved or
more fondly revered and appreciated. It is sacred to freedom and independence. The remains of these two patriots lie within the walls of Hopewell cemetery. Requiescat in peace! I wrote a suitable obituary of my
young kinsman and friend, Francis Ramsey Alexander, and a copy of it
will be appended if it can be procured.

In the meantime, with the concurrence of Colonel Torbett and other officers of the Bank of Tennessee, my Knoxville branch of that institution,
had been removed to Augusta and placed in the vaults of Mr. Metcalf's
bank in the care of my faithful cashier, Dr. B. Rush Strong. I remained
with the Confederate States depository at Atlanta. The enemy was making steady advances in the direction of that city. Seated at the breakfast
table at my boarding house, Mr. McCrosky's, I was beckoned to from the
door by a messenger from the telegraph office to come to the door. He
handed to me the telegram. It was from my old countryman and friend

and at the time the commander of three of my sons in the Confederate service, General J. C. Vaughn, and was dated "Blue Ridge, Virginia."

June 1864.

Dr. J. G. M. Ramsey, Atlanta, Georgia.

Robert safe. Alexander a prisoner. Arthur badly wounded—leg amputated.

J. C. Vaughn

I turned to Mr. Cleage and exclaiming, "Shocking. Terrible—terrible" and asked him, "Has the train left?" He ran down to the depot and ascertained that the morning train was gone. In his absence I had my trunk packed and already on the porch. Several of my Tennessee friends, and amongst the rest Governor Harris, came in. I inquired where Blue Ridge was? Could I reach it by railroad? Where had the battle taken place? Was it probably within the enemy's lines? Had other telegrams been received? With them I went down into town to the newspaper offices and to the headquarters of General _____, then commander of the post. I could ascertain nothing definite and had to await impatiently for further intelligence. The train could not go till next morning so as to make the proper eastern connection at Augusta. This interim I improved in so arranging my depository now in the Fulton Bank as to enable Mr. T. A. Cleage, now acting as my assistant, to have it carefully transported to Augusta, should unknown army contingencies in my absence render that measure necessary. In the afternoon Governor Harris and others called to see me again and to give me such further information as they could procure from every accessible source. Little of it was definite. The substance of it was that the enemy had made a sudden incursion from West Virginia, had met the Confederate forces in Augusta County and with a vastly superior force— capturing many prisoners, leaving many dead and wounded on the field of battle—were compelling the remainder of our armies to fall back into the interior for the protection and defense of Salem, Liberty and Lynchburg, and that some of these places were probably within the Federal lines and all railroad communication probably cut off. I was perplexed beyond measure what to do under these uncertainties. My poor wounded son might be suffering somewhere for such attentions and services as I could render him if I could but reach him. Governor Harris advised me that a further telegram might be expected and remonstrated against my venturing so far within the enemy's line as the hospital might be in which the wounded would be placed. But I determined to go by next morning's train, hoping to receive on my route such information as might make my way and my duty plainer. I did so. At Columbia I saw a dispatch in the morning paper that the enemy was at Staunton River and had been gallantly repulsed by Captain _____. This discouraged my further progress, as that point was over one hundred miles this side of where Arthur was wounded. On the train I learned that though our troops had prevented the crossing of the enemy at Staunton River, they remained still there and held the country beyond it. At Rock Hill I hired a private conveyance and deflecting a little to the left went by Mr. Pressley's, whose daughter was the wife of my son Alexander and who was, with her family, now at her father's. I arrived there and gave her the first information that Colonel Ramsey had been captured and his brother Arthur wounded. During the short time I was with her my granddaughter Nina was born. At early dawn Mr. Pressley sent me to Charlotte where I arrived in time to take the train. At Danville I heard where Piedmont battleground was, and tried to hire a private conveyance across the intermediate country so as to hasten my arrival for his relief. Neither horse nor buggy could I procure for love or money. I kept on in the train. Arrived at Burkesville Junction I found I was too late to get on the train for Lynchburg. It had passed three-quarters of an hour before. As I left the car a friend getting on recognized me and, unwilling to communicate what he knew, handed me a letter and hastily left me. Seeing it was from my beloved wife I stood in the hot sun and read it.

Bristol July 11 ___64

My dear Doctor,

I scarcely know how to write my heart is so sore I am crushed, my health is good. I have had a fatiguing trip but bore up through it all and hurried on to try and get to see my poor son. Now that hope is gone, and I don't care where I go it is so hard it is difficult to keep from murmuring. I have prayed so earnestly and suffered such anxiety for poor Arthur ever since he left me, the most I wished to come through the lines for was to see him. I received a letter from Alex—from camp Morton Indiana he wrote the day after he got there said he was a prisoner and dear Arthur wounded in the foot we were then at M. J. D. The flag of truce was to be sent out in two days and I was anxious to come. I was shocked when I heard that, but I dont know how I survived when I heard he was gone and we should never see him more. I often exclaim what have I done that I am made to suffer so much. I was often sick last winter and was sick after I came to M. J.s but felt better for two weeks before I started than for some time— it must be that I was being prepared for a greater affliction than I had yet endured—

O that God would comfort us under these severe bereavements—I had a distressing time before. Dear Ettie's health was bad all winter she never got over the shock she received when the little children died talked often about dieing said it would not make her die any sooner to think and be prepared. Mr. Park was sent for after the birth of her babe she had become worse he received her into the church and baptised the children the little boy was about 8 days old, after that she was all vain; she went to Heaven the 25th day May. Then the question often arose in my mind who will be the next? now it is answered my youngest and beautiful and good boy. Poor Ettie often during her sickness talked about you her brothers and sisters particularly Arthur prayed for all and talked to all of her many friends who came and nursed her. It has been a task to write this much. Our friends advise us to stay here Crozier is going to get us a house some friends say they will lend us furniture etc Crozier and Mck. are here and can get supplies. Wesley is here to assist us in the work. i have written to Sue. it will take but little to do us and we shall not want it long. My eyes are so weak I can scarcely see to write. May God have mercy on us all your affectionate M. B. Ramsey.

M. J. and the little boys were well—

I will not attempt a description of my feelings at the moment of reading this excellent letter from my excellent wife. No pen can describe them. It was nearly eleven o'clock. The intensity of the beaming July sun reflected from the arid space around me had not driven me to seek a cooling shade before I perused it. I had not heard before of the death of my favorite daughter Henrietta, much less of that of our Benjamin, my favorite son, poor Arthur, whom I was in vain trying to find and hoping to rescue and relieve. My heart was ready to break with agony indescribable and unparalleled. I was inconsolable and disconsolate. Oh, could I have seen these children die! Could I have taken leave of them with a father's fondness!

Could I have received a look of confidence and love and filial recognition from them! I stood there like a statue, inanimate from affliction, hardened by misfortune and lifeless from adversity. I stood surrounded by physical ruin. Burkesville was in ashes. The depot had been burnt. Standing chimneys and broken walls attested that the incendiary and vandal had been there to burn, to ruin and to lay waste. Not a vestige of Burkesville station was left. The charred trunks of branchless trees and leafless limbs stood there as spectres to intimidate and as ghosts to frighten the unfortunate beholder. The trains had left. Not a living being was in view. A death-like silence prevailed and all my surroundings were as quiet and noiseless as the grave. I stood some minutes amid these desolations motionless as if in a reverie. There was a stupid weight upon my senses—a strange apathy possessed me. I could not—I did not weep. If I could have shed tears, they would have given some relief to a heart oppressed by a burthen too heavy to be borne. A flood of grief had overwhelmed it and sorrow had well nigh stopped its pulsations. This stupor produced a feeling of syncope. If I had stood a minute longer in the hot sunshine I would have fainted. I looked for a shade. No one was in my reach. I carried my valise to the foot of a dead tree not far off and availed myself of the narrow shade its sapless trunk afforded me from the burning sun. Seated upon the valise my sight began to return and the tendency to syncope went off. I read and reread my wife's good letter and its pious tone and submissive spirit reanimated me. I began to look for my next step. I had not seen a single human being since the cars left. It was Sunday and the place bore the stillness and quiet of a graveyard. At length a Negro man came in view. I inquired the way and the distance to the nearest house. He told me all the houses were burned for two miles around but the hospital and pointed out the direction of it in the nearest forest. I walked up to the hospital, told the chief surgeon who I was and gave him a brief history of the past. I mentioned the sad contents of my wife's letter. I wish I could recollect so as to give his name. He was from a place which he spoke of as Black and Whites some place below. He had like myself been despoiled of everything and entered at once and with an earnest sympathy into all my misfortunes and bereavements. I found him to be a Christian gentleman, very hospitable to the extent of his scanty supplies—for the enemy's rapacity had been exercised even upon his hospital stores. I asked him to make me useful to the sick and wounded under his charge. He took me to see his most difficult cases. One of these awakened my deepest sympathy and secured my greatest vigilance and care. It was a knee joint wound received in the recent raid of _____ in the valley. Like my son Arthur he was yet a boy, little over eighteen. Like him, too, he was modest and retiring, evidently well raised and intelligent and anxious to recover so as to avenge the wrongs of his country. His countenance, his hair, his eyes, his stature all reminded me of Arthur. I went to see him the more frequently the day I stayed there so as to remind me of another youthful patriot and soldier who had fallen at Piedmont and to inspire this suffering patient with hope and encouragement. His mother had been sent for. I cheered him all I could. He was better when I left him and I hoped his convalescence would continue.

Sunday P.M. I telegraphed to Mrs. Ramsey at Bristol that I would arrive on the next train and to Sue, now at Liberty, that I would call for her there and take her on to meet her disconsolate mother and sister. Time can never obliterate from my recollection these occurrences at Burkesville Junction. They transpired nearly six years ago and yet the impressions they made on my mind and heart are as fresh and vivid as if they had taken place yesterday. The kindness of Dr. _____, the surgeon, and the interest I felt in one of his patients—the facsimile of my son Arthur—I can never forget.

I took the train. Marks of the recent raid met me everywhere. At Lynchburg I learned that, as Governor Harris and other friends at Atlanta had told me, the falling back of the Confederate forces from Piedmont and the consequent pursuit of them by the raiders would have baffled any efforts of my own to reach and assist my wounded boy, had I even known exactly at what point he would be found. I ascertained that for more than two weeks the country between Piedmont and the Staunton River had been in the occupancy of the enemy's cavalry. It was the fortune of war and incontrollable destiny that I should never again see my son Arthur.

The train passed a station called Blue Ridge, probably the office from which General Vaughn had telegraphed to me the disaster of June fifth at Piedmont. The high bridges near the Peaks of Otter were not yet repaired. The passengers walked around them. Coming in sight of Liberty I saw Sue standing ready with her trunks to go on with me towards Bristol. I did not get off the train though urged thereto by hosts of old friends who crowded around my car and manifested a generous sympathy in all that concerned me and mine. Some of Arthur's comrades spoke highly of his manly virtues and his gallant conduct in battle. Some of them had been slightly wounded at his side but had escaped capture and were now convalescent.

At length I neared Bristol. My telegram to General Ramsey had been received and he was at the depot awaiting my arrival. Without saying a word he pointed to the Lancaster House to me and leaving Sue and her baggage in his charge I hastened to the hotel. There I met my bereaved wife and disconsolate daughter, Mrs. Breck, dressed in mourning and drowned in tears. In a few minutes after, Sue came in accompanied by her brother Crozier. Such a meeting very rarely takes place even in this world of trouble, sorrow, affliction and bereavement. I felt, we all felt,—though I could not say it in words—"Surely I am the man that hath seen affliction." The first word I uttered was "Where is McKnitt?" I dreaded to hear the reply. Crozier answered, "At the head of a scout in Johnson County." I knew that was a position of imminent danger for a Tennessee secessionist to occupy in times and places of civil war: but still the answer gave me a sensible relief as he might be still alive. I next inquired, "Where is Robert?" "The last we heard from him, he was at the head of his scouting party, with General Early's command in the Valley of Virginia and surrounded by the Federal legions, with little probability of escape or of avoiding a desperate fight or capture." But I felt that the same kind Providence that in many a past conflict, had shielded and protected him unharmed, might still vouchsafe to him his further deliverance from danger and from death. "When did you hear from Colonel Ramsey?" "Not since his letter from Camp Chase announcing to us his own capture and the desperate wound of his poor brother Arthur." "How are you, Crozier?" "Still an unexchanged prisoner—paroled at Vicksburg and in the hospital here under treatment of my uncle Frank A. Ramsey, surgeon in chief of the Confederate States army of Tennessee. He and his family are now here in Bristol." "What have you heard from poor Ardie (Mrs. Dickson) and her two little boys?" "Still at Riverside—her fields of wheat and oats still pastured by the Yankee cavalry. No corn or other grain except a few bushels of the former secreted upstairs in her house—all her stock and provisions taken or destroyed but her family unmolested otherwise by the enemy encamped around the spring and the barn." General Carter had been so kind and polite as to give her a guard. "How are they at Lenoir's?" "Almost under a state of siege. Federal encampments all over their large plantation and the headquarters of the commanding general in the yard. An immense destruction of private property—many of their magnificent forests had been cut down and appropriated—fences burned, everything in the cribs, granaries, barns, smoke house and cellars had been seized and used or wasted by the invaders." These interrogatories and their answers occupied us the first few hours after this to us interesting meeting.

Afterwards I learned from Mrs. Ramsey and Mrs. Breck other details especially about our daughter Henrietta Lenoir and our youngest son Arthur, now both, as we trusted, gone to rest in Heaven. As mentioned in Mrs. Ramsey's letter, Mrs. Lenoir had never recovered from the shock she endured from the death of her two sons in the fall of the preceding year. That wound proved to be immedicable. Her depression was, as my wife now told me, much increased and aggravated when I and Arthur, her little brother, left her house for Longstreet's headquarters. No father was ever loved with a more filial fondness or a more dutiful affection, or a more partial admiration than she bore for me. For obvious reason she was devoted to her youngest brother. He was the pet of our household. He was amicable, intelligent beyond his years, manly, modest, courteous, obliging, obedient and passionately devoted and affectionate to his mother and sisters. His defect of vision only made him the object of higher interest and deeper solicitude for his safety. After our departure from Lenoir's in December Henrietta became very anxious for us both, often inquired for us and felt dissatisfied that she could hear nothing from us. She never mentioned and did not at all regard the loss of property, whether already inflicted or apprehended, but her anxiety for the absent members of our family was intense and persistent. No maternal kindness, no sympathy from sisters around her could assuage her grief or mitigate her sorrow. She had no melancholy, no discontent, no murmuring spirit. The heart was wounded. It was crushed. She laid hold of the covenant, joined the church of her fathers, offered her children to God in baptism, left her blessing and her farewell for absent friends and quietly fell asleep and woke in Heaven. . . .

Soon after her interment Mrs. Ramsey determined to carry into effect the purpose she had early made to join her exiled family in the South. At the solemn and earnest request of her dying daughter she had promised for herself and for me that we would take and raise her two children as we had raised and trained our own. The youngest was only seven weeks old and would require therefore the attention and care of its own nurse. My wife left the grandchildren, therefore, temporarily at least where they were and with Mrs. Breck came up to Riverside, intending to rest there with Mrs. Dickson a few days before setting out for the South. Before these ladies had recovered from the fatigues, anxieties and watchings necessarily undergone at Lenoir's a letter was received dated at Camp Morton, June 1864, from our son Francis Alexander Ramsey stating that he had been captured and was then in prison at a Federal camp, that his brother Arthur was dangerously wounded and left on the battlefield at Piedmont and asking his mother to send him some greenbacks, and to get other Tennessee friends to help him. Alexander also stated that Robert was in the fight but he had not seen him after it was over. This distressing intelligence hastened the preparations that were making at Riverside for the departure to Dixie. Mrs. Ramsey replied the same day she received this letter and inclosed to Alexander some money. General Carter had previously given my ladies permission to go out of his lines under flag of truce and take with them a bed and bedding and their wearing apparel. Their trunks were brought to town and subjected to the scrutiny of army officials at headquarters. Nothing wrong was detected and the United States seal was placed upon the trunks.

The flag of truce car was a very common box one without seats, no conveniences for carrying water, indeed with no appendages of comfort or convenience more than are found on every lumber or coal train. And yet there were Mrs. Ramsey, Mrs. Breck, Mrs. Vandyke the wife of Captain Vandyke of the Confederate army, Miss Anna Law, the poetess-laureate of Tennessee, Miss Mag. Williams and others. A decent respect to the commonest proprieties of life and the usages of honorable war would have required from the United States officers commanding at Knoxville to furnish to ladies entitled to consideration and respect from their age and position if not from regard to their sex a more decent and cleanly car. If the passengers were, as some of them were, exiled because of their disloyalty would that justify an officer wearing United States epaulettes to expose them to the further mortification of taking seats upon their trunks or upon the floor of a rough car exposed to the gaze of surrounding loyalists? It may have been all right on the part of the victorious invaders, to use this mode and this style of banishing from their native homes citizens of such character and worth. Who were they? One of the ladies, the oldest of the number—a sexagenarian and two—the daughter of one of the pioneers of Tennessee and of the founders of Knoxville—one of its first merchants, Captain John Crozier: He was one of its *patres conscripti*—who had *ab urbe condita* resided there, whose money and enterprise had liberally contributed to the growth, progress and enlargement of the young community then germinating into life, whose elegant and refined hospitality always welcomed the stranger and contributed to the comfort and encouragement of the immigrant and the friendless, whose munificence endowed and whose patronage supported all our early institutions of learning and religion, whose benefactions are even yet felt and acknowledged in the embellishment and material improvement of society and of the country, whose noble heart ever beat responsive to the spirit of an enlarged patriotism and the dictates of an unselfish public spirit, whose martial bearing designated him as the fit representative of ancient chivalry, to conduct the funeral ceremonials observed at the close of the last century upon the demise of the great Washington. "Conspicuous at the head of the funeral Cortege was the company of Dragoons under the lead of Captain Crozier —the hilts of their broadswords draped in black crape." He was the intimate companion and associate of the two governors, Blount and Sevier, and on the occasion of more than one affair of honor acted as the *friend* of the chivalrous Jackson. Such was the prestige of one of the ladies *boxed* out of the Federal lines by General _____ of the United States army at Knoxville. Who was another of them? A granddaughter of the patriot and soldier Isaac Shelby,—the Hero of King's Mountain and of the River Raisen—"Whose youthful patriotism first glowed under the genial influence of a Carolina sky, but retained its ardor undiminished by the cold and chilling temperature of a Canadian winter." (Ramsey's *Tennessee*, page 10 of Introduction.) Of the others it is sufficient here to remark they were all ladies of the highest respectability.

The flag of truce train was ready to depart. My ladies took a sorrowful leave of remaining friends. Many of them accompanied them to the depot. There was assembled a large crowd both of the loyal and the disloyal. No letters were allowed to be sent out, but oral messages and good wishes were whispered in the ears of the banished passengers. Very sincere tears were shed by many on the platform who wished for the privilege of exile too. The train was put in motion. It was the first day of July 1864, intensely hot. But the discomforts of a dark and crowded boxcar were not felt in the fond wish of soon getting beyond the enemy's lines and breathing again the free air of Dixie. Mrs. Ramsey and Mrs. Breck said they felt a relief they had not experienced for months from the cherished anticipation of finding our wounded son Arthur and of contributing their soothing care and attention in some tent or hospital wherever he might be found.

What was their disappointment and sorrow when, arrived at Strawberry Plains only fifteen miles from Knoxville, Major Smith entered their boxcar and announced that a telegram from headquarters required that the train should stop and the baggage and persons of each passenger aboard should be searched for contraband or treasonable papers. My wife apprehending that some delay might follow and thus postpone the principal object of her mission to Dixie, pointing to her trunk said to the major that it had been already searched and that it now bore the United States seal upon it. He replied that he had to obey his orders. An ambulance was improvised and the ladies were sent in it across the plantation and to the house of G. C. McBee, an old friend and patron of my own and a good Confederate. Arrived at his house the ladies were showed into a room full of strange men. The house had been stripped of all its furniture and everything movable. Mrs. Ramsey could not recognize our old acquaintance McBee—his attire and surroundings were so changed. She asked him for some water. As he handed it to her, he recognized my wife and told her who he was. She inquired for his family. They were all sick. He took her to Mrs. McBee's sickroom, where were also her grandchildren around her very sick. She alluded at once to my long professional services to herself and her family and inquired for me. Mr. McBee mentioned in an undertone their changed condition from profusion to want. An officer summoned Mrs. Ramsey into a private room. She was ushered into it and there met by two women picked up from the camp who said they were required to search her person. One of them seemed to know who Mrs. Ramsey was and not yet divested of all womanly instincts rather apologized and said in conclusion that, "You, Mrs. Ramsey, would do the same for your side." With her usual gravity and dignity she said, "I would do almost anything honorable for the South, but this I could never do: proceed though and execute your orders." This done, Mrs. Ramsey was allowed to retire again to Mrs. McBee's sick chamber. The searching process was carried into effect with each of the suspected ladies. When this was done the major again summoned my wife to submit to a closer search. There had been found on one of her co-passengers some articles—Confederate uniform—concealed under her clothing, and this had prompted the re-examination of my wife's person. But the ordeal was again submitted to with as a becoming spirit of self denial and gracefulness as was compatible with the exigencies of the occasion. She re-entered the private room as before and said to one of the august females in waiting, "You seemed to be satisfied with your first search —what do you consider contraband?" "Gold, pistols and medicine and *sich* like. Have you anything of the sort concealed under your dresses?" and pointing to the Confederate uniform still lying on the floor, exclaiming with an air of vulgar triumph, "See there what we got from Mrs. Van-dyke." Mrs. Ramsey carried around her person and wore two pockets which she produced. There were laid upon a table and the search further prosecuted with unfaltering loyalty and with a patriotic fidelity of research that should be rewarded by promotion or a pension.

I have had no opportunity to examine the official report of this daring achievement or the order book of some official, subaltern or principal at Knoxville, who telegraphed to Major Smith the search warrant, but in all conscience let the distinguished dictator of that famous telegram wear the laurels he has so gallantly won. But the search was still further prosecuted. My wife was an admitted rebel. She had refused the oath. Her five sons were or had been in the rebel service. There must be something further of treason, stratagem, and spoils concealed about her disloyal person. She must be searched *in extremis* and her criminality and guilt fully established and exposed. The virtuoso at the head of these inquisitorial transactions stooped to the servile duties of unlacing Mrs. Ramsey's shoes, scrutinizing them closely and replacing them on the pedal extremities of the suspected Southern lady, at her bidding relaced the shoes, and nothing discouraged by finding nothing contraband of war proceeded to rip open with a knife the hem of her outer garment. The seamstress that had made it, had taken very short stitches and after ripping the first yard of its circumference she found the task of ripping rather tedious and fruitless and she abandoned it in despair and was contented with the mere hasty manipulation and digital indentations of the remainder of the hem and retired from this scene of her glory carrying with her the two unopened side pockets as the legiti-mate spoils of war and trophies of victory. Mrs. Ramsey retired again to the sickroom of Mrs. McBee and awaited the decision of Major Smith.

That officer soon came to her and handed back to her her gold and other monies from one of the pockets and the entire contents of the other—her husband's *will* and some, to him, very valuable private and official papers. I had left them with her at Lenoir's when I bade her adieu there in De-cember—uncertain whether I could escape death or capture. The major had not looked into these official papers very closely. One of them was the official receipt of the secretary of the Confederate States treasury for be-

tween one and two millions of dollars canceled and forwarded to his department by me from Atlanta. My wife was aware of its value to me in
the settlement of my account to that extent and had taken the precaution
to burn the envelope containing it. This bore the official stamp of the Confederate States treasury and a hasty glance would have at once disclosed the
purport of the remittance. Major Smith must therefore have given a very
rapid inspection. But when he handed to Mrs. Ramsey her money and especially her gold she was not only surprised but delighted. She thanked
him very politely for returning it as she told him without that she could
not travel or go on to find her wounded son. He was evidently ashamed
of the participation in this ridiculous farce imposed upon him by his orders and had executed his part of the search with the delicacy and refinement of a true gentleman.

What became of the Confederate uniform never transpired. The Major
was more confused at its discovery than the lady on whom the grey had
been found and he was polite enough never to allude to it. It was apprehended at first that the great offense of carrying out to Dixie a few yards
of the grey would be considered as so capital as to demand for its punishment on the part of the United States transportation North. The telegraph
soon quieted this apprehension and the passengers returned to the train to
go again through the ordeal of examining their trunks, carpet bags, etc.
These had been left in the car surrounded by a guard. As she left the car
before going to the house, Mrs. Breck had slipped her silver and other valuables from her pockets into a large provision basket. It required some
ingenuity to contrive a replacement of her effects so as to conceal them.
She took the opportunity, as soon as the carpetbag of one of the ladies was
examined, to change her seat to her side carrying the provision basket with
her. While the search of the trunks was going on she found the opportunity to slip her silver into the carpetbag already examined and it was not
found.

The ceremony of the search was now over and the flag of truce train
was again in motion. Every minute appeared an hour to my two ladies
who were of course most anxious to get on. At Mossy Creek the railroad
was not yet so far repaired as to allow the car to go further. This was most
depressing news. Mrs. Ramsey remonstrated with Major Smith and reminded him that the transportation was to Greeneville. He desired my
wife to write to General Carter and assured her that if he got permission
to do so he would return immediately to Mossy Creek provided with am-

bulances to carry them forward to Greeneville. He obtained the permission and with little loss of time returned and with one ambulance and one baggage wagon took the passengers forward. He was indeed kind and obliging to my ladies, inquired for and procured the best places for their comfortable lodging and entertainment. On one occasion Mrs. Ramsey mentioned rather reproachfully the scenes and search at McBee's. He disavowed all agency in it. She added that the next time she was subjected to such an ordeal she could wish the officer would select ladies for her inquisitors. He felt the rebuke keenly and again exculpated himself from all participation in the selection of the women who executed the search warrant—said someone else had improvised them beforehand.

At Greeneville he rode forward before the arrival of the ambulance and procured lodging of the most comfortable character at the hospitable mansion of Mrs. Williams. There many of the best citizens called and paid their respects. General T. D. Arnold, whom we had known in earlier life, and a strong Unionist invited them to come to his house a short distance from town. But the Confederate flag of truce was hourly expected and the invitation was declined. General Lowry, another polite and patriotic gentleman of Greeneville, called in the evening at Mrs. Williams' and invited them to spend the next day and night with his family. It is pleasant to remember, to notice these acts of civility and kindness on his part to the Tennessee people. The night before this arrival of the pilgrims at Greeneville had been spent at Mrs. Shannon's, a widowed lady who had been broken up by the war. Mrs. Shannon refused to receive any compensation for the excellent accommodations furnished to my wife and daughter and was so interested in the narrative of their sufferings that she wrapped up a new cheese and made my wife take it as a present to her wounded son. It is pleasant to recount and remember these instances of sympathy and assistance so common throughout Tennessee. The early settlers of that country were the best people in the world.

At length the long-wished-for Confederate flag of truce arrived. Mrs. Ramsey had expected to receive through it some definite intelligence from her son Arthur. There was a vague rumor that after the amputation of his leg, the symptoms were favorable and that he would do well. Before leaving for Knoxville Major Smith called to see our ladies. He took an affectionate leave of my wife and was chivalrous enough to add, "I do hope after you quit our lines you will find friends who will tell you the young soldier is better." There was courage, patriotism, and chivalry, all three, in this parting farewell. It was soldierlike, officerlike, manly and humane as well as polite and considerate. His conduct contrasted well with that of some of the same command.

Our flag of truce as it came down to Greeneville had all along its route given circulation to the intelligence that some rebel ladies had been sent out from Knoxville and would soon pass up the road. As it returned, therefore, an intense interest had been excited and at every cabin, house and village the spectators were eager to catch a view of the exiled rebel ladies. The people were profuse in their offers of sympathy and kindness and as cordial and sincere as they were profuse. Lodging, breakfast, dinner, supper, everything, anything, the ladies needed. But all had to be declined. I was myself known to many along the route, Mrs. Ramsey to many who had never seen her. The colleges where I and two of my sons had been educated were not far from the road. We were all well known and not known only but highly esteemed and appreciated. The buggy in which Mrs. Ramsey rode was easily designated from the others. The attention of all was directed to it. The wound of one of her sons, the captivity of another, and the gallantry of all of them was well known in both armies and had been all the war the talk of the camps. Everybody wished to see the mother. At Leesburg an old and highly respectable lady, the widow of the late Matthew Stevenson and the sister of Judge Trimble, late of Nashville, came to her carriage as it passed her house, asked if that was not Mrs. Ramsey and being answered affirmatively insisted that she should alight, rest and take dinner. She said she had learned to be too good a soldier not to obey her superior officers, that the flag of truce was before her and she must follow it. After she had passed on Mrs. Stevenson inquired where our son Robert was. She had heard of his scouts all the last winter and she was afraid to hear from him and his brothers. At Jonesboro several of the most respectable citizens called upon the ladies under the flag of truce and kindly invited them to remain in the *neutral* (not occupied by either army) district a few days, but Mrs. Ramsey's anxiety to hear the fate of Arthur was hourly increasing and she insisted on the flag of truce proceeding on at once. The ladies although expressed what a change of feeling had come over them since they had left behind them the soldiers in blue and were everywhere cheered and saluted by those in the Confederate grey. All whom they now met were members of the Confederate States army. They recognized several from Knoxville, but if they knew anything of Arthur's fate they were unwilling to tell it. My wife described the crossing of the beautiful Watauga at night as the most interesting scene she had ever witnessed. It was the more so as she was told that Arthur's first feat of arms was achieved upon its romantic banks.

He belonged to a company of cavalry made up of the youngest sons of the best families of East Tennessee. His captain was A. L. Gammon of Jonesboro. His command was scarcely organized and but few in it had ever been in an engagement; a courier brought into camp information that a command of Federal cavalry _____ strong was at _____ on the west side of the river intending to cross it. Captain Gammon put his dragoons at once in motion and came in full view of the enemy across the river. Without reconnoitering or learning the number of the Federal force his command dashed into the impetuous stream, crossed it in good order, ascended the heights beyond it, engaged the enemy in a fierce onset, broke their ranks and drove them from the field. I saw Captain Gammon afterwards at Bristol and he told me that Arthur bore himself most gallantly from the time the courier arrived, that in crossing the river he kept his eye steadily upon his movements as he was nearsighted and the rapidity of the stream was so great as to require the utmost vigilance so as not to miss the opposite landing, that Arthur was cool and determined during the conflict while it lasted and in the pursuit he was one of the foremost and the very last to come from it. It was here Arthur flashed his maiden sword. Not strange, therefore, was it that in crossing its rapid waters, in the night his mother should be impressed with the romantic scenery along its banks.

The exiled ladies found lodging and excellent entertainment at the house of Mr. Devault. In the morning when the flag of truce was preparing to go onward, some Confederate horsemen rode up. Inquiry was at once made for the wounded soldier. At first a vague answer was given by one of the officers who knew that the inquiry came from his mother. He was reluctant to tell the sad news. At length one of his men who was from Knoxville—James White—disclosed the mournful intelligence that poor Arthur was no more. I leave the reader to imagine the heartbreaking effect this news had upon my wife and daughter. They had for many days deluded themselves with the vain hope of still finding him alive and of contributing to his comfort and soothing the agony of the wounded soldier that at the worst they would have the melancholy satisfaction of breathing Christian sympathy and peace into his ear and of shedding tears of sorrow upon his lonely grave. For this purpose they had sought expatriation and exile. They had endured fatigue, exposure, danger, discomfort, annoyance, which few before them have ever encountered. All was submitted to and borne with heroic fortitude and the calm spirit of resignation and hope. This hope had proven to be illusory and the dread reality had met them. Arthur, the obedient and dutiful and affectionate son, the fond and tender brother, the beloved Benjamin of his family was dead. Doubtful as had been the issue in this tragic scene, it was still difficult, almost impossible to believe its painful realization that poor Arthur was no more!

The scene around Devault's porches and gates was most impressive and affecting. The soldiers stood around in silent sadness. They had witnessed without being intimidated or disheartened the havoc and desolations of war and the horrid carnage of the battlefield. The missiles of Hunter and Sheridan excited only their courage and stimulated the spirit of revenge and retaliation. But here they were subdued by the grief of a mother and a sister's sorrow. The brave men expressed their sympathy and condolence by their tearful eyes. Some of them that had known Arthur in the camps or on the field wept and left the scene of mourning.

The two griefstricken ladies entered the ambulance followed by their sorrowing companions. Scarce a word was spoken. It seemed almost like a funeral cortege. The chief mourners were inconsolable. They arrived at Bristol. There a surviving son and brother met them. The sad interview renewed the scene of the morning at Devault's. There are some griefs so poignant and intolerable, some wounds so deep as to be curable only by the alleviation which *time* and *time alone* can bring to the sufferers. This was the case now. Six years have passed since these sad events transpired. The wound of the heart then inflicted is still bleeding, is not yet, can never, be staunched—it is immedicable. Time indeed may have assuaged the poignancy of a mother's sorrow, but time will never, can never, efface the memory of the young patriot, the gallant soldier, or the dutiful and affectionate son!

CHAPTER XVI

Some Atrocities and Some Adjustments

It is a relief though in the midst of such heavy and oppressive bereavements to receive the cordial condolence and sympathy of others. Such relief the survivors received abundantly at Bristol. Reverend James King, a Presbyterian pastor there, Reverend George Eagleton, a persecuted and almost martyred refugee from Jefferson county, Reverend John Doak, another exiled preacher from Greene, were all now at Bristol and called daily at the Lancaster House to offer to our afflicted and bereaved family the consolations of our holy religion. The resident and transient population of Bristol—now full of men and women suffering from similar inflictions —all came in to mingle their griefs, their tears, their sorrows and their consolations with our own. Before my arrival there, Captain Kain, then Confederate provost marshal there, had politely offered his headquarters in the Lancaster House for the accommodation, occupancy, and use of my destitute family. No supplies of household convenience and comfort could be had. But the resident ladies of Bristol, whose supplies had become scanty, soon supplied the deficiency. One sent a bedstead, another some chairs, another plates, another knives and forks, some one thing and some another. Colonel Goodson sent some wood and corn. Mr. _____, a printer, sent us every morning milk and butter. Our son Robert had left his boy Wesley; we extemporized him into a cook, house servant, steward, and woodcutter and we were soon fixed up comfortably if not tastefully. Everybody called to see the pilgrims, exiles, refugees, etc., and extended every courtesy and kindness possible. Amongst others Miss Sarah Boyd and Mrs. Cynthia Boyd came to Bristol from up towards Abingdon to see us. They had been close neighbors of ours and we appreciated this Christian and kind sympathizing visit under our afflictions and misfortunes. Mr. Boyd had been with me at Atlanta.

While at Bristol we heard of and saw many Tennesseans escaping from Federal aggression and insult at home. I can take time to mention only one or two. Reverend George Eagleton, in charge of the Presbyterian

Church near New Market, was warned to desist from preaching. He continued, however, to discharge as usual the important duties of his holy
calling. Sunday night he was called up from his bed, was seized by some
ruffians, taken some distance from his house, ordered to take off his
clothes as they intended to inflict a severe scourging upon his naked back.
He refused to denude himself. They proceeded to do this for him and to
wear out several hickory withes upon his nude person. With the stumps
of the withes left in their hands they struck him on the head and across
his face till he fell unconscious. He bled freely, which probably restored
him to consciousness, and perceiving how badly he was mutilated he took
the direction towards Dr. Blackburn's, one of his elders and neighbors.
The doctor dressed his wounds, put some clothes upon him, and sent him
a few miles up the country—advising him to get out of his neighborhood
before daylight for if it were known he had done anything for his relief
he himself would be exposed to a similar infliction or his house would
be burned. With great effort and caution he made out at length to reach
Bristol where I met him and saw deep wounds and scars still on his forehead and face. His only offense was that he preached in a rebel church.

Another case was that of Miss Turnley, daughter of J. C. Turnley, Esquire, near Dandridge, Tennessee. Miss Turnley was a highly educated
lady and extensively known. In 1863 she was a tutoress in some female
academy in Ohio. Her father was a Southern citizen, a lawyer and of good
character. The daughter was of the opposite politics. She obtained the
necessary passports and returned home. Arrived there she found his property destroyed and he himself banished into exile. He was then at Bristol.
She determined to follow him, and her little brother drove her buggy and
they arrived late at night and stopped at Greeneville. She was the guest of
one of the most respectable families in that town. During the night a band
of ruffians entered the house, procured a candle, inquired for Miss Turnley's room, entered it, told her she was their prisoner and must accompany them to camp. She replied she was not accustomed to make her toilet
before gentlemen and begged them to leave her alone while she dressed.
The leader refused to comply with this reasonable request and the poor
girl had to get up and dress before the leader and his gang. They took
charge of her baggage, ordered her fine horse from the stable, the chief
mounted him and ordered her to get also upon his horse behind him and
all started off in the dark. They went some miles to the house of a citizen whose wife happened to know Miss Turnley, left her there, and de-

parted saying that their leader would soon return. Soon after their departure the explosion of a gun was heard and not long after the gang returned bringing with them their leader badly wounded. He was taken into the house. The rest of the bandits disappeared in the darkness and were not heard of afterwards. The chief bandit was very penitent, asked Miss Turnley to forgive him for what he had done and for what he had intended to do further. He restored to her also her horse, the money he had taken from her satchel, and also made her take all that he had of his own—craved her pardon again and soon after became speechless and died. While the culprit lived, Miss Turnley gave every assistance to the wounded man and told him she forgave him but that he must look to a higher power for forgiveness. It was believed that some chivalrous rebel had pursued the ruffians from Greeneville and shot him. It is also possible that one of his associates in crime, dissatisfied with his portion of the spoils or perhaps disgusted with the baseness and infamy of the whole transaction, had assassinated his leader in crime and guilt.

Miss Anna Law, a coexile of my wife, was another case. She was a very true rebel and was suspected of course of communicating with the patriot army. She was arrested, brought to Knoxville, held and treated as a prisoner, watched, searched and expatriated. While we were at Bristol she composed those beautiful verses, afterwards published in the obituary notice of Arthur's death in the *Christian Observer*. . . .

I heard every day a recital of similar atrocities perpetrated by our enemies—superciliously, arrogantly, presumptuously claiming a higher civilization—the victims of which were my personal friends and acquaintances. I became so indignant as sometimes to feel (unchristian as it was) a spirit of retaliation. An eye for an eye, a tooth for a tooth. But our Savior said, "I say unto you love your enemies and pray for them which despitefully use you and persecute you." This is the highest proof that the Christian religion is divine. It is certainly not of this world.

But public duties required my services elsewhere. I kept myself in constant communication by telegraph with Atlanta. I found it necessary to return to my office as depositary. I tore myself, therefore, from my family at Bristol and went south. Taking the train I got to Staunton River. The bridge there was still unfinished. Passengers going or coming got out of the cars there on either side and were allowed a few minutes to walk over the bridge in its unfinished condition,—a mere skeleton, sills and sleepers without a plank or floor, with perhaps a space of eighty feet between the passengers and the river below you. I had, besides, a small money box in my hand. The young men all passed me on the bridge. The whistle had sounded and I must not be left. At the center there was an opening or chasm perhaps fifty or eighty feet across with a single streamer on which to walk. I kept the erect posture half across this chasm—the slightest vertigo or the smallest departure from the erect posture or the center of gravity and I would have been precipitated into the river below me. I realized this all. I steadied myself, set my money box on the streamer, got astride of it, pushed the box before me and thus crossed the bridge safely. A Confederate soldier helped me onto the car while on the point of starting. I have ever considered that in this crossing I underwent the greatest danger of my whole life.

Arrived at Atlanta I found the Federal army ready to invest the city. The wounded and sick had already been sent out to the interior hospitals and I could see other preparations to evacuate the place. I called again at the headquarters and the general commanding assured me he would give me timely warning of his movements. I made some heavy army payments, balanced my books, and packed up everything. Next morning the general sent one of his aides early to me saying that the enemy's shells were already falling within the city. I asked for a guard to come immediately to the Bank of Fulton. Mr. Cleage procured a dray. I put my assets on it—put them on the express car. With my guard I entered it, took leave of my friends and bade adieu to the Gate City. We were soon at Decatur, the first station. Here I noticed that while waiting for wood and water the enemy was erecting a battery on an imminence east or northeast of the village. I called the attention of the conductor to the battery. The whistle was sounded sharply and the train was at once in motion and before we had gone a mile the battery opened upon Decatur. We had made a narrow escape. During our trip some delays had occurred and we did not reach Augusta till nearly daylight. I waited at the depot till I could procure a dray. I took the depository to the bank of Mr. Metcalf who was also a Confederate States depositary. The doors were not of course yet opened. I put the chests on the steps of his vaultroom door, placed my guard around them and went and got my breakfast and returned and waited there till the cashier arrived and let me in. My funds were kept afterwards in this same vault of Mr. Metcalf, though my books, office papers and letters were kept in the counting room of General T. W. Flemming—on _____ Street near the river. Besides being a depositary he was also a commission merchant. His counting room had been extemporized by my cashier, Dr. Strong, as his place of business for our branch. He, however, deposited its money, coin, and issues with Mr. Metcalf. This now became the headquarters of all our Tennessee friends now in the South.[1] Amongst others my wife's nephew, E. W. Crozier, came in from the camp sick. He remained till he had recovered.

While at Bristol I had determined if the enemy got possession of Atlanta and should threaten Augusta I would move the two offices I held to Columbia first and afterwards to Charlotte, North Carolina, and there establish for a time at least the Confederate States depository and the Knoxville branch. It had become evident that Sherman's march to the sea would sooner or later take place, and in my own opinion Charlotte would be the last place in the South which could be held, and if I had to be captured or be forced to surrender I would as soon this should occur at Charlotte as any other point. When, therefore, Macon and Savannah fell it became evident that Augusta, vulnerable as it was both by land and water, must also fall before the invading army. Some of us had one small ray of hope that if the Federal forces should be so scattered and distributed as to favor the policy we would endeavor to strike through the intermediate country and carry our assets to the Trans-Mississippi, penetrate the best way we could, reach the headquarters of General Kirby Smith and thus escape to Texas or Mexico and thus keep the Confederate cause alive and its flag unfurled. Such a subdivision of the Federal forces though had not yet occurred and perhaps would not, and our funds were accordingly taken first to Columbia and then to Charlotte. I had written to the secretary of the treasury to give me permission to occupy the mint. He replied that that institution, buildings, vault and all, had been transferred to the Confederate States navy department and was now under the control of Captain Ramsey of the Confederate Navy. I called to see this officer

---

[1] From Augusta, Dr. Ramsey wrote to his son, Crozier, on September 1, 1864, that "The news are discouraging today from Atlanta, and I am on the point of leaving by this evening's train for Macon to bring away the specie of our branch to Augusta or perhaps to Charlotte. I will try to induce Torbett to bring off all his assets too. A big fight will come off at Jonesboro, Georgia today or soon. Crozier, if any raid threatens Bristol, let your Ma and the rest come in the direction of Charlotte in time to escape it." Later, Dr. Ramsey added a note to this letter: "This raid, though then apprehended by me at Augusta, did not take place till near the end of that year (1864). I was anxious all the time at the exposed and defenseless condition of my family then at Bristol. On this account I had removed them to Charlotte, though no entreaties of ours could induce our son Crozier to come more to the interior. I did not mention at the proper place that, as herein stated, I did go to Macon and persuaded Colonel Torbett to transport all his assets as well as the specie of the Knoxville branch from Macon, which he did."

at the mint in Charlotte, his headquarters, and was allowed to have part of his vault—the rooms all being occupied for other purposes. The assets had been temporarily placed by Mr. Fisher, cashier of our mother bank, Dr. Strong, my own cashier, Mr. Wilcox, cashier at _____, and other officials of the Bank of Tennessee in the vault of _____ on Tryon Street. Afterwards they were moved to the mint. I opened my depository by the kindness of Colonel Williams, cashier of the Bank of Charlotte, in his banking house.

In September (?) I went to Bristol for my family. While there I went below to the headquarters of General Vaughn and met several of the other survivors of the disastrous battle of Piedmont where poor Arthur fell, and learned some details of the fight I had not known before. The general had recovered from his wound. In my absence to Georgia he and Captain Gammon and others had called to see my family at Bristol. Captain Gammon said to my wife that Arthur was the favorite of his company and the idol of his officers, that when the order came to him to dismount his men and take the cars for Piedmont, he and his officers all wished Arthur, on account of his defect of vision and of his extreme youth, to remain behind and take care of the horses. The gallant boy replied he did not join the army to take care of horses and he declined that service. They afterwards, when taking the train, earnestly renewed the request for him not to go with them. He still persisted in refusing to remain in camp while others were going to Virginia to fight. They had to yield to his own preferences. After these dismounted cavalry left the cars a fatiguing march and countermarch had to be endured before they could reach the advancing enemy who outnumbered the Confederates in the proportion of four to one. General Williams was in chief command and determined to fight where he was, notwithstanding the disparity of numbers and the unfavorable nature of the ground and his position. General Vaughn dissented and advised him to fall back to _____ a more favorable position. The enemy advanced in full force and the battle took place. Our general fell early in the fight. General Vaughn was wounded but was able to conduct the retreat. Captain Gammon and his command received no orders to fall back and received the assault of the enemy in full force. They maintained their ground stubbornly, and lost, of course, a disproportionate number of men. Arthur was loading and firing in the most exposed part of the hotly contested field. Captain Gammon was near him when a cannon ball struck Arthur's leg near the ankle and he fell.

Though wounded himself the captain bore him a short distance to the root of a tree. He could be carried no further. But as our forces fell back and passed the tree where he lay he asked them not to let him be left so as to fall into the hands of the Yankees. Alas, such is the fortune of war! He did fall into their hands, was captured on the field and with two hundred fifty-four other wounded were scattered about the neighborhood in extemporized hospitals and left to the care of *two* army United States surgeons. This was the extreme of cruelty, inhumanity and dishonor on the part of a *victorious* enemy. Honor, humanity, civilization, would have assigned to the relief of two hundred fifty-four badly wounded soldiers left on the field where they fell gloriously and bravely fighting to the last, at least twenty-five competent surgeons. It will remain as a stigma upon the character of General David Hunter,[2] the Federal commander, that when thus victorious he could spare only two surgeons to attend to the vanquished and wounded. It was unofficerlike and exhibits little of genuine courage, magnanimity or chivalry. His epaulettes should be torn from his shoulders and tramped upon into the ground.

These indignant remarks will be fully excused when I add that though Arthur's leg was splintered and nearly shot off on Sunday the fifth of June his leg was not amputated till 10 the __th. Mrs. Ramsey, hearing the name of the kind family near _____ to whose house he was taken and where he died wrote to them to ascertain the details of his sufferings. . . . It was so ordered in the merciful Providence of God that one of our Knoxville neighbors, Wm. Engles, a venerable member of our church, was now in the neighborhood of the battleground, a refugee from vandalism at home. . . . He, Christian-like, visited him on his death bed, prayed with him, pointed him to Jesus our Mediator and Savior, and saw him decently interred at _____, Augusta County, Virginia.

From others, too, who survived the fight I obtained similar accounts of his gallantry and his devotion to the Confederate service. I met in Georgia a Mr. Taylor of Jefferson County with whom Arthur had boarded while at Mr. Wilson's school. Like most of the citizens of wealth and character he had expoused the Southern cause and was now with me a co-refugee and an exile. He refused to take any compensation for Arthur's

---

[2] Dr. Ramsey left a blank for the name of the Federal commander. Major-General David Hunter commanded the United States' forces in the Lynchburg campaign, May 26–June 29, 1864, and was in active command on the field at the engagement at Piedmont, Virginia, on July 5. Brigadier General William E. Jones, C.S.A., was killed on the field. *Official Records,* series 1, vol. 37, part 1, pp. 94–95.

boarding. He delighted in his company and that was compensation enough. He was so amiable, so polite, so mannerly, so diligent in his studies. He said further that Arthur always read his Bible, and especially on Sundays when his other boarders were visiting about, and that he was the best and most agreeable boy he ever saw, and that on one occasion when some Union men were depredating upon Southern men in his neighborhood he raised some volunteers and went in pursuit. Arthur proposed to lay down his books and go with them after these offenders. Mr. Taylor gave him one of his rifles and he went along, driving the culprits back into Sevier county. He shed tears when I told him Arthur was shot down with a rifle in his hand.

Arthur was under age when he died. I had not of course given him any of my real estate but had devised to him in my will an excellent farm above me on Holston. After his death I determined to give that farm on which to found an asylum for the education and support of the children of such Tennessee soldiers as had lost their lives in the Confederate service. When in March of 1869 I visited Knoxville I found that that farm had, with nearly all my real estate, been sold during Yankee rule there and was still alienated. If I should recover it, the sacred object to which I had consecrated it, shall still be carried into effect. It is a relief to even hope it may some day be accomplished.

Arthur had two other brothers in the same fight with him. One of them, Alexander, was taken prisoner and was the same day hurried off to Camp Morton in Indiana. The details of his march there and of his imprisonment will be given on a future page. The other brother Robert, captain of some scouts, was in another part of the field on horseback and of course not present when Arthur fell. After our forces retired he heard that Alexander was a prisoner and Arthur left on the field dangerously wounded. He immediately turned back and in the darkness of the night went over the battleground and the surrounding neighborhood where the wounded Confederates were but not a word could he hear of his wounded brother. His intention was to rescue him at the cost of his life. During his rambles he crossed some river twice, but could not find him. Next day he overtook our men, who being organized and reinforced were now in vigorous pursuit of the enemy, overtook them at Liberty, Virginia, pushed them through Liberty so earnestly as not to allow them time to plunder the noncombatants. His sister Sue was looking on the fight and route of the Yankees from the veranda of the house where she was with her aunt, Mrs.

Crozier, and her children looking on. It was fun and frolic to Robert who was avenging the disasters at Piedmont a few days before. It was as they passed "Blue Ridge" that General Vaughn telegraphed me at Atlanta "Robert safe, Alexander a prisoner. Arthur wounded," etc. Robert pursued them nearly to Lynchburg and eventually across the Blue Ridge into the valley.

While at General Vaughn's headquarters at Zollicoffer I met there, besides others, Mrs. Vaughn. The story of her wrongs ought to be preserved. It places in agreeable contrast Southern and Northern character. I can here only say by way of comment that if General Lee had captured Mrs. Meade in Pennsylvania and she, after her capture, had denounced the Confederacy and its civil and military officers and their measures *ad libitum,* even then the wife of General Meade would have been treated with the respect and consideration due to a lady. If she desired to be sent to the United States from the conquered territory General Lee would have sent her out, not in an old filthy boxcar, but in a splendid coach and four and under a guard of honor and the guard of honor would have been under the command of an admitted gentleman. What has become of the chivalry of the grand *old* army of the once United States? Contrast, too, the conduct of General Sam Houston when he captured Santa Anna with that of the United States authorities when President Davis was their prisoner. Although trained in the backwoods of Tennessee and at the end of the last century, General Houston had the manliness and the magnanimity to send his prisoner to Washington in a retinue of gentlemen with not one circumstance about him that was humiliating, much less degrading. What has become of the lessons taught to modern American heroes by George Washington, Andrew Jackson, and Robert E. Lee? Where is the civilization of our earlier periods? And echo answers, "Where?"

I left Zollicoffer and returned to Bristol impressed with the most painful apprehensions of the humiliating, degarding, oppressive, unjust and cruel treatment in store for the South should it be subjugated by the lowflung political leaders of Mr. Lincoln and the arbitrary and despotic chieftains of his army. These apprehensions I have lived to see realized. Political leaders, hatched into consequence by the accidents and contingencies of a revolution, army commanders hatched into power and authority by the sunshine of a tyrant's favor or the corrupt patronage of a venal department of government—what can be expected from them but misrule, tyranny, injustice, violence and wrong, venality, corruption and crime! Oh my country to what depths of infamy and ruin hath thou fallen!

"And in that deep, a lower deep,"
"Still threatening to devour us, opens wide."

A short time after this we left Bristol for the South. General Ramsey was still in the hospital then under the care of Dr. F. A. Ramsey. I advised him to come south with us. But he still hoped to be exchanged and enter upon his military services again and concluded to remain. I parted with him in sorrow. His lumbago it distressed us to see. Though still a young man he did not stand straight and erect. Using a staff he walked with us at night to the depot. I left him alone a minute with his mother. When I returned both were affected to tears. Our parting was painful. He promised to come to see us at Charlotte and we said good-by! At Liberty we spent a day with Colonel Crozier and his family. Next day we took the train. At Burkesville Junction I recalled to mind the mental sufferings and the parental griefs I had experienced there in July. We were soon at Charlotte. That place was crowded. We spent the night with a kinsman, Colonel B. W. Alexander—the next day with the family of a cousin of mine, Dr. Moses Winslow Alexander, now deceased. They were all dressed in mourning for the Confederate dead of their connections. At church the whole congregation wore black. Next day, leaving Sue at Colonel Alexander's, Mrs. Ramsey, Mrs. Breck and myself went to the country. We inquired for boarding but the country had scarcely subsistence for itself. We called at another kinsman, John Ramsey Alexander. They were all too in mourning for their brave son Captain Francis Ramsey Alexander who had fallen at Petersburg. We stopped at night at Mrs. A. B. Alexander's, the bereaved widow of another kinsman. Her sons were all in the southern army—as chaplain, surgeon, and commissary. One of her daughters about eleven years old and herself constituted her whole family except Mr. and Mrs. Chilton, an aged couple, refugees from Tennessee. The house was large, some better supplied with provisions and servants than we had yet met with. Mrs. Alexander proposed to board us for Mrs. Breck's services as the governess of her daughter Charlotte. I had to stay, of course, in Charlotte to attend to my depository and bank correspondence. Five nights in the week I was with Sue at Colonel Alexander's. The remaining two I was with my family at Mrs. Alexander's in the country, and to be more with them I often went out Friday night instead of Saturday night.

Once I took Mrs. Ramsey down to York District, South Carolina to see our daughter and her children—the family of our son F. Alexander Ramsey, now a prisoner at Camp Morton. I left Mrs. Ramsey there. While there she took sick and I was written to. I found her better but I brought her back to North Carolina. Confederate soldiers from Tennessee called frequently to see me in Charlotte and my family in the country. My pecuniary resources were small and daily becoming smaller. My salary was $1,500 as depositary and much smaller as president of a *bank on wheels*. But I was never so poor as to say to a transient Tennessee Confederate "No!" if he needed money. I was often in the hospital at Charlotte as surgeon, and took some professional cases in town and country. Mrs. Ramsey wished to employ her time more usefully and actively accepted an invitation from Mr. Theopilus Cannon near Concord to come there and give lessons to his children. He sent his carriage to take her and her trunks to Cabarrus. He was an elder of Poplar Tent and near to the church. She had been thoroughly educated at Salem, North Carolina, and was fully competent to discharge the duties and functions of a teacher. Besides, she was as loyal to the South as I was and could not hesitate to submit to annoyances and discomforts imposed by our exile. I never heard her murmur or complain. Throughout her whole life she had had not plenty only but profusion. But now, as bold as Julius Caesar and as calm as a Christian martyr she faced poverty and destitution with fortitude and resignation. One day before she left Mrs. Alexander's who should step in but our son Robert. He had been sent by General Wheeler from the mountains of Virginia to rest and recruit his horses in the grain counties of North Carolina. Next day he came on to Charlotte to see me. He overtook on the way a co-refugee from Chattanooga, Tennessee, Captain John, going also to Charlotte. They were soon well acquainted and came opposite to the office inquiring if I was within. I went to the door. Robert in a heavy winter overcoat captured from a Yankee I could scarcely recognize. It was a most agreeable surprise. I returned with him to the country. Several of his comrades joined us in the evening—amongst others Pryor Harris, ——— Morris, and others belonging to the company of scouts. They amused and interested us with a recital of their scouts and raids at and above Knoxville and old Mecklenburg the winter before. I do not mention them here. But must all these brave men did nothing which was not soldierly, chivalrous and honorable.

The same morning on which Mrs. Ramsey left to go to her new engagement in Cabarrus I saw J. H. Crozier passing up the road. He was without saddle or bridle, only a halter. His shoes were worn out. I said to him, "Jonny, you must be out of money." He replied, "So I am." I handed him $20.00. I wanted him to stop at Mrs. Alexander's but as I had told him his aunt had left for Mr. Cannon's he preferred to follow her carriage track and overtake her. He went on—did overtake her, and spent the night with her there.[3] Other soldiers from Knoxville and from Tennessee frequently called at Mr. Cannon's and met a cordial welcome.

----

[3] Mrs. Ramsey began a diary on the day that she entered on her new duties. She kept it with some regularity for a couple of years, and thereafter she wrote in it intermittently for some years. The last dated entry is September 23, 1885. A number of undated reminiscences relate to her experiences in Knoxville and Mecklenburg in 1863 and 1864.

The first entry was dated March 6, 1865: "Arrived here at Mr. Cannon's this evening. My son, J. G. McK, came with me. This is a pleasant place, kind and hospitable people. After dark my nephew John Crozier came. We were very glad to see him. The last time was at our own home almost two years. Then my dear son Arthur was with us. My heart yearned to this young boy. His presence brought up many sad recollections, and I wish I could do something for him. It is little I can do now for our soldiers. He was riding without a saddle, had no overcoat, was cheerful."

A typed copy of the "Journal of Mrs. J. G. M. Ramsey" is in the McClung Collection of the Lawson McGhee Library.

CHAPTER XVII

Exile's Retreat

Every alternate week after Mrs. Ramsey went to Mr. Cannon's I went by rail to see her. Sherman was advancing through and desolating South Carolina and my office was in such danger as to lead me to prepare for a further hegira. He made a feint towards Charlotte. Everybody was expecting his arrival there. Colonel Alexander and myself went up the Beatty's ford, as far as Hopewell. In passing I noticed several pits near the road which had once been dug in prospecting for gold but had been long since abandoned. I prospected some too and examined how far I could make these pits subserve the purpose of—not extracting golden ore from them but to deposit coin in them. A few, very few, of the *toil* were said to live in the neighborhood and I considered it rather hazardous to make even a temporary deposit of my assets there. I went to Henderson Ferry a few miles further and found a very suitable point below it on the Catawba where my treasure could be sunk in a deep place near its western bank. The surroundings were all favorable for concealing my operations in the darkness of the night and at a distance from any path or human habitation and perfectly secluded from sight even in daylight. No location could be better fitted for such a purpose as I contemplated under certain contingencies. I marked a tree on the bank opposite to which I intended to sink my assets.

On our return to Charlotte, news had arrived that Sherman had desolated Chester, that Stoneman's raiders were on the west side of the Catawba. Bank officers were hiding the contents of their vaults or preparing to remove them to other places. Railroad communication was in the direction of Virginia and that was the only avenue of escape left me. I adopted it. I wrote to my wife that I was going to _____, I knew not where, but that Sherman should not get either me or my money if I could help it, that she must take care of herself and not feel anxious for me, but that she should be kept posted as to my whereabouts. My clerk, Mr. Paxton, had my money, Confederate issues, and effects carried to the depot from the Bank of Charlotte. (Colonel Torbett, Mr. Fisher, and others had heretofore removed the Bank of Tennessee to Augusta.) My depository was placed on the cars and we started. At the depot near Concord I saw Mr. Cannon and sent word by him to Mrs. Ramsey that I might be in the Trans-Mississippi before she heard from me—exacted a promise from Mr. Cannon that he would take care of my family. Near to Greensboro, we encountered a wreck on the track in a very deep cut. My baggage was carried to a small house near to the place. A delay of nearly a day retarded our arrival at Greensboro. The town was more than filled with refugees from everywhere else—amongst others Mr. and Mrs. Gillespie from Charleston. I could get no lodging for myself but found room in a Mr. Lindsay's vault for my valuables. I met here W. A. Smith from Kingston, Tennessee who politely shared his bed with me and I got my rations as I could. Rumors of the approaching crisis at Richmond reached us. Raiders were said to be at Salem and near to Salisbury. A general stampede from Greensboro followed. We could get no further north and very little further south. We left for the latter and arrived late at night in a heavy rain at Salisbury.

Leaving the young men with my effects at the depot, I went up into town. I could find neither supper nor lodging. Every public and private house was full of people driven in from the incessant rain. At the mansion house I found a small space between the feet of a small table unoccupied. I crept into it. The entire floor of the room was covered over with men, some snoring, some drunk, some sober. I slept little and rested none. At daylight I left my narrow *bed,* observing as I left it that the planks of Rowan county were sawed out of very hard wood. I inquired for something to eat. Nothing could be procured there. I saw an immense crowd of hungry men besieging Mr. Buce's eating house, but nothing was to be had. I had eaten nothing for twenty-four hours. I went into the house, found the landlord. I beckoned to him and getting him away from the importunate crowd around him I whispered into his ear that I had silver to pay for my breakfast. It was soon on the table and I leave to the reader's imagination to tell how voraciously I ate it. I never relished breakfast before or since with a higher appreciation. I hastened to the depot, found the young men as hungry as wolves, told them I had spoken to Mr. Buce to provide a *silver* breakfast for them and that while they were gone to eat it I would guard the baggage. While sitting upon the depot I noticed an old gentleman standing near me—Dr. Long. I asked him to take a note from me to Mrs. Curry. I extemporized with a pencil on my knee. Dr. Curry had been our pastor at home in Tennessee, had become a chaplain and surgeon in our army, had been in charge of the United States prisoners' hospital in Salisbury, had died there suddenly a few days before and the substance of the note I sent was to inquire how she was provided for and if she needed assistance to let me know it.

I had scarcely handed this note to Dr. Long when the startling intelligence was received that raiders were within a few miles of Salisbury in large force. My young men had returned from breakfast. We went aboard at once. I afterwards was informed that within one hour Salisbury was in possession of the Federal cavalry. This was another very narrow escape.

At Charlotte I found Major Butt, chief clerk of the Confederate States treasury department, with many other officials from Richmond. He and others of the scattered cabinet of President Davis had passed me at Greensboro. I had corresponded with him officially and he knew all my antecedents but we had not been known to each other before. He disclosed to me his plans in part and said "You have had a long experience in such things. You have thus far been remarkably successful. We will take you into our council." He had along with him a captain in the navy (whose name I cannot recall) who commanded a company of marines. These constituted Major Butt's guard. I think there were sixty or eighty marines, besides cashiers and other fiscal officers, in charge of the Confederate States treasury and official papers, etc., etc. There was no well-defined plan in view as far as I was informed—only so far as to reach Augusta quickly and safely. Major Butt asked me to be his pilot. Sherman had deflected to the right, in the direction of Camden. Our way was open to Chester. That far the country was unoccupied by the Yankees. How it was between Chester and Abbeville, South Carolina and Washington, Georgia, was not certainly known and our best route was only matter of conjecture. It was determined to go by rail to Chester and then be governed by circumstances for the future. I embarked my own depository with Major Butt's treasury and we left on the train for Chester. Below that village the road and bridges were so burnt and destroyed as to forbid further railroad travel. We extemporized about fifty army wagons and other vehicles and transferring the cargo from the cars to the wagons we struck across the country to Abbeville or to a railroad leading to that point. Our first camp was at a church on the great road. There I for the first time ascertained that Mrs. Davis and young Jeff were with our train. She lodged in the church and the rest of us either slept in the wagons on top of the boxes and barrels or upon the ground. I slept in the wagon which carried my own depository and effects and no one disputed my claim to that privilege. I invited one of the marines or of the officers to occupy it with me. We observed the usual military regulations in our marches and our encampments,—posted out our sentinels at night, and had our advance guard and our rear guard, our sign and our countersign. The Confederate flag was not unfurled. I supposed though it was somewhere in our train.

Beyond Abbeville one night a courier brought to the camp information that upon our right a few miles off were some Federal scouts who intended to meet, or rather intercept, us as we crossed Little River on the bridge. Major Butt came with a lamp to my wagon about midnight to consult with me what was best to be done. Without hesitation I said, "If the courier's information is true let us start at once and pass the bridge before daylight and thus put Little River between us and the enemy. If the rumor is, on the other hand, not true we will have only progressed the further on our campaign." My advice was at once put into effect. Mrs. Davis was sent for at the hotel near our camps, our advance guard was sent forward, we advanced, crossed the bridge and were not pursued by the Yankee scouts. I heard afterwards that they were bushwhackers from the mountains of North Carolina and Tennessee under Captain Duncan whom I had so fortunately escaped at Piney September 1863. As we approached the Savannah River I suggested we should put our stores upon a boat or boats and descend the Savannah in them to Augusta. A messenger was sent forward to the river who brought back the information that no boat was to be found. Arrived at Washington, Georgia, we transferred our cargo to the cars and went down to Augusta. We left Mrs. Davis at Washington, and it was understood in camps (though Major Butt did not tell me so) that Mr. Davis and his faithful adherents, of which Captain R. M. Ramsey was one, were on our right and near to us every night and in communication with us daily. We found Augusta in hourly expectation of assault and probable capture. It was understood by the knowing ones that the authorities would surrender it on the first summons. Our cargo was placed in the upper story of some commissary or quartermaster's storehouse and our guards placed over it. We consulted what was best to be done. I suggested the Trans-Mississippi and General Kirby Smith as our new commander-in-chief. We slept upon it one night.

Going into town from the depot I found several of the Bank of Tennessee officials who had, as if by a common impulse of a despairing patriotism, concentrated at Augusta. I invited them down to our branch bank headquarters (Fleming's cotton commission house). Dr. Strong, my cashier, was in. We spent an hour in solemn deliberation. I said among other things that if we were to be captured anywhere I hoped it would not be in a city with fortifications around it and surrendered without a fight. I preferred to be overtaken by the enemy while making an effort to prolong the life of the Confederacy by trying to reach General Kirby Smith's headquarters. The following proceedings then took place.

"Augusta, Georgia, 26th April 1865

"At a meeting called by several of the officers of the Bank of Tennessee, at the counting room of Fleming and Wheless. Present Dr. J. G. M. Ramsey, Prest Branch Bank of Tennessee, Knoxville, B. R. Strong, Cashier, Jno. A. Fisher Cashr J. C. Rye, Cashr. J. R. Brown Cashr. Thos. Cleage Cashr. H. L. Claiborne, Clerk of the mother Bank, Joel A. Battle, Treasurer of Tennessee, Hon Thos. Meneers and N. W. Carter.

"On motion of Mr. Fisher, Dr. Ramsey was called to preside and H. L. Claiborne, appointed Secretary—

"The object of the meeting was explained—it being to take into consideration the safe keeping and disposition of the assets of the Bank of Tennessee, with a view to their being returned to the people of Tennessee to whom they belong.

"A letter was read from His Excellency, Isham G. Harris, giving his views, and offering some advice to the officers in charge of the valuables, in view of the present critical condition of the country,

"The following resolution was offered

Resolved That in view of the present condition of the country and the probability of an early peace, this meeting deems it imprudent to attempt the removal of the assets of the Bank of Tennessee, and is of the opinion that the assets can best be preserved for and returned to the people of Tennessee by keeping them in Augusta, in such places as may be deemed safest for storage.

"After considerable discussion the resolution was, for the present, laid on the table.

"The meeting then adjourned to meet at the same place at 3 O'Ck this evening.

3 o'clock, P.M.

"The meeting was called to order by its chairman, gentlemen (present as in) the forenoon except Cashr. Strong and Hon Thos. Meneers.

"The following resolutions were offered and after discussion were unanimously adopted.

Resolved That it is manifestly to the interest of the people of the State of Tennessee, that the assets of the Bank of Tennessee be immediately and quietly removed to the department of Mississippi for security, to be held for the citizens of said State.

Resolved That it is the opinion of this meeting at least one official from each Branch Bank who is in the Confederate States, shall accompany the assets of the Bank of Tennessee to such place of security as may be determined.

Resolved That Messrs. Rye, Brown, Cleage and Fisher be appointed a committee to secure transportation for the assets and that they have full power and are hereby instructed to proceed to the discharge of their duty with the utmost dispatch.

"The meeting then adjourned to meet at the Augusta Hotel at 9 o'clock, this evening.

Augusta Hotel 9 o'clock P.M.

"The meeting was called to order by Dr. Ramsey.
Same gentlemen present as in the evening, with the addition of Mr. S. B. Settle of Murfreesboro, Tennessee.

"The minutes of preceding meetings were read and approved. The following resolution was adopted,
Resolved That a copy of the proceedings of this meeting be prepared by the Secretary to accompany the assets of the Bank and a copy to be spread upon the minutes of the Bank of Tennessee.

"The Committee on transportation made a verbal report, of satisfactory progress.

"Adjourned until 10 o'clock tomorrow morning, to meet at J. A. Battle's room, Augusta Hotel.

"H. L. Claiborne   J. G. M. Ramsey,
        Secretary   Chairman"

[Inscription on back of Proceedings: "Last Meeting of Directors of Bank of Tennessee Augusta Ga. Apl. 26, 1865]

While Mr. Claiborne was making out the copy of these proceedings which is on this sheet as received from him, at my request I withdrew and went below and met a friend who informed me that two of General _____'s aides were in town and Augusta would in a day or two be surrendered without the firing of a gun and that these two aides were then at supper in the hotel.

I went immediately back to the room I had left and communicated what I had heard. It will be noticed that Dr. Strong was not present at the afternoon or the night sessions of the meeting, he having gone to his residence in the country, and so it was not fully settled which, he or I, should accompany the expedition as representative of the Knoxville branch. But I declared myself ready to start if it were tomorrow.

The meeting had not yet broken up and separated when I went back to their room, but it had now become painfully obvious that all attempt to escape under present circumstances from Augusta with the imposing transportation and guard such an undertaking would require would be alike fruitless and unwise. It was therefore abandoned, though the committee on transportation had acted promptly. They had selected their Confederate States quartermaster Colonel _____. He had procured some wagons and supplies. Captain _____ was to take command of the guard. The expedition was to go by Athens and Calhoun, Georgia, Decatur, Alabama—cross the Mississippi at some swamp below Memphis, strike for General Smith's headquarters wherever it should be, raise the Confederate flag, and keep the money of the people of Tennessee from the grasp of the Yankees.

I was content, however, to leave it where it was in the vaults of Mr. Metcalf and under the control of my faithful and honest cashier, Dr. Strong. He handed me the next day $50.00 in part of my salary as president. I heard afterwards that when it was captured Dr. Strong was allowed to go with it to Nashville but was not permitted to count it.

The Bank of Tennessee being thus disposed of I turned my attention to my other bantling—my Confederate States depository. It was almost out of town in a storehouse of some Confederate quartermaster in Augusta. I sought Major Butt, communicated to him what I had heard last night at our bank meeting and also what I had heard on the streets: viz., a rumor that stragglers from both armies were intending to make a run upon and appropriate it to their own use and their urgent wants and necessities. He said to me that day that as I had brought him there I must take him back. "Very well, Major," I replied. "The Southern Confederacy! Today, yesterday and forever I am at its and your service!" He inquired, "Which way can we go?" I answered, "Towards the enemy— the same way we came, via Washington, Georgia and Abbeville, South Carolina. Thence as best we can." "When?" was his next inquiry. "By tonight's train. The earlier the better. Load up this afternoon. The mob will notice your night movements." He seemed to acquiesce.

I thought the Confederacy was ended. But still Confederate States issues maintained some vitality. They were taken by the merchants at greatly reduced values. I had some shopping to do and asked Mrs. Schwab to go with me where she dealt. She did so, and bought a plain lawn dress for Mrs. Ramsey, Mrs. Breck and Sue each for $600.00 = $1,800.00—and some other light articles at corresponding prices. "Are you not afraid to hold

Confederate money?" I inquired. He answered "not while it will pay for cotton. I have a place to put it in. Can't I sell you some more goods. I want all the Confederate money you have." I put the goods into my trunk and my trunk and valise into the cars and next day found myself at Washington.

The Confederate States treasury had come up the previous night—the wagon train was still there, was soon reorganized, and we were again upon the road on our way to Abbeville where we arrived without molestation. I had to march on foot part of each day and was exceedingly fatigued and weary. It was Saturday evening and I determined to avail myself of enjoying the quiet and rest of a Christian Sabbath in the family of an old friend, Langdon Bowie, Esquire. His son was the Confederate States quartermaster and with him the Confederate States treasury was left under our own guard. He had exacted a promise from me when I passed up that if I did not go further than Augusta I would on my return visit his father's family. He drove me out to his beautiful country seat a few miles from town. It is a beautiful place, highly improved and tastefully cultivated. I had known him as a merchant in Charleston and New York, had often seen him at my own house and in Knoxville where Mrs. Bowie was born. I went with his family to church and heard an excellent sermon from Reverend Dr. Barne, I believe. I spent Sunday night in this social, hospitable, and Christian family. I really felt almost at home in Tennessee. When I left Monday morning Mrs. Bowie—fortunately for me as matters turned out—overburdened me with an abundant and excellent luncheon which, long as my journey was, lasted me to Charlotte. I bade the kind family farewell, returned to the village.

Our Confederate States treasury officers concluded to go no further than Abbeville. This place is classic ground and hereafter historical as once the residence of the great American statesman Calhoun. Here he had for nearly half a century forewarned the people of the United States that the government was rapidly tending to consolidation. That great catastrophe had now taken place. The treasury of the seceding states was here within the grasp of consolidationists and usurpers. The coercive policy had triumphed over the constitution, over state rights, over liberty. As I left my depository with the chief agent of the Confederate States treasury and retired from the door, I venerated more highly and appreciated more fully the character and services and virtues and statesmanship of Calhoun. I knew before that he was a statesman of unsurpassed ability, that he was a patriot of unequaled private and public virtue. But now I bowed down before and did homage to the memory of a *Prophet*.

When I turned my face toward Charlotte I felt a little depressed that I had left behind me two fiscal institutions that had long been confided to my care and supervision, but on the other hand I had before me still richer treasures—my wife and daughters, my family. I had done my whole duty zealously and faithfully in financing for Tennessee and the South. Other duties now devolved upon me. These were confined to domestic and social obligations hereafter falling upon myself. Under such influences I took the train and was soon at Newberry. I went down to the late Confederate States quartermaster's office and asked for transportation to Chester. Like an Irishman mourning over his deceased bride, the Confederate quartermaster was on a spree. I soon found him and showed him my now useless transportation papers. With a hearty embrace he said, "Dr. Ramsey, I cannot. It always gave me sincere pleasure to oblige or serve any gentleman who was true to our cause. But now I have no horses, no ambulances, no wagons, no buggies, no drivers, no nothing,—all gone home. I wish I could." But he went with me to a livery stable where, after several refusals, the proprietor promised to send me forward five miles early next morning. I found supper and lodgings with Mr. Malone of Greeneville, Tennessee whom I had known there. Mrs. Malone told me at supper that Captain Ramsey had been there with his scouts a few days before, had made some inquiries, was answered and dashed out of town towards Abbeville. I guessed his object.

Early next morning a horse and buggy came to the door. As I went the five miles to the appointed place the liveryman (he drove me himself) told me what I could see myself every step we took—that he was afraid to send his vehicles on the roads. The paroled soldiers from Lee's disbanded army met us constantly in crowds, tried to press his horse and buggy, and if he had not told them who I was they would have taken both. The day before they had jumped into and hung upon one of his carriages returning to town, broke it down, and took the horses from the wreck and rode them off. It was so afterwards till I reached Chester. All living on or near the great roads had to hide their horses and dismantle their vehicles or they would have been taken by the hungry, unpaid, and worn out paroled soldiers returning further south. I easily excused this apparent demoralization and from my heart sympathized with them.

The richest planters all along the route were without subsistence for themselves and if I had not been abundantly supplied by Mrs. Bowie's bounty I would have been under the necessity (which knows no law) to have done some pressing myself. At the end of my five miles I got out of the buggy. I had a small trunk beside my valise. I put them inside the gate, went to the house and asked for breakfast. I got only some buttermilk. Neither man nor horse was on the place. I waited hour after hour to find someone to take me forward. I waited in vain. I saw and heard nothing but the tramp tramp of the poor disbanded Confederates. At length a wagon hove in sight. It was going in the right direction for me. It had been pressed the day before and was now returning with the brokendown horses. The owner agreed to take me a few miles to the fork of the road where he left me at Dr. Webb's. The doctor was not at home. I waited till his return. He could do nothing for me but kindly invited me to take dinner and see if anything might turn up. In the P.M. a messenger arrived requesting a professional visit from him, miles off and in my direction. He improvised a rickety buggy and took me and my baggage to _____, where he left me afoot. There I hired a manumitted Negro man to carry my trunk on his head a few miles. I walked, too, carrying alternately in both hands my heavy valise. At length the Negro gave out. I hired another who carried my trunk till night. I stopped at a large plantation where the house had been eviscerated. Here one of the marines overtook me. In my valise I had a small package of tea and proposed to my comrade if he could make the tea I would supply the breadstuffs. He brewed it in a tin cup and without cream or sugar it really was excellent and refreshing. We had the privilege of laying all night upon the floor. At daylight we repeated the tea operation which, with Mrs. Bowie's luncheon, made us a good breakfast. I extemporized another Negro for the means of transportation till he became tired. I saw a wounded army horse ("U. S." was branded on him) on the road side. The Negro mounted him without bridle or saddle. I handed up my trunk and thus, I on foot and the Negro on the "U. S." horse, we traveled on till I broke down at a house where I went in and found a very sick Confederate soldier. The proprietor was on the point of starting off after a doctor nine miles forward on my road. I told him who I was. He asked me to examine the sick Georgian and prescribe for him. He was the son of _____ at Dalton whom I knew there. I gave him some medicine and told them that in eight hours after he would need some drops which he must send for at once. I asked about my further transportation. He fixed up his buggy and agreed to take me and my baggage as far as the doctor's shop.

Paying the Negro well for his services and, without leaving any equivalent for the U. S. horse, to the United States treasury, I got into the buggy and went on rapidly. We met as usual squad after squad of Confederate soldiers who attempted to press our establishment and were only withheld from doing so by the consideration which I urged upon them, of the sick Georgian's case. Arrived at Dr. _____'s on the road side I represented the case to him. He could not visit him till next day. I sent back the necessary medicine. I hope he recovered. By similar contrivancies and uncommon resources I at length reached Mrs. Mosby's, if I recollect right. There I found Colonel Wodfen, a refugee acquaintance and refugee from Asheville, North Carolina. I began to meet and see the Blue and the Grey —and if on one occasion, when asked by an armed scout dressed in the former, "What is your name?" I replied, "At home they used to call me McGready." "Huh! any kin of the McGreadys in Guilford?" "I believe there was one of them lived up there. I don't know that he was of the same family." The reader will excuse the harmless deception. My whole exterior was rather of the shabby-genteel order and did not much resemble that of a financier. I was not arrested. From Mrs. Mosby's I was sent forward in a carriage to Chester. Here while waiting for the train I met an old Knoxville acquaintance, now Reverend J. T. Helms, an Episcopal minister, once so jovial and blithesome a companion. He had heard of our afflictions and adversity. I was agreeably surprised when he, in a Christian spirit, administered to me the strong consolation of the Gospel.

When I reached Rock Hill I tried to procure conveyance to Mr. Presley's, where my son Alexander's wife and family were. Neither horse, wagon, nor buggy was to be had. I heard that our new authorities had established at, or rather on, the pontoon-bridge across the Catawba a rigid police and espionage. I had done nothing wrong but still preferred not to be arrested. Just as the train started an old lady, feeble and without attendant, asked some of us to take charge of her trunk and hire a Negro to carry it for her when we came to the bridge. I promised to comply with her request and did speak to one boy for her baggage and another one for my own. As we went down to and approached the bridge I noticed the United States functionary examining and catechising the passengers and their papers. I had the old lady and our two Negro porters in charge. We bore to the right and were not interrogated or otherwise molested. On the other side of the river passengers were subjected to the same ordeal. As soon as I was seated in the car I affected to be in a very profound sleep with my hat drawn over my face. I heard the conductor going through the car examining the people. He could not get me awake. After he came back I was still *asleep*. The train was not ready for some hours and I noticed a small wagon loaded with screws, bolts, etc., etc., taken from the ruins of the burned bridge. I inquired if they were going towards Charlotte? They replied, "As far as Fort Mills." I employed the owners to take me and my baggage that far. It was nearly night and in switching off the down-train a poor Confederate's leg and ankle were crushed. I was the only surgeon present, heard his cries of agony. A torch was lighted. I gave him a large dose of opium, dressed wounds, had him taken to an adjoining house on a cabin door pulled from its hinges, and directed the bystanders to send for a resident surgeon for his further treatment. Late in the night the up-train came to Fort Mills and carried me forward to Charlotte. I, with my baggage, was on a flat or open car. Colonel William Johnson recognized me in the moonlight and said "Great changes since you left." He could tell me nothing of my family. I found at Kern's every room occupied and the lights extinguished. My friend, W. A. Smith, heard me knocking at the door and recognizing my voice inquired from the window if that was not Dr. Ramsey and offered me half of his bed. I was more than glad to accept his kind offer. At daylight I went to Colonel B. W. Alexander's. I had not changed my clothes since I left Abbeville. Colonel Alexander could tell me nothing certain or recent from my wife. Mr. Davidson Alexander had got back from the army, happened to come to town that day, carried me home with him that night and next morning drove me up to Mr. Cannon's. My wife and Sue were there. They had not heard a word from me since I left and thought it not improbable that I was captured or possibly was en route for Texas or Mexico. But I was really broken down. Such an excursion as this last, such fatigues, exposures, responsibilities and dangers as I had endured, no sexogenarian and eight had ever before undergone.

I found Mrs. Ramsey cheerful and well. Her courage and fortitude had always sustained mine. She made a good tutoress. Employment congenial to her taste and her great capacity to instruct and her success in it encouraged and stimulated her. Then the consciousness of being useful to others was itself a source of, if not of emolument, certainly of a comfortable living. So also of Mrs. Breck. The scattered condition of the family was indeed a drawback upon their domestic happiness but when we did meet, as sometimes happened, our reunions were delightsome and enjoyed only with a keener relish. I felt that my public life was ended and that the remainder of my days was to be devoted to my family and the evening of my life was to be spent in the quiet of home and in the domestic circle.

But where was to be the center of that circle? We knew nothing of the large property we had left in Tennessee. From what we learned from the banished members of my household, from other exiles and refugees and from an occasional Union paper picked up by our scouts and brought to Dixie, the property was either burnt or destroyed or lawlessly sold, alienated, or confiscated. So that we had little to hope for and expect from that quarter. I had brought home with me from Georgia seventeen dollars all told of silver. My wife had still the twenty-five dollars of contraband gold which the generosity of Major Smith had restored to her at McBee's, making thus our joint fortune of forty-two dollars of available money on which to start in the world again—my wife at the age of nearly sixty-four and myself at the age of sixty-eight. Our daughters were not better provided for. Our four surviving sons were equally penniless. One of them had not yet got out of Camp Morton. Another had been captured, imprisoned and was now under trial (as will be presently detailed) in Knoxville. Another had clung to the fortunes of Mr. Davis to the last and had not yet returned. The remaining son had been paroled at Charlotte. He had a cavalry horse and saddle, his own property, worth all told perhaps one hundred dollars. We were in North Carolina among strangers and many of them as much impoverished as ourselves. The means of subsistence were very nearly exhausted by the wants and spoliations of both armies.

What was best to do? This was the question now to be solved. For a few days I rested and recruited my impaired energies at Mr. Cannon's. He was more despondent and discouraged than myself. So were all others I saw and conversed with, though on their own lands and in their own houses with stock and farming implements. I had, indeed, to cheer everyone I met. They had all desponded and were spiritless. Many stout men, not as old as myself, yielded to the pressure of adversity and died prematurely and without disease. I was surprisingly elastic. Necessity made me energetic. Under the circumstances I may be said to have been even buoyant and vigorous. *Nil desperandum* had always been one of my favorite maxims. *Labor vincit omnia* was another. In English, root, hog, or die. My wife and children had the same indomitable spirit. In a week it was determined that as we had not the means to get away from North Carolina we would stay where the waves of the revolution and disaster had floated us. We were as badly wrecked as mariners can be if they are not drowned. I had always been very fond of my profession and I determined to resume practice in the office of Dr. McKnitt Henderson of Mecklenburg. I put my card into the *Democrat*. This paper, I found afterwards, had few, almost no, readers in my neighborhood. The country was exceedingly healthy. Retired physicians had, like all other people, been ruined by the war. They were therefore forced to fall back on their profession. The army physicians and surgeons came in with rather close propinquity for the success of a stranger, and I therefore could expect little professional emolument but I borrowed a pair of medical saddle wallets, bought at least 37½ or 43¾ cents worth of medicine, and with McKnitt's cavalry horse and saddle was equipped for conquest not with Yankees but with disease. My wife and Mrs. Breck had still some of their five months session to fill out and while that term was being completed I rented an old farm. The house was comfortable and partly furnished. The stock, farming utensils and feed were also furnished. All we had to do was to furnish the labor. Fuel was abundant and convenient, water excellent. The season proved to be an average one and our third was about enough for a support for us five.

There were in the summer and fall of 1865 remaining in Hopewell besides others, refugees and exiles from New Orleans, a brother and sister, Mr. R. C. Kerr and Miss Mary Kerr. They were perfectly destitute. The former I had known during the war as an exiled printer and for the present as the foreman of Mr. _____ in the office of the _____ in Charlotte. The surrender had thrown him out of employment. Poor as we were, my wife offered him a plate at our frugal board and my son McKnitt offered to share his bed with him. He accepted their offer and this brought an addition of one more to our *good* society. For it was good. Mr. Kerr had a cultivated mind, sang well, had virtuous principles, was self-reliant, no croaker, was cheerful, polite and a man of business. Still no employment seemed to offer. Printers in North Carolina were all broken up by the war. No typographical enterprise was started till General D. H. Hill

proposed to publish at Charlotte *The Land We Love*. He needed a foreman for his business and one day, hearing of Mr. Kerr's qualification, came
out to our house to see and employ him. While there he became acquainted
with me and asked me to contribute to his journal.[1] I did so frequently,
for which he *paid me liberally*. I mention these unimportant details to
show how truly the promise has been in my case fulfilled—"Cast thy
bread upon the waters and after many days it shall be returned to thee."
If Mr. Kerr had not eaten my bread I might never have heard of General
Hill, nor received any money from him. Two only of my male acquaintances ever assisted us during these times of need. Reverend Ransom of
the Associate Reformed Synod had been a guest at my house in Tennessee
and sent down to us a bountiful supply of sweet potatoes—the best we
ever ate. I went one day in search of corn for bread. Reverend W. S. Pharr,
hearing that I wanted to buy, said he had none to sell but handed me
$5.00 and gave me his blessing with it. The ladies on the other hand were
more liberal or considerate. The daughters of Mrs. M. W. Alexander in
Charlotte sent a tailor to take my measure for a cloth cloak. The tailor
said he was directed not to tell who were the donors of the much needed
garment. My cousin, Mrs. A. B. Alexander, also gave me some domestic
cloth and some provisions. Mrs. Charles Jay Harris of Cabarrus gave me
a suit of Confederate grey for my constancy to the Southern cause. I
have enjoined on my family to bury me in it. The Lenoir brothers in
Tennessee loaned me money without security. Thus we made out to live
comfortably.

In May 1865, I believe, before I had yet left Dr. Henderson's, Captain
R. M. Ramsey stepped in, languid and broken down. From his recital I
take the following details. As before stated, he adhered to Mr. Davis' fortunes to the last and only left his escort when the ex-president begged
them as a matter of favor to himself to do so. He returned as far as Washington, Georgia, and from his exposure and his fatiguing services was
taken down with a violent bilious fever. Finding that he was seriously ill
he had to sell his fine and favorite horse. When he paid up his medical and

---

[1] Identifiable contributions to *The Land We Love* by Dr. Ramsey are: "Sketch of Mecklenburg County," by Mnemonika, 2:129–145 (December, 1866); "Battle of King's Mountain,"
3:381–400 (September 1867); "Duel Between Jackson and Dickerson," by A. Keosis of
Tennessee, 4:135–136 (December, 1867), and "The State of Franklin" 4:460–472, 5:13–22,
109–116, 216–229 which ran from April through July 1868.

hotel bills he had barely enough to bring him to Charlotte. He did as I had done a few days before—walked some, rode some, any way he could to get along. At Newberry, South Carolina, as he was yet very weak, he went at night into an empty boxcar which was at the depot. A comrade was with him. The town was in the occupancy of the Yankees and a force was stationed there. A cannon loaded and ready to fire was placed near the depot. The camp of the artillerists was not far off. After these were quietly asleep, no one being on guard, Robert got out of his boxcar, went noiselessly to the cannon, fired it off, retraced his steps in the dark, got into his own sleeping place and, weak as he was, enjoyed the fun of seeing the whole Yankee force thrown into terror and confusion occasioned by the firing and assault of two disbanded Confederates. The consternation was extreme. The Federals were evidently alarmed. The whole town was aroused and were unable to explain the treason and rebellion of the unexpected assault. If one of Wheeler's company had been at hand and had demanded it he believes the garrison at Newberry would have surrendered at discretion. As it was, he was satisfied with his own participation in scaring the Yankee conquerors so badly. This was the last gun fired, he believes, by the Confederates during the war. So that as the first gun in our revolution was fired in South Carolina so too was the last—and that by a defiant but invalid Tennessee Captain.

I went up with Robert to see his mother and sisters: and leave the reader to imagine their joy at seeing him. He, after resting and recruiting a few weeks, recovered. He became the manager and tenant of Reverend Mr. Watts in Rowan County. Being but twenty-two miles from us he occasionally visited us.

CHAPTER XVIII

Yankee Prisons

In June or July of the same year (1865) I received from my friend Captain Williams of Greeneville, Tennessee a note written on the Columbia and Charlotte cars that he had the day before met our son Colonel F. A. Ramsey returning from his imprisonment at Camp Morton, Indiana, and had told him where he would find us. A very few days afterwards he called at Dr. Henderson's and I went with him to Mr. Cannon's. We had not heard from him in several months and from what we had seen of the cruelties and inhumanity of the Federal prisons and especially of their treatment of Confederate prisoners at Camp Morton we were not without apprehensions that we would never see his face again. He told me that the reality exceeded the worst accounts we had seen of the rapacity, the injustice, the extortion, frauds, oppression, tyranny, cruelty, inhumanity and massacres at Camp Morton. His recital of these is undoubtedly truthful and reliable. He saw all the above catalogue displayed daily and there can be no mistake about it. It is all true. I enumerate only a few and these not the blackest of Federal *crimes* perpetrated by Yankee soldiers acting as they said under orders of superior officers bearing commissions in the United States army. When captured at Piedmont, Alexander was refused the privilege of remaining with and nursing his little brother Arthur whose leg was shattered and nearly cut off by a cannon ball (the wounded boy was left on the field and the foot was not amputated for four or five days—thus inducing tetanus of which he died as already stated). He with the other captured soldiers were then hurried off on foot, not withstanding the fatigue of the preceding marches and countermarches several days before the fight. The enemy were the conquerors and in *undisputed* possession of the whole country near them. Yet as if required by the exigencies of war or the least dread of pursuit or recapture the *officers* on horseback hurried up the men, with their drawn swords, and compelled their prisoners to a double quick over mountains and through water courses more than waist deep so rapid as to require that several prisoners should walk abreast to support one another from being overwhelmed by the impetuous stream. Some of the weaker and shortest men thus sunk beneath the water and, if rescued at all, were left on the shore. This flight —for it was a disgraceful *flight* (there were no Confederates to make pursuit)—was continued day and night, without intermission and with no halt only to eat scanty rations, till the prisoners arrived at _____ wearied, sleepy and hungry. Arrived at Camp Morton, what little money prisoners had was taken from their pockets. In that abundant country their provisions were stinted and unpalatable. Their comfort was never consulted. Their guards were insolent, cruel and revengeful. A letter arrived from his mother to Alexander inclosing, as the letter stated, $5.00. The letter was opened, the money taken out, and he never got it. Friends at Knoxville had written to Reverend McIntyre, once of that place, requesting his good offices in behalf of the Tennessee prisoners. That good man, once our frequent guest, was not permitted to see these objects of his Christian commiseration and sympathy. But anxious to serve them he addressed a note to Alexander and inquired what he needed? He replied clothes. A suit was sent to him. He was tantalized by the sight of the clothes, but they were withheld. Another application made some months later for a blanket was more successful. In many ways Mr. McIntyre tried to mitigate the sufferings and promote the comfort of the Knoxville prisoners but his kind efforts were thwarted.

Prison Life in Morton

When the soldiers captured at Piedmont arrived at Camp Morton they found many others there taken at other battlefields of the South. Some of these, by longer confinement and ill-usage, already emaciated, despondent—not sick enough yet to be sent into the hospital, but dreading that change of their condition and place of confinement the more from the fact that as yet no one hitherto sent to the hospital had ever come back to their companions. They had invariably died there and found relief from their captivity and sufferings only in the grave. Of these one was Major Corry with whom Alexander and all of us were acquainted. He was a gentleman of science and position—chief engineer on the W. and A. Railroad and had been captured. . . . After their first interview he found some solace from his imprisonment and separation from his wife and family and home in the companionship with Colonel Ramsey and seemed for the time to be trying to bolster himself and his co-prisoners against the adversities and debility consequent upon imprisonment. They were much together. He lost his appetite. His letters and money were withheld. Alexander tried to comfort him. The weather was exceedingly cold. Alexander lent him his blanket.

The stove was inadequately supplied with fuel. The jailor—I will not designate him as the prison regulations did, the curator—at length issued orders that messes of twelve each should alternately have periods of warming a given number of minutes around the stove. They were then required to give place to the next mess of freezing prisoners, retire to their bunks or cells or cots or berths as the case might be till the whole garrison had got warm and then resume the course again. Coal and other fuel were doled out most economically as if our prisoners, badly clad, some of them without a blanket, in that inclement winter of that cold climate could survive without subsistence and without fire. These deprivations were mentioned to the keeper without success. One replied our prisoners were better treated than those at Andersonville. Soon after this an order was given and carried into effect that rations should be issued in quantity barely sufficient to preserve life. This regimen was rigidly enforced. The stoutest survived this cruel diminution of bread. The weaker sank under it. The first symptom of this decadence was a melancholy, a despondence, a withdrawal from comradeship and a seeking after solitude. The subject of it would withdraw to a corner with a stupid gaze at the floor, a stubborn taciturnity, a perfect apathy and indifference to his surroundings—the extinction of the social principal, the extinguishment of hope. The hospital was next and the grave soon afterward. In the case of Major Corry, when these first symptoms were noticed, Alexander went to him and enticed him from his solitude and tried to recall into life his usual vivacity and to restore his wonted energy. He said he was aware what this languor implied and had been endeavoring all the time to fight against and overcome it. Alexander's continued efforts for a time seemed to reanimate and excite the dormant vitality of Major Corry. At length the curator ordered him to the hospital. Alexander asked permission to go with him. That was refused. He afterwards asked leave to visit. This, too, was refused. He never saw him again.

But this is not all of prison life in Camp Morton. One of the regulations there was that at _____ o'clock lights should be extinguished and the most absolute silence observed. On one occasion noises were heard in one of the rooms, arising, as the inmates conjectured, from the ravings of a maniac, the delirium of unsound sleep or the dreams of one accustomed to the foray and the battle. Silence was ordered from without. The noise was repeated. A volley from the sentinels killed two innocent men and wounded several others. Many other acts of similar atrocity could be here added. "Even the tender mercies of the wicked are cruelty." One day the keeper brought to a prisoner something palatable from a friend without. The prisoner, when his name was called, came forward. The keeper, in accordance with the Yankee code of ethics to the vanquished, said, "You damned coward and rebel! I ought not to let you have this. Eat it quick and if you open your mouth or say one word this bayonet will send you to Hell and then to Andersonville for your next meal of fire and damnation!" Such spirit and temper were once considered unofficer-like and cowardly. Used by a victor to an imprisoned and vanquished soldier they become contemptible, base, unmanly and little. Andersonville! The slaughter pen at Andersonville! Words often repeated to atone for Federal cruelty and inhumanity to our unfortunate prisoners in their own camps. What of Andersonville? I was never there. But I have seen Yankee prisoners and the wounded of the Yankee army in Georgia and elsewhere. I have dressed their wounds and have had the duty assigned to me to see their prisoners cared for, and I avow the truth when I assert that in not a single case on the cars, in the hospitals, in the prison at Salisbury, or on the march to the rear have I ever seen a cruelty perpetrated, an insult given, or an indignity offered to a captured enemy. I once heard the words *retaliation* and *the black flag* threatened but these words came from the mouth of a *bomb-proof* fireside patriot whose duties as commissary consisted in operating where there was neither danger nor self-denial. Far otherwise. The Confederates were brave in battle, generous in victory, and incapable of what was degrading or humiliating to any enemy disarmed or conquered. This is the pluck, these are the inborn principles of slave institutions and slave territory.

The prisoners were sent from Camp Morton according to alphabetical order and R. being far down in the alphabet Alexander did not leave till near the last. At Nashville he called upon his uncle and, receiving some help, was able to join his family near Yorkville, South Carolina.

In July of 1866 Robert was married in Rowan County. He had previously sold his farm in Tennessee. It had been sold under the existing

240
DR. J. G. M. RAMSEY

laws of that ill-governed state and rather than resort to tedious litigation he sold it below its value. He was thus in funds to take a bridal tour,—his sister Sue accompanying them. At Washington he saw the name of his brother Crozier on the hotel register. They arranged to meet on the same day at Richmond and to return together to our home in Mecklenburg. The bridal party went to Baltimore where they met several Tennessee exiles hunting business. Before their return to North Carolina they visited the disastrous battlefield of Piedmont, spent a night with the Christian family of Mr. Cline where their brother Arthur died. They visited his lonely grave, dropped copious showers of fraternal tears to the young martyr's memory, breathed a heavy sigh of regret when they left it for Richmond. There they met Crozier and together came on to our *Exile's Retreat* near Charlotte, as I had named our new home.

This was a most joyous meeting to all my family, as the reader will suppose when he reads the recital of the sufferings and the wrongs our eldest son, John Crozier Ramsey, endured after we left him at Bristol in October, 1864. The reader will bear in mind what has already been said —that he was paroled at Vicksburg, and was remaining in the rear of the Confederate States army anxiously expecting to be exchanged and to resume his sword. He had lumbago and though still young used a staff when on his feet. He was still in the hospital at Bristol and under treatment of my brother, Dr. F. A. Ramsey, medical purveyor of Tennessee. I had frequently after leaving him (October 1864) warned him of the dangerous proximity of the Federal cavalry and had urged him to come to our retreat in North Carolina and thus avoid the rigorous climate of the mountains and enjoy the milder winter of Mecklenburg. He thought and hoped he would soon be exchanged and preferred therefore to remain near the expected theater of future military service. At Christmas the Federal cavalry made a sudden dash into Bristol at night and captured what few Confederate soldiers were there—with the hospital, its stores, its invalids, its surgeons, and all. At the time of his capture he was in bed and in the same room was a comrade of his, J. A. Sperry, editor of the Knoxville (Atlanta, Augusta, Columbia, and, I believe, the Charlotte) *Register*. Sperry noticed first that the town was full of Yankees and communicated his apprehensions to Crozier. He took time by the forelock and before the captors had entered his room he sent across the street by his servant his gold watch and other valuables to a daughter of his uncle to be taken care of by her. The telegraph announced a great victory and the capture of most important personages.

Soon the prisoners were in motion upon the frozen and muddy roads to Knoxville. Crozier was permitted to ride a horse—so were, too, the army surgeons. The rest had to walk under guards. Crozier, riding near the superior officer, discovered somehow that he was a Mason and, sympathizing with Sperry who was afoot, made known to the officer that the latter was also a Mason and that he was unable to bear the fatigue and cold of his march. True to the obligations of the fraternity of Masons the commander furnished a horse to Sperry. Arrived at Knoxville these two and another prisoner Fox, formerly jailor at Knoxville in Confederate times, were paraded through the streets and marched to the jail and put in close confinement in a large room filled with convicts, felons, deserters from the United States army, men infamous for crime, desperate from their guilt and merited punishment. Intemperance, lawlessness, violence and crime were stamped on every feature of these desperadoes, thieves and murderers. Such were the inmates of this horrid prison. It was during the Christmas holidays. Bottles, jugs, canteens full of whisky, packages of cards, an old fiddle, etc., completed the outfit of the establishment with outbursts of profanity, ribaldry, and blasphemy on every tongue. Such were the surroundings of General J. C. Ramsey and J. A. Sperry when introduced by Federal authority to their prison house at Knoxville. The streets were in accordance with the prison. There was a general jubilee, a noisy rabble, an infuriated mob.

There is an instinctive deference to character and virtue which even bandits are not unwilling to pay. After the two Confederate prisoners were inaugurated into their new lodgings a comparative silence and quiet were restored. The drunken and outrageous became more calm. Crozier was interrogated by a dozen of clients as to the chances of each to escape punishment. He had in ante-bellum days become famous as a criminal lawyer. He found one there in jail for a repetition of the same offense of which he had been before acquitted. This one renewed his clientship and became the earnest patron of his old advocate and solicitor and advised all who wished to escape the halter to employ his old lawyer and friend. With all this patronage of the entire prison no fees were paid, I believe, though much was promised if they could be *clared*. Sperry, too, the editor was much interrogated about the news. Will the Rebels gain the day?

"Yes," said Sperry, "if they are not all killed, whipped, captured or imprisoned like we are. Very few are left and these few are scattered everywhere." At length all fell asleep. One of Crozier's clients lay so closely to him as to abstract from him a beautiful delicate pin made up of gold and diamonds. To this article of dress the owner always attached a special and peculiar value (hereto hangs a tale), but he never recovered it. Another trespass was committed the same night. His lady friends had sent to him an excellent luncheon and so abundant that he left much of it for morning use, concealing it as he lay upon the floor in a large pocket of his overcoat. It somehow disappeared and no questions were asked about the larceny.

Next morning the prisoners in the jail were, as usual, balled and chained and led along the principal streets to work upon the fortifications around town. Crozier's chain fortunately was so long as to allow him to carry the ball united to it in his hands and thus to let him walk erect. Sperry's, on the other hand, was so short as to shorten his steps and materially retard his movements. When they arrived at the fortifications it became evident even to the most obdurate and revengeful of the guards that Crozier was yet so much of an invalid and physically unable to work with a spade as to remit him from that duty. In the afternoon the line of march was resumed and the prisoners reconducted to their prison. This, like the morning display, was made for the purpose of gratifying the fiendish—not to say the infernal—malignity of two or three (perhaps not so many) ignoble and revengeful partizans in Knoxville. Along the pavements stood the virtue, intelligence and respectability of both town and country and of both sexes. They bowed a friendly recognition of the new and stranger *convict* as he trudged through the muddy street. Chained and balled as he was he acknowledged and reciprocated these recognitions from those who knew his worth and appreciated his high character by a graceful bow and a pleasant smile. He was amiable and he was popular and as he passed along not a jaunt, nor a jeer, not a word of reproach nor of unkindness was uttered in his hearing. The low and little means adopted and intended to humiliate and mortify his proud spirit had just the opposite effect both upon himself and the masses by which he was surrounded. A howl of indignant public sentiment could not be suppressed and spreading along the streets reached headquarters. An official order from the chief in command released the invalid prisoner and sent him to the hospital. By whose authority and at whose request this great indignity and wrong had been perpetrated remains unknown. General _____, the chief in command disavowed and revoked the order of some subordinate in Knoxville.

The enormity of this outrage against law, justice, decency, and honor will be the more clearly manifested when it is remembered that General Ramsey, the subject of it, had at the surrender of Vicksburg been paroled, had not been exchanged, was still not only an invalid but was captured while under treatment for a chronic lumbago and rheumatism first induced by service and exposure in the trenches at Vicksburg—that by the usages of honorable warfare the hospital of an enemy is sacred and the person of an invalid prisoner should not be exposed to inclement weather and the discomfort and suffering on the march—that imprisonment was unnecessary and especially amongst felons and outlaws—that the ball and chain were only cruel appendages to an unmerciful and unlawful punishment inflicted not by regular military authority but by an usurped and irresponsible power and that the march to and from the fortifications was only the exercise of a despotism as remorseless as it was dishonorable and unnecessary. This whole transaction from Bristol to Knoxville rests, will forever rest, as a stain upon the honor of the United States army and will forever tarnish the reputation and blight the fame and disgrace the epaulettes of any officer who inflicted the cruelty or even connived at or permitted the violation of the rules of legitimate and civilized war. General Jackson or General Scott would have cashiered such an officer as one every way unworthy of association with gentlemen of honor and true courage.

In the hospital General Ramsey received the kindnesses, civilities and consideration due to a gentleman situated as he was. Ladies of the first character visited him and contributed in many ways to his comfort and his loneliness. Mrs. Dickson, his only sister near him, asked admittance to his room. The keeper at first refused, saying so many called to see him that his door was always open and his room got cold. She replied that she had brought him a nice luncheon from the country. He replied "To my certain knowledge, he has had twenty-seven luncheons that day already." But learning that Mrs. Dickson was his sister, the door was cheerfully opened to her and admittance was never afterwards refused. At this first interview Crozier asked his sister to contrive word to us in North Carolina that he was very comfortable and feared no further molestation. He always showed himself the dutiful and affectionate son, more solicitous to allay our anxiety for him and to quiet our apprehensions for his health and his life than for his own safety and escape. All his subsequent letters are full of this filial spirit. He even contrived by verbal messages through union and secession friends who called to see him, to appease the uneasiness of his mother and me. Many of these reached us before and after the surrender. Well may his parents be proud of such a son. Well may the Confederacy boast of a patriot so true, so loyal, so brave, so honorable! He made many remarkable escapes during the war and after it. The evening after his parade through the streets, as already said, he was sent to the hospital and Sperry to a separate prison. This was not generally known. The populace believed they were both still in jail. Sometime during the night a mob obtained entrance and took out one of the prisoners and hung him. I have been told that the mob asked for Ramsey and Sperry. The tragic murder of poor Baker would have been the fate of the other two if they had been in the prison. Crozier had held civil office under Mr. Buchanan. He resigned it when Tennessee seceded and accepted both military and civil appointments under the Confederacy.[1] This constituted treason and a writ was issued and he arrested for that offense. He was also arrested and tried for murder under the false charge that he had been a member of a Confederate States court martial which had condemned some offenders to be hung. By the testimony of a leading Union man, a member of the Knoxville bar, it was proved that Crozier was not on the Confederate States court martial and, of course, he was acquitted. Other frivolous charges were stumped up for the occasion. When they came up for trial he was acquitted of them all. But during their pendency his life was in danger and threats of assassination were constantly made. Under these circumstances his friends of both parties advised him to withdraw from Knoxville until

"The fierce storm be overblown
"And its avenging fury cease."

He desired trial. He demanded it. He feared no verdict against him:

---

[1] John Crozier Ramsey had been appointed Confederate States District Attorney for the East Tennessee District. He held no commission in the Confederate army. His title of "General," which Dr. Ramsey always used, derived, after the Tennessee custom, from his having been "attorney-general" of Knox County before the war.

"Colonel" Francis Alexander Ramsey, too, seems to have served as an enlisted man, as his imprisonment in Camp Morton, almost completely reserved for enlisted personnel, would indicate. His title came, as Dr. Ramsey explained earlier, from his having been elected colonel of a militia regiment in ante-bellum days. Dr. Ramsey never conferred a military title on his son McKnitt, while Robert, who had been commissioned a lieutenant in the Confederate navy, served as a "captain" of a partisan company of scouts.

he had committed no offense. He, therefore, at first refused to accede to the advice of his friends to go away even for a time. One of his old clients told him at last that if he employed him again as he preferred to do his barns would be burned and his cause but prejudiced and jeopardized, and he, too, advised him to leave Knoxville. Crozier therefore reluctantly withdrew to Nashville and opened a law office there. Soon after this another writ was sued against him and but for the intercession of the excellent Mrs. J. K. Polk with General George H. Thomas my son would have been sent to a Northern prison. Such was the unrelenting spirit of persecution excited by two or three men against an innocent and inoffensive Confederate prisoner. But persisting in the determination already made and publicly expressed, Crozier wrote to me that he would face the music and yet demand a trial. He did so. On his acquittal he was invited by a friend to tea. The league, as they called themselves, heard of it and again threatened assassination. But the incorruptible Judge Conally F. Trigg had two of the parties arrested and bound in a large sum to keep the peace with J. C. Ramsey and all other persons.

This pleasant interview with our son continued several days. At the end of it he declared himself better rested, more recruited than he had been since the war. Postal communication was now (1866) fully established and hereafter his own letters to us will exhibit his great filial and fraternal regard and devotion to our family and their interests as well as his own affairs. . . . His sister Mrs. Breck returned with him to Knoxville. Her plantation had been despoiled by the invaders and was yet in the possession of others. It was therefore thought necessary for her to visit Knoxville. A *feme covert* was once considered incapable of the commission of treason—but new lords, new laws is now the order of the day. Mrs. Breck had refused to renounce her allegiance to the South and she must become the victim of Federal rapacity, aggression and wrong. After heavy costs and long delay and losses she was repossessed of her real estate though not of her back rents. Peculation committed by an individual makes him infamous. When perpetrated by the government it is no crime, but is justified by modern jurists as a public necessity and a fit chastisement of rebel women and it only whets the appetite for more plunder and greater injustice.

CHAPTER XIX

Return to Knoxville

At the end of the year (1866) I relinquished the lease I had at our first "Retreat" and formed another with Reverend Dr. Pharr a few miles nearer Hopewell. In some respects the location was better. The dwelling house was more comfortable and better furnished. A little income from Tennessee always sent promptly or in advance by our son Crozier, the emoluments derived from my practice, and my journalistic contributions—but especially the skillful labor and attention of our son McKnitt upon a small farm—furnished us an adequate support. The frugal and inexpensive habits of my family with their industry and economy required no heavy expenditures of money. In our secluded neighborhood there were no visits of ceremony, no show, no fashion. We formed our own society— had few associates and no intimate friends. We had not become more selfish, but evidently more domestic. The theater for the exercise of our affections was plainly more contracted, more centralized, not so expansive and widely diffused as before our exile and banishment from our early home.

This was more noticeable on myself. I had never since July 1817 been without office. I had had the professional charge of a very extensive practice, embracing several counties around my residence. I had had the charge of several farms beside the buildings and improvement of my town lots. My mills and ferry gave me additional care and trouble. I was one of the trustees of three colleges and two railroads, and the agent of Tennessee for the sale of her bonds and the purchase of the iron and equipments of the E. T. and G. Railroad. I assisted in building the first steamboat that was ever owned or used at Knoxville. I was state director of half a dozen banks and president of the C. and C. R. R. Bank and president of the branch bank of the Bank of Tennessee at Knoxville. I was also Confederate States depository and had the charge of and disbursed more than forty-two millions of dollars for the Confederate States government. Beside the pressure of these varied engagements I was a frequent contributor to the scientific, literary, religious and political journals of the country and the author of the *Annals of Tennessee*. In short, from July 1817 to April 1865 I cannot recollect that I was ever idle a whole day. *Omnis in hoc* was my peculiar characteristic. If I had anything to do I was *absorbed* by it till it was finished. *Labor ipse voluptas.* I took pleasure in my business. *Orave est operave.* It was part of my religion to achieve. Achievement was my idol: the good of others my purpose. I had endeavored, as age was advancing rapidly upon me,—having already reached my three score and ten,—to decline further public pursuits. I hailed the surrender of April 1865 with real pleasure and genuine satisfaction as the termination of my public life and public service—and public usefulness.

The reader may imagine—few though can realize—the vacuum thus created in my bosom. My affection and devotion to my country were prominent elements and principles of my nature. These had become a habit and a passion of my soul. But now I had no country to love. I felt that the Union was disintegrated and that its broken fragments could never hereafter be cemented. The coercive policy of Mr. Lincoln had annihilated the Constitution of the Fathers, of the country. Coercion was itself a political suicide, a *felo de se*. It was in direct conflict with the genius of republicanism and at war with the representative principle it-self. I felt that even Tennessee, which Mr. Jefferson used to claim as his favorite, had become almost insensibly and unconsciously a despotism: that other states had been reduced to a state of military vassalage and a provincial dependency: that freedom itself was there, only an *ignis fatuus* to mislead and bewilder while it brought neither heat nor light: that the waiting boy of Governor Harris had more political power than the chief magistrate of the former Volunteer State. That the foreman of General Pillow had become more potential in Maury than the hero of Cerro Gordo, and that my faithful carriage driver, Levy, had a controlling voice in the politics of Tennessee and the Union while I myself, the greatest benefactor of my native state, am disfranchised. Was this great revolution in state or Federal affairs brought in existence lawfully, constitutionally, and by the voice of the people—or by tyranny, usurpation and violence? There can be, there is, but one answer. Then have I a country to love, admire, and venerate? I had not.[1] Still I had duties to perform and affections to cherish,

---

[1] On November 10, 1865, Dr. Ramsey received a pardon from President Andrew Johnson. It was sent to General J. Crozier Ramsey in Nashville. On December 2, Dr. Ramsey informed Secretary of State William H. Seward that he had, in accordance with the presidential procla-mation of May 29, 1865 taken the amnesty oath. S. G. Heiskell, *Andrew Jackson and Early*

not diffused over a wide theater as heretofore, but centralized and intensified upon home and neighborhood, my family and friends, my books (borrowed of course), science, literature, etc., etc. These can still be my idols.
It was a relief to let go all the rest and cling the more steadfastly to domestic life and the social circle. I have found at our "Exile's Retreat"
near Charlotte and Salisbury a more genuine felicity than any other period of my diversified life. I enjoy in 1865–1870 the *otio cum dignitate* of
my old age in my quiet seclusion more than when disquieted with the
cares and responsibilities of public employment. "Man wants but little
here below, Nor wants that little long." Our natural wants are few and
easily satisfied, while our artificial wants are innumerable and insatiable.

On the seventeenth of October, 1867, our daughter Susan was married
to William Davidson Alexander, Esquire, of Alexandriana, Mecklenburg
County, North Carolina. His family was old and respectable. He was an
alumnus of Davidson College, went with his three brothers into the war
heartily and lost heavily during the conflict. He had industry, frugality,
and enterprise: is living on his own large cotton farm and near to a railroad and a good market and with the blessing of God the young people
will do well. They are in a good Scotch Irish Presbyterian neighborhood,
are both of them members of the Hopewell Church and within convenient distance of it and of Alexandriana Academy. Our son Crozier
had paid us a long and very pleasant visit during the summer and brought
back with him to our Exile's Retreat No. 2 his widowed sister Mrs. Breck.
He was urged to remain with us to witness the ceremony of his youngest

---

Tennessee History, (1920), 2:111. This act, however, did not preclude his appending to his
Autobiography a poem entitled "Lines by an ex-Confederate" which began:

> "Oh! I'm a good old Rebel
>   That is a Reb *"so-call"*
> For this 'Fair Land of Freedom'
>   I do not care at all;
> I'm glad I fit against it—
>   I only wish we'd won
> And I don't want no pardon
>   For anything I done"

After four stanzas which reiterated hatred for the constitution and the Declaration of Independence, and joy at the number of Yankees killed, the unknown author concluded:

> "I can't take up my musket
>   And fight 'em now no more,
> But I aint agoing to love 'em,
>   Now that is certain sure;
> And I don't want no pardon
>   For what I was and am;
> I won't be reconstructed
>   And I don't care a d_____."

sister's marriage but his duty to his clients at home called him to Knox-ville. I accompanied him to Charlotte and never saw him again.

Colonel F. A. Ramsey had invested the proceeds of his Swan Pond farm in a steam flouring mill not far from Rome, Georgia. He found the investment not very remunerating and while on a visit to us heard of a large property in Rowan County with mills and other machinery, all farming stock, implements, house furniture, etc., for rent. I went with him to see it. We determined to move to and occupy it. It was late at night when the Charlotte mail was brought in. A letter in a mourning envelope attracted my notice. It was from the Honorable J. H. Crozier, my wife's brother, and contained the distressing intelligence that our son General John Crozier Ramsey was dead. . . . I have previously said that our son was most devoted in his affection to all of our family, felt deeply the deprivations that we were doomed to endure and that while enduring himself far greater sacrifices on our account and for our benefit, he never thought of himself, the dangers to his own person, even to life itself. Ex-tracts from his many and excellent letters might here be introduced to this effect, . . . to furnish evidences in detail of the great, unparalleled and irreparable loss sustained by his parents and family by his premature and unexpected death. . . .

At the time of receiving the letter of Colonel Crozier announcing the death of General Ramsey I need not add that I was overwhelmed with grief. Mrs. Ramsey and Mrs. Breck happened that night to be absent from our Retreat on a visit to our daughter Susan, sick at her own house four miles off. McKnitt and myself endured the stroke of that melancholy night, of loneliness and desolation. What added to my grief was that next morning I had to be the messenger to bear the sad news to my wife and daughters at Mr. Alexander's. As I approached that place Mrs. Breck saw me first and before I had uttered a word ran to the gate exclaiming, "What is the matter? Is brother Crozier dead?" During the morning she told me she had had presentiments of this overwhelming calamity but had withheld them from us. Such presentiments I have often experienced. I have known several instances of the phenomenon in others which I cannot stop here to detail. I consider there is nothing in the belief of their truth either unreasonable or unphilosophical.

In a few days I tore myself from my afflicted family and went to Rowan County preparatory to the establishment of Exile's Retreat No. 3. In a few days Mrs. Ramsey and Mrs. Breck reached our new home. Though sensible in the highest degree of the extent of our late bereavement they devoted themselves to their new domestic duties and we passed our time away with heavy hearts and languid spirit. Oh, how we longed for some Tennessee friends who had known Crozier, our other deceased children, ourselves, and thus knowing could appreciate our loss and our affliction. But here we were in a double sense entire strangers. Not one came in to weep with us, or to cheer us, or to offer the consolations of religion. So true is it that "the *wretch* is always left to weep." Even the pastor of Thyatira, Reverend S. C. Pharr, D.D., only said on his first and last call at our house of mourning, "This is the common lot of humanity." And then alluding to an unfounded rumor that our son had made a very large fee very recently in a land speculation, added "all *that* you will now inherit. He had neither wife nor children. It will now be *your own.*" The sordid soul, the unsympathizing heart, and the vulgar breeding implied in such a remark were unbecoming his position and his sacred office and I resented it as such by telling him that instead of comforting us by his visit he had insulted and wounded our feelings and begged him never to speak to us again. Avarice had turned his heart to stone and a heathen would have had more religion and more manners, too. He felt the rebuke and never again entered my house.

The suits that had been instituted by my son in the state and federal courts at Knoxville for the recovery of my real estate made it necessary for me to go immediately to Tennessee.[2] I dreaded the visit to the scenes of my boyhood and of my manhood, and of my half-century of active public life and extended usefulness to my country. Six years of exile had reconciled me to our changed condition. But there was one change I had never contemplated or expected. How could I go onto Gay Street, to Ramsey's Block in which was my son's law office and find it vacant? There for twenty years or more I had always found him, and met him with the smile of filial affection on his face and of dutiful welcome and fond regard on every feature! That office was now closed!

But my duty could neither be delegated to nor performed by another. I must go there in person. I took the train via Atlanta. The season was

---

[2] Dr. Ramsey engaged former Congressman Thomas A. R. Nelson, prominent East Tennessee unionist, to prosecute his suits in District Judge Conally F. Trigg's court. Mecklenburg, with its three hundred acres and ferry, had been sold, March 20, 1865, for $3750.00 to satisfy a judgment of $300.00. Ramsey's Block, a three-story brick storehouse on Gay Street had been sold to satisfy a judgment of $362.00. It brought $5100.00. The briefs in Dr. Ramsey's cases are in the T. A. R. Nelson Papers in the McClung Collection of the Lawson McGhee Library in Knoxville.

inclement and it would be too cold in February for me to go through the mountains via Asheville. From Charlotte all the way a dim recollection reminded me at every station of some earnest effort to serve the South and to be useful to the country. But I saw them now with a stoical apathy. *Ilium fuit.* I arrived at Dalton in the night. Then taking the E. T. and G. train I was on my own road. Every step from there to Knoxville I knew like my own plantation. Of the entire work *magna pars fui.* From the first meeting of the new board at Athens in 184_ to the arrival of the first car at Knoxville I had been regularly and annually appointed by the governor a state director. This new board galvanized into life the old Hiwassee Railroad. By Governor Trousdale I was appointed state agent, sold Tennessee bonds at $104½ and with the proceeds bought its rails and equipments and completed my agency satisfactorily to the state, the community, and the company. This enterprise had revolutionized the trade of East Tennessee. I had sold corn in 1823 at twenty cents per bushel in June, wheat at thirty-three and one-third and beef and pork at two dollars and a half per hundredweight. Corn was now above a dollar, wheat a dollar and a half, and pork and beef five and six dollars. I found thriving villages all along the route and beautiful farms and enterprising farmers all over the country. A new creation had taken place. The metamorphosis was everywhere apparent.

It was night when I left Dalton. Day appeared as the train approached Cleveland. There I received the warm grasp of Tennessee friends who had not seen me since I went up December 1863 with Longstreet. It was so at all the stations we passed—a cordial welcome from Whigs and Democrats —Secesh and Union men.

I stopped at Lenoir's to see my two grandsons, now motherless. One of them I had never seen before: Henry Ramsey Lenoir bore the image of his sainted mother but looked upon me as a stranger. At Lenoir's I met quite a number of old friends and was received as in days of old. I walked with Doctor Lenoir to their private cemetery. I wept over the graves of poor Henrietta, my favorite child and of the favorite of everyone—and especially of my wife and me—James Ramsey Lenoir and his sweet little brother _____, who died on the same night and was buried in the same grave. Promising to return in a few days and make a longer stay, I next morning went on the train to Knoxville. At the depot I was met and surrounded by an immense number of old friends and neighbors, who gave me an intensely warm and enthusiastic welcome. Passengers on the train the day before had given the information that I was at Lenoir's and would be up the next morning. The concourse at the depot was immense and it was some time before we got into town. I went not beyond Colonel Crozier's office. I could not think of going as far down Gay street as Ramsey's Block and did not do so for several days. That same afternoon I rode out to Riverside with my grandson, Wilberforce Dickson, and remained with my daughter some days. The Sabbath intervened and I went to our old church, Lebanon. Reverend H. Brown was the stated supply. I occupied my old pew. I looked around for the old elders and the old members. Dr. Curry, our last pastor, I knew was dead and so of my brother J. M. A. Ramsey. A new set of elders and deacons had been formed in my six-year's absence—not to "the manor born." The pews were empty. The congregation exceedingly small, irreverent, vulgar looking—anything but Presbyterian people as of old. The church yard was broken down and burned but not much injury had been done to the building itself. But the greatest change was near the site of my old residence, Mecklenburg. Not a single building which I left there in August 1863 was now standing, not a structure left. Mansion, office, library, kitchen, smokehouse, cribs, barns—all either destroyed by fire or water. The sight was mournful. Still everyone present of the congregation greeted me cordially. Even some who had assisted in eviscerating my houses and looked silently on while the flames consumed them, had the effrontery to inquire if I was not coming back. The preacher himself said if I would settle there again he might be induced to retain the pastorate of Lebanon, but without this assurance he would shake off the dust of his feet and leave them at once. He did leave them shortly afterwards.

I had not yet been on the streets in town only as I came in from the train. But nearly a week after my arrival I went into Knoxville. Leaving Colonel Crozier's office I went down Gay Street. Every acquaintance I met bid me a hearty welcome back to my old home and seemed really anxious for me at once to bring back my family and settle again. Old and young, rich and poor, all political parties, all sects without an exception were delighted to see me. I could not without incivility get off the streets. It was nearly twelve o'clock before I reached Cumberland Street. No one can tell the sadness I felt when I went into the office recently occupied by my son and received from his physicians the incidents of his sudden death. Some of the circumstances lead to the suspicion of poison. The judgment of the Great Day will reveal it all. I found he had been robbed of his money. Some of his own papers, some of mine, cannot be found. The whole thing was shrouded in mystery. For a year before his death the country had become comparatively quiet. Crozier went anywhere without molestation. Once only was he assaulted in the streets. Once a pistol was fired through his window at night. In one of his letters he mentioned the great relief he had experienced. A heavy burden had been taken off him and he felt like a new man. The labor and toil which he had endured for years of investigating my land cases, of hunting up testimony and taking depositions, etc., etc., had come to an end and he had the satisfactory consciousness of knowing that everything had been done in preparation of them for trial and promoting my success. This he imparted to me cheerfully and he could look forward to the time when we all might return and live all together in one house again. Could some diabolical instrument of some of the parties concerned, who knew the thoroughness and extent of his professional preparation in the cases, have been bribed to perpetrate his murder by poison? I have said this much to no one. The Judgment Day will reveal it. In my own case I have always believed that the poor Michigan who fired my house was employed at and sent from Cincinnati to do the burning. Money has become potential for mischief ever since 1860. Its potentiality for the purpose of gratifying the malignity and stimulating the latent revenge of a devil incarnate is unquestioned. I may be mistaken. Time may not reveal it. Eternity will.

I, in company with Mrs. Swan, went one morning to Gray Cemetery where Crozier was buried. We planted some evergreens on his lonely grave. May angels guard his quiet resting place till the morning of the Resurrection.

I found a great change at Knoxville. Its commerce, its manufactures, its business had increased with its increasing population. Also a great change in its society which I had known intimately *ab urbe condita*. Its *unity* was gone. Its people were less homogeneous, perhaps was more heterogeneous. There was an undercurrent of discordant material, antagonisms were visible everywhere and in all pursuits—rivalries, jealousies, no fraternizations. There was less hospitality, less of the generous emotions and manly passions, more of the sordid love of money, less culture, much less refinement, a more vulgar taste. Less evangelical piety—more religious pretension. Less patriotism and, of course, more selfishness. Less of learning and, of course, more of pedantry. Less deference for age, character and worth and more boastful effrontery and upstart consequence. The people were ruder and coarser, less gentle, less amiable. Fewer gentlemen of the olden time—and vastly more parvenus and upstarts. Less of real respectability and more of the would-if-I-could. Yet there were elements at work in the material of society in Knoxville that may amalgamate and harmonize the antagonistic principles so as to produce in time symmetry and order and beauty. There are some model gentlemen, some model families that probably cannot be absorbed by the surrounding contact with the ignoble, the licentious, and the vulgar. Chemical affinities have much to do in the formation and growth of good society and its usages. For instance, if the low passion for money could, by any chemical process, be cultivated into an enlarged public spirit and thus come up to the dimension and proportion of a lofty patriotism, money may become the pabulum for the nourishment and support of the public good.

With such convictions of the present of Knoxville and with some doubt as to its future I hesitated still further as to the judiciousness at my age of life of making it again my home.

After remaining in Tennessee nearly two months alternately at Riverside, Knoxville and Lenoir's I bade them all adieu and returned via Asheville and Morganton to my Exile's Retreat No. 3. Our daughter, Mrs. Dickson, and her two boys came with me. They had stood the brunt of adversity and of isolation from us for five years. Mrs. Dickson unaided and alone had managed her farm so well as not only to support her own family well, but was able by her domestic habits, her skill, industry and frugality to bear the expense of such a journey. We came by rail to Wolf Creek. Thence to Morganton by stages and thence by steam again to our house. This journey up the French Broad—the very route I had projected in 1828 and assisted in surveying in 1836—brought to mind the frequent travels on horseback which I had made in the incipiency of the great work of connecting the South and West by railroad. The visions of my youth were nearly realized. Old friends at Asheville and Morganton spoke of it to me in very complimentary terms. Arrived at home I found all well. Mrs. Dickson spent the summer at our Retreat and during her stay on more than one occasion my entire family, consisting now of only three sons, three daughters, our grandchildren, were often all with us at one time. To this there was one exception. Dr. Lenoir and his two motherless boys were at their home in Tennessee. Such unions are not often seen after such separations, such dangers and such adversities. Such a re-union may not take place again on earth. The Lord prepare us all for a glorious union above—one where there will be no more separation, no more sorrow, no more affliction no more death: where those dear members of our flock who have gone before us to Heaven will be the first to welcome us there—a united family above!

Many men on arriving at the close of life, complain of all its pursuits and enjoyments having proven vanity and vexation of spirit; but to my mind this is just an intimation that the plan of their lives had been selfish, that they have missed the right method of doing good, and that they have sought for pleasure, not in the legitimate use but in foolish abuses of their faculties. I cannot conceive that the hour of death should cause the mind to feel, all acts of kindness done to others, all acts of benificence to one's country, all exercises of devotion performed in a right spirit, all deeds of justice executed, all rays of knowledge disseminated, all deeds of humanity and patriotism during life as vain, unprofitable and unconsoling, even at the moment of leaving forever this sublunary scene.

CHAPTER XX

A Return To History

Draper Correspondence

Exile's Retreat Near
Salisbury North Carolina
February 1, 1870

[Mr. Lyman C. Draper]

My Dear Sir,[1]

Your friendly letter of December twenty-seventh was forwarded to me from Knoxville and only reached me yesterday. Before I opened it I recognized your well known *chirograph* and was reminded—how painfully the present answer can but feebly express—how pleasantly none but congenial spirits and similar tastes and pursuits can estimate.

---

[1] Although Dr. Ramsey closed his Autobiography on a note of resignation and in the apparent belief that his days were drawing to an end, he had almost a decade and a half of life and usefulness left. Just before he finished writing his Autobiography, he heard again from his old friend and fellow antiquarian, Lyman C. Draper.

In a lesser way Draper, too, had suffered from the Civil War. He had been sympathetic with the South—or, at least, opposed to the "Black" Republican regime which had begun by ousting him from his post as superintendent of public instruction in Wisconsin, and had followed this by reducing his salary as corresponding secretary of the State Historical Society of Wisconsin. He remained true to his Democratic Party principles, and was, therefore, opposed to the coercive policy of reconstruction in the South. No great ideological gulf separated him from Dr. Ramsey, while their common interest in Tennessee history was a firm bond of union between them.

During the war Draper had continued collecting materials on the "old border" of Tennessee and Kentucky. In 1863 he made an extensive trip into Kentucky gathering manuscripts and lore of the Revolutionary period. The next year, he purchased the papers of another antiquarian, Reverend John D. Shane of Cincinnati. Among them he found a large number of notes and clippings relating to agriculture and domestic economy. Contemplating them, he conceived the idea of compiling a "family encyclopedia" of useful information for farm and home which, he hoped, would support him while he pursued his historical collecting and writing. He first wrote Dr. Ramsey to inquire the names of agricultural leaders in Tennessee.

Dr. Ramsey welcomed the renewal of his contact with Draper, and the two men mutually influenced each other to return to the historical studies which neither had ever completely forsaken. For a dozen years they wrote to each other. Soon Draper was on a search for the papers of South Carolina's Thomas Sumter and his men in the Revolution. Then he turned his attention to the Mecklenburg Declaration of Independence, and after that he completed a manuscript on "Border Forays and Adventures." Finally, Dr. Ramsey induced him to write a volume on the Battle of King's Mountain. On each of these subjects, Dr. Ramsey was a valuable source of information, and Draper essayed to draw him out on innumerable aspects of the Revolutionary period in North Carolina and Tennessee.

256

You addressed me *Mecklenburg Near Knoxville Tennessee*. Troy was —Mecklenburg has ceased to be also. In August (29) 1863 I, a depositary of the Confederate States and president of the branch Bank of Tennessee at Knoxville took my assets on the approach of the Federal army under Burnside, to Abingdon, Virginia and to Atlanta, Georgia for safe keeping —leaving the ladies of my family at our old home in the *tender mercies* of the vandals of the Union enemy. My five sons were all in the Confederate States army which, as I conceived, constituted the defence of my country and of freedom. Each one of them had the opportunity to show his gallantry and his patriotism and nobly did. They all suffered in the unequal conflict. My first born son, General J. Crozier Ramsey and my youngest boy (17 years old) Arthur Ramsey, our Benjamin, fell victims to the cruelty and violence of the bloody strife—and are mourned by us as martyrs to a great and glorious cause. The three remaining sons came out safe but not without wounds and imprisonment and (almost) starvation in Camp Morton and other prisons.

My wife and daughters occupied the old mansion for a few days only after I left them. Threats were made that the house would be burned as belonging to a confirmed rebel and a high officer in the rebel government (I had disbursed nearly fifty million in the Confederate service and in all my official acts never lost a dollar). My family therefore thought it prudent to leave the old place and did remove to Knoxville, taking with them little more than their wearing apparel. Everything else—including my museum (which I believe you saw), my private papers, my correspondent's letters, my three libraries (historical, medical and miscellaneous), the second volume of the *History of Tennessee* (from 1800 to the close of the American war) all ready for the press—not to mention the crops on several farms, my large stock of every kind, furniture etc., etc.

After a few days spent in a rented house in town my ladies received the expected information that the whole was stolen, confiscated or burnt. I and

---

Dr. Ramsey's letters, preserved in the Draper Correspondence and in the Draper Manuscripts in the library of the State Historical Society of Wisconsin, serve to supplement the *Annals of Tennessee,* to recover—through Dr. Ramsey's memory—some of the material lost in the destruction of Mecklenburg, and to enrich the record of early days in Tennessee by the memories of the "nursery tales" which Dr. Ramsey recounted in his letters. Moreover, the personal matter in the letters helps to round out and complete the doctor's Autobiography.

In the following chapters letters from the Draper Manuscripts are designated by the symbols under which the collection is classified. Those which do not carry these symbols are from the Draper and Wisconsin Historical Society Correspondence and are filed by date. For an account of Draper, see William B. Hesseltine, *Pioneer's Mission: The Story of Lyman Copeland Draper* (1954).

my sons were with the army in Georgia and Virginia. I, as a financial agent by day and a surgeon after business hours in the field, camps, or hospitals, doing all I could for the wounded Rebels—falling back before the victorious enemy. I made in all eight remarkable higeras and almost miraculous escapes but was never captured and did not lose a dollar belonging to the Bank of Tennessee nor to the Confederate treasury. Hopeful and true to the last, the surrender found me at Charlotte in Mecklenburg County, North Carolina—constant, loyal to the Southern Confederacy, and defiant to its enemies. So also were my wife and daughters in Tennessee. In 1864 our youngest daughter was sent south for "disloyal acts." The enemy would not indulge her in the wish to be sent to Atlanta where I then was but sent her under flag of truce to the mountains of Virginia. There I met her and soon after I met also Mrs. Ramsey and another of our daughters Mrs. Breck sent out for their well-known and candidly expressed sympathy with the South. They had come out in June 1864 so as to see and provide for our wounded son who survived 10 days the disastrous battle of Piedmont, Virginia. Noble boy! He fought like a soldier and died like a Christian. Thank God! I have the happiness to believe that my two heroic and patriotic sons are in Heaven where the wicked cease from troubling and the weary are at rest.

After peace came—such a peace—the joint capital of Mrs. Ramsey and myself was $42.00 all told of available money—left in a strange country, exiles and houseless in the midst of a community nearly as impoverished as ourselves. We had nothing here or elsewhere. I bought at least 37½ cents worth of medicine, borrowed my son's cavalry horse and saddle and from another, borrowed a pair of medical wallets and, still wearing the Confederate grey, fell back on my old profession. My wife became the tutoress in one family and my daughter, Mrs. Breck, the governess in another. Three of our sons came to us and thus have we continued to live comfortably. I have also recovered after tedious and vexatious delay and litigation two of my farms and one house and lot in Knoxville where some of us may probably return next fall. Others of us can never go back in safety. I have never heaved a sigh for the loss of property. That we can do without or can make another fortune. But I often do sigh for my lost children; two excellent daughters and two chivalric and patriotic sons, my manuscripts, my books and my museum. These can never be restored. But they were lost in a righteous cause though not *lost cause*. Our rebellion was a success

—is a success in this that it has disintegrated the union forever and forever. I do not believe that there is virtue enough left in the limited states ever to heal the wound inflicted by the *coercive* policy of the Lincoln dynasty. I speak deliberately the sentiments of the whole South.

Do not suppose me egotistic for this auto-biographical sketch of your old correspondent. In your letter you invited it and you have it.

My health is good—perfect at 73; see as sharply, hear as acutely, sleep as soundly, eat as heartily and love my friends as ardently as ever before. I write history as earnestly though not as hopefully as in ante-bellum times. I write for the secular and religious journals—"The Land We Love," "Christian Observer" and other papers. *Mnemonika* is my general pseudonym, sometimes an *Exile* and sometimes a *Tennessee Refugee* and occasionally *Agricola*. I am glad to see you have turned your useful attention to that greatest of all services, farming. But you must not let border biography cease to be your chief object. What has prevented you from publishing? Do not delay any longer. Others may write about fields and planting and stock raising but no one but Mr. Draper can write of Boone, Clarke, Robertson and Sevier but you. Finish and publish at once. I do not know who are the officers of the state or county agricultural societies in Tennessee for whose residencies you inquire. Address for this purpose Reverend C. W. Charlton, editor of the Knoxville *Whig* or General J. A. Mabry & Co. publishers, Knoxville, Tennessee. By the way, they have the best publishing houses in Tennessee and it may be the best place to issue your forth coming works. The paper is the successor of Brownlow's *Whig*—union radical and Federal—but Charlton was in our Confederate army and is all that he ought to be. I will put you in communication with him soon.

You enquire for Putnam. Poor fellow, he is dead. So is Judge Reese, president E. T. H. & A. Society. Its corresponding secretary is the only one that survives of the executive committee except Honorable J. H. Crozier and Reverend T. W. Humes, D.D., Knoxville.

I have a sore finger and can scarcely write legibly. Write me again and command me

Yours Very Truly
J. G. M. Ramsey
Perpetual Sec. E. T. H. & A. S.

This is mailed at Charlotte but address me at Salisbury Post Office Box 87.

Exile's Retreat Near
Salisbury, North Carolina
April 28, 1870

My Dear Mr. Draper,

I was delighted to receive your favor of the twentieth. I have already written to General D. H. Hill introducing or rather endorsing you to him and through him endorsing to Honorable Thomas D. Sumter of Statesburg, North Carolina your thorough adaptation to the performance of the pious and patriotic duty of writing the biography of his illustrious ancestor, General Sumter of South Carolina. I have the pleasure of knowing and of being known to General Hill and I know he will act promptly and intelligently in the matter. I went so far as to ask him to suggest to me the name of someone who could accompany you as pilot and cicerone in your visit to the Palmetto State. At home I was called at first The *Duke of Mecklenburg*—more recently, *Old Palmetto*. I supposed that it might possibly become your duty and your pleasure to visit and examine and perhaps make drafts of the places signalized by the valor of Sumter and his men first at Towers, Vegrassee, Fort Prince George—then at Hanging Rock and other battle grounds of the Revolution. I suppose you have read my footnote on page 55 of my *Tennessee* as well as the text. I had all the local histories of South Carolina at home but cannot say which of them (though I think Hewitt) furnished me the details of the arrest of Johannes as there stated. Sumter sprang upon him like a tiger and held him to the ground till he was tied and taken to Charleston. If General Hill gives me a name I will at once communicate it to you. If I were sixty I would seek the privilege myself of being your companion on this route. In some of these local histories—perhaps Drayton's—I found a map of Williamson's celebrated campaign against the Cherokees. It gave the towns, rivers, battlegrounds and encampments from the Saluda to Chota on the Tennessee. If I were younger and less impecunious than I am I would yet survey that whole route as I once fondly anticipated.

"Did you know *Colonel* Robert Campbell," etc., etc.? Yes and well. He was never colonel, only Lieutenant Campbell, at King's Mountain and in several Virginia campaigns against the Indians. All I know of him is given in my *Annals*. He was a brave soldier and quiet good citizen. Two of his sons, David and Edwin Campbell, lived at Knoxville, went to Arkansas and died. A son of the former, Robert H?, I believe, was working last May in Peoples Bank, Knoxville, there. A letter to him care of ——— Mitchell, cashier, will reach him.

Last May I came over the very route you propose to reach Salisbury. My daughter, Mrs. Dickson and her two boys came with me. Come from Knoxville to Morristown on E. T. & Va. R. R., then to end of the railroad near the Warm Springs, North Carolina then by close connecting stages to Asheville, North Carolina, and then by close connecting stages to end of railroad fifteen or twenty miles west of Morganton, then by rail to Third Creek depot or station sixteen miles west of Salisbury. Third Creek is five miles from me. Ask Mr. Allison or Mr. Clarke to bring you to my house early next morning where from the senior to the junior we will give you a Tennessee welcome. I came in two and one-half days. Be sure to come. You must come and stay at least a week.

Yours truly,
J. G. M. Ramsey

P. S. The stamps in your second letter were received and inclosed to General Hill. Be sure to come. I will take you to Salisbury.

P. S. Reading over your letter the third time I find I have omitted to allude, as I intended to do, to an expression in it about to this amount viz., that you do not see yet that you will make anything from your histories and biographies. How is this? Why in them I see a mine of wealth—now or hereafter or both. But it has cost too much time and labor to let your bantling suffer by no having an introduction to the present living age and peoples. I have wondered why you have not already published one of your subjects as an experiment. If Boone or Sevier or Clarke was before the reading public I know, impoverished as some of our western and southwestern states are, that would sell well. Suppose you, while at Knoxville, offer the copyright of one of these to Mabry & Co. of Knoxville, a very rich publishing house there and very *ambitious* of doing something large and enterprising in the book line. One of the firm is union, General Mabry; another intensely Southern or conservative, Reverend C. W. Charlton. Or suppose you finish Sumter and offer it in the Carolinas and Georgia. Evans & Walker of Charleston will buy the copyright. Poor as we Southerns are, any one of us can pay for a biography of our Southern men. At least don't you get discouraged yourself. *Nil desperandum. Dum spiro, spero.* These are my mottoes. I would have died at twenty-eight if I had not been actuated by them. This gave me energy in the past and now in my old age the Christian Hope—the anchor of the soul, sure and stead-fast, supplies what the world fails to supply and makes me at once cheer-ful and contented and enables me to resign my future to God's goodness.

Our ladies recollect you and hope to see you here.

Very Sincerely,

J. G. M. Ramsey

July 13, 1870

Your ever welcome favor of the seventh reached me last night. I have not heard a word of or from Colonel Sumter. I have not received any re-ply from General Hill but I feel certain that as far as *he* could do so he would put the Palmettos (Sumters) in motion after I enclosed your letter (to me) and the stamps to him. At the same time I wrote a communication for his paper on the general subject of your letter and introducing you, your border biography, and your proposed work on Sumter and his men to Southern readers. He gave to my communication a conspicuous insertion and to make it move he dropped my assumed name and put down my own without any authority from me to do so. But soon after I was in Char-lotte and several gentlemen and some ladies enquired when I looked for you, as it was determined that either Colonel William Johnson, President of the Charlotte and Columbia Railroad, or Captain Sydenham Alexander or Dr. Joseph Graham would accompany you into South Carolina and fa-cilitate your labors. The former especially, Colonel Johnson, seemed to be very earnest and told me I must bring you right to his house, that you must be his guest, and he mentioned several persons and places you must see, that I must come along and we would be able to hear and see all that remained untold of Sumter. I was highly pleased with his enthusiasm and I know they will all be disappointed when I tell them that you cannot come this summer.

Allow me now to suggest to *you* (and to none else till I hear from you) to allow me to say that you will be at King's Mountain on the seventh October and will there and then deliver an address or read a narrative of that great and decisive battle and recount the deeds of Sumter's contem-poraries if not of himself. Before the late war the seventh was always cele-brated every year. The custom can be revived next October if you will con-sent to be there. You can make it also subserve your further purposes. I would like myself to go with you. I think you could *enthuse* even the *frigid* Sumters of 1870. Don't say nay to my suggestion. I will have some of the Seviers and Shelbys there from East Tennessee. I finished last week my own Autobiography and wish very much to show some of its four hundred and eighty pages to you. It may be the last of my literary labors. Though I am at seventy-three very well—passing the evening of life *otio cum dignitate,* but in my exile I sometimes say "nunc domine tuum servium demittas." If I only had a country to *love* as I once did love Tennessee and the old union—but this disintegration will kill me if it continues longer. Everybody else of my own age and even younger has gone before me: W. Gilmore Simms, Dickens, Putnam, Reese. You are one of the few links that bind me to earth and to letters. God's will be done! May Heaven be our next home and our portion forever prays your old friend. . . .

P. S. Do you read the *Southern Home?* I wish you may have seen my article sent to General Hill about your intended visit.

Let me urge you if you can to come right to our Retreat and spend several days with us. A bed and a plate will always be at your service and no people will ever give you a more cordial welcome than my good wife, our widowed daughter, and J. G. M. Ramsey, our son. This constitutes all of the old large Mecklenburg family. The rest are near us and in Tennessee.

Charlotte, North Carolina
February 6, 1871

Your two letters of January 25 were received last mail—having been *forwarded* from Salisbury to this place. We were all sick in Rowan County. Sixty white and black lived on our plantation—fifty-nine of whom were sick of fever, leaving one Negress alone to hand us a gourd of cold water. Not one death occurred, but the malaria was so intense and persistent that we determined to go elsewhere—perhaps to Knoxville, Tennessee. If Mrs. Ramsey gets able to bear the fatigue of the cars and if this inclement weather moderates we may leave Charlotte this spring and possibly reach Knoxville to spend our golden wedding there March 1, 1871. I mention these things so as to let you know as far as I can my probable whereabouts when you set out on your southern trip. From your long silence I was afraid my last had failed to reach you. All of your friends were expecting to *greet* you and facilitate your objects in regard to Sumter and his men. Everytime I see any of them they inquire for you and desire to serve you and advance your objects.

Of *Thomas Sumter*—a Revolutionary pensioner in Knox County in 1840, or of James Sumter in some part of Tennessee I know nothing. This is strange as to the former. I was almost every day in Knoxville. The pension office was near my Bank and on the fourth March and seventh of September of every year dropped all other business to linger around the pension office for several days, take the old and feeble Revolutionary soldiers home with me, take down their services and their recollections of the past into my note book; and yet I [never] knew Thomas Sumter or heard of him. He must have been superannuated and probably drew his pension by proxy. If I go to Knoxville this spring I will investigate him in person. If I stay here I will write to my correspondents about him and James Sumter too and inform you fully hereafter.

I am glad to hear that you have made such progress in your Sumter researches. General Hill, myself, and others tried to stimulate his descendents and those of his men to aid your inquiries. I hope you will take me on your zig-zag route—either at Charlotte or Knoxville. I would live a year longer if I could see you and you would live ten good years longer in St. Augustine or almost any other point in Florida. Chronic catarrh and diseased throat are remediless where you are. Both become more tolerable and more curable in Florida. Get nearer to the sun as you grow older. Longevity is the natural result of this maxim of the Fathers in Medicine and Hygiene. Besides this, I hear from your own pen for the first time of another affliction of a different kind but common to us both —*impecuniosity*. On the St. Johns or on Indian River—indeed any place in Florida almost, east or west—a ranch costs you nothing. Your homestead is a gift from the government. An orange orchard is almost the spontaneous gift of nature. Deer, turkeys, aquatic birds, fishes of all kinds, oysters and all your necessary meats are cheap, abundant and easily procured. Rice and other breadstuffs cheap, too, and very procurable. What *labor* is needful for you is cheap as dirt. Our cook costs us from two to four dollars a month and they prefer cast off clothing to money. Their labor is often unsatisfactory and unreliable, but when one leaves you another is easily substituted. If they are well and justly treated by us Caucasians they never scruple about our supremacy. None of them aspire to equality. They are savages and barbarians, know it and submit to the inferiority it implies. Keep their stomachs full and with plenty of feed and sunshine they are more contented and less vicious than the white servants of the North. Many of our Carolina neighbors have gone there and

I hear are doing well every way. St. Augustine is no better than many other places—only Tallahassee has the better climate of the two. Several of my children have become fixtures in Carolina and Tennessee or I would have been settled in the everglades of the Floridas. Put yourself in reach of the United States mails and railroads of the South and you can live in Florida till you are four score. Go there by all means and stay.

I will today write to Dr. John H. Logan—still at Talladega, Alabama introducing you to him. He shall know you like a book and I will *make* him write to you at once, inviting you to call at Talladega and investigate him and his manuscripts thoroughly. I think he is the son of my old friend Logan of Charleston, South Carolina who in 1828 first introduced me to the Charleston Library. If so he will know me at once. This letter will have time to reach you before March first. I will suggest exchange of manuscripts and other matters in full. Did you receive the *Southern Home* containing an introduction from me to you to the Carolina people? I sent it to you. God bless, guard, guide, protect and defend and save you prays yours. . . .

Charlotte, North Carolina
April 6, 1871

I found this morning in my box 32 your kind favor of the second and now at 4 P.M. I am seated to reply to it. I have not yet gone to Knoxville and will remain here till May—say the fifteenth—perhaps a little longer. I will postpone our journey even at some inconvenience to us, for I must see you. I think you would hardly be repaid for the trouble of going by Knoxville to see Jack Anderson Bayless and Martin Cline Sumter. And I will (if you agree to my not unselfish advice to come on at once to Charlotte) undertake to see these Knox County Sumters and procure from them all they can furnish about their ancestor and his men. This I will do soon after I reach Tennessee and will communicate it to you by mail if after looking at our South you do not conclude to return by Knoxville. After I read your letter I called at General Hill's office and presented your respects. He lives in the country but comes to town every Tuesday P.M. and stays here till Saturday A.M. I mention this that if otherways practicable you may reach here Tuesday or Wednesday. If I hear the day I or Colonel Johnston will meet you at the depot and make you our guest. They and other friends are very desirous to make your acquaintance and will make your stay here very agreeable. I called to see Colonel Johnston but he is not at home, but on a former occasion he told me to take you right to his house and that he had sent you a *frank* on all his roads. We all received Judge Walker's address and thank you for it.

When I see you here as I hope to do in all of April I will in person modify the advice I gave you about Florida by enlarging the field from which to select your future southern home. In point of health, cheap living, cheap lands, good society, books, and educated gentlemen, Aiken, South Carolina ought to have been made prominent. But more of this when we meet. So then the matter is settled that you will write me, a few days before you leave Madison, when you expect to be at Charlotte, the route you prefer to take south of this, etc., etc. General Hill has already selected a Mr. Stowe to accompany you if you need or desire a cicerone. I have a little practice in Charlotte and have to *nurse* it for a living. Now seventy-four years old, but still active, vivacious, buoyant and feeling an unwavering trust in God's Providence as being the wisest and best for us. I got the other day your Hand Book, your Encyclopedia. How *do* you find time to work so much? *Omnis in hoc* has been always my motto, but I can't keep up with you.

May God bless, prosper, guide, direct you prays your old friend.

Draper Manuscripts 18 VV 261–2

Knoxville, Tennessee

May 6, 1872

Your favor of the fifteenth ultimo reached me soon after its date. I immediately walked over into North Knoxville to see Captain Jack Anderson and his wife. There I learned that he had removed somewhere over on the river at an inaccessible point to any but pedestrians. I wrote to him requesting him to come to my house. He did so today. I find he is not the Captain Anderson I once knew and promised to see. He died while I was in exile five or six years ago. This Captain Anderson is intelligent and truthful. His father-in-law, the nephew, was uninformed and illiterate, left no records. Even his family Bible is now beyond reach. Captain Anderson remained in my office today till after our dinner and has just now, three P.M., left. I am sorry to say that after referring to all the questions and points in your letter I could not succeed in gleaning anything more from him or his wife than the few gleanings which you will find on the other side of this sheet. I put a copy of my *Annals* in his hands to discipline or indoctrinate him on such matters. He will read it all and promises me that if anything further suggests itself to his recollection he will come back and communicate it to me and I will at once send it forward. I wish, my dear Mr. Draper, that I could have done you more service.

You inquire kindly how I am doing in mind and body. I am seventy-five years old since March 25. Am eight pounds heavier (118) than my usual weight, have not been sick an hour since we left the malarian region of North Carolina, am buoyant, hopeful, trustful, resigned, submissive (not to despotism, I mean, but to God), have as much practice as I can perform, at peace with all the world and especially with myself—*mens conscia recti*—a little impecunious comparatively but plenty to eat and wear. Though not able as formerly to establish literary institutions, steamboats and railroad lines, or erect churches and bridges and all that but about as well contented as at any period of my life, enjoy my *otio cum dignitate,* plenty of borrowed books to read, some very few and appreciative friends and no enemies that I know of, an increased taste for history, biography, and literature in general, a cordial invitation from Governor J. C. Brown to examine and cull from our state archives—so as to supplement my burnt volume in manuscript from 1800 to end of war with Mexico and, if life and strength last, to close up with the surrender in 1865. My autobiography is completed up to May 1871, the date of my return from an honorable exile. I must not ask you to write often but occasionally send me something in our line to read. Am glad you succeeded so well in South Carolina *Festina lente,* and let me see your work finished. And then I will say *Nunc Domine tuum servum dimittas!*

Draper Manuscripts 6 XX 72d

Mecklenburg Place,[2]
Knoxville, Tennessee
October 3, 1872

Yours of September 11 duly received. Have waited this interim to learn

---

[2] After his return to Knoxville in March 1872, Dr. Ramsey occupied a small colonial house on East Main Street which he christened "Mecklenburg Place." His subsequent letters carried this name at their head. (Cf. McClung Papers, vol. XIV, Part 3, p. 545. Lawson McGhee Library.)

something and inquire more extensively about *Coffee*. I am to hear here-after more minutely and from more accurate sources, but today I hasten to say that a Mr. Coffee did marry a daughter of General Sumter's sister and once paid a visit at a very early day to Beaver Creek settlement eight miles north of Knoxville, but as my informant thinks, did not settle there but passed on to *Pulaski,* Kentucky. Don't know whether that was the name of a town or county. His wife was a cousin of Mrs. Jack Anderson, of whom I once inquired and wrote you. Coffee never returned to Beaver Creek but it is believed remained permanently in Kentucky; is thought to be related to the Coffee associated with General Andrew Jackson. But I hope before long to see Colonel William Griffin, once sheriff of Knox County, and familiar with the old Beaver Creek settlers, and some others who may be able to help trace out the Sumter family; and when I hear anything material and reliable I will not fail to communicate it.

Soon after your letter, came also the welcomed and highly appreciated volume VI, 1869-72.[3] How have you achieved so much in the inauguration and erection of your historical society and in the accomplishment of so much other historical labor? If any living man should be proud, vain, or boastful of what he has done for that society, for Wisconsin, for the re-public of letters, for *history*—that man is L. C. Draper. May I hope to live long enough to see and read your *magnum opus?* Do publish soon. If I were less impecunious than I am since the war, old as I am I would next summer come to Madison to see and converse with you.

Of (my) The East Tennessee Historical and Antiquarian Society of which I was perpetual corresponding secretary only *three* members sur-vive and all our collections, transactions, cabinet, etc., burned or stolen and destroyed. What a wreck!—the Sevier and Blount papers, executive journal, private correspondence—all lost.

I reciprocate heartily your wishes for Greeley's election. Not that I like all his political antecedents. But Greeley and Brown now represent the press, journalism. That has become at least the *Third* Estate in our gov-ernment—the leader and manufacturer of enlightened public sentiment, the educator of our masses and in some considerable degree the instructor and evangelizer of our young people—a function of no small importance in the welfare of the country. Greeley and Brown represent that great organization which may promote the conservative principle that may still

---

[3] Draper regularly sent Dr. Ramsey the volumes of the *Collections* of the State Historical Society of Wisconsin as they appeared.

preserve liberty, law, order and right. That ticket I believe will be elected. Here in Tennessee the Democratic and Conservative party is a unit for them. Elsewhere at large our prospects are encouraging. The attempt by Andrew Johnson to disorganize our friends will signally fail. General Chatham will beat him as representative of the state at large.

I am half through your volume and am greatly obliged to you for it. I enclose you a genuine Confederate States treasury bill—that cost me par. I hold many such and like my two patriotic grandfathers who had trunks filled with Continental bills in profusion and left them as legacies to their children, so I have more than $10,000 besides as much of Confederate States bonds. I am proud of these wrecks of a fortune honestly acquired and gloriously lost in a patriotic devotion to independence and self government. Present this bill to your cabinet. When you can do so please send me more of your biographical and historical labors.

Did I heretofore send you a copy of my *Tennessee Annals?* Let me know. I have a few copies on hand. I am well and am making a comfortable living by practice, have a small circle of learned, educated and Christian friends near and around me and hope to go down to my grave in peace without one feeling of ill will to any human being. Our two sons, victims of the war we propose to reinter this fall in our Confederate cemetery— one of them from the Piedmont battlefield in Augusta County, Virginia.

Draper Manuscripts 15 VV 59

October 28, 1872

I received by last mail a letter from Mrs. J. K. Polk covering a communication from yourself to her making inquiries concerning Captain *James Knox.* I have today replied to Mrs. Polk, mentioning that during my exile in Mecklenburg County I had contributed in 1867–8 to the "Land We Love" an article headed *Charlotte and Mecklenburg* and other similar reminiscences of Revolutionary times, but that I had not today that magazine before me or in my reach but that perhaps these articles contained something of Captain Knox. I cannot recollect distinctly but think they do. Nothing though very specific. You may have that magazine in your collection. If so, you can examine for yourself. I also wrote, at the earnest request of the pastor and members of *Hopewell* Church a history of that congregation in which Captain Knox and his services are mentioned favorably. That is not yet published. When it comes out I will send you a copy. In the meantime I will send to a friend near Charlotte, North Carolina to procure for me an exact copy of the inscription on the gravestone over Captain Knox. I saw it myself and brightened it up and made what was illegible at first from moss and debris perfectly legible. The masonic emblems on it are finely sculptured and I suppose it to have been imported from abroad from its style and execution. I copied it in 1866 and sent to Mrs. Polk. As I never heard that it came to hand and as at that time there was an espionage on the letters of rebels, traitors, refugees and exiles, and some irregularity of the mails and post offices, my letter may have not reached its destination. The copy may contain place and time of his nativity and of his death. I know the traditions of the times in which he lived lead me to suppose that he emigrated from Pennsylvania with that large wave of population, principally Scotch Irish Presbyterians, that about the middle of the last century, 1750 to 1765, that came to the country lying between the Yadkin and Catawba who formed the infant settlements, founded churches and schools and embraced the cause of the colonies ardently in 1775, and with their co-patriots and co-emigrants in the co-terminous country a little further south in South Carolina helped to retard the invasion under Cornwallis, Tarlton, Ferguson, etc., joining Sumter, Shelby, Sevier, Davie in all their campaigns. Amongst these were Rutherford, Captain Knox, Captain William Alexander (known afterwards as Blind Bill), Ezekiel Wallis and many others.

Mecklenburg was truly designated by Tarleton the "Hornets Nest." Captain Knox was, I believe, one of the fourteen who under George Graham met and repulsed at *McIntire's Branch* a large foraging detachment September 1780. (See *Land We Love*.) He resided in that immediate neighborhood and was buried in Hopewell cemetery where his grave stone is still to be seen. In the same yard lie the remains of General William Davidson, Captain Frank Bradley, and many other Whigs, soldiers and civilians. Captain Knox has left in Hopewell the savor of a good name. He was remarkable for his piety, his extreme care and fidelity in the religious education and culture of his children in the doctrine and order of the Presbyterian Church. To this has always been ascribed the well known familiarity of his daughter (the late Mrs. Polk—mother of James K. Polk) with the creed and usages of presbytery. Her theological acumen, her vigorous and masculine intellect, her great tenacity of Presbyterianism made her a model in all the relations of life. The Bible, the

Confession of Faith, the Psalms and Watt's Hymns were her chief employment and her religious and spiritual aliment. Captain Knox was at once a hero and a saint, a patriot and a Christian gentleman. I lived four years in Hopewell and will write today to my correspondents and friends there for more minute information about him, his wife, his children. A kinsman Knox lives near [illegible] Ch. Rowan City, North Carolina. Another Knox lived before the war in Monroe or Polk County, Tennessee, Madisonville or Benton P. O.

I hear nothing further about the Coffee family. I wish to visit Nashville to examine state archives this fall or winter. Can't you drop down there and let us shake hands? My good wife is suffering from dropsy and for the first time in my long married life I feel apprehensive of the result. Lord God help us—have mercy—have mercy.

Send me occasionally something (of your own) to read. Have you in your collection Foote's *Sketches of North Carolina,* large octavo? It contains much history and biography. . . .

P. S. President Polk was specially proud of his maternal grandfather, J. Knox; of his record as a brave soldier, officer, patriot. He often spoke of him to me and when I last saw him in the White House he drew from me a promise that Mrs. Ramsey and I should accompany him and Mrs. Polk on a pious pilgrimage to Mecklenburg and Hopewell, North Carolina.

Draper Manuscripts 15 VV 75

December 4, 1872

Since my last to you I have procured from my son-in-law, W. Davidson Alexander, Esquire, a deacon of Hopewell Church in Mecklenburg County, North Carolina, an accurate and full copy of the inscription on the tombstone of Captain James Knox. I find it corresponds exactly with the copy I had hastily made one of the coldest days of December 1865. I enclose the copy to you. The hymn from which the poetry is taken is within your reach: therefore, only two lines are copied. On the tombstone the whole of the hymn is engraved beautifully. I have not copied the devices and emblems upon it but will add that the first two lines of the inscription form a half circle embracing the face and bust of a man draped in military costume, sword, etc. The line in Latin is in a straight line beneath the carving. This is artistically, even elegantly, done for 1794 and in upper

North Carolina. The widow had evidently left nothing undone which could at all manifest either affection or grief at her loss. I have endeavoured to ascertain her maiden name but have not yet learned it. I have a vague recollection that it was either Brevard, Davidson, Alexander or Springs Nelson. I know that President Polk claimed kinship with these several families. I will prosecute inquiry further on this point. I always heard that Captain Knox was noted for his courage and skill as an officer, his patriotism as a citizen, his zeal and piety, and his devotion to Presbyterianism. His widow has well described his characteristic virtues; *justice, generosity, probity,* and *sincerity*—traits which also eminently belonged to his grandson J. K. Polk, conspicuously so. If I have omitted anything please indicate the omission. I have sent Mrs. Polk a copy of the inscription and the traditions as far as I know them and as I said before I will inquire further.

Are you making progress in your *magnum opus?* Do let the world see it before 1876—a part of it sooner.

Poor Greeley died under a mistaken apprehension that a majority of the intelligence and virtue of the country had not voted for him. Deduct the Negro vote and the vote of the rabble North and South and he has a pretty majority. I was for him only in *spots,* as Ritchie said of Jackson's Union Proclamation (against nullification). While he endeavoured to benefit the Negro he has really done the race a great injury. Send me occasionally something to read. I get nothing further about Sumter or Coffey. . . .

Inscription copied from the Tomb Stone of Captain James Knox in Hopewell Graveyard December 1865 by *J. G. M. Ramsey.*

" 'Fond Man! The vision of a moment made Dream of a dream and shadow of a shade!'

Vivit post funera Virtus *

"In memory of Captain James Knox Who, in hope of a glorious resurrection to eternal life deceased Oct. 10, 1794 aged 42 years.

"To continue his memory in the minds of his surviving friends and to perpetuate a character in which were united the tender husband, the affectionate parent and good citizen and by whom were cultivated justice

----

* Anglice. Virtue survives the Grave.

generosity probity and sincerity this monument is erected by the faithful and grateful *partner of his life and affections."*

Then follows the well known poetic *effusion of Pope—beginning* "Vital spark of Heavenly flame, Quit, O Quit, this mortal frame" and so on through the hymn closing with "Oh Death where is thy sting." It is the 640th hymn as now found in the Hymn Book of the Presbyterian Church. I need not copy more of it. The inscription continues

"Cease then frail nature to lament in vain
"Reason forbids to wish him back again."

On foot stone of the same grave.   J. K.

The stone is fine—the sculpture and engraving excellent. They are found in Hopewell graveyard, Mecklenburg County, North Carolina. Captain Knox was a very pious member of this church—perhaps an elder. It was founded about 1756 when the Virginia colonists were driven there by outbreak of the Indians after Braddock's war.

I copy this for L. C. Draper at request of Mrs. Polk.

J. G. M. R.
Nov. 11, 1872

Draper Correspondence

February 3, 1873.

I received your last favors by due course of mail and with them the two valuable volumes and yesterday the annual *Report* of the Wisconsin Historical Society. I have read every word in them with great interest and a high appreciation of the zeal and energy and success with which *you* have inaugurated and carried into effect such a Herculean undertaking as you have done for your own state, the west, the country at large, and the world. I don't flatter you when I speak thus—but am sincere in the declaration that *you* have accomplished more for learning, science, and especially history and biography than any living man—perhaps I may truthfully say than any one that has preceeded you from Herodotus down. When I compare your achievements for Wisconsin with the little that has been effected for Tennessee I blush and feel mortified, exceedingly so. When you retrospect your own *past* you may exclaim with Ovid *"Jarnque opus exigi quod me finum"* etc.—but enough of this now.

I was glad to hear the name of Mrs. James Knox Gillespie. She was of a good family—not altogether unknown to fame. If I mistake not her father was a soldier—perhaps an officer—captain, I believe, under Greene at Guilford Court House, North Carolina—of the Scotch Irish Presbyterian stock in 1775 who did so much for liberty and the right of self government from the dawn of the Revolution at the battle of the Regulation at Alamance, 1771 I believe. "Oh," said an old man who was in that battle, "if John and Daniel Gillespie had only known as much about military discipline then as they knew a few years after that, the bloody Tyron would never have slept in his palace again." *vide Sketches of North Carolina* By William Henry Foote. D.D. page 61. I suppose you have that volume (large octavo pp. 557, N. Y., Robert Carter, 1846) in your library. If not let me know and I will express it to you at once. It contains much of Revolutionary history in the Carolinas and may help you in your "Sumter and his Men." I am promised something further of Captain Knox. When received it shall be sent promptly. You received, I hope, the beautiful and pious *Inscription* by his wife on his tombstone at Hopewell and also the several treasury bills inclosed you by mail. I have on hand some of the post office stamps, passports, orders for transportation, telegrams, etc., etc., of that renowned Confederacy—*quorum magna pais fini*. If they will interest you so much as to desire them let me hear from you early. When I am dead and gone they may be lost or destroyed. They are a part of history, to us in the South especially interesting if not valuable.

I am very well—seventy-six the twenty-fifth of March 1873 and you will be surprised to hear still vivacious and with some energy—fortune all gone—practicing medicine for a living—better contented than when sick, and with a more confiding and filial trust in God. A little bereaved again to hear of the death of a grandson, James Ramsey in North Carolina. [illegible] . . . and Eve Ramsey Alexander a grand daughter in Mecklenburg, North Carolina. I will go to them—They will not come to me. . . .

May 5, 1873

I read in the good Book "Avoid the appearance of evil." I am unwilling to seem even, to have forfeited your good opinion as a punctual correspondent—especially where I am requested to assist your research and investigation of Tennessee History or the biography of her people. And yet I will not say *"Peccavi! Peccavi!"* The day after your last favor came to hand I wrote to my friend J. T. Lenoir of Sweetwater in Monroe County, Tennessee to procure for your use the *old* maps and traditions of the localities you desired. Colonel Frank A. Ramsey, my nephew, handed him my letter; to whom he answered that he knew the man, *Colonel Johnson,* who was able to fill the bill precisely and should do it soon. All these gentlemen are competent and perfectly reliable. But after waiting thus long for their reply I have to add no reply has been received, and I begin to fear they may have sent the results of their labor directly to yourself. If so, I hope it will be satisfactory. If not, whenever it comes to my hands the whole will be duly forwarded.

In the meantime though I take the opportunity to add something myself—I once had an atlas (1800 I think was its date) when I began to study geography, 1808 or 1810, which contained a map of Tennessee as then known (and much of it except the rivers and Indian war and trading paths undeliniated because unoccupied—a seeming wilderness and *terra incognita*) some French settlements on our southern boundary. The great *Creek's* Crossing below what is now Chattanooga, and some Shawnee villages below what is now Nashville were pretty well delineated, but all of West Tennessee and much of Middle Tennessee a blank, one-third of East Tennessee still marked as unsettled. That atlas was burned with my library and house in September 1863 but copies of it are now extant. Will send you a copy if I can find the atlas, at least the page containing Tennessee. It will interest you some, if it does not answer your full purpose.

Again, when searching for the first approaches of civilization to Tennessee I procured the Memoirs of *Judge Drayton*—two volumes if I remember right. He and the Reverend Tennant were appointed in South Carolina to visit and address the back districts of that state so as to induce the settlers to espouse the cause of the colonies. In these volumes I noticed an old map and an account of the campaign of General Williamson against the Cherokees, 1774 or 1775, with his army. In that map are plainly given all their marches, their battles, the villages destroyed as well as visited or seen. The map is very full and minute. I know it can yet be had in South Carolina, perhaps elsewhere. My own copy was burned or stolen. Get a copy if you can. This is all I can do for you now. I will forward to you as soon as it comes to hand the answer of Lenoir and Johnson.

I am well. Our season and crops very unpromising but as more refreshing to us both a revival of religion in all our churches. Praise to God. May He continue to bless you and yours prays your friend. . . .

P. S. I do hope before I die that you may publish some of your *Border Warfare*. Especially Sevier, Robertson, Boone, Sumter, and others. Put one of them out now as a feeler. We are all satisfied about the work, but we old men in Tennessee want to see even a part of your *magnum opus*. P. S. second. I thank you for all you have sent me and will be thankful for more. I send you Nolichucky Jack (Anglice, John Sevier) being an address just out of press delivered by W. A. Henderson, Esquire, before the Knoxville Board of Trade. It is pretty good. I asked him not to mention my name in it.

August 5, 1873

I have been hoping to hear from you that Mr. Johnson or Mr. Lenoir, both of Monroe County, Tennessee, or others to whom I had applied for the old maps and other sources of historical, at least topographical, information had before this time furnished you something that would meet your wishes on the subject. Have they done so? They promised me to either send it to you or to myself. They have not sent me anything. Sincerely do I hope they have found something that will interest you and that they have forwarded to you.

I met yesterday on the street Colonel J. M. Flemming, our superintendent of state schools. He is neither a personal or political friend of mine but yet I desire to make his administration of the educational interest of Tennessee subserve the best interests of our people, and therefore suggested to him as most promotive of that great object to put himself at once in communication with you, informed him what you had done in this behalf for Wisconsin, gave him your address, etc., and authorized him to refer to me. If he knows his duty as I do he will write you.

We are all quite well. Cholera has visited many places in Tennessee with fearful fatality but thus far the epidemic has touched Knoxville lightly. I have not lost a single case. The apprehension still exists though that we will not altogether escape. Our whole people in Knoxville, with a spontaneity that was little expected and never surpassed, several weeks ago appointed a day of fasting, humiliation and prayer to God that He would avert His judgments from us. Thus far His hand has been stayed. Thanks to His goodness for the past. Let us hope in His Mercy for the time to come.

Send me anything of your own as soon as it sees the light. I have already written the Pulpit of Tennessee and have done something for its bench, its bar and its clinique. It is almost presumption in one aged nearly seventy-seven to expect to finish either of them—isn't it?

Your old friend.
J. G. M. Ramsey

CHAPTER XXI

Men of Mecklenburg

Draper Correspondence

Mecklenburg Place
Knoxville, Tennessee
May 15, 1874

L. C. Draper, Esquire
My Dear Sir,

I enclose you herein a part of the (Nashville) *Republican Banner* containing proceedings of the Historical Society of Tennessee at its last meeting. After fifteen years of inaction it has been resuscitated and galvanized into life. You will see that very unexpectedly to myself I have been unanimously elected president and that on motion of J. Berrien Lindsley, LL.D., a committee consisting of Doctors Ramsey and Foster and Judge Lea, was appointed to prepare and issue a circular address to the people of the state, soliciting the contribution of historic relics. Nearly an octogenarian, I at first felt unwilling to accept these high and laborious positions—president of the state historical society and chairman of its most important and responsible committee. But under the circumstances I could not consistently decline the honor and the labor implied by the compliment intended me. I had been invited to attend the called meeting, but being unable to do so I wrote a long letter in which I mentioned Lyman C. Draper and the State Historical Society of Wisconsin as having made the most perfect and successful historical achievement in that direction of any of her co-states. I pointed to your success and efforts as our model with a suitable comment, other suggestions on the general subjects involved, etc., etc. If my letter is published you will see it.

Before my library was destroyed in 1863 I could look into it and find almost anything I wanted. You had sent me several volumes of the proceedings and transactions of your society. One of them I recollect still with vivid freshness. It may have been one of your own reports as secretary, or of one of your committees, or of one of your earlier circulars, but it contained, I recollect, a full list or catalogue of the several *objects* and *purposes* and *aims* of your society, classified so perfectly as to enable each contributor to see for himself to what object to direct his attention. I think in the enumeration of its several objects were early explorations, first discoveries and settlements, voyages, biographies of your pioneers, battles, battle grounds, forts, stations, maps, the private files of the leaders in their days, early newspapers, relics of every kind, rare coins, aboriginal curiosities, etc., etc. This list was so well *classified* and *arranged* that I supposed you had a hand in it yourself. I admired it as being perfect of its kind. Now I wish to procure from you this circular, this pamphlet, this report or this volume as the case may be. I am now engaged on the *Circular* as required by the resolution of Doctor Lindsley, and will be greatly obliged to you to favor me with it at your earliest convenience. Address me at Knoxville, as heretofore (not Nashville, the seat of our state society). You are too busy, as I am, too, to trouble you today with anything further, only to say that after my sketch of Captain Robert Craighead, one of Sumter's officers, I found his name mentioned in Wheeler's *North Carolina* as having served under General Griffin Rutherford in his Cherokee campaign. Nothing further of him though is mentioned than his name as Captain Craighead. When will you publish? We are in our usual health, only again bereaved by the death of my excellent brother Colonel W. B. A. Ramsey, late secretary of state. He died in the Lord, April 27, at Nashville aged seventy-five. God's will be done!

Yours faithfully,
J. G. M. Ramsey

May 23, 1874

Your prompt reply and the enclosed circular with my earliest acknowledgment. The circular is the very thing I needed and asked for. Then I had found out by former experience as corresponding secretary of E. T. H. & A. Society that the suggestions you make—especially 1. 2. 4.—are very essential to our success. I will try to put them in practice.

Your inquiry whether our society would loan you their volume of South Carolina *Advertiser* 1789 shall receive my early attention. *I* was once (as Honorable Mitchell King said in his speech in Charleston) *the* E. T. H. & A. Society, being then its corresponding secretary. Now although presiding officer of the historical society of the state, I must consult others before I can answer affirmatively. I have called a meeting of the society for the sixteenth June here at Knoxville when I will meet at least a quorum of our body and I have no doubt I will be authorized to say yes to your inquiry—especially as you ask for the loan a brief period only. I hope that time will answer your purpose. It is Commencement day of East Tennessee University and that occasion brings together here the representative educators of the whole state. Can you by any possibility favor us with your presence on that occasion? If you could be here and tell us what your exertions have achieved for Wisconsin, and for history and biography in general, a new impulse would be given to our cause and a new life infused into our society. You will be formally invited. I hope and I beg you to accept. I do most ardently desire success in my new position but am not sanguine. Help me, advise me all you can.

Yesterday I made a professional visit to Sevier county to see one of the few surviving pioneers of Tennessee. He is living in the same house (a cabin modernized) that was occupied in 1786 or 7 when Sevier was Governor of Franklin and built by his father on that then frontier. The place almost inspired me.

To your other question I can only say all the collections of my (E. T. H. & A.) Society as well as my private collections were lost, burned or stolen by the vandalism of September 1863.

May 25, 1874

Your *second* favor of the twenty-first reached me yesterday. My reply to your *first* was a very hasty one, written after a fatiguing trip of a professional character to a distance patient, a pioneer of Sevier County last Thursday. But in imitation of your own promptness I answered it *emente calamo* and now scarcely know what I said. I desired though especially to thank you for your circular and the excellent suggestions you made me in my *new* position and duties. The circular though was the very thing I needed. You were right about the reference I had made to Captain Craighead. It was Hanging Rock. I found it again in Wheeler, ii, 194.

During my exile in North Carolina I did make the acquaintance, rather I renewed it, of Governor W. A. Graham. I have known him always. He is of *Hillsboro,* not *Greensboro* as you have it. Your letters may not have reached him. He is commonly prompt and obliging. Write him again that you must have the entire transcript of the Davie Manuscripts. If you fail, then write to Colonel William Johnston, or Colonel John Walker, both of Charlotte, North Carolina. The latter married Mrs. Swaine's sister (a granddaughter of Governor Caswell) and one or other of them will see that Ex-Governor Graham will furnish you the transcript. Refer to me. I think you will succeed. If not, I will write myself. Again you must have the loan of the South Carolina *Advertiser*. I will ask Judge Lea (who presented it to our society very recently) to bring it with him to our called meeting June 16 here in Knoxville. If he does so it can be expressed to you from here unless you may be present with us on the occasion of our educational and historical meeting. Please consider yourself as formally invited to attend. No one of our expected guests will be more cordially welcomed. I will send such of our proceedings as are published in the political papers as may be worth your notice.

I notice what you say to us of the necessity of money from the state or from endowments. We have neither. Indeed from an intimation of one of the officers I fear the society is in debt—amongst other things for painting the pictures of ten of our governors. I am apprehensive of failure from this very impecuniosity. Our state indebtedness is already great, and private benefactions are infrequent. The failure will mortify me the more as I never touched any public enterprise which did not succeed. I can only try. "In great attempts Tis glorious e'en to fail."

I know I have your good wishes. Your past example, your great success, stimulate me.

Did I tell you before that my heart is again heavy by reason of a loved brother's death. I am the only one left of my father's house. Olive plants of the same pious fireside, classmates, co-graduates, entering public life in the same community, members of the same communion—it is not strange that I feel like a pilgrim and stranger since his death. God help us!

July 8, 1874

With this please receive the "Circular" of the Historical Society of Tennessee. We hope to galvanize the old body into new life and activity. I hold up Wisconsin as our model for imitation. We are yet without funds, and Tennessee is so much in debt we cannot certainly count on a legislative appropriation or I would promise you our first volume of transactions.

During the late meeting of the society at the ancient capital of the state I brought to the attention of our officers your wish *by and by* to get the loan of the Southern *Advertiser* (if that was its title). Judge Lea said the reporter had made a mistake in the published account of the proceedings and that the series of the journal was not so extensive as reported. When you get ready for it address at Nashville Honorable J. M. Lea, J. B. Lindsley, D.D., A. Nelson, Esquire, Recording Secretary, or R. C. Foster, M.D., Vice-President, and it will be at once expressed to you. Have you ever seen the signatures to the Cumberland Association in May 1780? I had not time to copy them or I would send you a copy. Have you in your library the "Reminiscences of the Prominent Men of Alabama" by W. Ganett? The author promises me the mss of a Tennessee pioneer formerly of Cocke County, Tennessee. It will fill a gap in our history.

I practice in a limited circle to make my "daily bread" but I return to my first love, history and biography and regard it still *con amore.* Am in good health, buoyant and hopeful. Adversity has its blessings. . . .

Draper Manuscripts 2 GG 67

May 17, 1875

Yours of thirteenth instant received last night inquiring "about a facsimile of a hand bill publication at Knoxville by Heiskell and Brown and three of the Mecklenburg Resolves."

Yes. I know all about it. About 1824 or 1825 Colonel William Polk of Raleigh, North Carolina sent me by mail the Raleigh *Register* and a small pamphlet containing the Mecklenburg Resolves with names of delegates and others by whose influence and popularity the meeting had been gotten up May 19 and 20, 1775. Considering the perishable condition in which these documents were, I extracted from them three of the more prominent of the Resolves and had them, with the names, printed by Heiskell and Brown of this city. I had two copies printed on satin. Of these I presented one to General Andrew Jackson. The other I had neatly framed to hang up in my parlor by the side of the splendid picture of the battle of New Orleans where they have hung ever since. The state of the arts was at that early day in Knoxville behind the present style, but Heiskell and Brown made me a pretty picture or souvenir.

I had a few other copies printed on paper on the same form for keepsakes which I presented to such of the descendants of the 1775 patriots as were within my reach. It may have been one of these souvenirs which Dr. Joseph Johnson had seen. Though I do not know.

I always take a lively interest in my mother's old native country of Mecklenburg, North Carolina. I hope you will prepare your paper and publish it. Please send me a copy. Have you seen the Memorial and Argument of Ex-Governor W. A. Graham?

The Proclamation of Governor Josiah Martin from aboard his Majesty's ship Cruizer in Cape Fear River August 1774 refers to the Charlotte Committee and denounces them. See Wheeler.

I am still confined to my room and cannot leave it or I would be at Charlotte on the twentieth. Am glad to hear that Mr. Butterfield has joined you in book making. . . .[1]

Draper Manuscripts 2 GG 81

May 23, 1875

The copy of the Raleigh pamphlet which you have must be the same from which I extracted the three Resolves of my souvenir, though I have no copy in reach so as to compare number of pages, date, etc., etc. Mine was on perishable paper, very thin, I think about 16 pages. So I think you may fairly say that from this the three Resolves were copied. Then as to the *names* of the *delegates* (for there were no *signers*) the list given was the result of various combined recollections and thus varied a little. There were too many for the known number of captains of companys and in Colonel Jack's certificate he takes greater latitude by embracing those by *whose influence and popularity* the measure was adopted. Wheeler has the list *correct*. The legislative pamphlet I owned was burned in September 1863 or I would send it to you today. I think Wheeler has it too. I think Colonel William Polk's statement was in a previous number of the Raleigh *Register* introductory or a succeeding number containing the certificate and attestations of survivors, but I am not sure. Dr. Foote and Wheeler, you know, go into greater details. I wish you had material for sketches of the lives of these old patriots. There was not a trifler in the list. They were all men of mark, not one was a politician. In such times no one is elected but the wise and the virtuous. Foote says there were Pres-

---

[1] Consul W. Butterfield of Bucyrus, Ohio, moved to Madison, Wisconsin, to be Draper's associate in writing his histories and biographies. The association lasted only a short time, but they finished the manuscript of a book on "Border Forays and Adventures" for which they could find no publisher.

byterian preachers—Reese, Balsh and _____. Seven of the delegates were
Presbyterian elders. One delegate was a physician, Dr. Ephraim Brevard,
to whose cultivated pen the Resolves are always and by everybody ascribed
and by whose eloquence they were enforced. He was taken prisoner at
Camden, held so in a Charleston prison ship, released and got to the
house of his ex-secretary, John McKnitt Alexander, to die. Foote gives
a biography almost of him. Colonel Thomas Polk was a high souled Cavalier full of dash and courage, rich, hospitable and daring—a crown officer (surveyor, I believe) and McKnitt Alexander, also. The latter acted
in 1780 and 81 as aide and pilot to Greene on his retreat before Cornwallis
in pursuit of Morgan and his prisoners and was actively employed in destroying or sinking the ferry boats on the Yadkin and Dan Rivers. The
Tories remembered him long after and burned his house. You will find
some short biographical sketches of several delegates in Foote and Wheeler
—and when I have time I will copy from other sources the inscriptions
on some of their tombs. They are not in my reach today—such as you need
promptly.

I scribble off hastily now but *truthfully*. All these were Scotch Irish
Presbyterians of good mental culture and devotion to principle, cherished
loyalty to no one—king, prince, or chief—not even to majorities or King
Numbers. They were loyal only to right, conscience, liberty and independence—loyal to their creed and to Christ. It was they who after their
defeat in 1771-2 at Alamance shook the dust from their boots, crossed
the mountains and settled Tennessee. They were a remarkable race and
in 1860-4 with few exceptions were secessionists. I am sorry Governor
Graham has not written you. He has been very much occupied—is now
more genial and I hope you will try him again. He is occasionally from
home and his clerk may not take care of his letters in his absence.

One of the delegates was Duncan Ochiltre, a wealthy Scotch merchant
in Charlotte. He could save his goods and other property only by con-
senting to become Lord Cornwallis' commissary during his occupancy
of the village and thus became obnoxious to the Whigs and when his
Lordship was about breaking up camp at night Ochiltre went to the
house of J. McK. Alexander to propitiate the Whigs. He replied, "The
only way to save your life is to flee to Wilmington for safety." He did
so and escaped to Florida. But he never came back to Charlotte. His property was confiscated. Still his principles were believed to remain pure
—though the Whigs never forgave him.

Another delegate, very impecunious but true as steel, on one occasion attended Halifax or Newberne *walking* all the way to avoid the Tories and took his seat in the Provincial Congress. His name was Patton. See *The Land We Love* by General D. H. Hill, last volume. You ask for the likeness of Colonel Thomas Polk. I reckon none exists. These Scotch Irish were a curious people—they (some of them) did not hold that they should have "the likeness of anything" in their houses even to look at and there were no artists in those days. Polk died early. I have thus answered your letter hastily line by line. But as it is Sunday let me use one of its holy minutes by inquiring whether in all your various writings you have had to investigate the great religious awakening in the West—1795 to 1810? To me it is the most remarkable physiological (psychological, I almost said) phenomenon in our whole history of the past. I would almost be afraid to tell what I saw myself of it. Can you so far believe in Mesmeric influence as to think that a *revival* in the true meaning of the term could be propagated by mail in a letter from an unconverted man to a friend sixteen miles from him and when the letter was read from the stand the jerks—the exercise—the cries for mercy started forward a crowd of 2 or 3000? Resolve the strange work in your mind. . . .

Draper Manuscripts 2 GG 86

May 25, 1875

In my last of the twenty-third, after answering yours of the twentieth line after line, I added hastily some sketches of a few of the delegates and hoped by further reflection and examination to find more to send you. In this I have not succeeded. But now on thinking over what I said of John McKnitt Alexander as having acted as aide to General Greene I must request you to omit *aide*. He was my grandfather and it will look indelicate for me to call him that—though such is the tradition. He was so only *pro tempora*. He accompanied his army to the Yadkin and the Dan Rivers as pilot, being from his office (surveyor) he was familiar with all the roads, ferries, fords, etc., and went before Greene to collect first and then destroyed the boats. It is a small thing but as I pride myself on historical accuracy please erase the word *aide*.

It was suspected that the Tories set fire to his house in 1800 as they had threatened to do in 1780 and 1781 during the invasion but it was not known to be so. Perhaps they did not. I hear the centennial was a success. In haste. . . .

Draper Manuscripts 2 GG 93

May 26, 1875

Your inquiry is a very natural one and as I said about my souvenir or keepsake, cut, or plate containing the three Resolves, etc., I know all about it and proceed to give you the wanted information and I give it with great pleasure.

John McKnitt Alexander was the ancestor, the head of his family. He had two sons William Baine Alexander and Joseph McKnitt Alexander. Each was known in Carolina and especially in Mecklenburg. The senior as William Baine—the junior as Joseph McKnitt—even spoken to and spoken of and addressed as such, Billy Baine and Joseph McKnitt, and by no other name. The children of each son were called Jimmy Baine, Joseph Baine, Peggy Baine, and so down to the youngest of his fourteen children. So also the children of Joseph McKnitt Alexander. One was called Moses W. McKnitt. Why was all this? Mecklenburg was colonized about 1745-60 by a whole tribe of Alexanders and they were a prolific stock and today every alternate man is an Alexander and in Hopewell Congregation, where the McKnitt Alexander branch the tribe lived, almost every one is named Alexander—and only every fifth or sixth one is of another name. The commonness of the name produces necessarily great confusion and inconvenience. The people correct this themselves and speaking of W. Baine Alexander's children called them Jimmy Baine, Joseph Baine, and Peggy Baine, and so all over the county in all the other branches of the Alexanders.

So to come to the point of inquiry. J. McKnitt was the signature of Joseph McKnitt Alexander. His letters were addressed as McKnitt—he was addressed as such on the road, on the street and anywhere else— was never called or spoken of as Dr. Alexander. I have received not less than one hundred letters from him and each one is signed J. McKnitt —never by any other name. He was the active executor of his father's estate and in conveying title to his legatees for his real estate I believe he signed the deeds "J. McKnitt Executor of John McKnitt Alexander." Indeed I almost am sure of it but our deeds to my brother and sister and myself are in Shelby County in possession of those to whom we sold our lands. So you are right in supposing that J. McKnitt, Joseph McKnitt Alexander and Dr. J. McKnitt are one and the same person—perfectly identical. So numerous are the Alexanders in Mecklenburg that they are often designated by the office they bear or the trade or pursuit they follow: thus Governor Nat. is Governor Nathaniel Alexander; Fuller Nat.; Red Head Nat. Alexander, Clerk Isaac was used for Isaac Alexander; Long Creek Isaac Alexander. . . .

I never was surprised that Mr. Jefferson balked at J. McKnitt being the son of John McKnitt Alexander. It is natural that he should balk at that appearance of inconsistency and conflict.

I hope I have explained it to your entire satisfaction. You have seen or can see by reading Governor Graham's Memoir on the Mecklenburg Declaration that he gives this explanation. Professor Willing accepts it.

Reverend Dr. Martin of Atlanta has just left my room. He is the author of the poem to be read at Charlotte, May 20, '75, which I enclosed to you yesterday. I wish if it is published in your Madison papers you would have a copy of it sent to *Reverend Joseph H. Martin, D.D., Atlanta, Georgia.*

When your paper is prepared please send me a copy. You will have received mine of yesterday in which I asked you to erase the word *aide.* Work out the problem. Mr. *Howard* of Georgia who interviewed Mr. Rush has been written to and Dr. Martin thinks the paper Governor Josiah Martin enclosed to the British government will be found. If it is never found I am still a firm believer in May 20, 1775.[2] It is a nursery tale and a tradition with me.

Draper Correspondence

August 17, 1875

I preferred to see and consult with my pastor, James Park, D.D., before I would reply to yours of the third. He has been absent and has not yet returned. I will wait no longer but give you only *my own* recollection and observation now and if Dr. Park gives me further or different light on the subject I will write again.

---

[2] Draper completed a book-length essay on the Mecklenburg "declaration of independence," using a great deal of the material which Dr. Ramsey supplied. He apparently never divulged to Dr. Ramsey his own conclusion that the so-called "Resolves" were spurious. He was never able to find a publisher for his work.

Southern Presbyterians especially in Virginia, the Carolinas and Tennessee have always used Saturday as preparatory as far as temporal affairs are concerned to the sacred duties and observance of the Sabbath. The wood was cut and piled near the door. What cooking was necessary for the Sunday's consumption of the family was all done Saturday evening. Even the boots and shoes were blackened and ready to put on Sunday morning. Even cracking walnuts was not allowed on the Lord's day and the family worship of Saturday night something like this concluded that service: "Help us now to dismiss all our worldly cares and prepare to keep thy Sabbath holy which is approaching. May we be in the spirit on Thy Sabbath. May we make at least a Sabbath day's journey heavenward. Help us to read Thy word with care and profit, having faith mixed therewith. May we lay it up in our hearts, practice it in our lives. And if Thou shouldst give us or any of us an opportunity of meeting with Thy people in Thy house of prayer, graciously meet us there in mercy and bless us. Let Thy stately steppings be seen in the sanctuaries of Thy grace. Give us Thy convincing, converting and sanctifying grace and prepare us for that Heavenly Sabbath above which shall never end." These simple petitions were offered up in nearly every Presbyterian home in the South. Parents, children and house servants all joined in the service. But Saturday was never *the preparatory day*. In the olden time and now in all country congregations, on communion occasions four days were appropriated to the solemnities of the supper, from Friday morning till noon on Monday. Friday was observed as a fast and on that day every communicant at least in the congregation was expected to be present at church and to hear *the preparation* sermon. It was for believers only and pointed out the duty of self-examination, personal religion, spiritual mindedness and self-consecration. Thus *Friday was preparation day* as far as I know and believe in all Presbyterian communities. More recently, and especially in cities and large towns, the fast day has been omitted and a communion service is confined to Saturday and Sunday only. The preparation sermon is unfortunately too often omitted. Have I comprehended your inquiry and answered it?

In a former letter I told you that I believed that *J. McKnitt* signed that name to title papers, deeds, etc. I believe so still but do not assert it to be so. I send you his signature *es nominee* as a witness to a bill of sale for a slave which in Wisconsin will be considered almost a curiosity and worthy of presentation to your society. In North Carolina and elsewhere in the South Mr. Jefferson's skepticism on the subject no longer excites surprise.

You say rightly of Mr. Johnson that he was *honest*. I admit it but his course on *coercion measures* caused more bloodshed and other mischief than Napoleon ever did.

I am glad your Mr. Butterfield meets your expectations. *Border Forays and Adventures* will be a good introduction to your future enterprises. I am almost tempted to turn critic in advance upon its merits. Williams Sturgiss and Company of this city are reliable booksellers. I am still a cripple but otherwise am quite well. Did you complete your papers on Mecklenburg Declaration of Independence? . . .

September 20, 1875

I have this moment read the second time your favor of the 16th just received and proceed without delay to answer in their consecutive order your several questions, occasionally adding something else suggested by them. First, I have no knowledge of Colonel Elijah Isaacs of North Carolina. I think there has been a Judge Isaac in West Tennessee. I will inquire for one of that name and if I hear anything of him will hereafter write you. Second, I knew Clark Isaac Alexander well half a century since. He was known only as Clark Isaac and never was called by any other. As I wrote you heretofore, so numerous were the tribe of the Alexanders, they had to be designated by their office—their trade or their middle name —in the case cited to you Jos. McKnitt for Jos. McKnitt Alexander. This Isaac Alexander was, as far back as I can recollect, clerk of Mecklenburg County and retained the office while he lived. His chirography was elegant, his attention to official duty never was surpassed. I think he was a member of Sugar Creek (Presbyterian) Church and perhaps an elder. Everybody confided in him as a patriot, a neighbor, citizen, head and priest of his own household. His official and private integrity, his capacity and fidelity were proverbial.

John Flenniken emigrated at an early day from Mecklenburg to Knox County, Tennessee. He died before my recollection, left descendants, with one of whom, Major Samuel Flenniken, I was intimately acquainted. Have heard from him his recollections of what he had heard his father narrate of the Mecklenburg Convention, May 20, 1775. He was, I believe, of the seceder (Presbyterian) faith and lived south of Holston amongst that denomination in a congregation called Salem, near the Andersons, the Wilsons, McCalls, McBaths, etc.

You do not inquire for Zacheus Wilson, one of the delegates of the Charlotte Convention, but I will add that soon after the Revolution he came west and settled near Gallatin, Tennessee, on the Cumberland. Lived to become superannuated but still recollected 1775 and his participation in the measures of that day. Colonel Thomas Boyers, well known in that neighborhood, may be able to ascertain whether he left any important papers, etc., etc. I can't give you his P. O.

I think there has been published a map of Tennessee with all the county lines but not an Atlas made up of county maps. I have not kept up with these new and money making enterprises, called school books, school geographies, etc., etc. Have found some of them erroneous and unreliable. *W. T. Berry and Company,* booksellers, Nashville, Tennessee, can inform you better and if you will say that you had been referred to them by me they will tell the truth and not cheat you either. I have thus replied to your several inquiries—imperfectly it is true but still as fully as I can today. Write again and often when I can do anything for you. Am sorry that you do not find publishers. Northern houses, as I have learned by corresponding with them, do not like to touch anything wearing Southern features or promotive of Southern interests and character. I am impatient to see before I die something from your pen. But *festina lente* is a good maxim and I must not hurry you.

I inclosed in my last a bill of sale for a slave, witnessed by *J. McKnitt* as Dr. J. M. Alexander always signed himself. Did you receive it?

Considering that I am a cripple, I have been rather successful lately in collecting for the Tennessee Historical Society. Beside this Dr. Lindsley of Nashville and myself hope to bring out soon "Ramsey's *Annals* abridged for the use of Schools." [3] Can you give me some of your wise suggestions about it? May our good father in Heaven bless, guide and save you!

---

[3] Dr. Ramsey, too, was the author of an unpublished manuscript. His "Abridged History of Tennessee, for the use of Common Schools" bearing only his name on the title page, contained the outline of seven chapters—discovery and exploration, Watauga, North Carolina in the Revolution, the state of Franklin, the Cumberland settlements, the territory South of the Ohio River, and the history of the state of Tennessee to 1860. The last chapter was not written, and the others consisted of introductory notes and references to passages in the *Annals* which were to be incorporated in the abridgement. A note, dated December 7, 1875, read: "I will explain all this to Rev. J. Berrien Lindsley, D.D., when he arrives Dec 25 or 27 and he can then explain it fully to our publishers." A typewritten copy of this manuscript is in the McClung Collection.

P. S. I enclose for your collection of autographs that of my grandfather John McKnitt Alexander cut from a business letter to James [obscure] dated May, 1800. Its date if nothing else makes it valuable.

[Inclosure]

Biographical

John McKnitt Alexander, whose autograph is herein enclosed, was a native of Pennsylvania and migrated about 1750–5 from that then Province and settled near the Catawba River at his well-known farm, Alexandriana, on the head of Long Creek where he ever afterwards resided. His wife was Jane Baine, also of Pennsylvania. They were members of the Presbyterian Church. He was the founder and one of the first elders of Hopewell Church in what afterwards became Mecklenburg County. He often represented this county in the provincial legislature at Newbern, Halifax, etc. He was also a crown officer—a surveyor, it is believed. But from the commencement of the oppressive and unconstitutional measures of the British parliament and ministry, such as the Stamp Act, the tax on tea and the Boston Port Bill, etc., he boldly and unselfishly took a decided stand in favor of the colonies—favored the Regulators in their resistance against illegal taxes, the official magnificence of Governor Tyron's officials and on May 20, 1775 was present as a delegate to the Charlotte Convention—noted as one of its secretaries—and throughout the Revolution which ensued he was an active officer in the army. If not a member of General Greene's staff, certainly his pilot driving the retreat of the Americans in the direction of Virginia in 1781. His familiarity with all the roads in the up-country of North Carolina led General Greene to select him to destroy all the boats and ferries in the Yadkin and Dan Rivers. He was wealthy and gave of his money freely to the cause of independence and liberty. He died in 1817, is buried in Hopewell, aged eighty-four. A true patriot and a good Christian.

CHAPTER XXII

Pioneers of Tennessee

Draper Correspondence

Mecklenburg Place
Knoxville, Tennessee
September 25, 1875

[Mr. Lyman C. Draper]
My Dear Sir,

Yours of the twenty-first is just received. I hasten to say in reply that I have not seen the *traditionary* narrative you speak of in reference to the siege and capture of Fort Loudon. I know if anything *new* and *authentic* about it has been published and especially in a Tennessee paper it could have hardly escaped my notice or my recollection. I wish to see all such things and I have outside friends everywhere in Tennessee and the Southwest who never fail to watch for me and forward everything to me that meets their eye. If I find anything more will promptly report it to you. But I cannot let this opportunity pass unimproved of sending you this enclosure. I had intended it for our Tennessee Historical Society but having duplicates you shall have one of them. You are no stranger to the autograph of General Jackson, but may not have the signature of *Judge* Jackson. You will also notice that of Hugh Lawson White—afterwards Judge, Senator, and Vice-President White. Also Henry Brazeale, writer of the little Book "Life as it is," one of the early publications of Tennessee.

Have you seen the accounts of the Harps—two notorious thieves, robbers and murderers of Tennessee and Kentucky—published early in Tennessee and the West?

Success to you and your Mr. Butterfield on your undertakings and Heaven's benediction on yourself prays your old time friend.

J. G. M. *Ramsey*

P. S. I answered former favor a few days since and inquired if you had received a former letter and its *inclosure*.

P. S. No. 2. Samuel Houston is the Reverend S. Houston mentioned in

my *Annals* as the member of the Convention who introduced the consti-
tuion of the Commonwealth of *Frankland*.

October 2, 1875

Yours of the twenty-eighth ultimo received late last night. I will try to
explain the puzzle as well as I can. Mr. W. Shakespeare Harris and others
have doubtless given you the correct statement about *John Flenniken*,[1] the
delegate from Providence. When I showed the Raleigh pamphlet to Major
Samuel Flenniken he said that his father had often told him that he was
present at Charlotte and witnessed all that was said and done there on
the nineteenth and twentieth of May '75, and the reading of the pamphlet
brought vividly to his recollection all that it contained as having been
narrated to him by his deceased father. But the Major may have been
mistaken in saying that the father was a *delegate*. There may have been
two Flennikens of the same name in the neighborhood. I never saw this
Knox County John Flenniken—he died long before my interview with
the son Major Samuel Flenniken whom I knew well as a man of truth
and perfectly reliable. The father, I have no doubt, *was present* but not
as a *delegate*. This may explain the apparent discrepancy. I think Harris
has given the true version of it and I still have no doubt that our John
Flenniken told his son that he was at Charlotte and witnessed the declaration.

Let me here say while I think of it that I had in my possession a letter
to myself from *Reverend Richard H. King* formerly of Iredell County,
North Carolina in which he states that he was visiting at the house of
J. McKnitt Alexander and found him copying the Mecklenburg Declaration of Independence for the use of *Dr. Hugh Williamson,* the historian
of North Carolina. I cannot recollect the date of this visit of Mr. King
though I think it was early in this century. His letter I sent to his grandson, Major Richard Nelson of Rockford in Blount County only a few
months since. I ought to have made a copy of this part of the letter but
did not. If it is of any service to you I will. . . .[2]

---

[1] Variously given as Flanagan, or Flanigan.

[2] King's letter to Dr. Ramsey is not copied, but is to be found on the back of Dr. Ramsey's
letter to King in the Draper Manuscripts, 2 GG 5. Dr. Ramsey's letter to King was dated September 4, 1822,—revealing how early he had begun to gather material on North Carolina
and Tennessee history. It read:

"Rev. R. H. King.

"Dear Sir,

"It has been asserted on testimony which I feel no hesitation in pronouncing competent

Can you describe the locality of Fort Loudon? Not very certainly, though I have been on the ground. On another piece of paper I send you a rough diagram of it as I recollect it in 1846–8. Dunmore[?] and his men were massacred not at Loudon but at Telico Plains, a few miles—one day's march—from it. The spot is still pointed out. The Telico Plains is a notorious place and if I had the money as I once had I would procure a civil engineer and go with him and delineate both the plains and the site of the old fort for your own special use: but I am impecunious and so is also my society and I must be content with the rough draft I enclose.

Hezekiah Alexander was a full brother of John McKnitt Alexander, the clearest headed magistrate in his county. He had other full brothers and sisters there and some half brothers. Ezekial Alexander was one of these, the youngest son. He died in Middle Tennessee. Adam, Abraham, Ezra and Charles Alexander were cousins of John McKnitt Alexander. Someone told me that Abraham and Adam were his brothers but I could not ascertain the exact genealogy. Mrs. Jemima Sharpe, Mrs. Betsy Samples, and perhaps Mrs. Bradly were his half sisters. The mother of Dr. Ephraim Brevard I have been told was of the McKnitt stock. The two secretaries were probably cousins—certainly they were bosom friends. When Dr. Brevard returned from his captivity and imprisonment in Charleston, South Carolina sick, emaciated and forlorn, almost moribund, he sought the hospitable house of his kinsman or friend J. M. K. Alexander; was kindly nursed by him and his family and died there. This may have given rise to the belief that Dr. Brevard was interred in Hopewell graveyard, which was the place where J. M. K. Alexander worshiped and buried his dead. But the popular tradition is that the remains were carried nine miles to Charlotte and buried there by the side of his wife previously deceased. I resided five years from 1865 to 1870 in that country and it surprised me much to find how much is lost, how little is well known of these family chronicles and incidents.

I don't know who was the father of Major Thomas Alexander. It might

that the first Declaration of American Independence was made by a convention that met in Charlotte, Mecklenburg County, North Carolina, in May 1775. The fact has, however, been called in question in Massachusetts and other places; and I have determined to collect and embody all the evidence I shall be able to procure at this late day in order to convince the most skeptical. And as you once resided in and are perhaps a native of the county in which the convention met and were acquainted with some of its most active members and especially with my grandfather, John McKnitt Alexander, who was their secretary, I have taken the liberty to request you to get me a written account of anything you know on the subject or may have heard from such a source as you think entitles it to credit.

I am, Sir,
Very Respectfully yours
J. G. M. Ramsey."

be found out in Sugar Creek where he lived in quite a late period. I have often been at his house. It was in 1825 near the residence of my uncle, Reverend Samuel C. Caldwell, and is still standing, but out now of his family. One of his daughters, a Mrs. Wilson, was living in 1869 in Hopewell. I will write to my son-in-law, W. Davidson Alexander, near Hopewell Church and learn more details, though you cannot receive his information on this and other points for several weeks. Major Tommy Alexander, as he was called, was an excellent character in church and state. Governor Nat. Alexander belonged to the Alexander tribe, but which branch of it I do not know. Did I not send you the genealogical register of James Alexander, the father of Mr. McKnitt Alexander? I think I did. I know it is amongst my papers. He was twice married and left a numerous set of descendants. I will look up that register.

The snow campaign of December 1775 was carried on against the Scovillites in South Carolina. General Thomas Polk is said to have conducted it. I have heard that his brother, Ezekial Polk, was one of his captains and had in his company and under his command his nephew Devil Charley Polk, son of General T. Polk and also William Polk, another nephew afterwards distinguished at Eutaw where he was a column captain. Devil Charley married the daughter of Hezekiah Alexander and was a dare-devil kind of man, perfectly fearless and reckless. One of his sons was General Thomas Independence Polk, more recently of Fayette County, Tennessee who has a son Charles and another son Colonel H. M. Polk, late the delegate to twentieth May centennial on the part of Tennessee Historical Society and also the Tennessee legislature. Both William Polk and Charley must have been boys in '75. President Polk told me that though they were boys they were both in service under his father Captain Ezekial Polk in the snow campaign.

I forgot to say when speaking of the Alexanders—that Captain Black Bill Alexander, or as he was afterwards known, Blind Bill, was chief at the capture and burning of the British powder before the war of '76. Whose son he was I did not ascertain, but he was a relative of the Alexanders and a brave scout all around Charlotte. I have written you a long letter with little information in it. . . .

November 1, 1875

I have not heard from Major Nelson since I last wrote you that I had requested him to examine further for Reverend King's letter and to send it *entire* to you. I presume therefore that he has before this enclosed it. I hope he has done so. I thank you for your last and the communication of and the picture of L. C. Draper. Three or four decades have made great changes on both of us as you will see from the picture of *J. G. M. R.,* your old friend of seventy-eight—nearly an octogenarian. Born at Swan Pond, Knox County, Tennessee, March 25, 1797. Please give me your nativity—where and when, your parentage, etc., in full. I want to use it soon. Receive for your *Mr. Durrie* [3] note of Reverend Dr. J. B. Lindsley, who has been my guest for a week. I have just finished 56 closely written pages on *Lebanon Church* [4]—containing biographical sketches of its pioneer members—General James White. Captain or Dr. James Cozby, Captain Thomas Gillespie, Captain Robert Craighead, Squire George McNutt, Squire John Adair, Colonel F. A. Ramsey, Governor John Sevier, his son-in-law, Archibald Rhea, and others.

I hope you will not perpetuate the mistake that *Sevier* was one of our *elders.* He was not and I have so declared in my reminiscences of Lebanon. His last wife *was* a member but he was Gullis-like and cared for none of these things. But he *attended* our church and always occupied the pew of his old friend and comrade Captain and Surgeon James Cozby while his ladies sat in Squire Rhea's pew. Some of Sevier's biographers persist in the error that he was a Presbyterian elder. I know you will have it all right. General White, Captain Gillespie, Colonel Ramsey and Squire Rhea were the elders—Squire Adair, McNutt and others were also but Sevier never—not even a communicant.

I have read *Crawford* by your associate Butterfield. It is a model of typographical excellence, the whole mechanical execution perfect, and that is not half its *merits. Your* wealth of material—I suppose so—has enriched its pages. He has done his work well. It fills up a hiatus that has been long wanting in our American History. The *Atlantic* part of it has been pretty well preserved and sufficiently dilated upon and expanded but who but Draper has analyzed the northwestern and western incidents of our early history? *Crawford* makes a happy beginning to the wanting links of the long chain. George Rogers Clarke (You see I retain the final *e* as I learned it fifty years ago) ought to have preceded *Crawford* but no doubt you have your reasons for letting Crawford take the priority, but

---

[3] Daniel S. Durrie was librarian of the State Historical Society of Wisconsin.

[4] Dr. J. G. M. Ramsey, *History of Lebanon Presbyterian Church "In the Fork," Five Miles East of Knoxville, Tennessee.* (Pp. 24) was first published in 1918 and reprinted in 1952.

it whets my appetite for Clarke. Give my respects to your Mr. Butterfield and say that some of these days I will give him a favorable and friendly and longer review in some of our journals. At this time I am very much occupied with Dr. J. B. Lindsley in abridging my *Annals* into a school history for our Tennessee normal and common schools. I write with some pain. I cannot yet sit close up to my table so as to make my writing legible. Otherwise I am very well and capable of a great deal of labor and *labor ipse voluptus* especially history and biography. Your picture shows you well preserved and possessed of your old time vigor and energy. I hope you may never suffer the ignoble accident from an unruly horse that has been inflicted on me. Command me freely. Thank you for your enormous catalogue. . . .

November 10, 1875

I write again to Major Wilson *enjoining* upon him to look up the last letter, for I know he has too much *veneration* in his composition to have destroyed it. But having a long list of cousins and other kin he has probably handed or sent it to someone else than Miss Fonte or his aunt as he supposed he had done. I think he will come up with it yet, but it may be too late though for your purpose. Last summer I wrote for the Christian *Observer,* Louisville, Kentucky a memoir of Reverend R. H. King which is now before me and would be sent now entire but that to tear it out of my scrapbook would disfigure and mutilate it too much. (Everything I write for the press it is my habit to cut out and paste in a book kept for that purpose.) But I copy for your use or gratification an item or two to meet your inquiries. During my late sojourn in North Carolina, the daughter of Reverend D. Carruthers of Greensboro, North Carolina requested me to prepare and revise for the press a long and full biography of Reverend King written by his colleague in the ministry, Reverend Carruthers. I did so. This manuscript would make a volume itself, giving in detail the formation, progress and growth of Presbyterian Churches in North Carolina and some revolutionary incidents, etc., etc. From the perusal of this manuscript biography I took dates enough to form my article for the *Observer*—which will answer your inquiries.

R. H. King was the eldest son of James King and his wife was Sarah Hall, sister of Reverend James Hall, D.D., a captain and chaplain in the Revolutionary army. R. H. King was born July 22, 1767 in Iredell County,

North Carolina and graduated at Princeton in 1788. Was a subject of the great revival and felt called on to preach. His presbytery required him to study divinity a certain length of time: he was too impatient to wait so long and he applied to and was licensed to preach by Bishop Asbury then passing through the country. He became a powerful preacher and was usefully employed on his circuit a few years when his presbytery felt authorized to license him to preach in the mother church. This took place about 1808-9 when he took the pastorate of Concord and Bethel Church, which he relinquished early in 1815 when he removed to Knox County, succeeding Reverend S. G. Ramsey in the pastorate of Ebenezer and Pleasant Forest churches. Becoming too corpulent to preach in his churches he removed to Blount County where some of his daughters had married. His weight was 404 pounds. He died in 1825. His letters to me—exact date not recollected—were probably written in 1823 or 1824. In one of them he said that he recollected that on a former visit to J. McKnitt Alexander he found him copying the Mecklenburg Declaration of Independence for Dr. Williamson, the author of a history of North Carolina. Alexander died in June 1817 and had been blind several years, say five or six before his death. I suppose the visit alluded to was before Mr. *King* began to preach, or before he assumed the pastorate, but I do not know—perhaps the lost letter mentioned the date. I am not certain that it does. I will continue to press Major Wilson to hunt it up. I know he would not destroy it. But he is full of business, not very methodical, and has only mislaid it or forgotten whom he sent it to. He valued them very highly. Mr. King was somewhat scientific as well as pious and spent once a considerable time in excavating the tumulas in rear of my house. By the help of my Negro man he sunk a shaft from the summit to the base in these researches.

Your Mr. Butterfield has been more industrious and more skillful than I supposed one of his age could be since I find he had not the benefit of your assistance. He is to be the more commended. I wait impatiently for your *Border Conflicts and Adventures*. I am now on my abridgment for the use of schools. If I were by you I would ask you for a hundred suggestions about my little bantling—250-300 pages octavo. Is that large enough for nearly ninety years? I only bring it down to 1860, for fear I would tramp on somebody's toes, hurt the feelings of some modern Democrats such as A. Johnson. *De mortifs nil nisi bonum.* Am glad you have *Rupp's* work. Some of the *Resolutions* come very near to the Mecklenburg's proceedings, though not quite. I was the more interested in them as the Mecklenburgers, as many of them emigrated from that section in 1760 to Carolina—as some of the Ramseys, Alexanders, McGimpseys and other Mecklenburgers did. I thank you for the dates and localities you sent me.

New Hampshire and Vermont will do—. Not much Puritanism in them. Did you ever compare the rejected constitution of Frankland with that of Vermont—almost cotemporaneous and the two countries almost facsimiles of each other?

Am quite well, but have still to use my crutches. My crushed limb is less painful but very little stronger. . . .

November 28, 1875

I wrote to Major Wilson that I knew he had too much veneration to have destroyed his grandfather's letters which I had sent him and that I supposed he had only put them in a very *safe* place so that he could not find them on first hunt for them. It turned out to be so. He writes now that he did find them in his son's safe in his store here in Knoxville and that he had enclosed that one to you which had the statement that he had seen: J. M. Alexander copying the Mecklenburg Declaration of Independence for the use of Dr. Williamson. I hope you have received it. Please let me hear if you do not get it.

The Major also sent back to me Reverend R. H. King's other letters. Looking them over I find one giving a list of genealogies of the Polks and Brevards which may interest you. I have no authority from Major Wilson to tell you to keep it or I would say so. Perhaps he will expect me to return it.

As you probably see the *Southern Home* I do not this morning send a letter contained in it from Edward Wallis to *National Intelligencer* on some general subject in 1853 I believe. Nor have I ever sent to you *my own* recollections of nursery tales derived from my mother and General White and others of the olden times. I prefer not to say and have never written a word of what I know myself. It is not necessary, but I have heard it all my life and never allowed myself to doubt a single word J. McKnitt Alexander ever said or wrote. Jefferson himself has never asserted that it was not genuine but the suggestion about the father and the son not having the same name did create some suspicion in the minds even of candid men. I have heretofore explained all that obscurity and misapprehension to you in a former letter. I suppose that came to hand. In North Carolina it is all understood and there it has never been misconceived.

I am on my *Abridgment* and need very much a wise suggestion from you about the *size* of the volume. It stops at 1800.

Wisconsin has done nobly and Will Allen of Ohio is the only one who can carry his state in 1876. Allen and Vance of North Carolina or Harris of Tennessee make a strong team. God bless you, prays yours truly . . .

January 18, 1876

My last informed you that Major Wilson had written to me that he had found and forwarded to you his grandfather's letter and inquired whether you had received it, and also inclosed another letter from Reverend R. H. King which contained some genealogical lists of the Polks, Brevards, etc., which I supposed might interest you a little. I have been ever since anxious to hear from you. Did you get Major Wilson's letter concerning Mr. King's lost letter? Please let me hear at once. I have feared that you were sick—perhaps you are gone somewhere to publish your *magnum opus*. I am distressed to think the former, which would be a great public calamity and would leave me in a state of *historical orphanage*.

I write today to inquire how and where you are? and to assure you that in my opinion you are one of the most important personages now living. Do relieve my anxiety and write me at once. . . .

P. S. It is a nursery tale with me that on the occasion of a wedding in his neighborhood Colonel Thomas Polk, though the invitation was to him and family, positively forbade his son Charles from accompanying him to the house of the bride, saying, "You are so much of a Devil I can't allow it." His coach and four went, leaving *Devil Charley* behind. He, however, was not easily thwarted. He hitched two old shabby horses with plough harness to a sled in the wood yard and just as Colonel Polk drove up to the house—here came Charley hooping and hallooing at his team, passed the coach containing the family, arrived at the gate first, dressed in an unbecoming suit but was well received by the host, etc., etc.

The colonel had drunk freely and was telling of his war exploits and his courage to the guests. Charley withdrew, waylaid his father's coach, disguised—came out of the woods, stopped the driver and the coach, demanded the colonel's pocketbook and naturally received it and returned it to him next morning at breakfast. Other such tales without number.

January 31, 1876

I unite my thanks with your own to Almighty God for your preserved life and health. It was in no vain spirit of adulation that I said in my last that your life appeared to me to be more important and valuable than that of anyone else. I really felt it to be true. Take care of it. You have no conception of the loss which a suspension of your great and useful labors would inflict upon this age and country. Your letter shows how well preserved you are. The hand steady, the mind clear, the purpose determined. Happy and fortunate Wisconsin! When can Tennessee aspire to and reach your encouraging example? I thank you for the able and satisfactory *Report* of your State Historical Society and the memorial you sent me. I am sorry that the sixteenth state of our union lags so far behind her younger sister. While you have such able coadjutors—a cabinet of which you are chief—I stand nearly unaided and alone. I received last week a contribution of old papers and documents which fill a box 5 x 3 x 2 feet deep—some of them very valuable—and all of them old. These I am arranging for our collection at Nashville, believing that no one else would have the patience to do it right but myself. *Labor ipsi voluptas.* I can transfer it to no other and undertake it cheerfully.

Consider the letters of Reverend R. H. King as presented to yourself from me. Major Wilson authorizes this. I have others but of less value.

I have a request to make which I hope you can grant without much interruption of your persistent labors. I am investigating the career of General Griffith Rutherford. To save you unnecessary research I will say in advance that he commanded the Mecklenburg militia in May 1771 called out by Governor Tyron to put down the insurgent Regulators in Alamance, but sympathizing with the justice of their cause *failed* to join the royal army under Tyron; was the commander of the North Carolina troops against the Cherokees in 1776, penetrated into what afterwards became Tennessee and devastated their Over-Hill villages, was a decided Whig, was captured at Campden in 1780 and sent to prison at Charleston and St. Augustine and some years after the peace of 1783 secured lands for the North Carolina soldiers in (I believe) 1786 on Sucahatchee River in the present Shelby County near Memphis where he located military warrants for my grandfather's Revolutionary services 3,660 acres and for many other North Carolina officers and soldiers and *perhaps* located General Nathaniel Greene's large grant on Duck River, Maury County, held civil office under the territorial government and the state. About this time I lose him only that our Rutherford County and that in North Carolina and Rutherfordton also in North Carolina were all so called for him. Can you help verify these items of his biography and further tell me where *he was born and where and when did he die?* Further. For whom was our Williamson County called? Was it for General Williamson who went to the Over-Hill Cherokees in 1776 in command of a similar expedition (from South Carolina) to Rutherford's—though not *with* him till they reached the center of the Nation where their commands met? Please solve these questions and excuse me for troubling about them.

Dr. Hunter (Cottage Home, Gaston County, North Carolina) is preparing biographical sketches of Mecklenburgers and gives that of one of the men as *Captain* J. McKnitt Alexander. My grandfather was above the military age in the Revolution but acted as pilot and one of General Greene's aides on his celebrated escape from the pursuit of Cornwallis in February 1781. His claim for land warrants was that of a colonel, 3,660 acres, of which I inherited a part. Do your Mecklenburg papers mention his grade in the service? Dr. Hunter may refer to another of same name. The tribe was the largest of that Israel.

I have fatigued you and can only add that I am making satisfactory progress in my *Abridgment.* Can you refer me to a similar work anywhere which you can recommend to me as a model? . . .

April 29, 1876

I am always so glad to hear from you as I did yesterday by yours of the twenty-second. I am always ready to answer historical or biographical questions but cannot today give you anything definite about *Colonel Elijah Isaacs* but will get on a better track, will inquire and if I hear anything will write you again. But I think I have heard from some source of such a man as Colonel Isaacs over in Burke County, North Carolina. When I was a boy I knew the McDowells (Colonel and General) Colonel

Wrightstill Avery, Colonel McGimpsey,—the Irvines and the Martins all patriots of the Revolution but am not certain as to Isaacs. After writing thus far Honorable T. Nixon Vandyke of Athens, Tennessee came over to see me and while he was here I inquired for Colonel Elijah Isaacs. Judge Vandyke says he thinks that a congressman of that name once represented the Winchester district in Middle Tennessee; does not recollect his first name, nor does he know further about him but that Judge J. T. L. Sneed or Judge Turney of our Supreme Bench will hold his court here soon and that he can tell all about him. I have not at hand the list of congressmen from Tennessee to refer to. You doubtless have one. After seeing Judge Sneed or Turney and further inquiries, I will write you again with more accurate and reliable details. I have heard the name, I know. A biographer, Dr. Cyrus Hunter of Cottage Home P. O., Lincoln County, North Carolina is preparing and will soon publish a work on the Revolutionary men of Western North Carolina and is writing me very earnestly about a family named *Jack*. Had heard that a descendant of one of them once lived in upper East Tennessee and was a circuit court judge here many years since. Our *Jacksboro* in Campbell County may have been named for him, but I cannot get on the trail and beg to ask you whether you have anything of that family? He is said to be a connection of Captain Jack, the bearer of the Mecklenburg Declaration of Independence to Philadelphia in '75.

What I have said of Evan Shelby I must have got from Haywood as the *Shelby papers* in my hands before my house and office were burned in 1863 referred only to the son, Isaac Shelby, and did not mention the father, Evan Shelby, at all if I recollect right. When the latter undertook his campaign against the Chickamaugas by water he was supposed to live in Virginia, under whose authority the nautical enterprise was undertaken and on his return he was made Brigadier General by Virginia. I have been at his old place in Sullivan County, and it is several hundred yards this side of our state line and near Bristol, Tennessee. Across the line and in exact contact with it is *Goodson,* they really are parts of the same town, one of whose streets follows the state line through the town. Finding that he did not live in Virginia, he would necessarily become *frinctus officire* and was not known as General Evan Shelby afterwards though he retained the title ever afterward and is, I believe, so designated on his monument which I have seen. In 1784? or near that date Sevier was commissioned by North Carolina Brigadier and Evan Shelby could not be a

Brigadier at the same time. Every county in North Carolina had its own regiment and of course when Sullivan County was struck off of Washington County the new county had to have its colonel commandant and thus Captain Isaac Shelby became the colonel—say in 1779. I will look further into this some other day as I happen at this moment to be very much engaged.

I write this early so as to add one thing more to yourself about your Mecklenburg, still on your shelves as you cannot get a publisher to undertake it. Have you ever tried the Methodist Publishing House at Nashville, Tennessee? Eastman and Company? These Methodist people are very clannish and have made a success of everything (even Calvinistic and nonsectarian works) which they publish. They have the *machinery* in their circuit riders to give popularity and éclat to all their publications. Tennessee is the best field you can find anywhere for your bantling—everyone nearly in it being of North Carolina descent. Their terms are: The author furnishes the manuscript, they stereotype and manufacture it into a volume, put it into their *machinery* for selling, retain enough of the proceeds of sale for the extinguishing of the expense of manufacture first, and then each party is equal in all the sales, author retaining the plates. They will publish my abridgment or *Manual of Tennessee History* on these terms. Yours will sell better than mine. Suppose you write them. The Burke County people, except W. Avery, were from Pennsylvania, as probably Isaacs was. I will see _____ and write you.

I am preparing a paper on the prerevolutionary and the revolutionary history of Tennessee, for the next meeting of our state historical society. Do you ever see the *Christian Observer,* Louisville, Kentucky? In the last number you will find an article, "Mnemonika" on Old Lebanon-in-the-Fork. God bless, guard, guide and direct you prays your sincere friend. . . .

P. S. Before I had sealed this letter, yours of the sixteenth reached me. *Gap Creek* is a large tributary of Watauga, still known by that name and on this side of the Alleghenies. *Brights Trace* was, I suppose, one of the blazed paths across the mountains and so called for one of the first hunters or explorers, and did pass directly through the *Bald Place* that gave that name to the mountain. In 1805 the place was still *bald* and may be still so. I saw it so when eight years old and can still recollect it well. *Brights*

Place: I don't know where it was. He may have *blazed* the trail but may have lived elsewhere. This was done with a tomahawk of a hunter or pioneer. I don't think the Bald Place showed any marks of having been cleared when I saw it. Not a cabin was then on it nor a fence, but on the edge of the Bald Place was a camp and ashes, etc. The men may have paraded there. Mr. Andrew Cresswell told me they were ordered to discharge their rifles and load and prime afresh—Tories might be waylaying them. They did discharge them but made little explosion. *Trace,* as I understand it, meant a blazed line of considerable length say from the eastern base of the Blue Ridge clear across the high mountains to their western base. At the same time, 1805, this trace crossed *Lindle* Ridge, perhaps Linnville, a considerable elevation east of Yellow (Bald) Mountain. Not far from its foot we crossed Catawba River (small), came to the house of Colonel Wrightstill Avery (one of the members of the Mecklenburg Convention). He lived near the present Morganton, Burke County. Lindle Ridge was abundant in izing glass and attracted the notice of an eight year old boy from Knoxville.

I fatigue you with these boyhood recollections. I saw near the trace we traveled the place where a noted Tory was followed and I asked years afterwards who had with three others waylaid and murdered a Whig over in Hopewell. That county is full of history.

I hope *Paulette* may not disappoint your Mr. Thomson. He is experienced in book enterprises and travels extensively. If he comes to Knoxville soon I will try to see him.

June 20, 1876

I have been busy lately preparing a centennial offering to the people of Tennessee. *"Tennessee in the Revolution"* is the title of the address. It will be read at the next meeting of the historical society of the state on July 4 in the capitol. I am one of the first born of the sons of the *State* of Tennessee and I thought that occupying the position I do in the society, and especially as I am the connecting link between the pioneers and their successors in the Volunteer State, it would be very appropriate and well timed for me to seize the centennial occasion to make the offering. Am I right? But having now finished the last line of it, I take up your favor of the twelfth, knowing that you can now see and appreciate the cause of *apparent* delay.

Your present *chronology* about Evan Shelby must be accurate from other circumstances than those you enumerate. I briefly refer to them: On examining the "Annals" I see they do state that Shelby was made General by Virginia. I cannot now recollect on what authority this statement was made. At first he seemed to be a citizen of that state but after the line was drawn it became evident he lived in North Carolina. I know his old residence and have been at it—not a quarter of a mile from the dividing line. As he was invested by Virginia with the *chief* command in providing for and carrying on his Chickamauga expedition, as he had the regiment of Colonel Hamilton placed under him, etiquette or courtesy would concede to him the title of general, or perhaps Virginia may have appointed him or offered to appoint him general, which, of course, he could not accept as he lived out of her territory and of course had to decline it. How and when did he become General under North Carolina? Colonel Sevier, you recollect, was appointed general in 1784 when the Franklin difficulties began in order to oppose these discontents and in fact, after this appointment of Sevier was made, he himself used it as an argument why the malcontents should drop all idea of separation or a new state. But becoming soon afterwards the head of the revolt he became incapacitated to be a general under North Carolina and at the same time governor of the new state. He may have resigned or been deposed—perhaps both. At all events there became a vacancy in the brigade and none was better qualified to fill that vacancy than Evan Shelby. See *Annals,* page 3, 5, 7, 8 and elsewhere in my chapter on Franklin. Then the gap you find, in the Shelby letters you refer to from 1783 to 1787, is easily explained. Colonel to 1784 and in 1787 a general under North Carolina wishing to resign. The dates correspond exactly. Shelby was and had been a friend of both parties. I do not mean a fence man. Far from it. He had tried to heal the breach between the old and new state by negotiation with Governor Sevier. The latter would not yield and the other could not fight unnecessarily with his countrymen and best friends. Hence his request to be allowed to resign. I concur with you in dating his commission about 1786 and wishing to resign in 1787. These dates all agree to this hypothesis. See *Annals.* 1799 is the proper date of his death, in December.

I do not know that Charles Robinson went to Chickamauga with Evan Shelby, nor that it was a joint expedition between Virginia and North Carolina. "Our early history needs a good deal of honest revision" you say truly. I have not yet received answer from our Judge Turney about

Colonel Elijah Isaacs. When received you shall certainly hear from me promptly.

Did you receive my letter stating that Eastman, Tarvel and Company of Nashville are publishers, etc., etc? They are executing our *Manual of Tennessee History for Schools, Academies,* etc., etc. I think they would be suitable publishers for your Mecklenburg. I still hope to see it before I depart home. Dr. Cyrus L. Hunter of *Cottage Home,* Lincoln County, North Carolina expects to bring out his volume on the same subject in all this month. It will be well done.

One word on politics. The convention at Cincinnati has done the Democrats great harm by nominating Hayes. He is a negative man, but all the worse to us for that. It will require all our wisdom and virtue to repair the mischief or prevent complete disaster.

God bless, keep, protect and save you prays your old but sincere friend!

J. G. M. Ramsey

CHAPTER XXIII

Interests of an Octogenarian

Draper Correspondence
Mecklenburg Place
Knoxville, Tennessee
January 14, 1877

My Dear Mr. Draper,

Yours of the eleventh I received yesterday. Adopting your language fully, "Thank the good Lord I have entered upon a new year in reasonable health"—in March (25th) a full octogenarian, with all my faculties and all my external senses as perfect as ever, though still unable to walk without both crutches—a cripple probably for life but not otherwise much of an invalid, using the same glasses my son General J. C. Ramsey presented me from Washington, D. C. during Mr. Polk's administration, hearing accurately, sleeping full eight hours, enjoying society, company of friends and my borrowed books *con amore*. I try to be—I ought to be—thankful to our Heavenly Father for his continued kindness and manifold blessings to me. How is it, my dear friend, that even under these rare blessings and mercies I so often *distrust* Him? This *is* a great sin and I have to repent of it often and painfully. If we grow in grace at all our trust in our Heavenly Father should increase too.

I am glad to hear that the seventh volume of your society's *Collections* will be out soon and I look for it impatiently. Strange that my publishers at Nashville did not respond to your letter. I had already told them who Mr. Draper was. They, as other publishers elsewhere all are, are timid and cautious. Everything hangs fire, and will do so till after the fifth of March. If Tilden is not inaugurated there will be further usurpation, tyranny and lawlessness, perhaps empire, another civil war. Our Democratic resolutions on the eighth in Ohio speak out significantly, and portend much. This is no Union now—only a fragmentary patchwork. Throw a brickbat or a sledge hammer into one of Stuart's largest and most brilliant mirrors on Broadway, New York and no power of Alchemy, no chemical skill, no artistic genius and no power of combination known to philosophers or statesmen can restore its . . . unity. Reconstruction, Johnson's Restoration —"my policy," as he called it,—have all failed alike to remodel us into one whole people. Tilden may restore some of our lost features so as to last a term or two. There is but one and only one method to regenerate the republic into one homogeneous body out of the existing discordant and heterogeneous materials of which we now consist and that is this—*Reassociation*. That word will explain itself, implying the equality of all the activities and agencies of all the peoples making up our whole; holding out the old idea of state sovereignty and denying almost totally the idea of congressional supremacy. Wipe it out. It is the great source of our national danger.

[I wish I had consented to go into the Senate with] [1] I. G. Harris and other old time Democrats. [We] could have put the ball in motion and possibly have saved the country from ruin. It is the only proper combination of the Federal and elective principles that can be framed, but I may not now enlarge upon or explain the idea. I sent you a most imperfect account of our last meeting at the capitol. A fuller will be out tomorrow which may be in time for this letter.

Your letter has done me good and I thank you for it.

God bless you prays

J. G. M. Ramsey

Draper Correspondence

Mecklenburg Place
Knoxville, Tennessee
July 30, 1878

Mrs. James P. Irwin
Charlotte, North Carolina

My Dear Madam,

Your polite favor of the twenty-eighth is to hand. All the traditions of my mother's family have invariably assigned the *residence* of her Uncle Hezekiah Alexander to Sugar Creek and to the very locality so graphically

---

[1] Dr. Ramsey drew his pencil through the words in brackets.

described by H. M. J. in the *Southern Home*. When I first read the lines to which you cite me on page 201 of Foote's *Sketches,* soon after their publication in 1846, I thought there was an error as to Hezekiah Alexander being buried in Hopewell. When I came to page 204 I read again that a like error had occurred in assigning Hezekiah Alexander as an elder of Hopewell. I came to page 211 and there found the names of the elders in both Sugar Creek and Hopewell,—congregations then united under the pastorate of the then incumbent Reverend S. C. Caldwell. This explains in part the inaccuracy as to Hezekiah Alexander's place of burial and the name of his church.

As to Ephraim Brevard's reputed burial in Hopewell it may have been inferred by those from whom Dr. Foote received the information, that, as on his return from prison in Charleston to his old place in the Brevard settlement (now Iredell) he reached the house of J. M. K. Alexander and there died, and hence it may have been inferred that Dr. Brevard was buried in Hopewell. I have heard traditions both ways but incline to the belief that as Mrs. Brevard had been interred at Charlotte so the remains of her husband were taken to that place too for interment. But I *know* nothing, of course, further on the matter but what tradition has brought down to us.

When I saw the first number of H. P. J. in the *Southern Home* my good wife and myself had no difficulty in ascribing the production to your facile pen. And I can here not abstain from congratulating the readers of that able journal that so beautiful and interesting a theme as "the homes of the signers of the Mecklenburg Declaration" has fallen to such a competent and graceful writer as Mrs. Irvin. The last number which I have just read is the most succinct, concise, and satisfactory article on the general subject which the whole discussion has elicited. I await the future of your labors with impatience. I was tempted once or twice to put you in possession of additional material.

The public taste will demand that your work be continued and that your several numbers be embodied in a volume. Thousands of Tennessee readers, descendants from the old Hornets Nest and the Seven Churches of Mecklenburg will appreciate its merits.

With great respect,

Your Obedient Servant
J. G. M. Ramsey

Draper Correspondence

August 7, 1878

[Lyman C. Draper]
My Dear Sir,

Your very welcome favor of July 31 is to hand. I appreciate it the more as I have not for so long a time had the pleasure of hearing from you. Your letters, while they always instruct me, never fail to comfort and encourage me. To your kind inquiries I reply almost in your own words. Publishers ask too much payment in advance and there has been no positive contract yet made to publish either my abridgment or the entire work. It hangs fire but may go off some of these days.

My society is doing better and we are more encouraged and hopeful. Dr. Drake's enterprise (*Annals of the Army of Tennessee*) will be an auxiliary and in part supply the great want of an organ of our own. You have no doubt seen his monthly.

To your question about my health I can only say that a month ago I met with another fall—not from my horse for I never ride now—but from my crutches. This fall slightly increases the discomfort from my fractured neck of the femur. I cannot sit upright against my table and do much of my writing with a pencil and on a board across my lap. You would be surprised at my power of endurance. On a recent occasion I wrote eight pages foolscap in one day. I am a wonder to myself. In my eighty-second year I sleep well (full eight hours in continuous sleep), eat heartily, retain my former avoirdupois 108 pounds and the use of all my external senses, a full degree of vivacity and cheerfulness, and I must add, a wish to be useful with a calm trust in God and a fond hope of rest in Heaven.

Am glad to hear you are still actively employed, even if it is on Brant,[2] and that you are making additions and corrections on your Mecklenburg. I hope your society receives the *Southern Home* (Charlotte, North Carolina) and other journals of the Old North State. I have noticed in them several articles for the last three years on this theme. Some of them are already pasted in my scrapbooks and others filed away. I don't know that any of them are new to you but I inclose to you today the third of a series

---

[2] Although at the moment Draper had two manuscripts nearly completed, he had turned his attention to Samuel Brant, the Mohawk chieftain, and was diligently gathering material on Indian affairs during the American Revolution.

of articles that are being published weekly in the *Southern Home*. They are from the facile pen of Mrs. James P. Irwin of Charlotte, a lady of the highest character in the South and not of kin to any of the Alexanders as far as I know. After reading the number I will thank you to inclose it to me again as I preserve in my scrapbook everything that I meet with on that subject. Otherwise you might retain it. The more I look into this subject the more thoroughly do I believe in the entire authenticity of the Mecklenburg Declaration. I also inclose to you a copy in writing of another scrap of history which I found in a North Carolina paper but which is already posted on my scrapbook. It is an exact copy. Read it. John Sevier is mentioned. Our John Sevier may have been over there on some public occasion. I will inquire and procure if possible the original paper. I can speak for the *signature* of three or four of those named.

The Chickamaugas was an association of lawless Cherokees and Creeks, implacable, revengeful, bloodthirsty—the Barbary Powers of the interior country—the Ishmaelites of our aborigines, allies in war and malcontents in peace. They observed no *treaty* stipulations; they were freebooters and desperadoes. The Cherokees as a nation discarded and disowned them. The Nickajack campaign dispersed and destroyed the association. A *treaty* was not always authorized by North Carolina, the Federal government, or even by a formidable military force, but often by a commander of a small force and scarcely deserved the name of a treaty. Wheeler's date is probably wrong. My collateral authorities were all destroyed in my house and I have nothing to refer to.

I copy from some newspaper the following as printed and now pasted in my scrapbook or it would have been inclosed in its original form.

Copy

"An important Revolutionary paper has been found by Captain Appleton Oaksmith of Carteret County, North Carolina. It is in the handwriting of Richard Casswell, being signed by him and one hundred and eighty-five prominent patriots of the state—among whom are Willie Jones, Cornelius Barnett, William Graham, Hezekiah Alexander, Robert Irwin, Zacheus Wilson, John Brevard, Wrightstill Avery, Joseph Hewes and John Sevier. The following is a copy of this document: 'We the subscribers do declare that we will bear faith (sic.) and true allegiance to the independent State of North Carolina, and to the powers and authorities which may be established for the government thereof and we will to the utmost of our powers, maintain and defend the same against Great Britain and all other Powers, enemies to the United States of America. And this we do most solemnly and sincerely declare without any equivocation, mental evasion or secret reservations whatever.'

"This paper was signed at least a year before the Mecklenburg Declaration was drawn up."

The black lines embrace the whole scrap, without any date, name of paper, or place of issue. I will write to Captain Oaksmith of Cartaret County, North Carolina and try to get on the right track of this strange paper. Can you help me unravel it? In clipping it, my amanuensis left off something perhaps that would explain the mystery. I think it was cut from a western North Carolina paper but am not sure.

Do your notes enable you to say where General Griffith Rutherford died? I am investigating him. Excuse me. If you have them please answer.

Yours most cordially and truly,

J. G. M. Ramsey

P. S. Please reinclose to me the article now sent of Mrs. Irwin as I preserve all such in my scrapbook. Three or four of her numbers have already appeared in the *Southern Home. Ephraim Brevard* is promised in a future **number.**

J. G. M. R.

August 19, 1878

I duly received your former letter and replied to it inclosing some *one* of the series of papers now being issued in the *Charlotte Home* by Mrs. Irwin. I hope you received the letter. And now I received your favor of the ninth asking for the numbers of the series, etc. Yes, my dear sir, with all my heart. If you have not already received them from the editor as you have written for them, please let me hear and the numbers I have will be cheerfully inclosed as a temporary *loan* to you as I intend them for a place in my scrapbook, number four. I would inclose them today but will wait to hear that you have not been able to procure them from Charlotte.

Have you ever read the memorial address of the North Carolina bar on the life and death of the late Governor William A. Graham? I have it pasted in my scrapbook but as you may not have read it, I make a short extract from it for your eye. ". . . Some writers had seized upon that event and in that spirit of historical suspicion so rife in our day, had undertaken out of a few discrepancies to deny the genuineness of the Declaration or that any meeting was held on the twentieth of May. William Graham had been often solicited to place that event upon the proper basis. He had heard it often talked of at his father's (General Jos. Graham's) fireside, he knew all the traditions connected with it, he had known and talked with many of the subscribers of that declaration, he was well acquainted with public opinion regarding it, in that section where the event occurred, down to the date of its republication in 1820. For a long time motives of delicacy, growing out of his connection with some of the principal actors, restrained him. But at that time all the actors had passed away, they could no longer be heard. A just regard for their fame urged his acquiescence. He embodied his vindication in the form of an address which he delivered on this occasion. No fair synopsis of that address is possible. It is a solid compact argument which would be greatly impaired by any attempt at abridgment. Let it suffice to say that the evidence is arrayed in the spirit of the philosophical historian and with the skill of a consummate lawyer. It will not put to silence the mere caviler: no amount of evidence will on this or any other subject. But the candid inquirer will rise from the perusal with the conviction that few events in history rest upon a firmer foundation than the Mecklenburg Declaration of Independence." I am almost ashamed to send such writing to the *Plutarch of the West*. Excuse me. Since my second fall early in June I have to adopt various expedients to write at all. I am again improving even with our thermometer at 93 and nothing would distress me more than for you to think that I can't answer your ever welcome letters.

I am doing pretty good work considering that I am a cripple. Any other man but me would lay on his back and grumble, moan and complain at his lot. Goodness, Mercy have followed me all my days.

Let me hear if copies of Mrs. Irwin's papers are wanted. . . .

September 14, 1878

I have been so long time witness to your promptness—punctuality—that I am now really uneasy, anxious for your health, and must inquire this morning for you. I promptly replied to your former letter inquiring about treaties, etc. In that reply I inclosed to you one of Mrs. Irwin's numbers (on the homes of the signers of the Mecklenburg Declaration of Independence) and requested you to send back to me that number of the series—as I preserve them in my scrapbook number three. I afterwards wrote you a brief note. But I am distressed not so much on the return of the printed slip as I am to be assured that sickness of yourself or your family is not the cause of your silence. Do relieve me and if you are done with the slip taken from the *Southern Home* please inclose it to me. Let me also hear whether others of Mrs. Irwin's numbers have been received. *Mine* are not yet pasted in my book and are carefully preserved for *loan* to you if you desire them.

I have replied only this morning to an invitation to be the guest of the Essen Institute on the commemoration of the twenty-eighth of September 1628—the landing at Salem of Governor Endicott. But I must not trouble you further today. You may be only convalescent. God bless, preserve and save you, prays your sincere friend. . . .

P. S. Knoxville and East Tennessee are free of all disease.

December 21, 1878

I received on the nineteenth your catalogue of the library of the State Historical Society of Wisconsin. What cannot the industry and diligence and zeal and the *will* of one man do? *Exegi monumentum perenius oure* may you well say in bringing out this splendid volume. Are you a dictator in the Northwest? or how do you achieve so much at Madison? Our society has the same date (1849) with yours and yet it has done nothing, literally nothing. You have certainly something of magic about you which I dare not aspire to. And yet I am *omnis in hoc* and am never idle. Can you put me on another track? I am discouraged, wholly so. I see no fruits, no harvest, no growth. Will it ever be otherwise? In my correspondence I often allude to your success and to Wisconsin but get no responsive cheer here at home. Tennessee is in debt and can give us no help not a single dollar and we have no rich men to fall back on and no public spirit in that direction. But I must thank you for this volume. I will keep it on my table and call to its contributions the attention of everyone whom I see with the hope of exciting in some humble degree a similar spirit.

And then yesterday your letter of the sixteenth is received and noticed. I was before the war a large farmer and hog-raiser and had often amongst them the hog cholera. As far as I know there has been no *successful treatment* of that disease. I am satisfied of its contagiousness but know it also to be indigenous, i.e., of domestic origin. I know no cure, no preventive.

Our hog raisers just gave up to its ravages and agreed to bear the loss which they never estimated at less than 20 per cent, sometimes more.

While I was in exile in North Carolina, 1865 to 1871, it appeared in Rowan and Mecklenburg Counties. A neighbor farmer thought the best treatment was to keep his hogs in larger inclosures *without water* but he boiled the roots of pine very strong in a solution of coperas and confined them to this for their drink. He fed sparingly. This seemed to cure curable and incipient cases but in advanced cases some of his hogs died, but very few. I tried it with my hogs and it did not reach a single one of them. The same neighbor told me that hogs which were not allowed when pigs to run on clover pastures never took cholera. I think there is something in this and such is prevalent opinion here now.

I am sorry to answer your inquiries so unsatisfactorily. I have read much in the agricultural department of the *American,* Nashville, Tennessee on this subject. William Killebrew of that city has written a good deal on it and he is good authority when he speaks of his own knowledge and is perfectly reliable on many branches of husbandry. The nostrums he gives on the authority of others fail sometimes. But I will see some of our best Dutch hog raisers in the hog region above us on French Broad and will inquire diligently of their experience of cholera and will write you at once the result of my conference with them. What they pretend to know they know practically and well.

I know of no publication on this subject to refer you to. If I hear of any I will hereafter write you. I hope you will succeed in getting out your book. It will be eagerly read by the farming community and others. I wish it great success.[3]

Your Volume VIII of your *Collections* will be waited for impatiently in 1879. Its predecessors have always interested me. This one will increase my *self* reproach—not exactly that either, but it will make me more dissatisfied at the apathy of Tennessee and our South. There is nothing even since 1860 which we need be unwilling for posterity to read; even the disaster and defeat of our lost-cause. "In great events 'tis glorious e'en to fail." My society is struggling to live but it is yet alive and some of its members are alive. "Eureka!" exclaimed your old friend the other day writing to our vice president, Honorable J. M. Lea giving a résumé of our transactions.

---

[3] Draper's "family encyclopedia," called *A Helping Hand for Town and Country* had been published in Cincinnati in 1871 but had been in litigation almost since its date of publication. Periodically he hoped to rescue it from the courts, revise it, and sell it by subscription.

He said, "After the vain research of thirty or forty years I received very recently from Miss S. Houston of Rockbridge County, Virginia a printed copy "A Declaration of Rights or Form of Government on the Constitution of the Commonwealth of Frank*land* [sic] by the Convention of the Freeman thereof—elected and chosen for that particular purpose in Convention assembled at Greenville 14 of November 1785. Philadelphia printed by Francis Bailey at Yoricks Head 1785. Attested by my father Francis A. Ramsey, clerk." This copy is probably the only one in the world—(The copy used in my *Annals* was burned in 1863 in my house or stolen or lost). This copy contains nothing new but it is yet a great curiosity. Reverend Mr. Samuel Houston was believed to be in possession of all the records of Tennessee. I wrote to him. He died soon after. This year I renewed my correspondence with his executor with the above result. The granddaughter promised me other valuable papers. I hope to get something of historical importance in our earliest periods. Mr. Houston was a leading member of the convention and when this convention failed to adopt his hobby he returned to Virginia and never returned to this country.

The failure of the Nashville publishing house has postponed the publication of the abridgment of my *Annals*.

The weather is so cloudy and dark that I can scarcely see so as to make my writing legible. I have nothing to send you but a historical sermon by my pastor, Reverend Mr. Park. . . .

April 30, 1879

Your ever welcome and esteemed favor of the twenty-fifth instant duly received. I have waited two days to look over my books, pamphlets, etc., with the hope of finding my copies of the "Land We Love." From August 28, 1863 to April 1870 I was in honorable exile in Georgia, South and North Carolina and Virginia—with the Confederate army, as president of the branch Bank of Tennessee at Knoxville and Confederate States depositary for Tennessee to the surrender. And then my family (wife and unmarried daughters having been sent out of Tennessee to Dixie) joined me in North Carolina when we lived in other people's houses as tenants. There I contributed several articles for the "Land We Love." I had the whole series as the numbers came out and until your letter came, supposed they were on our shelves or perhaps in some of our trunks. I find they are not here and that I must have left them in Mecklenburg, North Carolina. I will write at once to Mrs. Alexander or Captain R. M. Ramsey, both of whom reside there yet, and who being our children will doubtless have taken care of the whole series. I think they will be found there and as soon as I receive them they shall be forwarded to you, only I must retain the *pages* on which my own contributions shall be found. Before the war I had carefully preserved everything that had been published from my pen under my own name or Clinton or 76 or A Young Believer, or Presbyterous, or Mnemonika or Tennessee or Mecklenburg, etc., etc., but these were all burned September 1863 by Burnside. Since the surrender I continue to preserve them in my scrapbooks. I have not a single number of the North Carolina University magazine nor of the *Southern Literary Messenger* or they would be now sent.

"I am not seemingly making any progress." You are mistaken, my dear friend. You are doing and have done more than any *ten* men in this wide world. The Plutarch of the West[4] shall not say this to me who knows all about this matter. You are overworked and have been so ever since I knew you. Hence the neuralgia in your right arm, your dyspepsia, and the consequent debility. I must volunteer a prescripton for you: Not to quit work— that would be fatal. But to come this very summer to Knoxville. The travel itself will be beneficial. The change of climate and scenery and then the fact that everywhere you go, every face you see, every town you visit, every ruin you pass in Tennessee at least has its own history and is not only instructive to the tourist but will be so utilized by him as to *teach history*. I am in earnest, my dear friend, and so are also Mrs. Ramsey and my daughter Mrs. Breck and my son McKnitt Ramsey who constitute our whole family. We keep one room always for a prophet's chamber, with a table, a candlestick, a few books, a genealogical record and a list for autographs; a fine chair made in London before 1773 and bought in 1774 by J. McKnitt Alexander whilst a member of the provincial legislature of North Carolina and given by him to his daughter, my mother, in 1789; her wedding shoes (an exceedingly antique and queenly article of dress). Her funeral sermon preached by Reverend R. Henderson, D.D., in 1805 and printed at Abingdon, Virginia. My grandfather's staff (R. Ramsey), a soldier of Washington and in his army at Princeton and Trenton, and a

---

[4] Draper's title, "Plutarch of the West" had originally been conferred on him in 1844. It had been revived and confirmed in a biographical sketch of Draper published in the New York *Graphic*, October 16, 1876.

part of the Constitution of the Commonwealth of Frank*land* (sic) printed in Philadelphia, Pennsylvania 1785, and many other things rare, curious, antique and historical. I hope these all and our unmalarial climate will cure you. Beside this your benevolence will be gratified by adding (perhaps) one year more to my own advanced life. I repeat I am in earnest and hope you will come. Drive right to my gate in East Knoxville, Mecklenburg Place.

You say "I hope the *Father* is dealing gently with you." I like your emphasized word *Father*. For eighty-two years he has been indeed a kind and indulgent Father to me. My surroundings are all pleasant even yet. An excellent wife aged seventy-six in comfortable health, of congenial taste, fond of books and especially of her Bible, of the traditions and history of Tennessee sits often as my amanuensis as she has done for fifty-eight years assisted by our widowed daughter Mrs. Breck. Another widowed daughter Mrs. Dickson and two grown sons only three doors from ours both alike dutiful affectionate and kind. Our son—J. G. McKnitt living with us and devoted to our care and comfort most thoroughly. You know, I believe, that I was in 1875 incurably crippled by my horse. That accident still confines me to my room. But I have the perfect use of all my external senses, eat and sleep well, and am otherwise quite comfortable with a slight though perceptible failure of my memory especially of recent events. But my friends in every part of the South never pass through town without paying me a call. The chairman of some public committee called the other day and on coming in remarked that I was recognized everywhere as one of the institutions of the country and that he had concluded not to return home without offering me his respects. Scarcely a day passes without a similar civility. To all this list of blessings should be added this further one that clergymen and private members of all denominations besides my own pastor all frequently call to see the Old Pilgrim. So that the good Father is leading me gently down to the grave in peace with all the world.

You did send me the fourth volume of catalogues. I ought to have acknowledged it sooner. Our Tennessee Historical Society is hardly alive. It needs some Galvani like yourself to galvanize it into life. I have done what I could.

The *Father* guide, bless, comfort and save you prays

Your sincere and affectionate friend. . . .

September 22, 1879

By direction of the committee for that purpose I have the pleasure of inviting you to be present at the Centennial of Jonesboro, Tennessee on the third of October 1879 and to express the ardent wish and hope that it may not be inconvenient to you to favor us with the presence and aid of one who is so familiar with the rich memories and hallowed associations this occasion will furnish to the student of Tennessee history and of one who has done so much in behalf of our common West and Southwest.

Please allow me to add to this official duty, that of begging you to furnish me as a *personal favor* first the *names* of the captains and other officers of Colonels Sevier, Shelby, Campbell, Chronicle, Hambright, Clarke and Williams who were in command October 7, 1780 at King's Mountain. I assure you in justice to yourself that as far as they will be used on this centennial, *Lyman C. Draper* shall have full credit for the information thus given. *You alone* are able to do this great favor to me and the general public. If I am asking *too much* I know you will generously forgive me. Perhaps you can find time to send me something appropriate to the occasion to be read or exhibited in your own name, some original or duplicate if you have it, which shall be returned safely by me. Again I ask, am I begging too much? Can you send me the *Autographs* of some of our Western heroes, adventurers and pioneers? George Rogers Clarke (sic) D. Boon, Robertson, Sevier, Shelby, William Campbell, Hampton, Sumter, General Griffith Rutherford, William Cocke or others. I will exchange with you hereafter when I have duplicates. . . .

January 30, 1880

I lose not one mail in replying to yours of January 26 received last night. I have been sick, very sick, since December. Pneumonitis—not only pneumonia, as was common here during the dark, black, damp weather of our warm winter. But my simple life and temperate habits have given me a remarkable recuperative power and now am not only an established convalescent but in good health, except some slight debility. I will, twenty-fifth of next March, enter on my eighty-fourth year. My grandfather J. M. McKnitt Alexander, of whom in stature, weight, complexion, temperament, intellect, tastes, everybody that knew us both always said I was his exact *facsimile,* died at eighty-four. Like causes produce like effects. He became blind several years before his death. I use the same glasses (peri-focal—made of the Brazilian glass got at Washington, when Mr. Polk was yet in the White House) which I have used ever since and read now with no perceptible abatement of good sight and other external senses. I use no stimulant only tobacco and that moderately—only incessantly when I am well—sleep sound and eat enough and enjoy society with a keen relish and my books. I allow myself, as through life, never to be unemployed, never to be idle, only the yet sweet hours of domestic enjoyment and a serene old age and tranquility and hope in God.

After this long introduction, let me answer your inquiries seriatim. The centennial proceedings at Jonesboro were promised at first in pamphlet form and I bespoke several copies for exchange with you and others. This has never been done, and only yesterday week I wrote to W. E. Mathis, corresponding secretary of the centennial, on the subject, but have not received his reply. There was some conflict of opinion between the *agricultural* and the *historical* features of the celebration and I expect the race horses and the Grama chickens carried off the palm over antiquities and our state history. The present over the past, as is too common everywhere except in Madison and Wisconsin. Still there was in several secular journals an occasional notice, sometimes a list of antique and rare historical articles borrowed or sent to the exhibition, but no full account has been published or I would have sent it at once to *you* and if a pamphlet is got up I will certainly send it by mail. There was only a synopsis of Mr. Doak's oration printed and nothing new in it. The secretary of the centennial sent to me two photos of the famos Boon Tree with the Boon inscription very plain and legible,—now neatly framed and hung up in my study near the lithograph of S. Doak, D.D., the apostle of learning and religion in Tennessee and the Southwest. The secretary, W. E. Mathis, Esquire, promises to present me soon with a staff made of a log of the first church ever erected in Tennessee for Presbyterian worship. The associations awakened by this staff are very solemn and even sacred to me. My parents worshiped in it and one at least of my deceased brothers was offered to God in holy baptism in that primitive log church and log college built as early as 1779. Salem Church and Martin Academy are historical now and will ever be so.

Yes Sir. The King's Mountain Centennial will be the great event of 1880—Nashville not excepted. It was not at my suggestion that *April 27, 1880* was made the Tennessee Centennial. I suggested October 7 and I only acquiesced in the other date in conformity with the preferences of Middle

Tennessee friends who think that the arrival of General Robertson at the salt lick now Nashville January 1, 1780 was a greater event than the most decisive victory of the Revolution. Though I have consented to prepare a paper on "Tennessee in the Revolutionary period" for the April centennial, not one line of which has yet been written, and hope yet to meet the expectation of my friends, yet Nashville will not draw like King's Mountain would have done. Half of our people prefer to go there. These Palmettos never do anything without a whole hearted purpose. It will be so next fall. They already begin to talk of a grand celebration, a sham fight in which Virginia, the Carolinas, Georgia and Tennessee will be present. It will require good management to get up much enthusiasm at Yorktown. There will be less nationality, nobody will attend north of Norfolk. Such is still the passion for state pride and state rights. That feeling grows every year. Still when Governor Albert S. Marks last fall offered me the Commissioner to Yorktown I thanked him but declined the honor. That centennial does not occur till 1881 and Imperialism or Caesarism, alias Grantism, may then have brought on another revolution. Besides this, if the mad policy becomes a reality that Tilden is now to be cheated again out of the Democratic nomination our grand old party will be split asunder and go to pieces. We are and have been constantly a unit for Tilden in Tennessee. The masses and our statesmen are still for him, while our *politicians* are against him and will ruin the party.

Before I close let me request you to send me your photograph if you have one to spare. The *Plutarch of the West* I must have to hang up in my study and look at again. How old are you and where born and educated? Another request, if it is not wrong to make it, is to ask you to send me a full list of the volumes you have written, their titles and sizes. It seems that some besides yourself should know this and make with your permission a prudent use of the information.

You will be formally invited to attend our Tennessee centennial next April at Nashville, and also that at King's Mountain October 7, 1880. Come to both if possible.

I have fatigued you and myself too and close by invoking the blessing of Almighty God on yours and you!

Faithfully yours

J. G. M. Ramsey

CHAPTER XXIV

King's Mountain Men

Draper Correspondence

Mecklenburg Place
Knoxville, Tennessee
March 11, 1880

My Dear Mr. Draper,

My mail late last night brought me your favor of March 8. I read it twice and endeavored to grasp the whole subject. I seldom give advice without first examining it carefully. *Festina lente* is a good maxim, and one which I have through life adopted. Make haste deliberately, or, as Crocket used to say, "Be sure you are right—then go ahead." So in the present instance, after the second reading of your letter, I laid it on the table, slept on it, looked on it in all its bearings and aspects and now give you my deliberate opinion that the present is the auspicious moment to lay down everything else and give *King's Mountain and its Heroes* to the press.

I think there will never be a more suitable or opportune an occasion to *inaugurate* the business of your *life*—your *Border Warfare*—your *Robertson, Shelby, Sevier,* even your *Sumter,* and a host of others. All these have some day soon to be *inaugurated* and all the surroundings of the situation point out 1880 as the *very time* for beginning of the ceremonials. First the Nashville Centennial opens up the ball in the west—this brings into consideration Virginia, good old North Carolina and with her, her gallant daughter, East Tennessee, whose pioneers at Alamance in 1771 were the first armed force that opened resistance to colonial oppression and misrule of any of the British Colonies. Driven from the field for the want of ammunition and an experienced leader, their pioneers, as Bancroft says, shook the bolt from their brow and crossed the Alleghenies and settled Watauga and in a state of political orphanage, in a secluded wilderness, formed the *first self-governing association* known in America—a free and

323

independent little Republic, a gallant little Swiss Canton in the mountains of Tennessee—and all this against the proclamation of the king inhibiting any settlement or purchase on the western waters. (King's proclamation dated 1763.) Watauga then petitioned North Carolina for annexation to that state under the condition and pledge of bearing her full share of the expense to be incurred in the war for independence. This annexation was made, and the representatives of Watauga took their seats in the convention which formed the state constitution of North Carolina. Then came King's Mountain, the most decisive battle of this revolution. Then the surrender of Yorktown and independence. After October 7, 1880 will come the Cowpens, Eutaw and Wapetau.

So we have a historical epoch—a garland of brilliant victories within the next two years. Your part in the whole series is the publication of your book. This being admitted, your Cincinnati enterprise comes next. You ask me if I know any reliable, experienced and energetic canvasser. I know some who will do as side agents under a competent chief. But for such a one please give me a little time. When this letter is finished, say this P.M., I will write to my friend Anson Nelson, Esquire, my recording secretary (and whose name you will find on this letterhead page [1]) and explain confidentially to him your purposes and desire to procure the services of a competent canvasser in Tennessee for your volume. Mr. Nelson, though somewhat busied *officially* these centennial times, will I know be able to find a suitable chief for you and perhaps some sub-agents. He has heretofore had something to do with the publishing houses in Nashville and two years since when I was making an (abortive) attempt to bring out an abridgment of my *Annals,* told me he was well acquainted with canvassers who were experienced and competent and would exactly suit my purpose. I will say to him further that I have given his address to you and advised you to write to him immediately. I know he will obey your request. We have a bookseller here, an agent of Colonel J. B. Killebrew (author of his *Resources of Tennessee*), whom I will consult this P.M. if he is at home. He knows all the canvassers in Tennessee and can perhaps promote your purposes in this behalf.

If you can get the volume out against October first your agents and yourself will have achieved a remarkable success. I know it will sell well everywhere in the South. When you inquired if Yorktown would absorb

---

[1] Nearly all of Dr. Ramsey's letters to Draper were written on the letterhead of the Tennessee Historical Society.

King's Mountain I thought the places and the dates intervening were too far apart to interfere much with either celebration. I think so yet. The latter is isolated, insulated rather, in the woods thirteen miles from York-ville, South Carolina over mountain roads, with a sparse population and very limited accommodations. But though somewhat desolated and se-cluded, these Palmettos are, as in 1780, determined to do their whole duty in 1880. They are exerting every energy to have a good celebration. They will have a sham battle—orators from every state that participated in the fight. In upper East Tennessee troops will assemble September 25 at Wa-tauga Old Fields and some of them march over the old Brights Trace in the old frontier costume to the battleground. And here in Knox County we are trying to form an association of the descendents of the old time Whigs of 1776 to attend this centennial jubilee. I hear Governor Marks is invited and will attend with the executives of Georgia, South and North Carolina and old Virginia. So that, as far as I can now see, it will be a good celebration. Since I began this letter Reverend Lathan writes me under date Yorkville South Carolina March 6, 1880 that my name had been placed at the head of the historical committee and that this com-mittee is charged with the duty of preparing a sketch of the battle and of the lives of the prominent actors on that occasion. He is silent as to anything he expects to perform then. Says nothing of his *pamphlet.* I once knew Mr. Lathan. He will not interfere in your book at all as you will cover the whole ground while he will only skim the surface of the mountain itself. Therefore, I repeat my advice to you to go on at once and publish your volume. Four hundred pages is a good size and five hun-dred is better. The subject is broad and comprehensive and ought not to be too much condensed. Cincinnati is a good place, too, now when she is sticking out her iron hands to Tennessee and the South. When the proper time arrives for the Tennessee Historical Society to endorse your great enterprise and give its small prestige to its success, if I am still living it shall be most cheerfully conferred.

Your name is already before our committee of invitation of which Hon-onable _____ Guild is chairman. Come if you can. It may help you greatly in many respects. Is the next volume of your *Collections* out? I must have fatigued you as I have fatigued myself.

Your Friend Truly
J. G. M. Ramsey

P. S. I have not intended to omit the mention of South Carolina and

Georgia. Have you seen the old time correspondence between Governor
Isaac Shelby and Senator William Campbell Preston, his grandson?

March 23, 1880

Hearing that Mr. Paulett had arrived at his headquarters (Knoxville),
I sent for him this morning to call over and see me. He is a book agent,
canvasser, sometimes chief agent of publishers, or of authors—having sub-
agents or deputies over a given territory. In this capacity he has canvassed
some years back the whole of Tennessee and adjoining states and has very
successfully introduced Killebrew's *Resources of Tennessee* and other
smaller works. His limits are extensive, from Chicago to New Orleans
and all the South. He is a native of Anson County, North Carolina, but
has been in every county of Western North Carolina, South Carolina,
North Georgia and Western Virginia and all of Tennessee. The very field
for your book and (I think) the very type of such an agent as you need
to introduce *King's Mountain and its Heroes*. He is no Yankee but a true
Southern man, prudent, discreet, and wise and ready to work now. I
mentioned (*inter nos*) your present purpose and plan of operations. As far
as I could judge, he thinks very favorably of your enterprise, and thinks
the time very opportune to take up subscriptions—now when the centen-
nials of 1880 are the theme and the talk of the day.

He will write to you this P.M. This letter and his will reach you together.
If you have not contracted with others you will perhaps mature something with Mr. Paulett. Whomsoever you employ, your subscription papers
should be at our Nashville celebration April 24.

I have received from our friend Nelson information that when you
write to him on any subject he will attend promptly to your request, such
as agent or sub-agents to take up subscriptions for your book. . . .

P. S. I am often applied to for the exact route of the Mountain Men from
the camp on Watauga across the mountains to Ferguson's camp, or
rather, camps. It will greatly add to the interest of your book if you could
give in detail every trace and encampment from Watauga to the seat of
the battle and even of the returning route of the victors.

What is Brights Trace? Which *Broad* River did our troops cross on
the fifth and sixth October? What became of the spoils taken on the
seventh and were they auctioned off on the eighth and ninth? Their march

to Hillsboro was necessarily hurried. Where did they cross the Catawba and the Yadkin and where and to what American officer were the prisoners given?

April 20, 1880

I received your kind favor of the fourteenth and by next mail your society's annual report. I need not say to you how much your success rejoices me while I also feel so mortified at the comparison between the results of my efforts in the Tennessee Historical Society and your progress in that of Wisconsin. I have done what I could. We may do better at a future day. I have an excellent cabinet—my field is broad and long and all but two of us officers are poor, broken down by the war. We have never received a single donation, devise, bequest, legacy,—little state aid and little more hoped for as the state treasury is impoverished indeed. Bankrupt, we don't even ask the state for a dollar. Our centennial exposition expenses are paid by our own voluntary individual contributions. But being a very proud people we are going to succeed in making a big show. I am glad to hear you will be at Nashville. May you enjoy it fully.

Now as to private business. I am glad to see you are so hopeful. The preliminary commendations of myself and your other friends will be forthcoming any time you may think proper to name. Please be specific even as to the minutiae. There is a great policy in this whole thing. I am generally very careful what, when, and how to speak, but in your case anything you wish me to say for you, your book, your capacity to write history accurately, truthfully, it will be said cheerfully and without stint. Indicate when, how and to whom. And so of my society and of my historical and personal friends in Tennessee and anywhere else. I will endorse you from A to Z, from Alpha to Omega, and I know I risk nothing by doing so. Your subject, King's Mountain and its Heroes, just meets the emergency now present. Have it on the ground October 7 ready for distribution to every point in the South and Southwest. I think it will take. You should have some sure friends at Washington to speak in the social circles and to colleagues for it. That is an emanating point, potential and effective. When you get *started* I will write to my friends (Harris, Bailey, Vance, Ransom, Atkin, Dibnot, and all the rest) and get them to look at King's Mountain as a matter heretofore neglected and little known even in the South and by general historians (except Butler) ignored. Even

Bancroft (in first edition) treats it as a backwoods *skirmish* and those we call *Heroes* as a *Banditti*. Ferguson thought thus of Sevier, Campbell, Shelby, and Chronicle etc. I comprehend what you say about the conference at Charlotte. It is a big thing and a capital idea. I am corresponding with Vandyke at Athens. I nominated him to Governor Marks. He is to be here to see me this week. I know him like a book and will dissect that whole subject with him.

No doubt about your material. *Forty* years research as to the extent and then the *con amore*—the *heart* which animated and prompted the seeker.

When you go to Nashville see and investigate Judge Lea and Mr. Nelson. They are safe councillors. Command my services at all times and ways. You must make this book introductory to future volumes. God bless you!

May 19, 1880

Yours of the fourteenth has been received. I am glad to hear that you have made an arrangement with Peter G. Thomson for the publication of your work; and it affords me a sincere pleasure to promise *in advance* any commendation of the enterprise which may promote its success in development and preservation of American history of our Revolutionary period. How can I do this most efficiently? If I had the address of your publisher I would enclose to him a short note on the subject, which he may use as he thinks proper in securing to the work a wider circulation and a more remunerative patronage of his enterprise. I enclose it to you herein. I am little acquainted with the forms of such things. You may think the enclosed too long or too short, not in sufficient detail of what I know of the author, his familiarity with the whole field he investigates, his patient research, his untiring diligence, ability, accuracy, etc. You may see much to amend, reject, some additions, some changes to make in the phraseology. I here give you a *charte blanche* to make it longer, shorter, more in detail, more or less specific as to your place of nativity, past publications, pursuits, etc. Whether thus amended or changed or in its present form consider it as addressed to *yourself,* or, what may be better, to the *Publisher* and to be used as he may think best either in his prospectus or some literary journal.

I will also write to Judge Lea and other historical friends to unite with me in this or a like commendation.

No. All my Knoxville and other newspapers were burned in September 1863 by the enemy. But I have already sent over into town asking Colonel Moses White (who has the dates you gave me, 1812–13 and 22) to *loan* them to me for you. I guaranteeing their safe return. After a few days, if they are found, they will be forwarded to you.

I notice what you say of appending the whole *Preston-Shelby correspondence* to your volume. It will add greatly to its interest and will, at the same time, awaken the slumbering ires and animosities engendered by the correspondence in 1821. I had it all before me in 1852 when my *Annals* came out. I found other material too abundant to allow the insertion of the correspondence. The truth of history may require another course proper now. I do not advise either way. Virginians are very sensitive. Some of them thought me at fault in not making Campbell the hero of King's Mountain. I did not.

General John S. Preston has not yet replied to my letter to him.

May 20, 1880

I have just received and herein send you answer of General Preston to my former letter to him. I hope you will soon receive the Shelby and Preston correspondence.

I wrote yesterday in full to Judge Lea and think he will cooperate fully and cordially in commendation of your Book.

Colonel White has not yet sent the Knox Papers. As soon as he finds them they shall be forwarded promptly to you.

June 15, 1880

I think I promised you that after I could see Judge Vandyke I would write you. He came to Knoxville, came over at once to see and confer with me, stayed all day and dined with me. He had determined before to go to Charlotte on the twenty-first. Saw some of his colleagues *here*. I gave him letters of introduction to several of my friends in Charlotte and promised to write others (which I will send him today). I mentioned to him your book especially, agreed to *commend* it fully and if found best to get all the commissioners to unite in some commendatory notice of *your* work when they adjourn and to send me, yourself, or your publisher at Cincinnati a copy of it. If he does this I will hand over what the commissioners say to a Knoxville paper and send it to Madison or Cincinnati.

If this is all right be it so. If not, write in time for me to act on the matter.

Our heated term is on us in all its intensity and am able scarcely to write this much.

Draper Manuscripts 15 DD 69

Mecklenburg Place
Knoxville, Tennessee
July 12, 1880

My Dear Mr. Draper,

Your favor of the ninth has just been handed to me, two P.M., and as my constant habit has long been to leave no duty undone before I go to sleep I am already *in medias res* by way of reply.

You are right. I did recently write a hasty P. S. to you in which I said "It is an invariable tradition all over East Tennessee that on the point of the march of the rifleman from Sycamore Shoals on Watauga, the troops engaged in divine service and were adressed by a Presbyterian clergyman then present." This minister is said to have been Reverend Samuel Doak. He was then or soon after the founder and president of Martin Academy, the first academy chartered by law west of the Allegheny Mountains (has since been succeeded (1795) as the present Washington College—of which he became the founder and first president.) The tradition has preserved this further that in his prayer or address he used the words or petition "Teach our hands to war and our fingers to fight." and also "The Sword of the Lord and of Gideon!" I have heard this tradition from my boyhood and from all my knowledge of the man I believe it substantially true. Dr. Doak was my father's pastor and I am an alumnus of his college.

You say "I wish I knew more of the route of the King's Mountain Men." So do I. I have encountered the same difficulty. *Brights Trace,* which the army pursued, is indefinite now. As far as I know or can certainly say is that the riflemen crossed the Yellow Mountain where it was also called the Bald Mountain. Several of the soldiers have told me that when they reached the very top, *the acme of the ridge,* the army was ordered to shoot off their rifles and in so doing there was little or no *report.*

Such was the rarity of the atmosphere that when the rifles fired there was almost no explosion heard. They must thus have crossed the Bald Mountain Gap and when, after the escape of the two deserters (see my *Annals*), the army deflected to the left and thus left Brights Trace till they fell in with Cleveland and Winston at the foot of the mountains. These *Traces* are very indefinite and often mislead both the writer and reader. Tilden's Ridge was also on Brights Trace—some short distance from Morganton. I wish I could speak more accurately of the *route*. Shelby's officers: John Sawyer, I think, was one of them—then of Sullivan, afterwards of Knox County. In 1774 he decided the fight at Kanawha. I think Jesse Walton was a captain of Sevier. Colonel Maxwell was one of Shelby's captains. Major Tipton, I think, was of Sevier's men. If I can *ascertain* any thing further will write soon. I wish you could describe the route and print the map to accompany it. It adds greatly to its value. I had not seen Major Dunlap's name before. Give us all you can find of the *Tories*. As far as I can learn their descendents were with few exceptions opposed to the South in 1860 and 65.

Draper Correspondence

July 14, 1880

Yours of the eleventh came to hand last night and as there is no time to be lost, I wrote at once (at seven A.M.) this morning to General John S. Preston, Columbia, South Carolina, telling him of *you,* your purpose to issue a volume on *King's Mountain and its Heroes,* and that you greatly needed and desired to obtain the *loan* of statements collected by Honorable William Campbell Preston about the battle October 7, 1780—and that he would at once gratify and oblige me greatly by granting the loan and furnish thus a tribute to history and to science and reminded him that in 1852–3 I had met him at a club in Charleston, had heard his lecture, and was introduced to him by Honorable Mitchell King, etc., etc. I know he will lend you at once the statement.

You did not, like myself, get to Nashville. We both missed a *treat.* Colonel Henderson, one of our members, has just returned and came right over to see me and told me that Judge Lea had assigned Dr. Draper and Dr. Ramsey specially as his own guests—that we had almost spoiled the entertainment and the centennial by our failure to attend etc., etc.

You may have seen all the speeches and the proceedings in the northern papers.

The celebration at King's Mountain will wind up the centennial and will indeed be its most *prominent* feature. If your publisher can get out the volume and have some of them on hand the sixth, seventh, and eighth the book will be *canonized* at once—its fortune assured. I will not be there. You will be, I hope. Can't you take Knoxville in your way? Drive right to my gate and some of us will go with you after a night or two in my cell. I have read your last report. It is excellent and is on its circuit round town. Command me *ad libitum*. . . .

Draper Manuscripts 15 DD 70

July 29, 1880

I think Matthew Talbot's mill was not far up the creek then known as Big Creek. If I recollect right it is a tributary of Watauga, but it may be of Big-Doe. It must be *this* side of Yellow (Bald) Mountain. Crab-Orchard, I think, is on the east side of it. But there are several Crab-Orchards in all the ranges and on all the traces. This may produce confusion and error.

Paulette may decline the general agency because that would lead him off into Virginia, the Carolinas etc. and interfere with his main pursuit of Tennessee schoolbook enterprises. While he sat in my study he spoke of your book as the biggest of the two jobs as it is certainly. A picture such as you describe of Shelby, Sevier, McDowell and Hammond etc. will make your book popular for another century.

If Paulette is here soon I will take the opportunity to set him right. By the way what costume will you put upon the *officers?* McDowell had been a *Colonial* officer and was a grand old fellow, dignified and aldermanic in his dress, his person, and his bearing and used to walk about the Quaker-Garden (the Pleasant Gardens as afterwards called—*Carsons* still later) as if he were a duke, while the western colonels all wore the back-woods hunting shirt. I am describing the expatriated and exiled McDowell, and not the brother who commanded October 7.

Doctor Sevier lives at Jonesboro but not Dr. G. W. Sevier. Colonel J. W. Sevier, the governor's son once lived here but afterwards at Nashville where he died. I do not know the initials of Dr. Sevier of Jonesboro. He will get your letter there.

I can hardly tell you *who* now represents the old Carter family at Elizabethton, Carter County, Tennessee. A greatgrandson, Honorable Robert L. Taylor is the present member of congress. He lives at Jonesboro,
Tennessee. Reverend Nathaniel Taylor, his father, lives at Elizabethton
and Colonel Alfred Gillespie, another grandson, lives here. Any of whom
will represent their ancestors or Colonel H. L. McClung here:—all first
rate gentlemen.

Bear one question from myself. Were any Tennessee soldiers with General Morgan at the Cowpens? They write to me from South Carolina
and I can't tell. I know you can. If there were any such, who were they
and their names, especially if they were officers? I don't think there were
any. Morgan's men were not militia from this side of the mountains.
But if any were there I want to give them a place in the picture. . . .

P. S. They are getting up a commemorative monument at Cowpens and
their committee asks our Governor Marks for the names and he asks me
to answer their letter. Please tell me the names, especially of officers.

Draper Manuscripts 4 DD 42

August 2, 1880

I wish you to have every opportunity available for perfecting your King's
Mountain enterprise. So after I wrote you last week I sent to my neighbor
Major Webb, whose wife is a great-grand-daughter of the *ancestor* of all of
the Tennessee Carter family. Major Webb took your letter over into town
showed it to Major Taylor, Colonel McClung and Colonel Alfred Gillespie (who all are of the Carter stock and who got their wives on Watauga River and of course are familiar with the locations you inquire
about). Please find on the next page two paragraphs which he has written
for you. He also informs me that Reverend Nathaniel Taylor of *Elizabethton* P. O., *Carter County, Tennessee* is the now accredited representative of the Carter family. He is able and very willing to aid your inquiries
on any subject connected with King's Mountain and that he would ap-
prise him of your wishes. Reverend N. Taylor lives there on the spot and
is the very man for your purpose and is capable, reliable, and a gentleman of leisure.

Several of this *tribe* will take tea with me this evening and I will take
that opportunity of enlarging on your book. Honorable R. L. Taylor of

Jonesboro is the congressman of that district and we hope will be re-elected this year.

Don't be discouraged about Paulette. He is no thermometer on this matter. There is as good fish in the sea as *were* ever caught before. Command me when I can serve you. Hancock booms. Better and better than even Tilden or Seymour. God directed him in December 18, 1876 to write that letter to General Sherman. I believe in the designs of God even about presidential elections. . . .

P. S. I enclose an extract from the *History of Montgomery County* by Goodpasture. The last letter was *first* published from the original letter in my *Annals*.

The troop made only a short day's journey first day. The beeves disliked to leave their *own home range* and most of them had to be left and were abandoned as the *Annals* say. Can Thomson give us a plan or even an imperfect map of the route on both sides of the mountain? I hope he can make it more perfect than has heretofore been done.

Draper Correspondence

August 6, 1880

Yours of the second is received. The dark places and the uncertainty on the *western* part of the route I hope will be somewhat relieved when you shall have conferred with the Reverend Taylor (Elizabethton, Tennessee) with whom my last put you in communication. The *Crab Orchard* you are after has been identified satisfactorily.

You don't know how much you have relieved and gratified me about Tennesseans at Cowpens. I knew *where* to turn my eyes for help. *Wisconsin-ward* means, as everybody knows already, her corresponding secretary of her historical society. I had heard before as traditional that Moses Shelby, wounded on or under a wagon on King's Mountain, went before his wound was perfectly healed to Cowpens—but now I know it on Wisconsin authority and his obituary. Will not that enable me to put his name on the Cowpens monument as the *senior* in command of the volunteers from Tennessee in Morgan's great victory? Yes; unless Wisconsin tells me I ought not to do so. The enemy burned or stole my Johnston's *Life of Greene* and also Dr. Charles Caldwell's biography of the southern Washington and all my other historical works and I cannot procure another copy in Tennessee. The plate of Johnson's Cowpens battle may throw some further light on this point. Please tell me. Evan Shelby, Jr., if tradition is correct, went with his wounded uncle (?) and he will not compete for the seniority in command.

I am very exacting in this troubling now when you are so busy on a subject so important and so imperative. But you are so methodical, so systematic and hold so much, everything nearly, in your head that I venture to ask a monosyllable or two.

I knew George Nelson, the editor of our Knoxville *Gazette,* the first journal I ever read, and have some recollection yet of Mr. Greer, his father-in-law and his brother, Andrew Greer, our then Sheriff, etc.

I think there is no *Atlas* of Tennessee by *counties.* But Killebrew's new map of Tennessee is just out. I have not seen it. They speak highly of it. You are progressing exceedingly well to be reading proof of four chapters. . . .

I must tell you that yesterday our sheriff's election took place. We elected our Democratic candidate. Anderson was elected by *one* majority—the vote of the Radicals more than four hundred votes. Tennessee Republicans recollect 1829 and refuse to endorse the Hayes fraud of 1876. We claim it as a Hancock victory. I voted in 1819 for the grandfather of Anderson and yesterday for his grandson. I was carried to the polls and one vote saved the Democrats and now they say *Ramsey* decided the election. This old heart rejoices. It will be still better in November.

Success to King's Mountain and its Heroes. . . .

August 16, 1880

I must intrude upon your time once more if I do so in pencil.

I have answered, at Governor Marks' request, the letter to him from W. A. Courtney, chairman of Cowpens Committee on Monuments. I sent a copy to Governor Marks of my answer to this chairman and now write you in the absence of a copy, the *substance* of it only. I began in your cautious words "There was no embodied party probably at Cowpens from what is now Tennessee. These western soldiers had, after the defeat of Ferguson and the capture of his whole army, taken the prisoners and the spoils of war to a place of safety in the interior and the Wataugans with Sevier and other officers at their head had returned to their homes in the West and found their frontiers invaded by a large force of Cherokee warriors. Without stopping to rest a day, Captain Russell's company continued their organization and without disbanding they and their comrades from King's Mountain started on another expedition." Here I gave the strong points of page 262 *et sequento* of the *Annals,* closing with the remarks that at the time of Morgan's fight the western soldiers were too much occupied in the wilderness with the Cherokees to know that Tarleton had thrown down the gauntlet against Morgan or that the latter needed a reinforcement.

But, I added, "It is still satisfactory to know that a few, a very few, were in the Cowpens engagement. Amongst these Moses Shelby (brother of Isaac), in his intemperate eagerness for victory at King's Mountain, charged either under or over the line of wagons used by Ferguson as a defense of his encampment in which he was wounded and had not yet recovered when he dashed again over the mountains and encountered another corpse under a different leader. It is claimed further that Evan Shelby, Jr. was at his side and supported his kinsman still only partially recovered from his former wound. To these named we add *Jordan Roach* and *Alexander Greer* on the verbal authority of an old editor of Knoxville, George Wilson, who has since died in Nashville. There may have been others. But these four, I believe, went from Tennessee to Cowpens and participated in Morgan's victory on traditional testimony authentic and unquestioned.

"But as to the *seniority* of these four, I cannot answer. The one previously wounded at King's Mountain and, when not yet wholly recovered, volunteered for a second campaign and second fight would seem to have won his spurs for the seniority.

"There was a force of 700 with Sevier. They went as far down Coosa as to see the long leaf pine—nearly three hundred miles from their homes."

I have heard here this further. That when Moses Shelby declared he *would* go Evan Shelby said he would go too and take care of his wounded kinsman. So you see I have turned my eyes Wisconsinward by incorporating your traditions with my own. Will it do?

Yes. I did once write for some data of your life and for a very good purpose and I wish even yet to see them. If Rasmus B. Anderson writes soon I hope to see his sketch.[2] But if not, there will come an occasion

---

[2] Rasmus B. Anderson prepared a "Memoir" of Draper for a volume on the history of Dane County, Wisconsin. Draper had the memoir reprinted and bound by his Cincinnati publisher, Peter Thompson, and circulated it widely.

before long I hope when another of your friends and one who knows something of your historical zeal, diligence, ability, and success, and knows how to appreciate and admire them will wish to scribble, if it is only a newspaper paragraph about "King's Mountain and its Heroes" and its author's merits. I have too often intruded and taken you from your important work, and must not again seduce you—but that you can do for me in half an hour if you have that much leisure. . . .

September 6th, 1880

My mail did not reach me till today, and then came in a *heap*. One letter was to be answered instanter and now my attention will be directed to yours of the first September. Yes. I can recall my authority for the statement on my 230 page referred to in your letter. I received it from Mr. Love, Jr. (one of the good families then living near or at Elizabethon, Sparta County). He was a member of the East Tennessee Historical and Antiquarian Society of which I was *perpetual corresponding* secretary, Chancellor Reese, president, and Reverend Stephen Foster vice-president. Mr. Love was well educated. I think his father was in the army that went to King's Mountain and perhaps some of his uncles also. He had always lived up there and seemed to know everybody and every place on Watauga. He corresponded with me and the society and died forty years ago. I copied what he wrote and as he had the pioneers and soldiers for what he wrote I always thought him correct. I know he was truthful and had good chances to be accurate.

Then I have heard from others the great difficulty of getting beeves just from the canebrakes and the wide range so tame as to be driven along a crooked road—path or trace. At the point of starting the beeves (as mentioned in the text) they took a *stampede* and had to be left behind. Some of the soldiers, too, slept at home the night before they started. Then the religious services in camp would occupy some time and thus it might have consumed the whole day to reach Talbot's. W. B. Campbell is very good authority for what he says. Mr. Love I consider equally in getting the truth. I have never heard one reader of the *Annals* say there was any inaccuracy in my text about staying the first night at Talbot's. Next morning the drivers, having after the stampede all rejoined their comrades, they were all fresh and, nothing impeding their rapid march, would reach their second camp across the top of the mountain. Take these thoughts for what they may be worth. Nothing more than that.

I see that we are invited October 7. I wish you could be there. I think it would help the celebration greatly and your sales still more. Will your book be out on the ground on the 7 October.[3] Paulette has not been here and I see nothing in the papers and I am too cautious to say anything, I do not know to be authentic. But I would be glad for you to give me the *data* about yourself which I believe I asked for two or three years ago. Don't forget that.

The Cowpens Committee say the three or four names I and you have mentioned shall be cut on the memorial column at Cowpens. I find *Alexander Greer,* the father-in-law of our old friend George Wilson, was in 1794 a citizen of Knoxville. We are unveiling some hidden things. God bless you prays your friend.

October 20, 1880

Your favor of the sixteenth reached me an hour ago and I reply at once not that I have much to give you in answer to your inquiry but to tell you at the earliest moment all that I know of Ensign Robert Campbell. He was one of Colonel William Campbell's relatives—perhaps his brother or cousin and one of his truest soldiers in the King's Mountain campaign and battle. He was an emigrant about 1826–5 to Knoxville from Washington County Virginia, bought a plantation near town and died here 1832. He was known as Ensign Robert Campbell and was reputed as the capturer in the fight on the seventh of one of Ferguson's officers—McGinnis, adjutant of Colonel Ferguson.

I regarded Ensign Robert Campbell as a very truthful and reliable man. I have never read the narrative you ascribe to "Colonel Robert Campbell" but think he was the same individual as Ensign Robert Campbell. I have seen in the newspapers some reference as to his narrative but never read the narrative itself and never heard in the whole Campbell clan of any other Robert than the Ensign. There was some very chivalrous incident in the capture of Adjutant McGinnis. But I do not recollect it accurately

---

[3] Despite Dr. Ramsey's high opinion of his ability to accomplish his objectives, Draper was always dilatory about writing. Although his publisher was urging him to hurry, Draper had stopped writing half-way through his book. It was not ready on October 7, 1880, the centennial anniversary of the Battle of King's Mountain. When it appeared, nearly a year later, the enthusiasm of the centennial celebrations had waned and it met a poor reception.

and will not try to recall it only to say that Ensign Robert Campbell had the credit of achieving the incident. He left three sons; David, Edwin and Robert. They left home about 1840. The two first moved to Arkansas and soon died. The youngest, Robert, when I last heard from him, was a clerk in Nashville, Tennessee and may now be dead. Probably they left no papers. I know no one to refer you to. The senior Robert Campbell I think was referred to in the correspondence of Shelby and Senator Preston.

The delay in the appearance of your expected work will only make it the more *perfect*. N. Dickson, Esquire, my grandson was present during the centennial of King's Mountain and heard frequent inquiries about your book and were very desirous to see it. We are all so here in Tennessee. There was a "beggarly account of empty bones" from Tennessee and Virginia. As to Tennessee it was owing to intense political excitement prevailing all over the State. Hancock and English are safe. But our state debt has created much doubt as to the governor, legislature and members of congress. Our platform ought not to have touched state indebtedness. It has divided our people and may ruin our prospects in future. These modern Democrats affiliate badly with the *old Democracy*. . . .

November 5, 1880

Yours of the first received late last night. The youngest son of Ensign Robert Campbell has come back to Knoxville and is now a resident clerk in the office of Colonel C. M. McGhee, president of East Tennessee and Virginia and Georgia Railroad, Knoxville, Tennessee. Thus addressed, your letter cannot fail to reach him.

You have estimated Reverend D. C. K., D.D. of Nashville exactly. He was appointed by Governor Marks as one of our state commissioners to King's Mountain Centennial but failed to attend after promising to do so.

Much of what I say in my *Annals of Tennessee* about Captain Edmondson I have from the lips of Andrew Cresswell, John McCrosby and many other of the King's Mountain fight who had the best opportunity of knowing the truth of every incident I mention. They were privates under Edmondson and each of them men of unquestioned integrity and truth. I knew them well, practiced in their families forty years ago. So also of Grimes, one of the *very* few Tories on Watauga. I heard all the details about him from the same source and others. Captain Robert Sevier tarred and feathered him before the King's Mountain campaign and then drove him across the mountains. He was hung as a desperate and cruel Tory.

Honorable William A. Courtenay, mayor of Charleston, South Carolina is the chairman of committee of invitation for the celebration of the battles of King's Mountain and Cowpens. Charleston, South Carolina, is his proper address.

I cannot recall to mind from whom I got the statement of the King's Mountain campaign. It was, I think, a contribution to the E. T. H. and A. Society of which Honorable W. B. Reese, chancellor, was the president, Reverend Stephen A. Foster, professor in our East Tennessee University, was vice president, J. G. M. Ramsey, corresponding secretary and custodian and Honorable J. H. Crozier was recording secretary. I probably got it in this way or possibly it was sent to me from some other contributor or some historical friend in Kentucky or Tennessee or, as Haywood's book was printed in Knoxville, it may have been received from the publishers here. Haywood quotes largely from it in 1820 and must have seen it and it is not impossible that he may have handed it to me himself. I think the statement was in Shelby's hand and bore his signature. It was among the collections of my society and was burned or stolen by the enemy in September 1863 with all I had when my house and office were burned.

A. A. Anderson, Esquire, lived here in 1823–6, son of United States Senator Anderson in 1786, removed to Frankfort, Kentucky, married the granddaughter of Isaac Shelby at Frankfort, Kentucky and, if still living, is there now. I don't know further about him.

Wishing you a great success in your books. . . .

P. S. I am not quite well today but desire always to answer you promptly and to assure you how much I appreciate your historical enterprises.

Draper Manuscripts 15 DD 86

November 20, 1880

I enclose this letter and its enclosures to you that you may see them before you finish your volume on "Kings Mountain and its Heroes." Please return them to me, or what is better, to *Anson Nelson* Recording Secretary Tennessee Historical Society. Nashville, Tennessee.

I could point out some inaccuracy in them but am too feeble to do so today. God bless you prays your old friend.

Draper Correspondence

January 27, 1881

I have this moment received the prospectus of your forthcoming volume "Kings-Mountain and its Heroes." I thank God that I have hopes still to see it and enjoy the privilege of reading it.

I will send at once to one or two of our principal editors and ask them to give it the proper notice. I like the style or plan of the *Prospectus*. Nothing extravagant, high faluting, take-in, or deceptive about it. No. It is all truth, sober truth. The public will so view it. No clap-trap or falsehood in it. It speaks for itself and will be heard.

I will write to the publishers at Cincinnati. He says "it will be published by *subscription*." Of course he will need *agents* and I will write him in behalf of my grandson *Wilberforce Ramsey Dickson* of this city who desires to be one of his agents. He is aged twenty-six years, has not heretofore acted as a book canvasser and of course has had no experience in this business: but believes that he will be able to give full satisfaction in the premises. *My* own ambition will be to show that Tennessee will give the largest patronage to your book than any of the sister states. Success and Prosperity! . . .

P. S. I am a little better than I was when your last letter was sent.

January 29, 1881

I thank you for the two prospectus received from you yesterday. I immediately wrote to Mr. Thompson, the publisher, that if he needed an agent at Knoxville to take subscriptions for his work I would suggest the name of my grandson Wilberforce Ramsey Dickson, aged twenty-six or twenty-seven, an intelligent native of this county, well acquainted with our people and rather a favorite with them. But that he had no experience in *book canvassing business*. But that if that was not an insuperable objection he would address him here to my care. This much I had written to Mr. Thomson when your favor of the twenty-fourth January reached me. I at once added a *Post Scriptum* in which I gave him a list of perhaps thirty gentlemen all over East Tennessee counties who I think will make good book agents or advise and suggest such as will be so and gave their post office address.

The delay in getting the book out has done you no harm if, as you say, it has enabled you to straighten up some crooked narratives, either verbal or printed. Your well known accuracy and cautious care, will shield you from any apprehension as to this.

I was uneasy and even anxious lest the delay would come from *over-work and hurry*. The book will be the better for it. I would have inquired earlier for your health but that I knew you so well. Let me not trouble you for answer one minute only when I can serve you.

The cold weather has not made me worse. Indeed I am perhaps better.

Draper Manuscripts 14 DD 3

March 8, 1881

Some several weeks since I received the long and valuable catalogue of your state library. A few days since the sketch of your biography by Professor Anderson followed it, and late night before last, your appeal to the Wisconsin legislature and your welcome letter of March 1 completed the series. Thanking you for all and each of them and apologizing for *apparent* tardiness in acknowleging some of them I hasten to tell you what I recollect of Colonel John Sawyers. . . .

I thank you for the sketch of your biography and will use it. There is no *vanity* at all in it, incomplete though it be. Yes, your Mr. Thomson promptly did appoint my grandson Wilberforce Dickson agent for Knox County. The young man's modesty, perhaps his ambition to do you full justice lead him to decline the civility implied in the appointment. I had another in view and at my suggestion Mr. Thomson sent me the appointment of Mr. Francis Asbury Butler of this city as his successor. I sent for him immediately. He came at once, accepted the position, and in twenty-one days secured sixty-six of the elite of our city as subscribers —all good and true and solvent men while our streets are filled with Yankee peddlars of trashy vulgarity and light scribling. I think Butler will make it a success. I have sent to Mr. Thomson a long list of names of thirty or forty gentlemen in other counties outside of Knoxville suitable for similar agencies. I have also suggested to Honorable J. M. Lea, Anson Nelson, Esquire, and others in Nashville to take good care of your interests in our metropolis. It is now too late probably to ask you whether I ever informed you of a very strong tradition or camp-talk in 1780 that Kusick, one of Sevier's men, was the sharp-shooter who killed Ferguson? or that equally strong conviction that Colonel James Williams of South Carolina achieved that great success?

Probably both are true as Ferguson had more than one fatal shot in his front. I believe this.

P. S. Your picture really has surprised me when I saw it in Anderson's Biography of L. C. Draper—the Plutarch of the West. You look like you were only thirty-five.

Draper Correspondence

March 19, 1881

I enclose to you this letter of Mrs. Douglas—lady friend of ours at Nashville, Tennessee. I fear it will reach you too late for her purpose now. Her enclosure may give you *names* that may interest you in the future as to sales of your books but they afford little unknown to you heretofore.

P. S. You will hear before long more of Colonel Sawyers.

Draper Manuscripts 14 DD 6

March 14, 1881

I have just read over the pages 240-1 of the *Annals* to which you refer me in your last. I concur with you in the conclusion to which you seem to have arrived, that I refer to *Captain* William Edmondson as the officer who fell on that occasion. I was in communication with Governor David Campbell when I wrote but his letters are not within my reach—having been burned in my house in September 1863. But your understanding is doubtless correct on the matter.

In the first copies of my book *Sawyers* was spelt with the last syllable omitted *Saw*. The rest of the edition had its correct *Sawyers*. He was known after the war as Colonel Sawyers by courtesy probably or possibly by our military promotion.

I hear from our friend Anson Nelson at Nashville that Thomson's agent there, a Mr. Price, has commenced an auspicious canvas in Davidson County. F. A. Butler in Knox still meets with encouragement.

Since Spring has dawned in East Tennessee I feel somewhat rejuvinated. . . .

P. S. While this was being written your second letter of March 10 came in time to answer in this. I will this P.M. ask W. A. Anderson, Esquire, who lives near Colonel Sawyers' old place and where he lies interred and will promptly investigate all the questions you ask me to enquire about. He is probably the only living man who can give you any further information authentic and reliable on that subject. Colonel Sawyers had been in service somewhere north as I read in some book on which his name was introduced. What book or account I may never recall. But he was commisary or quartermaster in furnishing army supplies at or near to Fort Duquesne and had military experience.

Draper Manuscripts 14 DD 4

March 25, 1881

Excuse my pencil scribbling on this my eighty-fourth birthday.[4] (March *25, 1797*). The enclosed comes from a granddaughter of Colonel John Sawyers; and is supposed to be authentic—though incomplete and im-

---

[4] This letter, written on his eighty-fourth birthday, ended the long correspondence between Dr. J. G. M. Ramsey and Lyman C. Draper. It had served to keep alive Dr. Ramsey's interest in the history of Tennessee and it had enabled Draper to preserve many items, bits of information, and matured opinions which would otherwise have been lost.

There was but one further communication between the two historians. In 1883 Draper wrote to ask another question. More than thirty years before, Dr. Ramsey had sent him a tracing from a tree upon which had been carved "D. Boon Cilled A Bar on tree 1760" Draper had gathered many another carved record of Daniel Boone's prowess as a bear-hunter. Now he wanted to know if Dr. Ramsey had himself seen the tree. The answer came from Mrs. Ramsey, replying to the question and giving another glimpse of Dr. Ramsey's last years:

October 6th, 1883

Mr. L. C. Draper,
Dear Sir,

In reply to your question did Dr. Ramsey ever see the Boone bear tree? He desires me to say he visited that locality at least forty years ago, does not exactly remember the year. His old friend Nathan Gammon wrote to him he had been to see the Boone tree. Dr. Ramsey went to the place described by Gammon, it was 106 miles from Mecklenburg Tennessee the Doctor's old home. He saw the camp grounds sheltered by a cliff of rocks, one of the rocks still retained marks of the fire built by Boone against it. Dr. Ramsey has a photograph of the Boone tree—presented to him from the centennial celebration at Ganesborough. If you would like to have the picture will send one. He has two. Professor McAdoo expected to go on the Watauga during the vacation but was prevented on account of some unpleasant difficulties in the University. He was not concerned himself in the trouble but thought it best not to be absent. He still thinks of going when he has time, will no doubt gather up something valuable which Dr. will forward to you. Although very feeble he is always pleased to render any service he can to his long-time friend in his useful and interesting work. Dr. Ramsey is not able to be out of bed only for a short time.

He enjoys the visits of friends when they call. Many old friends from a distance and

perfect in its details. I give its *pages* as they come to me from others. The remains of the ancestor are buried in the graveyard of Washington Church, Knox County, Tennessee.

[*J. G. M. Ramsey.*]

---

strangers when they visit the city come to see him. He takes an interest in all public affairs of both church and state. I know you feel an interest in all that concerns Dr. Ramsey, therefore I say so much about him. We were glad to get the magazine which contained the sketch of your life and picture.

Dr. Ramsey desires to be kindly remembered and prays your strength both mentally and physically may be continued for many long years.

Very truly your friend
M. C. Ramsey

Dr. Ramsey lived for another six months, dying in Knoxville April 11, 1884, seventeen days after his eighty-seventh birthday. He was buried in the churchyard of Lebanon-in-the-Fork on the hillside overlooking the site of his beloved "Mecklenburg." Mrs. Ramsey survived him five years. Lyman Draper, his long-time correspondent, retired from the State Historical Society of Wisconsin in 1886, and died in 1891 at the age of seventy-six.

Index

Abbeville, S. C., 185, 222, 223, 226, 227
Abingdon, Va., 64, 108, 109, 112, 115, 116, 123, 145 note, 208, 257
Adair, John, 296
Adams County, Pa., 1
Adams, John, 93
Adams, John Q., 22 note
Advertizer, The South Carolina, 279, 281, 282
Agnew, Judge, 12
Agriculture, conditions in East Tennessee, 17–18, 38–39, 158, 251; in South, 85 ff.; Draper's interest in, 256, 259; hog cholera, 315–316; mentioned, 276
Aikens, Mr., 22 note
Alabama, preface, 123, 156–157 note
Alamance, battle, preface, 284, 301, 323
Alexander, Mrs. A. B., 217, 218, 234
Alexander, Abigail Baine, 4
Alexander, Abraham, 189
Alexander, Adam, 189
Alexander, B. W., 217, 218, 220, 231
Alexander, Charles, 189, 294
Alexander, Clark Isaac, 289
Alexander, Eve Ramsey, 274
Alexander, Ezekiel, 3, 294
Alexander, Ezra, 189, 294
Alexander family, preface, 3, 4, 102, 272, 286–287, 289, 299, 312
Alexander, Francis Ramsey, 190–191, 217
Alexander, Fuller Nathaniel, 287
Alexander, George W., 4
Alexander, Hezekiah, 3, 189, 294, 295, 309–310, 312
Alexander, James, 295
Alexander, James Baine, 286
Alexander, James McKnitt, 4
Alexander, John, 13
Alexander, John McKnitt, 3, 5, 189–190
Alexander, Mrs. John McKnitt, 3, 5
Alexander, John Ramsey, 4, 217
Alexander, Joseph, 4

Alexander, Joseph McKnitt, Charlotte convention, 4; daughter marries, 8; mentioned, 284, 285–287, 288–289, 290–291, 293–294, 295, 298, 299, 302, 310, 318
Alexander, Moses Winslow, 217
Alexander, Moses W. McKnitt, 286
Alexander, Mrs. M. W., 234
Alexander, Naomi, 1–3
Alexander, Nathaniel, 287, 295
Alexander, Peggy, 4
Alexander, Peggy Baine, 286
Alexander, Robert D., 4
Alexander, Sydenham, 262
Alexander, Thomas, 294–295
Alexander, William, 270, 295
Alexander, William Baine, 4, 5, 286
Alexander, William Davidson, 231, 248, 249, 271, 295, 318
Alexandriana, N. C., 4, 12, 248, 291
Allegheny Mountains, 7, 10 note, 17, 24, 323
Allen, Carey, 2
Allen, Pynem, 157 note
Allen, William, 300
Allison, Mr., 261
American, The Nashville, 316
American State Papers, 80
Anderson, Alexander, 38
Anderson, Colonel, 154, 155, 161, 163
Anderson, Doctor, 115
Anderson family, 290
Anderson, Jack, 266
Anderson, Mrs. Jack, 268
Anderson, John, 80
Anderson, Rasmus B., 336–337, 342, 343
Anderson, Sheriff, 335
Anderson, So. Carolina, 156–157 note
Anderson, W. A., 344
Anderson, W. E., 35
Andersonville Prison, 238 f.
Annals of Tennessee, sketch of J. M. Alexander, 5; of F. A. Ramsey, 16;

347

ing, 26 ff.; Columbia meeting of, 1839,
37–40; conventions in Knoxville, 50
note; Ramsey's acquaintance with,
55; his activities, 62; Memminger interested in, 101; bank of Georgia,
105; in East Tennessee in the Civil
War, 112; Holston bridge, 115; Tennessee bridge burned, 118; in Civil
War, 120; Ramsey's interests, 146,
254; in wartime Tennessee, 146; in
North Carolina during war, 190–191;
bridges destroyed, 210–211; Knoxville, 251

Raisen River, 200

Raleigh, N. C., 69, 282

Raleigh pamphlet, 283

Ramsey, A. B. C., 139

Ramsey, Arthur Crozier, preface, 152,
156, 196, 197, 198, 200–201, 205 f., 219
note; at school, 115; returns home,
116, 159; leaves father, 148; joins
army, 151, 155; in Knoxville, 160;
first skirmish, 206; in Piedmont battle, 213–214; wounded, 192, 199, 204–
205, 236; death, 186, 193–194, 206–
207, 257; grave, 240, 269; character,
215

Ramsey, Captain (C.S.N.), 212–213

Ramsey, Charlotte Barton, 108–109, 116,
124, 164–165

Ramsey, "Colonel" Francis Alexander,
acquires Swan Pond, 10, 137; hunts
Confederate counterfeiters, 104–105;
accompanies father from Knoxville,
116 ff.; visits Lenoir's, 118; heroism in
flood, 126–127; scout for Kirby Smith,
131; early career and California trip,
134 ff.; Confederate service, 137–138;
marries, 137; with Bragg's army, 143;
at Campbell's station, 149; at Jonesboro, 155; captured, 186, 192, 197,
199, 215; and prison experience, 236–
239; in business, 249; mentioned, 115,
116, 119, 151, 152, 193, 218, 230, 232

Ramsey, Colonel Frank A., 275

Ramsey, Dr. David, 2

Ramsey, Eliza, 14

Ramsey family, preface, 1–9, 299

Ramsey, Francis Alexander, the elder,
2–3, 53, 296, 317; migration to North
Carolina, 6–7; migration to Tennessee,
7; surveyor, 7; remarried, 12; death
of children, 12; patron of schools, 13;
death of second wife, 14; remarriage
and death, 15; character, 15–16; bank

president, 35, 44; trustee of Blount
College, 52; on Sevier, 79

Ramsey, Francis Alexander, Jr., 12

Ramsey, Frank A., 11, 117, 197, 217,
240

Ramsey, James, 274

Ramsey, James Gettys McGready, career,
preface; historian, preface; writes obituary of uncle, 3; born, 9; mother's
death, 11–12; education, 13–14; studies in Philadelphia, 14; begins practice
of medicine, 17; marries, 17; Mecklenburg politics, 17 ff.; promotes railroads, 19–20; visit to Charleston, 20–
22; writes under name of "Clinton,"
20, 21 note; in Knoxville railroad
convention, 23; president, Knoxville
branch of railroad bank, 24, 35–36;
financing railroads, 24 ff.; markets
railroad bonds, 27 ff.; operates ferry,
35; director, Knoxville branch of
Bank of Tennessee, 35–36; at Asheville railroad convention of 1831, 38,
40; writes *Annals of Tennessee,* 41;
trustee of Bank of East Tennessee,
41–43; president, branch Bank of Tennessee, 42–43; opinion of Parson
Brownlow, 42–43; school commissioner, 46, 49; political principles, 47;
efforts to entire Draper to Tennessee,
49–50 note; opinions on schools, 49–
50 note; family, 50 note; college
trustee, 52; received M.A. degree, 52;
memorial to Dr. Doak, 54–55; Tusculum College board, 54–55; honored
by societies, 55; receives M.D., 55;
practice of medicine, 58; offers Draper partnership, 58; Polk appoints to
Mexico, 62; attitude on commerce,
63; daughter marries, 66; in 1852
campaign, 67; progress with *Annals,*
70; has Shelby Mss., 72; *Annals* in
press, 73–75; plans second volume,
77; has Sevier Mss., 77 note; letters
on slavery and slave trade, 83–97; on
secession, 95 ff., 98 note; practices
medicine, 99 note; attends bank convention in Richmond, 100–102; un-
official representative in Congress,
101–102; appointed Confederate depositary, 103; evacuates money from
Knoxville, 107 ff.; guide, 111–112;
abandons Mecklenburg, 115 ff.; personal description, 118 note; buries
cousin, 139–141; surgeon at Chicka-